The Economics of Commodity Markets

For other titles in the Wiley Finance series
please see www.wiley.com/finance

The Economics of Commodity Markets

Julien Chevallier
Florian Ielpo

WILEY

Registered office
John Wiley & Sons Ltd, The Atrium, Southern Gate, Chichester, West Sussex, PO19 8SQ, United Kingdom

For details of our global editorial offices, for customer services and for information about how to apply for permission to reuse the copyright material in this book please see our website at www.wiley.com.

Library of Congress Cataloging-in-Publication Data

Chevallier, Julien.
   The economics of commodity markets / Julien Chevallier, Florian Ielpo.
     pages cm
   Includes bibliographical references and index.
     ISBN 978-1-119-96791-0 (cloth) – ISBN 978-1-119-94539-0 (ebk) – ISBN 978-1-119-94541-3 (ebk) –
ISBN 978-1-119-94540-6 (ebk)   1. Primary commodities.   2. Commercial products.   3. Financial futures.
I. Ielpo, Florian.   II. Title.
   HF1040.7.C4684 2013
   332.64′4–dc23
                                                                                          2013018144

A catalogue record for this book is available from the British Library.

ISBN 978-1-119-96791-0 (hbk) ISBN 978-1-119-94539-0 (ebk); ISBN: 978-1-118-71009-8 (ebk)
ISBN 978-1-119-94541-3 (ebk) ISBN 978-1-119-94540-6 (ebk)

Set in 10/12pt Times by Aptara, Inc., New Delhi, India
Printed in Great Britain by CPI Group (UK) Ltd, Croydon, CR0 4YY

To our families

Contents

Preface

As a consequence of the strong recent growth of commodity markets and especially their substantial future growth potential, a dynamic financial industry with hundreds of participating firms, asset management firms, brokers, consultants, verification agencies and other institutions has developed. To address this large and still strongly growing market, universities and business schools have launched dozens of courses on commodity markets to date. Additionally, the Chartered Financial Analyst program (CFA) includes aspects of Commodity Markets in its certification.

This book aims at covering recent topics on commodity markets based on empirical applications and the latest developments in financial economics/econometrics. It draws on the authors' professional, as well as teaching, experience of commodity finance and commodity markets at the University Paris Dauphine (France). In terms of intended audience, the book is equally suited to professionals (chief investment officers, portfolio managers, strategists, commodity traders, commodity analysts, energy analysts, quantitative analysts) and academics dealing with commodity markets, financial economics and econometrics.

Useful comparators for this book would be Geman's (2005) *Commodities and Commodity Derivatives: Agriculturals, Metals and Energy*, and Schofield's (2007) *Commodity Derivatives: Markets and Applications*. While these previous titles provide essential textbook material on the functioning of commodity markets, our book provides new quantitative insights in the field of econometric modeling and risk management that could be useful to academics and professionals. Besides, we adopt a broad coverage of commodity markets including the energy, agricultural and metals markets.

The material presented in this book is primarily dedicated to investors seeking a thorough analysis of the key features of commodity markets over the past twenty years. While the mechanics of commodity investment vehicles have been well covered by previous titles, the stylized facts motivating investors to increase their investment in commodities as an alternative asset class have received more limited attention. This book aims at filling this gap. We aim at covering recent topics on commodity markets based on empirical applications and intuitive economic reasoning. Therefore, the originality of our approach lies in the application of up-to-date financial econometric techniques to the analysis of commodity markets, by making the conclusions and analyses appealing to investors.

To accomplish this, the book is composed of three parts:

1. Part I is dedicated to the descriptive analysis of commodity market dynamics. Chapters 1 and 2 consider three main categories of commodities: energy, metals and agricultural

products. For each category, we detail their individual dynamics (in terms of momentum, risk premium, occurrence of jumps, etc.), and their linkages with other assets thanks to factor modeling and the construction of volatility spillover indices. This introductory section of the book may be of interest to a wide audience of readers, including undergraduate and graduate students, and working professionals including non-specialists of commodity markets.

2. Part II details how commodities react along the business cycle. It is composed of original econometric applications to the sphere of commodity markets. Chapters 3 and 4 seek to characterize the different regimes in commodity markets, as well as their reaction to macroeconomic news. Together, they constitute empirical financial analyses of commodity markets that are essential to investment decision makers.

3. Part III contains an in-depth analysis of the commodities' fundamental value, from a longer-term perspective. Chapters 5 to 7 contain a cointegration analysis across the various categories of commodity markets (agricultural products, metals and energy) in conjunction with traditional asset markets (equities and bonds). These chapters provide a long-term view of the evolution of commodities over time, and the extent to which their price path may converge to a fundamental value based on market-specific characteristics and the global macroeconomic environment.

In sum, this book provides interested readers with a presentation of up-to-date financial economic/econometric methods related to commodity markets. Readers will therefore find a strong value added to this book through the up-to-date information of market trends for commodities, and a strong emphasis on the quantitative treatment that turns data into information. While discussing the key insights of these methods without falling into technicalities, this book is designed to be as self-contained as possible: every explanation is designed so that the reader with a basic background in mathematics and finance should not need any additional reading to make his way through the chapters. Applications to various commodity markets (metals, energy, agriculture) are developed and discussed.

Last but not least, we wish to thank very warmly colleagues both at work and at the university for many interactions on the topic of commodity markets which led us to write this book. Among them, we wish to thank more particularly Frederic Peltrault, Philippe Bernard, Benoit Sevi, Yannick Le Pen, Sofiane Aboura, Sophie Meritet, Colin Rowat, Michalis Drouvelis, Mathieu Gatumel, Chafic Merhy, Arnaud Bitoun and Chloe Koos. We warmly thank Ling Ni Boon for research assistance on specific sections of the book. We also thank Dr Patrick Zweifel for having inspired the organization and various aspects of this book. We thank the University Paris Dauphine for providing access to the data used throughout this book. We wish to give special thanks to our editors and external referees at Wiley Finance for all the hard work they have put into the preparation of this book. All errors remain our own. This book does not reflect the views of any of the past or current employers of the authors.

J. Chevallier and F. Ielpo
Paris, France & Geneva, Switzerland
November, 2012

List of Figures

List of Tables

Acronyms

ADF	Augmented-Dickey–Fuller Unit Root Test
API	Argus/McCloskey's Price Index for Coal
CAPM	Capital Asset Pricing Model
CCAPM	Consumption Capital Asset Pricing Model
CBOT	Chicago Board of Trade
CCI	Consumer Confidence Index
CME	Chicago Mercantile Exchange
COMEX	Commodity Exchange
CPI	Consumer Price Index
CRB	Commodities Research Bureau Index
CRBRI	Commodities Research Bureau Raw Industrials Index
CSCE	New York's Coffee, Sugar, and Cocoa Exchange
CTA	Commodity Trading Advisor
DCC	Dynamic Conditional Correlation Multivariate GARCH Model
ECB	European Central Bank
ECM	Error Correction Model
ECT	Error Correction Term
EGARCH	Exponential GARCH
EGARCH MN	Exponential GARCH with a mixture of normal distributions
EM	Expectation-Minimization algorithm
EMU	European Monetary Union
EVT	Extreme Value Theory
FAVAR	Factor-Augmented VAR
Fed	US Federal Reserve
Fox	London's Future and Options Exchange
FX	Foreign Exchange Markets
GARCH	Generalized AutoRegressive Conditional Heteroskedasticity
GDP	Gross Domestic Product
GH	Generalized Hyperbolic Distribution
GSCI	Goldman Sachs Commodity Index
HAC	Newey–West Heteroskedasticity and Autocorrelation Consistent Estimator
HH	US Henry Hub Natural Gas Price
HSFO	High Sulfur Fuel Oil

ICE	InterContinental Exchange
IFO	Munich Society for the Promotion of Economic Research
IMF	International Monetary Fund
IPE	International Petroleum Exchange
ISM	Institute for Supply Management
JOC	Journal of Commerce index
KPSS	Kwiatkowski, Phillips, Schmidt, and Shin Unit Root Test
LIFFE	London International Financial Futures Exchange
LME	London Metal Exchange
LOP	Law of One Price
LR Test	Likelihood Ratio Test
LSFO	Low Sulfur Fuel Oil
MCAPM	Money Capital Asset Pricing Model
MCCAPM	Money Consumption Capital Asset Pricing Model
NBER	US National Bureau of Economic Research
NCE	US National Cheese Exchange
NYMEX	New York Mercantile Exchange
OECD	Organization for Economic Cooperation and Development
OLS	Ordinary Least Squares
PBOC	Public Bank of China
PCA	Principal Component Analysis
PJM	US Pennsylvania–New Jersey–Maryland Interconnection
PMI	Purchasing Managers Index
PnL	Profit and Loss
PP	Phillips–Peron Unit Root Test
PPI	Producer Price Index
PPICM	Producer Price Index for Crude Materials
PPP	Purchasing Power Parity
QML	Quasi Maximum Likelihood
RBOB	Reformulated Regular Gasoline Blendstock
S&P 500	Standard & Poor's 500 Equity Index
SDF	Stochastic Discount Factor
SENSI	Conference Board's Sensitive Materials Index
SMI	Swiss Market Index
TGE	Tokyo Grain Exchange
TOCOM	Tokyo Commodity Exchange
USD	US Dollar
VaR	Value-at-Risk
VAR	Vector AutoRegressive Model
VECM	Vector Error Correction Model
WCE	Winnipeg Commodity Exchange
WGN	White Gaussian Noise
WTI	West Texas Intermediate Crude Oil Futures Price
WTO	World Trade Organization
ZEW	Mannheim Centre for European Economic Research

Part I
Commodity Market Dynamics

A proper understanding of commodity markets should start with analysis of the first kind of information at hand, i.e. the historical evolution of prices and returns on these assets over time. This first section aims at providing the reader with the most important insights to be gained from these data series: what are the main stylized facts one should be aware of when investing money in these assets? Which characteristics do they have when compared to the usual asset classes? How do they interact with each other and, more importantly, with the basic building blocks of a traditional asset allocation? Financial econometrics has now provided us with the necessary tools to answer these questions, and we will apply them in a systematic way to help us build a list of the most interesting features. The attention of academics has been increasingly focused in recent years on the understanding of the potential risks and patterns observed in commodity markets. To address the problem any investor is faced with, this section steps into this recent evolution and will be mainly devoted to measuring regularities in commodity markets by using a large dataset of commodity indices. We will follow a thorough analysis of commodity returns, both from an individual and from a cross-asset perspective. In the meantime, Part I of the book tackles three different types of problem that investors are confronted with.

The primary focus of our investigation in Part I of the book is to help the reader obtain an increased understanding of the formation of returns on commodities, both from an individual and from a cross-asset perspective. Recent books such as Ilmanen (2011) have put massive efforts into the listing of the salient features of excess returns, as they are the reason why investors would increase their exposure to any risk factor. This investigation of the past has one purpose: improving the ability of investors to estimate expected returns of this asset class. Studies like Gorton and Rouwenhorst (2005a) or Erb and Campbell (2006) geared investors toward commodities mainly by emphasizing the 'equity-like' performance over the period they consider, as well as the strong diversification impact of adding portfolios of commodities to standard assets in a global portfolio. Part I of the book aims to build on their work, by improving it in two directions. First, by using a more recent dataset that incorporates the 2008 crisis, we confront their findings to this major event and confirm or not their original findings. Second, we use a large set of new econometric tools as a magnifying glass to provide the reader with a more detailed analysis of these returns than previous studies. We tackle, for example, the two key aspects of commodities that are the forecasting power of the term structure of futures and the existence of a momentum effect in commodities.

Beyond the essential theme of expected returns, a second topic is the measure of the risk exposure that any investor has to deal with when investing in commodity markets. Building on 'What every investor should know about commodities' by Kat and Oomen (2007a; 2007b), there are a couple of stylized facts that an investor should keep in mind when entering commodity markets: for instance the nature of volatility patterns in commodity markets, the jump activity and its impact on upcoming returns, and the behavior of correlations among commodities and with other assets. These three elements aim at helping the reader become familiar with the complex mechanism of returns on this asset class. A continued comparison to standard assets will enable readers that are familiar with such assets to get a faster grasp on the salient features of commodities.

A final aspect that is essential from a diversified portfolio perspective is the nature of the relationships between commodities and the assets traditionally included in a balanced portfolio. This aspect should matter both to hedge fund managers and to those in charge of deciding the nature of portfolio mixes to be used in pension funds. Two aspects here are rarely disentangled: first, the instantaneous cross-sectional dependency as measured by correlation is a key aspect of those cross-asset linkages. Such correlations vary through time, as illustrated in Longin and Solnik (2001) or Ang and Chen (2002). Diversification by itself is usually looked for in this part of the linkage measurement issue. Second, dynamic linkages are also important; that is, the way shocks from an asset can spread across other assets. The 2008–2011 Euro crisis is a very good example of how such shocks can spread in markets and endanger the whole financial system. Measures of such dynamics have been proposed in the literature, as in Diebold and Yilmaz (2012). We apply this approach to commodities, and bring forward evidence that commodities are not as insensitive to such shocks as one would assume.

PLAN OF PART I

This first part of the book is divided into two chapters. Chapter 1 covers the individual dynamics of commodities, investigating first expected returns on commodities from different angles, before turning to risk metrics. On expected returns, our investigations are focused on the forecasting power of the term structure of commodity futures and on the momentum of commodities. The section dedicated to risk questions the existence of leverage effects in commodities, before turning to an analysis of the jump activity in commodities. Chapter 2 investigates the cross-asset linkages both within commodities, and between commodities and standard assets. This analysis is performed from two different perspectives: first, we analyze the factors implicit in the cross-section of returns on commodities and standard assets, before considering the dynamic spillovers that are potentially found in such datasets. The first approach is thus somewhat an analysis of static linkages, whereas the second one can be seen as an analysis of the dynamics of these returns.

1
Individual Dynamics: From Trends to Risks

Starting with the asset-by-asset investigation of commodity returns, the salient features under our assessment will be first the nature and persistence of returns on commodities, moving next to the analysis of higher order moments – that is volatility, asymmetry and extreme events.

One of the first attempts to try to bring together cross-asset conclusions regarding commodities can be found in Kat and Oomen (2007a). Investigating between 22 and 29 commodities over the period 1965–2005 (when such data is available), they reach the following empirical conclusions:

1. First of all – and consistent with the results of Erb and Campbell (2006) – individual commodities do not provide investors with a risk premium on average. This conclusion has to be differentiated from the basket of commodities case: Gorton and Rouwenhorst (2005a) show how such a risk premium is associated to a basket of equally-weighted commodities by using the Commodity Research Bureau dataset covering the 1959–2005 period and including 36 commodities.
2. The persistence in commodities is found to be important: a positive or a negative shock to commodity prices usually has long-lasting effects, unlike equities and bonds. This is an essential feature for trend-following investment strategies.
3. The volatility of commodities is not found to be excessive when compared to the volatility of equities over the period under consideration.
4. They also find a limited asymmetry of returns in their dataset: the skewness of commodity returns is usually found to be close to zero.
5. Finally, one of the key properties of commodities is the frequency at which extreme events occur. Kurtosis being a natural way to measure such a tail event activity, they find excess kurtosis for most of the market under the scope of their investigation.

This list of empirical features seems, however, to be somewhat specific to the period covered by each dataset. More recently and by using various kinds of continuous time models encompassing time-varying volatility and jumps in the returns and volatility dynamics, Brooks and Prokopczuk (2011) studied in a more quantitative way the law of motion of commodities' returns. Their empirical findings show that jumps are an essential building block of the underlying data-generating process of such markets. The frequency of appearance and the size of the jumps in returns are found to be very different from one market to another. Finally, the correlation between returns and their volatility is found to a have a sign that is specific to each market: for example, a large negative return in the crude oil price should trigger a surge in its volatility that is larger than in the case of a similar but positive return. Such a pattern does not hold in the case of gold, silver and soybean, following Brooks and Prokopczuk (2011). This goes against the fifth conclusion from Kat and Oomen (2007a; 2007b), but the period covered by both studies is quite different.

Two additional aspects should be mentioned here.

1. First, as for any financial market, commodity markets are affected by time-varying volatility. This stylized fact has been investigated in many research articles such as Serletis (1994), Ng and Pirrong (1996), Haigh and Holt (2002), Pindyck (2004), Sadorsky (2006), Alizadeh *et al.* (2008) and Wang *et al.* (2008). Most of them use various specifications close to the Generalized Autoregressive Conditional Heteroskedastic (GARCH) model initially presented in Engle (1982) and Bollerslev (1986). Bernard *et al.* (2008) present results regarding the aluminum market. Whereas these contributions were based on discrete time models, continuous time finance also focused on the addition of stochastic volatility to the basic model by Schwartz (1997), as presented in Geman and Nguyen (2005) and Trolle and Schwartz (2009).

2. Second, the tail and jump issues that seem to be so important in the literature drove many attempts to build models combining time-varying volatility, persistence through the convenience yield and jumps. Deaton and Laroque (1992) found empirical evidence that agricultural prices are agitated by jumps, while Duffie *et al.* (1995) also reported fat tails found in the dynamics of returns on commodities. Pindyck (2001) finds jumps both in the commodity prices and in the inventory levels. This triggered numerous theoretical contributions based on the continuous time finance models proposed in Brennan and Schwartz (1985), Gibson and Schwartz (1990), Schwartz (1997) and Schwartz and Smith (2000). An application to agricultural markets can be found in Sorensen (2002), and to natural gas in Manoliu and Tompaidis (2002). Hilliard and Reis (1998) wrote one of the first articles adding jumps to the model by Schwartz (1997). Deng (1999) brings jumps, mean-reversion and stochastic volatility together. Casassus and Collin-Dufresne (2005) also include explicitly discontinuous jumps in their model. Liu and Tang (2011) relate the convenience yield with its volatility. Dempster *et al.* (2010) propose a continuous time model that encompasses both short- and long-term jumps, highlighting how these aspects are important to the pricing of options on commodity futures.

We now turn to the analysis of descriptive statistics computed over a set of 22 commodities and of four sub-indexes from the Goldman Sachs Commodity Index (GSCI) universe. Table 1.1 presents the annualized returns over 1995–2012, as well as the volatilities, skewness, kurtosis, minimum and maximum returns, and the estimated autoregresssive parameters of an AR(1). We compare the results obtained for commodities to those obtained for other asset classes such as equities, currencies and interest rates over the same period. The main conclusions from Table 1.1 are:

– As explained in Kat and Oomen (2007a), the realized return and the volatility profile of commodities are very similar to what equities are capable of. The average return on the four GSCI sub-indexes ranges from −1.8% for agriculture to 9.6% for precious metals. This is very similar to the range of −4.1% (Nikkei) to 16.6% (Bovespa) found in our equity sample. The returns on commodities have been positive over the 1995–2012 period for most of the commodities, as well as for the sub-periods considered in the table. This is, however, not true for the agricultural products over the 1995–2003 period: during this period, the return on sugar was −10.4% for example. Positive returns have also been delivered by the various equity indices presented in the table, but for the Eurostoxx 50 case from 2003 to 2012. There is an ongoing debate about the existence of a risk premium in commodities that would be similar to what can be found in equities: for a large majority of them at least,

Table 1.1 Descriptive statistics on commodity, stock, currencies and rates

		Ann. Returns (%)			Volatility (%)			Skewness	Kurtosis	Extremes (%)		AR
		Total	1995–2003	2004–2012	Total	1995–2003	2004–2012			Min.	Max.	
Commodities	Gold	0.089	−0.002	0.188	0.168	0.13	0.199	0.067	7.352	−0.072	0.102	−0.017
	Silver	0.112	0.005	0.232	0.301	0.215	0.368	−1.119	10.509	−0.204	0.132	−0.022
	Platinum	0.079	0.063	0.095	0.224	0.21	0.237	−0.379	5.498	−0.097	0.1	0.042*
	Aluminum	0.002	−0.04	0.046	0.206	0.153	0.248	−0.325	2.753	−0.082	0.059	−0.026
	Copper	0.061	−0.06	0.198	0.268	0.185	0.331	−0.213	4.536	−0.104	0.119	−0.044*
	Nickel	0.04	0.005	0.077	0.363	0.285	0.428	−0.186	3.903	−0.181	0.131	0.009
	Zinc	0.033	−0.041	0.114	0.288	0.176	0.367	−0.3	3.517	−0.121	0.091	−0.025
	Lead	0.069	−0.037	0.186	0.312	0.187	0.4	−0.262	3.961	−0.128	0.127	0.055*
	WTI	0.109	0.061	0.16	0.358	0.346	0.37	−0.094	4.475	−0.165	0.219	−0.008
	Brent	0.122	0.054	0.196	0.341	0.334	0.347	−0.144	3.19	−0.144	0.129	−0.042*
	Gasoil	0.117	0.051	0.188	0.32	0.318	0.322	−0.165	2.661	−0.157	0.112	0.004
	Natural Gas	0.018	0.129	−0.082	0.548	0.566	0.529	0.388	5.717	−0.222	0.346	−0.016
	Heating Oil	0.113	0.05	0.179	0.347	0.344	0.349	−0.246	2.335	−0.14	0.103	−0.031*
	Corn	0.061	0.005	0.119	0.287	0.245	0.324	−0.71	15.701	−0.284	0.092	0.036*
	Wheat	0.03	−0.007	0.067	0.314	0.256	0.362	0.21	2.269	−0.1	0.11	0.002
	Coffee	0.004	−0.095	0.114	0.386	0.444	0.318	0.075	4.984	−0.15	0.212	−0.011
	Sugar	0.018	−0.104	0.158	0.35	0.326	0.372	−0.236	3.549	−0.154	0.143	−0.002
	Cocoa	0.032	0.03	0.034	0.311	0.298	0.324	−0.065	2.407	−0.1	0.107	−0.001
	Cotton	0.001	−0.029	0.032	0.297	0.274	0.319	−1.362	26.364	−0.34	0.09	0.028
	Soybean	0.059	0.006	0.114	0.249	0.208	0.284	−0.42	3.17	−0.099	0.065	−0.009
	Rice	0.05	0.015	0.085	0.278	0.284	0.273	0.279	19.437	−0.219	0.255	0.047*
	GSCI Agri.	−0.018	−0.042	0.006	0.197	0.146	0.237	−0.119	2.696	−0.075	0.072	0.024
	GSCI Energy	0.079	0.151	0.012	0.319	0.307	0.331	−0.223	2.197	−0.144	0.098	−0.019
	GSCI Ind. Metals	0.049	−0.031	0.136	0.226	0.147	0.284	−0.28	3.154	−0.09	0.076	−0.041*
	GSCI Prec. Metals	0.096	0.016	0.183	0.178	0.13	0.216	−0.143	6.363	−0.082	0.088	0.013
Equities	Dow Jones	0.074	0.109	0.04	0.191	0.186	0.196	−0.154	7.394	−0.082	0.105	−0.062*
	S&P 500	0.066	0.095	0.038	0.203	0.191	0.214	−0.233	7.578	−0.095	0.11	−0.07*
	Nasdaq	0.085	0.108	0.062	0.27	0.304	0.232	−0.054	4.729	−0.102	0.133	−0.021
	Canadian TSX	0.064	0.07	0.059	0.182	0.165	0.199	−0.704	8.949	−0.098	0.094	0.003
	Mexico IPC	0.177	0.148	0.206	0.255	0.285	0.222	0.052	6.181	−0.143	0.122	0.092*
	Brazil BOVESPA	0.166	0.158	0.174	0.364	0.419	0.301	0.458	12.751	−0.172	0.288	0.03
	Euro Stoxx	0.033	0.084	−0.016	0.236	0.239	0.233	−0.052	4.553	−0.082	0.104	−0.009
	FTSE	0.037	0.037	0.037	0.195	0.19	0.2	−0.155	5.69	−0.093	0.094	−0.022
	CAC 40	0.031	0.062	0.001	0.238	0.242	0.235	−0.016	4.422	−0.095	0.106	−0.013

(continued)

Table 1.1 (Continued)

		Ann. Returns (%)			Volatility (%)			Skewness	Kurtosis	Extremes (%)		AR
		Total	1995–2003	2004–2012	Total	1995–2003	2004–2012			Min.	Max.	
	DAX	0.07	0.064	0.077	0.248	0.266	0.229	−0.12	4.126	−0.089	0.108	−0.009
	IBEX	0.048	0.097	0.001	0.237	0.237	0.238	−0.023	5.139	−0.096	0.135	0.022
	MIB	−0.035	0.039	−0.105	0.251	0.239	0.262	−0.096	4.278	−0.086	0.109	0.005
	AEX	0.029	0.069	−0.01	0.238	0.25	0.226	−0.132	5.594	−0.096	0.1	0
	OMX	0.078	0.09	0.066	0.252	0.262	0.242	0.083	3.33	−0.085	0.11	−0.009
	SMI	0.05	0.085	0.016	0.199	0.209	0.188	−0.081	5.478	−0.081	0.108	0.033*
	NIKKEI	−0.041	−0.072	−0.009	0.246	0.241	0.252	−0.272	5.669	−0.121	0.132	−0.037*
	HANG SENG	0.059	0.039	0.079	0.279	0.289	0.267	0.093	9.271	−0.147	0.172	0
	ASX	0.051	0.065	0.037	0.16	0.131	0.184	−0.484	6.115	−0.087	0.057	−0.029
Currencies	Euro	0.004	−0.009	0.016	0.099	0.096	0.102	0.128	1.822	−0.026	0.039	0.005
	Canadian Dollar	−0.02	−0.001	−0.038	0.084	0.056	0.105	−0.162	5.984	−0.058	0.028	0
	Japanese Yen	−0.013	0.018	−0.043	0.111	0.117	0.105	−0.479	4.692	−0.063	0.034	−0.003
	Australian Dollar	0.017	−0.021	0.056	0.127	0.101	0.148	−0.68	12.189	−0.087	0.069	−0.018
	Hong Kong Dollar	0	0.001	−0.001	0.005	0.003	0.006	−2.711	44.815	−0.006	0.003	−0.051*
	Singapore Dollar	0.078	0.146	0.014	0.359	0.356	0.362	−0.889	12.402	−0.301	0.133	0.009
	New Zealand Dollar	0.014	−0.012	0.041	0.129	0.104	0.15	−0.3	5.343	−0.063	0.065	0.018
	British Pound	0.002	0.001	0.003	0.09	0.077	0.101	−0.068	4.26	−0.035	0.052	0.014
	Swiss Franc	−0.021	0.007	−0.049	0.113	0.11	0.116	0.224	8.122	−0.054	0.091	−0.028
	Swedish Krona	−0.006	0.014	−0.025	0.119	0.1	0.135	−0.242	3.583	−0.065	0.031	−0.023
	Norwegian Krone	−0.01	0.012	−0.031	0.12	0.097	0.14	−0.234	11.1	−0.094	0.082	−0.025
	Indian Rupee	0.03	0.048	0.014	0.056	0.041	0.067	0.274	10.529	−0.03	0.034	0.061*
	Vietnamese Dong	0.037	0.037	0.038	0.04	0.041	0.039	9.875	228.613	−0.04	0.065	−0.117*
	Brazilian Real	0.048	0.158	−0.049	0.158	0.149	0.166	0.671	18.853	−0.119	0.114	0.01
	Mexican Peso	0.057	0.098	0.019	0.143	0.169	0.11	−0.926	99.598	−0.207	0.137	−0.143*
	Polish Zloty	0.016	0.059	−0.026	0.133	0.096	0.162	0.159	5.154	−0.069	0.048	0.027
Rates	US 2	−0.43	−0.663	−0.197	0.545	0.308	0.706	−0.025	10.397	−0.301	0.303	−0.078*
	US 5	−0.406	−0.506	−0.305	0.387	0.241	0.491	−0.163	7.377	−0.23	0.146	−0.055*
	US 10	−0.342	−0.389	−0.294	0.263	0.191	0.319	−0.224	6.533	−0.171	0.105	−0.025
	US 30	−0.275	−0.307	−0.244	0.195	0.142	0.237	−0.255	6.212	−0.114	0.08	−0.006
	German 2	−0.372	−0.468	−0.274	0.531	0.2	0.724	−0.577	31.917	−0.409	0.409	−0.025
	German 5	−0.389	−0.457	−0.32	0.32	0.181	0.414	−0.364	12.079	−0.197	0.164	0.031*
	German 10	−0.345	−0.398	−0.293	0.203	0.136	0.254	−0.072	8.856	−0.136	0.113	0.045*
	German 30	−0.325	−0.35	−0.299	0.161	0.117	0.196	0.015	4.995	−0.076	0.064	0.084*

we find a positive annualized return over the three types of periods considered here. On this debate, see Kat and Oomen (2007a), Gorton and Rouwenhorst (2005b) and Erb and Campbell (2006).[1]

– Commodities are supposed to exhibit a volatility that is larger than those of the usual equity index. On this point, our figures agree with those from Kat and Oomen (2007a) – and despite the inclusion of the 2008 crisis in our sample we do not find that commodities' volatility is higher than equities'. On average, annualized commodity volatility ranges around 30%. Three singular cases must, however, be distingished from the others: coffee (38.6% of annualized volatility), sugar (35%) and heating oil (54.8%). Beyond these cases, the rest of the figures look very similar to stock indices for emerging or developed equities.

– The skewness figures presented in Table 1.1 should help the reader gain some intuition about the potential asymmetries in the distributions of returns on commodities. Two conclusions arise from those figures. First, the sign of the skewness depends on the type of commodity considered: while in the case of gold (0.067) and wheat it is positive (0.21), the skewness associated with cotton is large and negative (-1.362). Equity indexes conversely are primarily affected by negative skewness, but for a couple of emerging markets such as Brazil and China. For example, the S&P 500 has a negative skewness over 1995–2012 that is equal to -0.233. A similar case can be made out of the interest rate figures: the skewness obtained from the variations of the 5-year rate is equal to -0.577. When considering the results obtained from the foreign exchange rates, we obtain a picture that is very close to what is obtained from the commodity dataset: the skewness can take various signs. For example the Australian Dollar vs. the US Dollar has a skewness equal to -0.479, whereas the Euro vs. US Dollar has a skewness equal to 0.128. The US Dollar vs. the Polish Zloty has a skewness equal to 0.159, whereas the US Dollar vs. the Mexican Peso has a skewness equal to -0.926. In this respect, the commodities – considered as an asset class – appear closer to the currencies than to any other asset classes presented here. A second conclusion from this table is related to the scale of the skewness value: despite a few extreme values, the absolute value obtained from the commodities looks very similar to what is obtained from any other asset class. In this respect, the asymmetry of commodities is very close in terms of magnitude to the rest of the financial markets. The main difference here is that the sign of the asymmetry looks asset-specific.

– Turning to the kurtosis analysis, two conclusions again should be drawn from the table. First, when considering individual commodities, we find large kurtosis. This is in line with the previously quoted articles such as Kat and Oomen (2007a) emphasizing that the main difference between commodities and the rest of the asset classes lies in the extreme events found in the variations of the prices of raw materials. Their kurtosis ranges between 2.269 for coffee and 26.364 for cotton. On average each of these kurtose are higher than 3, the threshold to be reached for the empirical distribution to depart from the thin tails obtained from a Gaussian distribution. The magnitude of these kurtose is broadly speaking in line with the figures obtained on the equity side, yet with a higher degree of heterogeneity. In this respect, it is again closer to the currency markets for which we obtain high variations in kurtosis from one currency to the other. The magnitude of the kurtosis obtained with the basket of currencies considered here is, however, much higher than the one obtained from

---

[1] Finding a positive return for most of the commodities over the period considered here is not proof that commodity holders receive a risk premium for being long of such markets. Part II of this book will cast light on the possible macroeconomic fundamentals explaining positive or negative performances of such markets.

the commodity dataset. The second conclusion from the kurtosis computations is reached when comparing the results obtained from individual commodities and from the baskets of GSCI indices: the kurtosis associated to the latter is, on average, lower than the one computed from part of its components. For example, the WTI has a kurtosis equal to 4.475 whereas the GSCI Energy sub-index has a kurtosis equal to 2.197. A similar pattern is obtained from the GSCI Agricultural sub-index: its kurtosis is equal to 2.696 when cotton has a kurtosis equal to 26.364, and rice a kurtosis equal to 19.437. This has to be related to one of the key stylized facts about commodities: the weak correlation between them, even amongst a given commodity sector. We will discuss figures around this issue later.

– A last point must be mentioned when analyzing the basics of returns on commodities: following Kat and Oomen (2007a) and a very prolific literature that we will detail later, commodities are known to be affected by a high degree of persistence. In other words, commodities are known to exhibit sharp trends that were one of the reasons for the development of the well known trend-following industry that tries to benefit from trends in financial markets. A first way to gauge these persistent trends is to estimate a regression of the following type:

$$r_t^i = \phi_0 + \phi_1 r_{t-1}^i + \epsilon_t^i, \tag{1.1}$$

where r_t^i is the daily logarithmic return on the commodity i, ϵ_t^i is a random disturbance with an expectation equal to 0 and standard deviation equal to σ^i. ϕ_0 and ϕ_1 are real-valued parameters that can be estimated by Ordinary Least Squares (OLS).[2] The last column of Table 1.1 presents such estimates along with an asterisk for each parameter significantly different from zero. Out of the 22 estimates, only eight are different from zero. To observe persistent trends, we need to have ϕ_1^i positive: this is only the case for platinum, lead, corn and rice. These numbers are obtained by using daily returns that are thus less persistent than weekly or monthly returns. Still, when comparing these results to those obtained in the case of other assets, we have trouble finding sharply different conclusions. In the case of equity, we find two significant and positive parameters (Mexico IPC and SMI) and three negative and statistically significant ones (Dow Jones, S&P 500 and Nikkei) out of the 18 indices considered here. A similar picture is obtained in the currency case. The case of interest rates is a bit different: for these series, we have five out of eight series that yield significant estimates. From these preliminary estimates, we fail to find a picture as striking as the one presented by Kat and Oomen (2007a): over the past 15 years, there is limited evidence of a higher persistence in commodities than in other asset classes.

This preliminary analysis casts light on the key aspects we are going to focus on in the coming pages: the nature and the number of trends in commodity markets, the origin of the asymmetry in returns on commodities and finally the jump activity in commodities. These seem to be the aspects for which our preliminary analysis pointed out differences between commodities and the usual asset classes. The next section deals with the complex relationships between returns on commodities and the term structure of futures. This question has been the center of much of the academic attention over the past 30 years. We revisit this problem, as it is one of the keys to forecasting returns on raw materials. We move then to an extensive trend analysis in commodities, of the asymmetry in returns, and finally of the tail activity observed over the past 20 years.

---

[2] We refer any reader interested in these time series models to Box *et al.* (2008).

1.1 BACKWARDATION, CONTANGO AND COMMODITY RISK PREMIUM

Beyond the themes that will be analyzed in the coming pages, a large part of the academic literature has been devoted to the understanding of the existence of a slope in commodity futures. Basically, futures are financial contracts that entitle the buyer (respectively the seller) to buy (sell) a given amount of a certain asset at a price that is set in advance for a given maturity. Unlike options, which allow holders to exercise or not the contract, futures involve a commitment to deliver or to buy the underlying asset. These futures contracts are actively used by commodity traders – and their clients – either to hedge future flows or to speculate over the future stance of a given market. In the case of equities, this slope is solely driven by the risk-free rate through arbitrage arguments. The case of commodities is unclear: commodity futures are bought both by producers and buyers of such products to hedge their natural exposure to market fluctuations. For example, when an oil-producing company wants to hedge – i.e. wipe out the risk in its balance sheet that is purely related to the fluctuation of oil prices: its exposure – it can decide to sell futures six months in advance in order to know exactly at what price it will be able to sell its planned production in the future. On the other side of the market, a company that needs to secure the price of its buying of raw products can decide to buy such futures. Depending on the balance of hedgers – buyers and sellers – the slope of the term structure of futures would be upward or downward. When this slope is upward, market participants say that the market is in a contangoed position. Conversely, when the term structure of future prices is downward sloping, the market is said to be in backwardation.

Although this problem is of little relevance for investing in commodities,[3] it still matters from a financial economics point of view. What is more, when the trading of commodities involves the actual delivery of the underlying asset, this term structure of commodities implies some sort of a 'risk premium'; that is, the fact that it is possible to buy, for example, a given amount of raw product for a future price that will be below the actual spot price on the day of the settlement of such futures. Several theories have tried to explain the existence of such a slope. Keynes (1930) developed a theory of 'normal backwardation': in a world where risk-averse commodity-producing companies are the main market participants, their need to hedge price risk should drive future prices lower. By doing so, the future price of commodities should be structurally lower than their spot prices, and such markets should be regularly backwarded. A side effect of this theory is that by buying futures and selling the spot asset, an investor would be able to generate a profit: this potential profit is usually regarded as a 'commodity risk premium'. However, as shown in Table 1.2, such an average pattern simply does not exist: different commodities have different slopes, and through time a given commodity can either be backwarded or contangoed. This table presents the results obtained when computing $s(t, T)^i$ the future curve's slope for asset i:

$$s(t, T)^i = \frac{F(t, T)^i}{S(t)^i} - 1, \tag{1.2}$$

where $S(t)^i$ is the spot price at time t for commodity i and $F(t, T)^i$ the corresponding future with a residual maturity equal to $T - t$. We use three different generic futures contracts,

---

[3] When a private or an institutional investor wishes to have an exposure to the commodity universe through futures, this regularly requires rolling the position from a future with a maturity that turned out to be short to a longer dated future. As pointed out in Gorton and Rouwenhorst (2005a), this rolling procedure of futures has, by construction, no impact on the performance of an investment in commodities provided that the net amount of this investment remains unchanged.

Table 1.2 Average difference between the 3, 6 and 9 month futures and the spot price of commodities expressed as percentages of the spot price

	All sample			1995–2003			2003–2012		
	3M slope	6M slope	9M slope	3M slope	6M slope	9M slope	3M slope	6M slope	9M slope
Aluminum	0.37*	0.66*	0.84*	0.32*	0.58*	0.68*	0.41*	0.74*	1*
Brent	−0.08*	−0.23*	−0.44*	−0.67*	−1.36*	−2.03*	0.52*	0.89*	1.15*
Cocoa	1.2*	2.27*	3.28*	1.56*	2.95*	4.37*	0.84*	1.58*	2.2*
Coffee	1.5*	2.97*	4.36*	0.68*	1.65*	2.69*	2.31*	4.3*	6.04*
Copper	−0.09*	−0.21*	−0.36*	0	−0.09*	−0.19*	−0.18*	−0.33*	−0.53*
Corn	2.32*	4*	5.16*	1.8*	3.39*	4.59*	2.84*	4.61*	5.73*
Cotton	1.82*	3.19*	5.14*	1.98*	3.42*	4.57*	1.67*	2.95*	5.7*
Gasoil	0.05*	0.11*	0.18*	−0.18*	−0.33*	−0.47*	0.28*	0.55*	0.82*
Gold	0.25*	0.24*	0.42*	0.29*	0.7*	0.65*	0.2*	−0.22	0.19*
Heating Oil	0.19*	0.29*	0.33*	−0.24*	−0.42*	−0.61*	0.61*	1.01*	1.27*
Natural Gas	1.93*	3.32*	4.37*	0.56*	0.79*	0.96*	3.29*	5.85*	7.78*
Nickel	−0.12*	−0.29*	−0.61*	−0.08*	−0.17*	−0.5*	−0.16*	−0.4*	−0.72*
Rice	2.05*	3.8*	5.23*	2.34*	4.55*	6.45*	1.77*	3.05*	4.01*
Silver	0.26*	−0.05	1.1*	0.32*	0.66*	1.21*	0.2*	−0.76*	1*
Soybean	0.2*	0.09	−0.16	0.11*	1.00E-02	−0.1	0.29*	0.17*	−0.22
Sugar	−0.21*	−0.67*	−0.95*	−1.49*	−2.54*	−2.89*	1.06*	1.2*	1*
Wheat	2.62*	4.14*	5.36*	2.14*	3.5*	4.67*	3.1*	4.77*	6.04*
WTI	−0.06	−0.22*	−0.42*	−0.83*	−1.6*	−2.31*	0.71*	1.17*	1.47*

Note: An asterisk indicates that the average is statistically different from zeros at a 5% risk level.

ranging from 3 to 9 months by periods of three months. This provides us with a dataset of slopes expressed in terms of percentage increases over the spot price for three maturities: 3, 6 and 9 months. By doing so, we can bring some statistics not only around the 3 month slope as is generally the case, but also check whether the sign of the slope is consistent across maturities.

This table confirms previous results: commodities are both affected by backwardation and contango. For example, aluminum exhibits on average an upward sloping future curve: every 3 months of maturity increase leads on average to a future price higher by 0.3% over the period considered here (1995–2012). Conversely, Brent is typically a commodity for which the future slope is negative: 3 months of additional maturity lead to a future price lower by 0.1 to 0.2%. Out of the 18 commodities reported here, only 5 of them have been backwarded on average over the period. Consistent with that, Kolb (1992) investigated 29 commodity futures, finding that there is no 'normal backwardation'. Bodie and Rosansky (1980) ended up with a similar conclusion. What is more, over the full period, the sign of the slope is consistent across the three selected maturities. One of the only exceptions is silver over the 2003–2012 period: its 6-month slope is significantly negative (−0.76%) whereas its 9-month slope is significantly positive (1%). Finally, the sign of the futures slope can change depending on the period: for example, heating oil has a positive slope over the 1995–2003 period, and a negative one over the subsequent period. This holds across all maturities of the futures on heating oil considered here. A similar case can be made with sugar.

A natural way out of this conundrum is to assume that commodity producers are not the only hedgers intervening in such markets. Cootner (1960) and Deaves and Krinsky (1995) have formulated the 'hedging pressure hypothesis': depending on whether hedgers are net long or net short, this slope of the term structure can either be negative or positive. For example, Bessembinder (1992) found that over the 1967–1989 period, the return on futures was influenced by the net position of hedgers. With this theory, there is a commodity risk premium, and its sign depends on the net hedging pressures: when producers are dominant, the risk premium is positive, as buying futures and selling the spot asset should deliver a positive return to the holder. Conversely, when commodity consumers are the main hedgers, the risk premium should be negative overall. The evidence presented in Table 1.2 is somewhat more consistent with the conclusions of this theory, as it makes it possible to have both upward and backward sloping futures curves.

Finally, a third theory attempts to explain the existence of such a slope. The 'theory of storage' links the level and cost of commodity inventories to the shape of the futures curve. We owe this theory to Kaldor (1939) and Brennan (1991): it tries to explain why inventories are observed in periods of downward-sloping futures curves, as such a pattern implies a future spot price that should be lower than the current level and therefore a lower nominal value of the inventories held. Holding inventories helps in handling the varying demand: disruptions on the production chain would have a limited impact on the ability to meet the global demand. This stock buffer improves somewhat the comfort of the commodity producer, hence generating a 'convenience yield'. However, by doing so, the producer has now to face a market risk, linked to the fluctuations of the market price of its commodity. Such a risk is higher when storage is low: for such a case, the convenience yield should be very important and the term structure of futures downward sloping so as to provide the inventories holder with a positive risk premium. Conversely, when inventories are high and the convenience yield is therefore low, the term structure of futures should be upward sloping, merely reflecting the interest rates paid when borrowing cash to build the storage space and the actual cost of storage. Gorton *et al.* (2012) provide an empirical assessment of the impact of inventories over 31 commodity futures curves: as they point out, accessing such a dataset is difficult, especially over extended periods such as theirs.[4] They conclude that inventories have a strong explanatory power over the 'basis' of many commodities; that is, the difference between the first future and the spot price of each commodity. Inventories seem to robustly predict the sign and magnitude of risk premium in commodities, whereas the net position of traders – that measures where the hedging pressure is – has limited – if any – explanatory power. This long-standing debate is, however, still in discussion: here, the length and depth of datasets matters.

Beyond the potential explanations of such a phenomenon, there is one interesting question to be raised and answered here: a large part of the literature expects that the risk premium earned from holding commodities can be explained by the slope of these futures curves. Let $r^i_{(t,t+h)}$ be the return realized over the t to $t + h$ period by holding asset i. Table 1.3 displays the following correlations:

$$\operatorname{cor}(r^i_{(t,t+h)}, s(t, T)^i). \tag{1.3}$$

In the case of Table 1.3, h is equal to 3 months.[5] When there should be a relation between the term structure of futures and the expected returns on a given commodity, this relation should

---

[4] They study commodity risk premium over the 1969–2006 period, therefore limiting the impact of shorter datasets on the estimation results.

[5] The results presented here are, however, weakly dependent over the choice of this period. With this 3-month period, we simply put a larger emphasis on the stylized fact we are trying to measure.

Table 1.3   Correlation between rolling 6-month returns and the 3 to 9 month slopes

	3M slope	6M slope	9M slope
Aluminum	0	−0.03	−0.01
Brent	0.04*	0.05*	0.05*
Cocoa	0.03*	0	−0.01
Coffee	0.09*	0.1*	0.09*
Copper	0.05*	0.05*	0.05*
Corn	0.32*	0.28*	0.18*
Cotton	0.23*	0.27*	0.76*
Gasoil	0.12*	0.13*	0.14*
Gold	−0.18*	0.04*	0.03*
Heating Oil	0.14*	0.16*	0.19*
Natural Gas	0.28*	0.38*	0.4*
Nickel	0.06*	0.05*	0.02
Rice	0.45*	0.42*	0.36*
Silver	−0.02	0.01	0.23*
Soybean	0.34*	0.38*	0.36*
Sugar	0.29*	0.44*	0.36*
Wheat	0.14*	0.12*	0.09*
WTI	0.1*	0.09*	0.09*

be negative: a negative slope implies a positive return on average obtained from buying the future and selling the spot asset. From Table 1.3, we get the impression that this correlation is, however, more positive than negative. We obtain a negative correlation only in four cases, and only one of them is significantly different from zero. For the rest of the cases, this correlation is significantly positive, implying that a positive slope forecasts a positive return on commodities. What is more, the scale of this correlation ranges between 0 and 0.2 for most of the cases, which is rather low for a correlation. There are, however, four commodities for which this correlation is higher: corn, cotton, soybean and sugar. Beyond them, the correlation remains weak but significant. Hence, the commodity risk premium is poorly explained by the term structure of futures, and the sign of the relationship goes against the theory that the risk premium is negatively correlated to the slope of futures.

Cochrane and Piazzesi (2005) found that the term structure of futures has a forecasting power over the realized future variation of the underlying interest rates. By regressing those realized variations over a basket of futures with various time to maturities, they found 'tent-shaped' coefficients across futures' maturities. Combining these futures through these coefficients, they obtained a new factor that explains one third of one-year ahead excess returns. Their finding has been confirmed in Kessler and Scherer (2009) and Sekkel (2011) for non-US markets. One way to reconcile the relationship between the slope of the term structure of futures and the realized performance of the spot asset is to run a regression similar to Cochrane and Piazzesi (2005). Within this approach, the slope is assumed to contain elements that forecast future returns. The slope would therefore be driven in part by financial market participants' expectations. By using previous notation, we run the following regression:

$$r^i_{(t,t+h)} = \alpha^i_0 + \sum_{j=1}^{3} \beta^i_j s(t, T_j)^i + \epsilon(t)^i, \tag{1.4}$$

with $\epsilon(t)^i$ being a centered disturbance with volatility σ_ϵ and T_j for $j = 1, 2, 3$ being the various maturities for the slopes considered here. Here, we consider various h, from 1 week to 6 months. Given the overlapping nature of our sample, the asymptotic volatility for the OLS estimates of the previous regression has to be modified. Following Cochrane and Piazzesi (2005), we rely on a Newey–West approach to the robust estimation of those volatilities. Results are presented in Table 1.4 along with R^2. Figures 1.1, 1.2, 1.3 and 1.4 chart the β_j across futures maturities obtained with the 3-month returns, when both the realized returns on the spot asset and the slopes of the future curve have been scaled to make the parameters comparable across commodities. Our results confirm that of Cochrane and Piazzesi (2005) in terms of interest rate futures: in the case of agriculture and energy, we find tent-shaped β_j^i across maturities.[6] Most of the estimated parameters are found to be significantly different from zero at a 5% risk level. In the 3-month case, those regressions come with an R^2 that is greater than 0.1 for 6 of the 18 cases considered here, confirming that the slope of the futures curve contains information that can explain the commodity risk premium. From these results, it appears that the relation between the commodity risk premium is more complicated than the previous theories predicted. Interestingly, despite the non-financial aspect of such assets, we still find properties that are consistent with what is usually found for the standard assets. By comparing the results obtained for various h, we cast light on the dependency of our results upon the period over which the returns are computed. From the analysis of Table 1.4, when increasing the period over which the returns are computed, we obtain a growing explanatory power of this simple regression. For example, in the case of cotton, the R^2 associated with this regression is equal to 0.06 in the 1 week returns case, and to 0.663 in the 6-month case. Hence, following these regressions, the slope of the term structure of commodity futures can incorporate information that helps predict the commodity risk premium. Figures 1.1, 1.2, 1.3 and 1.4 clearly display tent-shaped parameters across maturities. The forecasting power of this regression does not seem to be as important as the one obtained in the bond market case. However, for some of the markets investigated here, we obtain an R^2 that can reach 0.6, as in the case of cotton. However, the variability of this R^2 is higher than in the bond case. Such results tend to show that the term structure of futures is a variable of interest to investors, as it expresses at least partly participants' expectations – as for other purely financial assets.

1.2   UNDERSTANDING COMMODITIES' MOMENTA

This section will focus on the measurement of trends in commodities. Trends are one of the backbones of the quantitative fund management industry: 'trend followers' are funds whose main strategy is to invest in assets with positive trends. These trend-following strategies all started under the label of Commodity Trading Advisors (CTAs), investing primarily in commodities. The name has remained, but the scope of investment possibilities has increased, extending to futures and options written on any type of asset. Still, commodities may have been the birthplace of the trend-following industry. When reading the main conclusions appearing in Kat and Oomen (2007a; 2007b) regarding the persistence of trends, the consistency between these trend-following methods and the persistence found in commodities definitely makes sense. The objective of this section is to assess the nature of these trends in commodities through their measurement.

---

[6] Unlike Cochrane and Piazzesi (2005) who use forward rates from 2 to 10 years, here we can only rely on the most liquid short-term contracts.

Table 1.4 Regression results of the 1-week to 6-month returns over the slopes of the future curve

	1-week returns				1-month returns				3-months return				6-months return			
	3M slope	6M slope	9M slope	R^2	3M slope	6M slope	9M slope	R^2	3M slope	6M slope	9M slope	R^2	3M slope	6M slope	9M slope	R^2
Aluminum	0.003	−0.001	0	0.001	0.007*	−0.004	0	0.002	0.002	−0.009*	0.004	0.002	0.011	0.002	−0.005	0.001
Brent	−0.004	0.004	−0.001	0	−0.017	0.033*	−0.016*	0.003	−0.065*	0.061*	−0.017	0.006	0.049	−0.129*	0.078*	0.014
Cocoa	0.004*	−0.003	0.001	0.001	−0.002	0.009*	−0.005*	0.002	0.033*	−0.016*	−0.002	0.013	0.06*	−0.005	−0.02*	0.037
Coffee	−0.002	0.005*	−0.003*	0.004	−0.021*	0.035*	−0.017*	0.03	−0.039*	0.064*	−0.03*	0.041	−0.073*	0.079*	−0.025*	0.046
Copper	0.001	0.007*	−0.005*	0.003	−0.004	0.013	−0.006	0.004	−0.007	0.006	0.002	0.003	−0.067*	0.027	0.013	0.007
Corn	0.002*	0.001	−0.001*	0.012	0.008*	0.001	−0.003*	0.051	0.014*	0.011*	−0.008*	0.124	0.008*	0.02*	−0.005*	0.195
Cotton	0.002*	−0.001*	0.001*	0.061	0.007*	−0.005*	0.003*	0.205	0.006*	−0.009*	0.008*	0.624	−0.014*	−0.002*	0.012*	0.663
Gasoil	0.001	0	0	0.003	0.012	−0.012	0.007*	0.014	0.031*	−0.064*	0.039*	0.029	0.111*	−0.215*	0.114*	0.046
Gold	−0.009*	0	0	0.003	−0.04*	0*	0.002*	0.021	−0.09*	0.001*	0.002*	0.04	−0.148*	0.001*	0.001	0.051
Heating Oil	0.004	−0.006	0.003*	0.009	0.014*	−0.016*	0.009*	0.028	0.04*	−0.065*	0.037*	0.052	0.042*	−0.092*	0.054*	0.035
Natural Gas	0.001	0.003*	−0.002*	0.041	−0.004*	0.015*	−0.007*	0.132	−0.018*	0.015*	0.002*	0.174	−0.002	−0.003	0.01*	0.08
Nickel	0.006	−0.001	−0.001	0.001	0.013	0.002	−0.007*	0.002	0.076*	0.023*	−0.039*	0.019	0.133*	0.045*	−0.063*	0.032
Rice	0.002*	0	0	0.033	0.009*	−0.002*	0.001	0.124	0.011*	0.005*	−0.001	0.207	0.005*	0.001	0.009*	0.221
Silver	−0.005*	0*	0.003*	0.16	−0.002	0	0.004*	0.062	−0.02*	0	0.006*	0.053	−0.058*	0	0.007*	0.041
Soybean	0.002*	0.001	−0.001*	0.03	0.011*	0.003	−0.003*	0.109	−0.009*	0.022*	−0.004*	0.149	0.017*	−0.029*	0.03*	0.18
Sugar	0.001*	0.002*	−0.001*	0.029	−0.001	0.012*	−0.006*	0.126	−0.013*	0.029*	−0.01*	0.248	−0.028*	0.032*	0	0.297
Wheat	0.002*	0	0	0.006	0.004*	0.001	−0.001	0.016	0.006*	0.001	−0.001	0.02	0.003	0.004	−0.001	0.019
WTI	−0.007	0.014	−0.007	0.003	−0.025	0.054*	−0.028*	0.012	0.07*	−0.06*	0.019	0.012	0.157*	−0.19*	0.081*	0.015

Note: The first three columns present the estimated parameters and the final column displays the R^2 obtained with the full regression. An asterisk indicates a statistically significant relation at a 5% risk level. We used a Newey–West estimation to the parameters' volatilities.

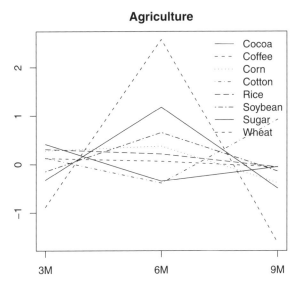

Figure 1.1 Tent-shaped regression for agriculture products

When it comes to analyzing trends in commodities, a first question must be raised and answered: should we consider working on the prices or on the returns of financial assets? Following Ghoshray (2011a), there seems to be mixed evidence of unit roots in commodity prices: returns are usually considered as they are, by construction, trend-stationary. Prices are the results of the combination of positive and negative trends: the combination of those two types of trends is not always trend-stationary. Hence the diagnostic of trend-stationary prices depends on the dataset used, as the various conclusions obtained in the literature demonstrate.

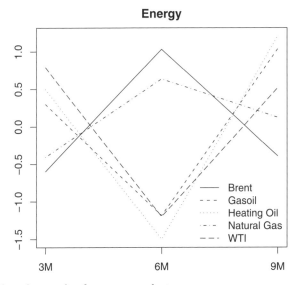

Figure 1.2 Tent-shaped regression for energy products

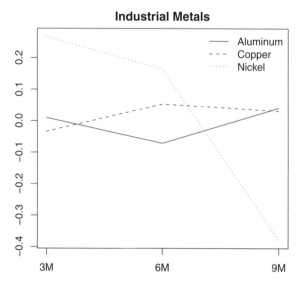

Figure 1.3   Tent-shaped regression for industrial metals

For example, Sapsford (1985), Grilli and Yang (1988), Helg (1991) and Ardeni and Wright (1992) found evidence that commodities are trend-stationary. Conversely, Cuddington and Urzua (1989), Cuddington (1992), Bleaney and Greenaway (1993) and Newbold *et al.* (2005) used empirical tests showing that commodities are difference-stationary. This question of stationarity will be investigated in Part III of this book. Here, we aim to consider commodities as any other financial asset: in this respect, we will work in this section with returns on commodities. Let p_t^i be the logarithm of the price of asset i at the closing market session at

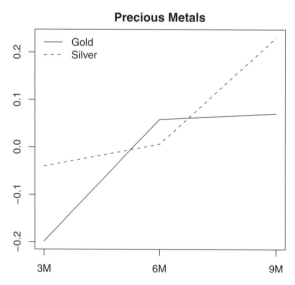

Figure 1.4   Tent-shaped regression for precious metals

time t. The return obtained from investing in asset i between the date $t - 1$ and t r_t^i is therefore calculated as follows:

$$r_t^i = p_t^i - p_{t-1}^i. \tag{1.5}$$

In a similar fashion to the presentation in Ghoshray (2011a; 2011b), a trend in the asset i can be represented in the following way:

$$p_t^i = a_0^i + a_1^i t + \epsilon_t^i, \tag{1.6}$$

where ϵ_t captures the deviation from the trend. The sign of a_1^i decides the nature of the trend. Moving back to returns, this equation turns out to be

$$r_t^i = a_1^i + \epsilon_t^i - \epsilon_{t-1}^i. \tag{1.7}$$

When a_1^i is positive (respectively negative), the asset is driven by a positive (negative) trend. The first three columns of Table 1.1 displayed estimates for a_1^i across commodities from 1995 to 2012, using daily data. Obviously, the sign of long-term trends varies depending on assets. For example, from 1995 to 2003, the price of sugar seems to have been affected by a negative trend, while the price of natural gas has been affected by a positive trend. A large literature tries to assess whether a constant sign affects the price of commodities. Ghoshray (2011b) examines the Prebisch–Singer hypothesis[7] that commodity prices should be decreasing over the long run, using recent advances in unit root testing in the presence of multiple breaks. While Leon and Soto (1997) found that 17 commodities were affected by negative trends, Ghoshray (2011b) only found seven negatively trending commodities. Cuddington (1992) found that five out of 22 commodity prices had negative trend commodities over the 1900–1983 period – and that 16 of them were diagnosed as trendless. Wickham and Reinhart (1994) found a long-term negative trend that is shared by many commodities. Bleaney and Greenaway (1993) found that the sign of trends actually depends on the kind of commodities investigated. More recently, Cashin and McDermott (2002) found evidence of persistent negative trends in commodities over 140 years.

The main issue here is that these trends have a low probability of being stable: world-wide business cycles, political events or technical innovations can have various effects on these trends that are difficult to foresee. This section is not focused on the rationale behind these trends: we will discuss those points later in the book. Table 1.1 gives some hints regarding the variation of these trends. The question now is to discuss how persistent these trends are – and how many types of trends affect the dynamics of commodities.

Before turning to this, a necessary question to be answered is how useful to investors this kind of knowledge is. In a recent contribution, Miffre and Rallis (2007) present evidence that trend-following strategies perform well for commodities, consistent with previous results on the equity market. Similar findings are obtained in Fuertes *et al.* (2008). Erb and Campbell

---

[7] The Prebisch–Singer conjecture states that commodity prices should exhibit a persistent negative trend relative to manufactured products. Different explanations have been proposed: first, unions in the manufactured product sector are stronger than unions in the production of raw products – essentially because these products come from developing countries – implying that in return the price of manufactured products will have to be increased more often than commodities' in reaction to an increasing labor cost. A second explanation states that the sensitivity of the demand for commodities to a wage increase is lower than those of manufactured products, implying in turn that commodity prices should increase at a slower pace than manufactured products. These are the two explanations proposed respectively by Prebisch (1950) and Singer (1950). It seems that the Prebisch–Singer conjecture is also used as a loose designation for a negative long-term trend in commodities.

(2006) use a momentum strategy that invests in the best-performing commodities against the worst-performing ones. Irwin *et al.* (1997) showed how a channel trading system makes it possible to generate abnormal returns on soybean over the 1984–1988 period. Lukac *et al.* (1988) obtained similarly a positive return from various technical trading rules. Szakmary *et al.* (2010) obtained positive returns from trend-following strategies from 22 out of 28 futures on commodities. The basics of such investment approaches should push investors to hold a long position (respectively short) into commodities with a positive (negative) past performance. Despite the apparent simplicity of the approach, many issues need to be solved, such as the horizon over which to compute the past performance of each asset – that is the past momentum. There are a lot of alternative investment strategies that track this momentum effect in commodities, such as filters, moving average or channel breakouts: the trend-following methods are in fact strongly related to technical analysis. Here again, evidence of the presence of a stronger momentum in commodities is, however, not fully consistent. Marshall *et al.* (2008), for example, do not find that quantitative market timing strategies are consistently profitable over 15 commodity futures. Wang and Yu (2004) find that short-term contrarian strategies deliver a positive return to investors. The underlying issue here is, of course, to be able to estimate trends from financial returns and to discuss how stable these trends are.

Building on Equation (1.6), there are two potential origins of trends in assets:

1. Trends can be understood as a natural tendency for returns to have one particular sign, regardless of the period considered or of the frequency used to compute it. This is measured in Equation (1.6) by a_1^i.
2. Beyond that, $\eta_t = \epsilon_t - \epsilon_{t-1}$ can be affected by a positive autocorrelation – that is to say that when η_t goes through a shock, this shock will have long-lasting effects on the returns themselves. This implies that when $\eta_t > 0$, η_{t+1} stands a higher chance of being the same sign although with a more limited scale. Understanding the origin of trends requires disentangling these two potential origins.

In this section, we use time series models to estimate and characterize the trends and momenta in commodities – and we compare these results to similar estimates of standard assets.

1.2.1 Persistence of Shocks in Commodities

A first simple and intuitive approach to gather evidence that commodities exhibit persistent trends is to compute the autocorrelation of returns of order h; that is, for a given asset i:

$$\rho_h^i = \frac{cov\left(r_t^i, r_{t-h}^i\right)}{V\left(r_t^i\right)}, \tag{1.8}$$

where $cov(.,.)$ stands for covariance and $V(.)$ for variance. An asset with persistent returns will stand a greater chance of being affected by trends: when receiving a positive shock over a given period of time, an asset with positively autocorrelated returns will stand a greater chance of displaying a performance of a similar sign over the following periods.[8] We compute these autocorrelations using a dataset covering the 1995–2012 period, using closing returns at daily, weekly and monthly frequencies. Table 1.5 presents such estimates along with a

---

[8] On this point, see the standard forecasting procedure of an Autoregressive (AR) model as presented in Box *et al.* (2008).

Table 1.5 Autocorrelation coefficient over various assets from 1995 to 2012

	Daily			Weekly			Monthly		
	1995–2012	1995–2003	2004–2012	1995–2012	1995–2003	2004–2012	1995–2012	1995–2003	2004–2012
Gold	−0.02	−0.02	−0.02	−0.01	0.02	−0.03	−0.16*	−0.08	−0.23*
Silver	−0.02	−0.05*	−0.02	0.01	−0.02	0.02	−0.12	−0.25*	−0.09
Platinum	0.04*	0.02	0.06*	0.03	−0.03	0.07	0.2*	0.04	0.26*
Aluminum	−0.03	0.03	−0.05*	−0.03	0	−0.04	0.14*	−0.18	0.26*
Copper	−0.04*	0.04*	−0.07*	0	0.11*	−0.04	0.19*	−0.15	0.29*
Nickel	0.01	0.02	0.01	−0.01	−0.01	−0.01	0.07	−0.04	0.11
Zinc	−0.02	−0.01	−0.03	−0.06	−0.02	−0.06	0.02	−0.11	0.04
Lead	0.06*	0.05*	0.06*	−0.08*	−0.05	−0.08	0.08	−0.15	0.11
WTI	−0.01	0.03	−0.04	−0.07*	−0.05	−0.09*	0.07	−0.06	0.21*
Brent	−0.04*	−0.02	−0.07*	−0.04	−0.03	−0.06	0.17*	0.04	0.3*
Gasoil	0	0.02	−0.01	0.01	0	0.02	0.12	0.04	0.21*
Natural Gas	−0.02	−0.01	−0.02	0	0.06	−0.05	−0.02	−0.03	−0.01
Heating Oil	−0.03*	−0.03	−0.03	−0.04	−0.04	−0.04	0.08	−0.02	0.19*
Corn	0.04*	0.03	0.04	−0.07*	−0.14*	−0.04	−0.01	0.01	−0.03
Wheat	0	0.04	−0.02	−0.03	−0.06	−0.02	−0.08	−0.05	−0.1
Coffee	−0.01	−0.01	−0.01	−0.03	−0.06	0.03	−0.18*	−0.16	−0.23*
Sugar	0	0.01	−0.01	0.03	0.08	−0.01	0.1	−0.02	0.17
Cocoa	0	−0.02	0.02	0	0.02	−0.02	−0.2*	−0.14	−0.27*
Cotton	0.03	−0.02	0.06*	0.04	0.04	0.03	−0.06	−0.16	−0.01
Soybean	−0.01	0	−0.01	0.01	−0.08	0.07	0.01	0.11	−0.03
Rice	0.05*	0.03	0.06*	0.03	0	0.05	−0.12	−0.13	−0.11
GSCI Agri.	0.02	0.06*	0.01	−0.01	−0.01	−0.01	0	0	−0.01
GSCI Energy	−0.02	0	−0.03	0	0.03	−0.02	0.18*	0.08	0.27*
GSCI Ind. Metals	−0.04*	0.04*	−0.06*	−0.03	0.02	−0.05	0.19*	−0.19	0.29*
GSCI Prec. Metals	0.01	−0.01	0.02	−0.03	0	−0.04	−0.19*	−0.15	−0.23*
DOW JONES INDUS. AVG	−0.06*	0	−0.11*	−0.08*	−0.08	−0.08	0.05	−0.05	0.17
S&P 500 INDEX	−0.07*	−0.01	−0.12*	−0.08*	−0.1*	−0.06	0.11	0	0.24*
Euro Stoxx 50 INDEX	−0.01	0.01	−0.03	−0.06	0.02	−0.13*	0.12	0.07	0.18
HANG SENG INDEX	0	0.02	−0.03	0.01	0.03	−0.02	0.07	0.02	0.14
EUR-USD X-RATE	0	−0.02	0.03	0.01	−0.01	0.03	0.01	0.06	−0.02
USD-CAD X-RATE	0	−0.01	0	−0.01	−0.04	0	−0.08	−0.01	−0.1
USD-JPY X-RATE	0	0.02	−0.03	−0.05	−0.03	−0.1*	0	0	−0.02
AUD-USD X-RATE	−0.02	0.01	−0.03	−0.04	−0.04	−0.05	0.05	0.02	0.06
British Pound Spot	0.01	−0.02	0.04	−0.02	0	−0.03	0.04	−0.17	0.17
Swiss Franc Spot	−0.03	−0.04*	−0.02	−0.01	−0.02	−0.01	−0.06	0.03	−0.13

Note: * denotes a statistically significant autocorrelation at a 5% risk level.

breakdown for the 1995–2003 and 2004–2012 periods. By comparing results over these various periods and frequencies, we will be able to obtain some hints about the persistence of market episodes. Should ρ_h^i be positive and significant at a 5% risk level, this provides evidence that asset i exhibits persistence. Conversely, when ρ_h^i is negative and significant, asset i has a mean-reverting behavior, rapidly correcting its trajectory in case of a large positive or negative return.

As in the previous tables, we compare the results obtained in the case of commodities to those obtained with more traditional assets. From Table 1.5, there is almost no persistence in the returns of standard assets: the only case for ρ_h^i positive and significant is obtained in the case of S&P 500 at a monthly frequency for the 2004–2012 period. The rest of the significant figures are negative, unveiling some mean-reverting properties in financial returns. Turning to commodities, the results are clearly different: we obtain a higher number of significant figures – not necessarily positive. At daily and weekly frequencies, we respectively find a statistically significant autocorrelation for 7 and 3 of the commodities in our dataset – not necessarily the same ones. Weekly returns that have a statistically significant autocorrelation have a negative sign at a weekly frequency, implying some mean-reversion properties. When breaking down the samples into subsamples, we find limited evidence of stability of persistence at weekly or daily frequencies. Now, turning to monthly data, we do find a higher number of positive autocorrelations that are different from zero. Platinum, aluminum and copper are fair examples: a positive shock of these has a greater chance of being long-lasting when compared, for example, to zinc. However, here again, the stability of such figures is rather limited.

From Table 1.5, we are able to reach two conclusions:

1. Weak evidence exists that the alleged trends in commodities come from persistent shocks. When one of these commodities goes through a shock – such as a shortage on production for various reasons – there is no statistical evidence that this shock should turn into a persistent trend.
2. Still, Table 1.1 presented figures showing that commodities have, on average, a non-zero performance, whose sign can change depending on the period. This implies that a proper way to track these unobservable trends is to use a proper time series model that would allow us to measure how commodities switch from one trend to another over the years.

Markov switching (MS hereafter), as initially presented in Hamilton (1989), makes this possible: in the next section, we will make use of it to evaluate the presence of changing trends in commodities. We will then be able to diagnose whether commodities exhibit more persistent trends than traditional assets.

1.2.2 The Nature of Momentum in Commodity Markets

Now[9] that persistence can be somewhat discarded as a source of trends in commodities, we move on to measuring trends dynamically. Trends are now considered as being made of a combination of an expected such return as a_1^i in Equation (1.7) and a corresponding volatility. This question is well known and discussed in the case of equity markets: bull, bear and range trading periods are usually disentangled. A bull market is a market phase during which expected returns are positive and volatility is low. A bear market is, on the contrary, characterized by

---

[9] We are thankful to Mathieu Gatumel for his valuable help on the building of this section.

a strongly negative return and a higher volatility. A range trading episode corresponds to a period for which the market has no clear trend, ranging in a low volatility environment between two levels. For an investigation of such phases, see, for example, Maheu *et al.* (2012). When it comes to commodities, there is no clearly identified evidence of the existence of bull, bear or range trading episodes, despite the obvious interest of the trend-following industry in such empirical works. These different types of trends underlie the momentum strategies of CTA funds, from which they are trying to gain a benefit. The key issue here is, of course, to be able to estimate these market phases, and above all to be able to determine how many of them are usually necessary for commodity markets. Markov switching models, as presented in Hamilton (1989), are typically the kind of time series modeling approach that makes such a task achievable. These models had significant success in the financial industry, as they made it possible to accommodate the intuition accumulated so far in terms of trends and momenta within a simple statistical model. In the coming sections, we present the MS model along with the estimation of the number of regimes required to model commodities.

1.2.2.1   A Brief Presentation of the Markov Switching Model

We provide the reader with a short presentation of Hamilton's (1989) Markov switching model. This model was initially introduced in the literature by focusing on the US business cycle. Its use to estimate the regimes[10] driving financial markets has since been developed in various articles such as Chauvet and Potter (2000), Ang and Bekaert (2002) or more recently Maheu *et al.* (2012). This time series model aims at modeling and estimating the changes in regimes that affect different kinds of economic series. It relies on the assumption that the probability of moving from one regime to another varies over time, while the transition probabilities[11] are constant. Ang and Beckaert (2002) present an asset allocation strategy based on an MS(2) model, underpinning the economic performance of such a model when compared to a single regime one. Maheu and McCurdy (2000) present a variation of an MS(2) model that provides evidence about the duration of each market cycle. Chauvet and Potter (2000) use this modeling approach to build coincident and leading indicators. However, most of these articles focus on equity markets: investigating returns on commodities by using this modeling approach should therefore provide us with very interesting insights.

We present the basic intuition of using a two-regime MS model before turning to a more general case. Let r_t be the logarithmic return on a given asset at time t, for the holding period between $t-1$ and t. Let s_t be an integer value variable that is equal to 1 (respectively 2) at time t if regime 1 (respectively 2) prevails in the economy. Given that the regime i prevails, the conditional distribution of returns is as follows:

$$r_t | s_t \sim N(\mu_i, \sigma_i). \tag{1.9}$$

The probability to be in regime 1 at time t can be written as:

$$P(s_t = 1) = P(s_t = 1 | s_{t-1} = 1) \times P(s_{t-1} = 1) + P(s_t = 1 | s_{t-1} = 2) \times P(s_{t-1} = 2). \tag{1.10}$$

---

[10] As explained later, a trend or a momentum in this respect can either be considered a regime, or a combination of regimes.
[11] Transition probabilities are the fixed probabilities of switching from one regime coming with certainty from another.

$P(s_t = 1|s_{t-1} = 1)$ is assumed to be constant and equal to p, and $P(s_t = 2|s_{t-1} = 1) = 1 - p$. With a similar argument, $P(s_t = 2|s_{t-1} = 2) = q$ and $P(s_t = 1|s_{t-1} = 2) = 1 - q$. These transition probabilities can be gathered into a transition matrix as follows:

$$\Pi = \begin{pmatrix} p & 1-q \\ 1-p & q \end{pmatrix},$$ (1.11)

such that

$$P_t = \Pi P_{t-1},$$ (1.12)

with $P_t = (P(s_t = 1), P(s_t = 2))^\top$. The parameters driving the model are thus the moments associated with asset returns for each state and the matrix Π. The usual estimation strategy is a maximum likelihood one, based on the filtering approach developed in Hamilton (1989). This two-regime case can be generalized to an n-regime one: in such a case, s_t can take integer values ranging from 1 to n, and the Π matrix becomes an $n \times n$ matrix.

It would be possible to consider that r_t follows a more sophisticated conditional model, like a switching GARCH model. Nevertheless, as presented in Aingworth et al. (2006), increasing the number of states in the Markov chain allows us to obtain a sequence of models that gets closer to a stochastic volatility model. In addition to that, the unconditional distribution of an MS model is a mixture of Gaussian distributions – as presented in Hamilton (1989). This distribution is consistent with fat tails and the asymmetry usually found in financial return datasets (see Bertholon et al., 2007). As straightforward as our modeling approach looks, it is still consistent with the stylized facts of financial returns while being parsimonious – an essential feature when one tries to test for a higher number of regimes, given the rapidly growing estimation difficulties when this number increases. Beyond this, the weak evidence of persistence in shocks on commodities or standard assets does not make it necessary to add an autoregressive parameter to the conditional means for each state.

1.2.2.2 Testing for the Number of Regimes in an MS Model

Beyond the insight regarding the time series dynamics of returns, one of the main issues with the MS model is to select the proper number of regimes. This is all the more important as our primary interest here lies in providing evidence around the nature of trends in commodity markets. Gatumel and Ielpo (2011) present a test around this issue making it possible to estimate the number of regimes in a financial time series. A large part of the literature assumes that markets are driven by two types of trends:

1. a trend up – with a low volatility in the case of equities, and
2. a trend down – with a large volatility.

Uptrends are known as 'bull' markets and downtrends are 'bear' markets. Many articles assume that two regimes are enough to correctly capture the evolution of the main equity indices. See, for example, Henry (2009), Al-Anaswah and Wilfling (2011) or Dionne et al. (2011). Maheu et al. (2012) and Gatumel and Ielpo (2011) present evidence that in financial markets there are more regimes than just bulls and bears.

Before turning to the presentation of the test, we need to understand what can be expected from this 'more than two regimes' approach. The cross-asset empirical analysis built by Gatumel and Ielpo (2011) shows that different kinds of regimes can be obtained:

- The first kind of regime is a 'trend regime', i.e. up or down regimes. In this kind of market configuration, prices are either trending upward or downward – which is why these can be labeled trend regimes. The volatility associated with such regimes can be of various magnitudes: in the equity case, the uptrend usually comes with a low volatility, unlike the downtrend. Both these regimes last the longest of all regimes, as measured from the diagonal of the transition matrix.
- The second kind of regime is a regime that captures extreme or tail events in financial time series. The associated expectation and volatility – once annualized – are usually very large. However, such events do not last for long, being associated with a low diagonal element of the probability matrix.
- Finally, two to three regimes can have a low diagonal element in the transition probability matrix, but they can be part of a sequence of events. For example, one regime with a positive trend and one regime with a negative trend can form a sequence. Returns will go from one to another of these regimes very rapidly: prices will then rise and fall over short periods. By doing so, MS models are able to mimic a key market momentum, i.e. trendless market episodes with small-scale oscillations. Practitioners usually refer to such episodes as 'range trading' as prices evolve between a low and a high range.

These are the three types of trends found in the literature. The global estimations performed in Table 1.1 are just the result of the combination of these types of trends. The literature provides us with various tests to estimate the number of relevant regimes driving the time series. Three types of tests can be found in the literature:

1. penalized likelihood tests,
2. Kullback–Leibler distance based tests, and
3. tests based on the empirical likelihood surface.

We do not put much emphasis on these approaches, as the interested reader will find an up-to-date literature review in Gatumel and Ielpo (2011). Psaradakis and Spagnolo (2003) consider methods based on complexity-penalized likelihood criteria. Smith *et al.* (2006) present a Kullback–Leibler divergence based criterion. Finally, Gatumel and Ielpo (2011) use a density-based approach. When discriminating between one and two regime situations, both Psaradakis and Spagnolo (2003) and Smith *et al.* (2006) provide accurate results. However, when this number of regimes increases beyond three, the accuracy of the estimation of the number of regimes can drop sharply. The test proposed by Gatumel and Ielpo (2011) provides accurate estimates over the Monte Carlo tests, which is why we focus on this approach here.

Let $f_{n_1}(r_t; \hat{\theta}_{n_1})$ be the likelihood function associated with an estimated Markov-switching model with n_1 states. Let $f_{n_2}(r_t; \hat{\theta}_{n_2})$ be a similar quantity in the case of an MS model with n_2 regimes. θ_{n_i} is the vector of the parameters to be estimated by maximum likelihood in the n_i-regime case. The two specifications are compared through their associated log density computed with the estimated sample. Let $z_t^{n_1, n_2}$ be the following quantity:

$$z_t^{n_1, n_2} = \log f_{n_1}(r_t; \hat{\theta}_{n_1}) - \log f_{n_2}(r_t; \hat{\theta}_{n_2}) \tag{1.13}$$

The approach proposed here is based on the following test statistics:

$$t_{n_1,n_2} = \frac{\frac{1}{T}\sum_{t=1}^{T} z_t^{n_1,n_2}}{\hat{\sigma}_{n_1,n_2}},\tag{1.14}$$

where T is the total number of available observations in the sample used to estimate the parameters, and $\hat{\sigma}_{n_1,n_2}$ a properly selected estimator of the standard deviation of $\frac{1}{T}\sum_{t=1}^{T} z_t^{n_1,n_2}$. Several methods have been proposed in the literature to estimate the standard deviation. We use a Newey–West (1987) estimator with different lags.

Under the null hypothesis that both models provide an equivalent fit of the returns' distribution, Theorem 1 in Amisano and Giacomini (2007) provides the asymptotic distribution of this test statistic:

$$t_{n_1,n_2} \sim N(0,1).\tag{1.15}$$

The correct number of regimes is the one that delivers the best fit from the previous statistics point of view, while being as parsimonious as possible. We retain the optimal number of regimes, $\hat{n}$, such that : $t_{\hat{n},\hat{n}-1} \geq q_\alpha$ and $t_{\hat{n}+1,\hat{n}} < q_\alpha$, with q_α being the quantile for a given risk level of $\alpha\%$. Monte Carlo simulations show that this risk level should be set to 1%.

1.2.2.3 Estimation Results

We use the previous estimation scheme for the number of regimes using a dataset of daily closing returns over January 1995 to April 2012. This dataset includes various commodities, commodity indices, equity indices, currencies and interest rates. With this dataset, we first estimate the correct number of regimes necessary to adequately describe the behavior of each asset.

Figure 1.5 summarizes these results, charting the sorted number of regimes for each asset. When commodities exhibit marked trends (up or down), the test simply diagnoses that a two regime model is enough. When just two regimes alternate, a trend-following mechanism could generate abnormal returns – assuming that the persistence of each regime is high enough. When the number of regimes is higher than two to three, abnormal returns are likely to fade out, as range trading periods prevent the trend-following mechanism from capturing the correct trend.

The results reproduced present globally mixed evidence that trends in commodities are stronger than those in equities or currencies, for example. Still, we find that in the cases of WTI, heating oil, corn, wheat, cocoa and cotton, a model with three regimes is enough to capture the key trends. Among the nine series for which we find that a three regime model is accurate, eight are series from the commodity universe: on top of the six commodities previously mentioned, the GSCI indices for the agricultural and energy sectors also match this type of market behavior. In the meantime, rice should be characterized by six different regimes: behind the 5% annualized return over the 1995–2012 period presented in Table 1.6, there are many different market episodes behind this single figure.

Globally speaking, out of our subset of 21 commodities, six are characterized by two regimes, six by four regimes, eight by five regimes and just one is characterized by six regimes. The period considered must indeed have a large influence over such results, but when comparing the results presented in Gatumel and Ielpo (2011) the basic intuitions remain:

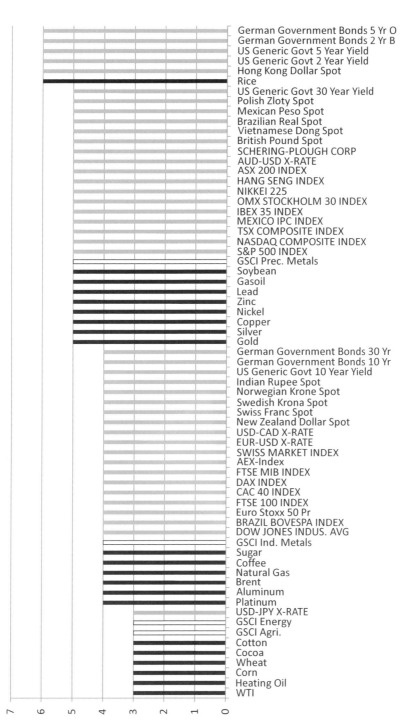

Estimated number of regimes 1995–2012

German Government Bonds 5 Yr O
German Government Bonds 2 Yr B
US Generic Govt 5 Year Yield
US Generic Govt 2 Year Yield
Hong Kong Dollar Spot
Rice
US Generic Govt 30 Year Yield
Polish Zloty Spot
Mexican Peso Spot
Brazilian Real Spot
Vietnamese Dong Spot
British Pound Spot
SCHERING-PLOUGH CORP
AUD-USD X-RATE
ASX 200 INDEX
HANG SENG INDEX
NIKKEI 225
OMX STOCKHOLM 30 INDEX
IBEX 35 INDEX
MEXICO IPC INDEX
TSX COMPOSITE INDEX
NASDAQ COMPOSITE INDEX
S&P 500 INDEX
GSCI Prec. Metals
Soybean
Gasoil
Lead
Zinc
Nickel
Copper
Silver
Gold
German Government Bonds 30 Yr
German Government Bonds 10 Yr
US Generic Govt 10 Year Yield
Indian Rupee Spot
Norwegian Krone Spot
Swedish Krona Spot
Swiss Franc Spot
New Zealand Dollar Spot
USD-CAD X-RATE
EUR-USD X-RATE
SWISS MARKET INDEX
AEX-Index
FTSE MIB INDEX
DAX INDEX
CAC 40 INDEX
FTSE 100 INDEX
Euro Stoxx 50 Pr
BRAZIL BOVESPA INDEX
DOW JONES INDUS. AVG
GSCI Ind. Metals
Sugar
Coffee
Natural Gas
Brent
Aluminum
Platinum
USD-JPY X-RATE
GSCI Energy
GSCI Agri.
Cotton
Cocoa
Wheat
Corn
Heating Oil
WTI

Figure 1.5 Number of regimes in commodities

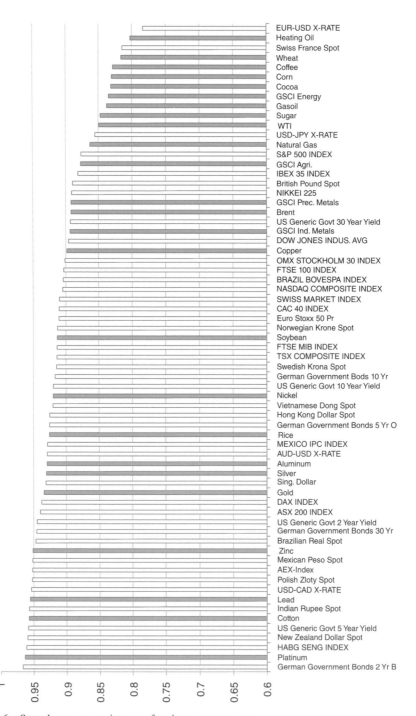

EUR-USD X-RATE
Heating Oil
Swiss France Spot
Wheat
Coffee
Corn
Cocoa
GSCI Energy
Gasoil
Sugar
WTI
USD-JPY X-RATE
Natural Gas
S&P 500 INDEX
GSCI Agri.
IBEX 35 INDEX
British Pound Spot
NIKKEI 225
GSCI Prec. Metals
Brent
US Generic Govt 30 Year Yield
GSCI Ind. Metals
DOW JONES INDUS. AVG
Copper
OMX STOCKHOLM 30 INDEX
FTSE 100 INDEX
BRAZIL BOVESPA INDEX
NASDAQ COMPOSITE INDEX
SWISS MARKET INDEX
CAC 40 INDEX
Euro Stoxx 50 Pr
Norwegian Krone Spot
Soybean
FTSE MIB INDEX
TSX COMPOSITE INDEX
Swedish Krona Spot
German Government Bods 10 Yr
US Generic Govt 10 Year Yield
Nickel
Vietnamese Dong Spot
Hong Kong Dollar Spot
German Government Bonds 5 Yr O
Rice
MEXICO IPC INDEX
AUD-USD X-RATE
Aluminum
Silver
Sing. Dollar
Gold
DAX INDEX
ASX 200 INDEX
US Generic Govt 2 Year Yield
German Government Bonds 30 Yr
Brazilian Real Spot
Zinc
Mexican Peso Spot
AEX-Index
Polish Zloty Spot
USD-CAD X-RATE
Lead
Indian Rupee Spot
Cotton
US Generic Govt 5 Year Yield
New Zealand Dollar Spot
HABG SENG INDEX
Platinum
German Government Bonds 2 Yr B

1   0.95   0.9   0.85   0.8   0.75   0.7   0.65   0.6

Figure 1.6   Sorted average persistence of regimes across assets

Table 1.6 Annualized expectations and volatilities across regimes

		GSCI Agri.	GSCI Energy	GSCI Ind. Metals	GSCI Prec. Metals	S&P 500	10Y US Rate
Regime 1	μ_1	0.064	−0.733	−0.050	1.962	−3.439	−0.155
	σ_1	0.266	0.528	0.117	0.113	0.126	0.109
Regime 2	μ_2	−0.075	0.507	−0.354	−0.066	0.261	−0.126
	σ_2	0.130	0.253	0.420	0.075	0.091	0.275
Regime 3	μ_3	0.079	−6.240	0.064	−1.360	2.998	0.062
	σ_3	0.266	0.245	0.167	0.228	0.134	0.202
Regime 4	μ_4			0.185	0.057	−0.315	−0.014
	σ_4			0.237	0.344	0.423	0.529
Regime 5	μ_5				−0.350	0.053	
	σ_5				0.101	0.109	

commodities are among the assets with the lowest number of regimes – that is with the strongest trends – and energy commodities typically display a low number of regimes.

When turning to the case of the commodity indices, we find three regimes for agriculture and energy, four for industrial metals and five for precious metals. Table 1.7 as well as Figures 1.7 to 1.12 provide additional details about the nature of these regimes. We detail here each of these cases and then compare them to the case of the S&P 500 and the US 10-year rate:

– As noted previously, the agriculture and the energy GSCI indices share the same number of regimes. An analysis of Table 1.7 gives us hints regarding the nature of these regimes. For both cases there are two very persistent regimes – which are regimes whose corresponding value on the diagonal of the transition matrix presented in Table 1.7 are very close to 1. Both these two persistent regimes' expectations have an opposite sign. In the case of the GSCI agricultural sub-index, regime 1 has a 6.4% annualized performance for an annualized volatility equal to 26.6%. When entering such a market regime, the probability of remaining in this kind of regime is 0.99. Regime 2 has a negative expected return (−7.5% for a volatility equal to 13%), and the probability of staying in this regime is 0.96. Thus, on average, the most common regime over the 1995–2012 period is one for which agricultural prices have been rising with a larger volatility. Drops in agricultural prices also occured, but with a lesser volatility. This is clearly the opposite of what is usually found in equities. The main risk for agricultural products comes from bad harvests which have a tendency to pull prices higher, with a greater amount of volatility. The last regime (regime 3) is thus a regime with a much weaker persistence (0.32), a higher expected return of 7.9% and a volatility equivalent to regime 1. When entering this type of regime, the probability that the market enters a downtrend – i.e. regime 2 – is estimated to be equal to 0.68. This type of regime should be regarded as a tail event: a stronger than expected return that is on the risk side of the market when prices rise. However, from Figure 1.7, such a regime never received a probability higher than 50%. Hence, it has been selected to help fit the tails of the returns on such an index.

– The structure of momenta in the GSCI energy index is very similar to what we uncovered from our estimations when using the agricultural index. The energy index is also characterized by two persistent trends, one positive with an expected return of 50.7% (and a

Table 1.7 Transition matrices

GSCI Agri.

	Regime 1	Regime 2	Regime 3	Regime 4	Regime 5
Regime 1	0.99	0.01	0.00		
Regime 2	0.00	0.96	0.04		
Regime 3	0.01	0.68	0.32		
Regime 4					
Regime 5					

GSCI Energy

	Regime 1	Regime 2	Regime 3	Regime 4	Regime 5
Regime 1	0.95	0.05	0.00		
Regime 2	0.00	0.95	0.04		
Regime 3	0.09	0.80	0.11		
Regime 4					
Regime 5					

GSCI Ind. Metals

	Regime 1	Regime 2	Regime 3	Regime 4	Regime 5
Regime 1	0.37	0.00	0.63	0.00	
Regime 2	0.00	0.97	0.00	0.03	
Regime 3	0.60	0.00	0.40	0.00	
Regime 4	0.00	0.01	0.00	0.99	
Regime 5					

GSCI Prec. Metals

	Regime 1	Regime 2	Regime 3	Regime 4	Regime 5
Regime 1	0.22	0.00	0.03	0.01	0.75
Regime 2	0.02	0.97	0.00	0.00	0.00
Regime 3	0.30	0.04	0.32	0.00	0.34
Regime 4	0.01	0.00	0.01	0.98	0.00
Regime 5	0.37	0.00	0.29	0.00	0.34

S&P 500

	Regime 1	Regime 2	Regime 3	Regime 4	Regime 5
Regime 1	0.07	0.00	0.20	0.03	0.69
Regime 2	0.02	0.98	0.00	0.00	0.00
Regime 3	0.06	0.07	0.15	0.00	0.72
Regime 4	0.00	0.00	0.03	0.97	0.00
Regime 5	0.34	0.00	0.30	0.00	0.36

US 10Y Rate

	Regime 1	Regime 2	Regime 3	Regime 4	Regime 5
Regime 1	0.61	0.00	0.38	0.00	
Regime 2	0.00	0.99	0.00	0.01	
Regime 3	0.55	0.00	0.45	0.00	
Regime 4	0.00	0.00	0.00	0.98	
Regime 5	0.00	0.02	0.00	0.00	

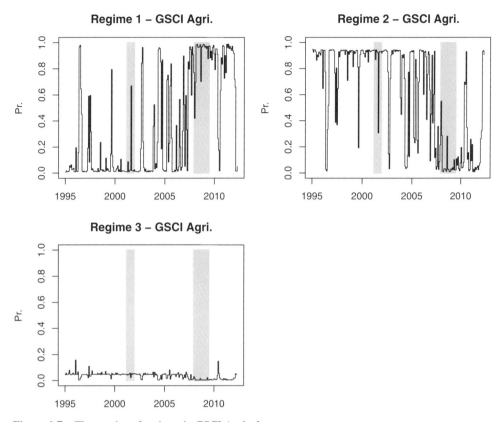

Figure 1.7   Time series of regimes in GSCI Agriculture

corresponding volatility of 25.3%) and one negative with an expected return of −73% (for a volatility of 52.8%). Contrary to agricultural markets, the regime with the highest volatility matches the negative return. From Figure 1.8, such a trend typically occured in 2008 during the sharp drop in energy prices over the third and fourth quarters of the 2008 crisis. These two regimes are highly persistent, as their corresponding probabilities on the diagonal of the transition matrix are close to 1. As in the agricultural case, a third regime is selected that accounts for a tail event: regime 3 has an expected return equal to −624%: when entering such regime on a given day, the probability of staying in this regime is equal to 11%. This is more of a one-day event, that is usually followed by a market episode of regime 2 type. As in the case of agriculture, we find here that trends are strong and of only two varieties, which in turn should imply positive and abnormal returns for the trend-following industry. Again, these results depend on the period covered in the dataset.

– Industrial metals have a structure different from trends. As in the two previous cases, there are two main persistent trends in industrial metals: one is a positive trend with an expected return of 18.5% (for a volatility of 23.7%), and one is negative with an expected return of −35.4% (for a volatility of 42%). These two trends are very persistent, as in previous cases. The largest volatility is obtained for the trend affected by a negative return. Beyond these two, regimes 1 and 3 articulate one with another: when in regime 1 (with an expected

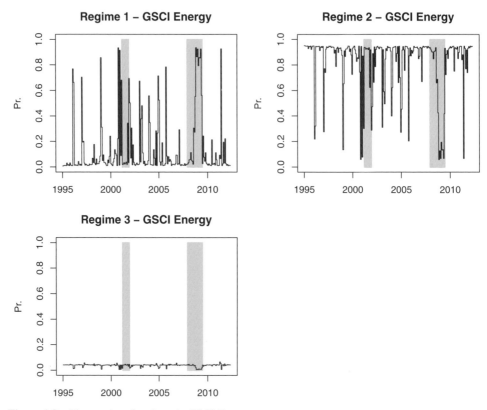

Figure 1.8   Time series of regimes in GSCI Energy

return of −5%), the market statistically stands a 60% chance of going to regime 3. Coming from regime 3, the market now stands a 40% chance of switching back to regime 1. By switching from one of these regimes to another, the MS model simply reproduces a period of range trading, with typically a low average expected return – and an even lower return for trend-following strategies, given the number of switches from one regime to the other.

– Finally, the most complex structure of trends is obtained for the commodity group celebrated for its high diversification effect (Hillier *et al.*, 2006). In the case of precious metals – as represented by the GSCI sub-index – five regimes are estimated over the 1995–2012 period. As for previous cases, two regimes with expected returns of an opposite sign are found. In the case of regime 2, the expected return is −6.6% (for a volatility of 7.5%), and in the case of regime 4, this expected return is 5.7% (for a volatility of 34.4%). From Figure 1.10, this regime matches the 2008 crisis period: the expected return is not that high but volatility is large. Beyond these two regimes, regimes 1, 3 and 5 articulate with each other to create a chain of extreme variations: their respective expected returns are 196%, −136% and −35%. Their persistence is very low: the probability when entering each of these regimes of remaining in this type of market trend is below 35%. Still, the estimated joint articulation can be read in the transition matrix in Table 1.7: regimes 1 and 5 are related, and regimes 3 and 5 as well, creating two kinds of very volatile range trading patterns. Here again, this type of configuration is a drag on the returns on trend-following strategies.

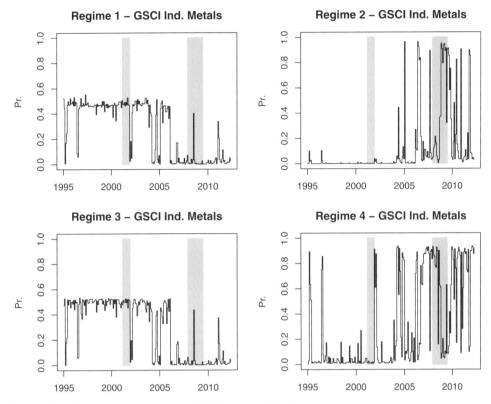

Figure 1.9 Time series of regimes in GSCI Industrial Metals

Finally, when comparing these results to those obtained for the S&P 500 and the US 10-year rate, we find similarities and key differences. First, as for every commodity, these standard assets exhibit two persistent regimes with expected returns of an opposite sign. The rest of the regimes are either used to account for extreme events or for range trading situations. There are two major differences between commodities and standard assets:

1. In the case of commodities, the average number of regimes is lower than for standard assets. This should pledge for higher returns of trend-following strategies when they are using commodities as an investment vehicle.
2. However, a second difference appears from our empirical analysis: Figure 1.6 presents the sorted average persistence of regimes; that is, the average of the diagonal of the transition matrix. When analyzing how persistent regimes are on average, we clearly see a strong heterogeneity across commodities. While gold, platinum, zinc and cotton are characterized by persistent trends, sugar, cocoa, corn and coffee exhibit the lowest degree of persistence, materializing the Erb and Campbell (2006) statement that commodities are indeed a heterogeneous asset class that can hardly be regarded as a whole.

In the next section, we discuss how these characteristics impact the performance of trend-following strategies, as these are widely used and applied to commodities in the financial industry.

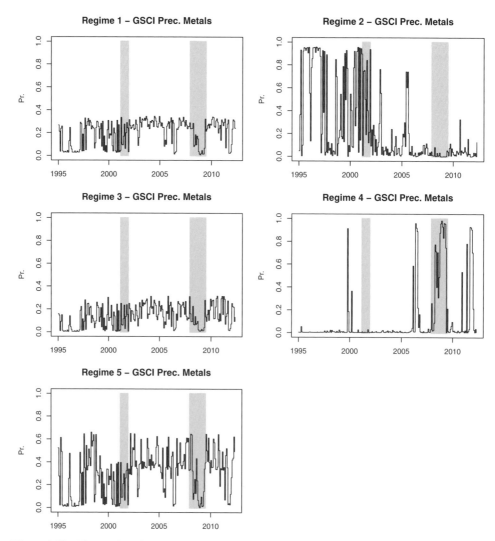

Figure 1.10   Time series of regimes in GSCI Precious Metals

1.2.3   Time Series Momentum and the Number and Nature of Regimes

Based on the previous analysis, there are only weak chances that commodities would be a more suitable asset class for trend-following strategies: the nature of trends in these markets is very close to those observed in other asset classes. Yet, a thorough analysis is required here to judge whether commodities can deliver similar risk-adjusted returns to trend-followers. We focus our research here on the concept of 'time series momentum', as developed in Moskowitz *et al.* (2012).

1.2.3.1   Time Series Momentum

Momentum strategies are one of the most well-known strategies on equity markets: they amount to overweighting stocks that were top performers in the past, and underweighting those with the lowest past returns. Such a strategy had a tendency to generate positive returns – 'abnormal returns' – which should be arbitraged away by market participants. This cross-sectional effect in the stock market has been largely documented in the academic literature. On this point see, for example, Jegadeesh and Titman (1993) and Asness (1994) for the US equity case and the extension to other asset classes presented in Asness *et al.* (2010).

Moskowitz *et al.* (2012) present evidence of another type of momentum effect that is closer to the typical CTA investment strategy: they find persistence in the performance of a wide variety of futures, including stocks, bonds, currencies and commodities. When a given future delivers a positive (respectively negative) performance over past months, it stands a greater chance of also having a positive (negative) performance in the upcoming months, creating persistence in the performance. It generates, in turn, again an 'abnormal' return when applying a trend-following strategy.[12] To show this effect, they use the following investment strategy: they propose to hold a long (respectively short) position in assets having experienced a positive (negative) performance. The return from such a strategy $r_t^{\text{strat},i}$ at time t obtained from asset i is computed in the following way:[13]

$$r_t^{\text{strat},i} = \text{sign}(r_{t-12,t}^i)\frac{40\%}{\sigma_t^i}r_t^i,\qquad(1.16)$$

where $r_{t-12,t}^i$ is the return on asset i over the past 12 months, as in their article they use monthly data. The investment strategy has a constant risk exposure, with a targeted volatility of 40%. In order to reproduce their results with our sample, we use a slightly different estimate of volatility. Instead of theirs, we use a 30-day rolling estimate: beyond the appeal of a simple and widely used estimate in the industry, our results should be seen as a robustness check of theirs. To this strategy, we add a second one, still belonging to the trend-following methodologies: a breakout investment strategy. Again, this is a simple strategy that aims at capturing trends in financial asset prices. The logic is as follows: starting from a neutral position, an investor would take a long (respectively short) position in a given asset i when this asset's price reaches a value that is higher (lower) than the maximum over a given period of time. Once the investor enters the position, it is held until the converse signal is observed: such strategies are sometimes referred to as 'stop-and-reverse' strategies. Similarly to the time series momentum strategy, there is no neutral positioning once the investor is in the market. For additional development on such strategies, see, for example, the recent paper of Clare *et al.* (2012). In the same spirit as the time series momentum strategy, we consider the minimum and maximum computed over the past 12 months of data: by doing so, we hope to make the two trend-following strategies as comparable as possible.

1.2.3.2 Empirical Results

Running the previous investment strategies over our sample[14] of commodities, stock indices, currencies and rates, we obtain the results presented in Table 1.9 for the time series momentum

---

[12] It remains an abuse to think that such an effect can be 'arbitraged away' by market participants: such patterns were exploited during the 2003–2007 period by using currencies: the carry – that is the fact that a lower interest rate is paid over the funding currency than the interest received from the currency used as an investment vehicle – was the main reason for the trend on the GBP. Even though this trade seemed 'riskless' over this period, the reversal that occured in 2007–2008 reset most of the profits accumulated by the average of the trend-following industry. An arbitrage requires that the trade is strictly riskless, which is clearly not the case here.

[13] We follow as much as possible the notation in Moskwitz *et al.* (2012).

[14] The original dataset of daily data has been turned into a monthly dataset by sampling only the end of month prices for each market.

Table 1.8 Average Sharpe ratios by asset class

		Mean Sharpe Ratio		
		Full sample	1995–2003	2004–2012
Trend-Following	Commodities	0.30	0.33	0.30
	Equity indices	0.85	1.07	0.67
	Currencies	0.42	0.96	−0.19
	Bonds	0.31	0.43	0.17
Breakout	Commodities	0.24	0.18	0.29
	Equity indices	0.85	1.11	0.62
	Currencies	1.40	2.39	0.41
	Bonds	0.06	0.08	0.03

approach, and in Table 1.10 for the breakout strategy. In the case of the time series momentum strategy, most of the Sharpe ratios associated with this investment strategy are positive. They range from −0.297 in the case of soybean to 0.943 in the case of gold for the commodities data. For other asset classes, Sharpe ratios are quite similar in terms of scales except for a few remarkable assets, most of which are emerging currencies: in the case of the Vietnamese Dong the Sharpe ratio is equal to 9.2 and in the case of the Real, it reaches 5.9. These extraordinary figures are outliers coming from extreme movements on these markets. From this preliminary analysis, our results are quite consistent with those in Moskowitz *et al.* (2012): for most of the assets, the return on such a time series momentum strategy is positive, with an average value that is close to 0.45. The breakout strategy results are very similar to those that we have just described, confirming that both strategies are actually tracking the same market premium. When gathering data by groups of assets, we get the results presented in Table 1.8. If we had to rank asset classes along their suitability for momentum based strategies, commodities would never come first, even when slicing the full sample into two sub-periods: commodities come last, except for the 2004–2012 period. With a volatility budget equal to 40%,[15] the average expected return would reach 12% per year, which may seem to be an interesting final return and is quite low given the large risk exposure.[16] This fact is obvious from Figures 1.13 and 1.14: those figures present the sorted Sharpe ratios computed from the full sample for each asset for both methods. Most of the commodities are found in the weakest half of the sample. The average 0.30 Sharpe ratio that we obtain in the momentum strategy case is actually very close to the results obtained in Miffre and Rallis (2007).[17] They, however, found higher risk-adjusted returns: as mentioned previously, the nature of the results is dependent on the period that is covered in the empirical study. The Sharpe ratio obtained in the commodity case for the breakout strategy is slightly below those of the momentum strategy. It remains, however, of a similar magnitude. Finally, very interestingly, the average of the Sharpe ratios obtained from the commodities is the most stable over all the assets. This is especially obvious in the results obtained with the momentum strategy: in such a case, we obtain a Sharpe ratio that remains around 0.3 for the three samples considered. The diversification effect – coming from the weak

---

[15] That is when building a portfolio of futures with an *ex ante* volatility of 40%.

[16] A typical *ex ante* risk exposure in the hedge fund industry would be around 20%, with an expected Sharpe ratio ranging from 0.5 to 1, thus generating larger *ex ante* expected returns.

[17] They find a Sharpe ratio ranging from 0.42 to 0.57 depending on the length of the period used to compute the past average return. In their study, they allow it to vary between 1 and 12 months. See their Table 1.

Table 1.9   Returns on the time series momentum strategy of Moskowitz *et al.* (2012) across assets

	1995–2012		1995–2003		2004–2012	
	Avg. Return	Sharpe Ratio	Avg. Return	Sharpe Ratio	Avg. Return	Sharpe Ratio
Gold	0.377	0.943	0.145	0.362	0.6	1.501
Silver	0.044	0.11	−0.078	−0.195	0.187	0.467
Platinum	0.203	0.508	0.202	0.505	0.228	0.569
Aluminum	0.015	0.037	0.168	0.421	−0.11	−0.274
Copper	0.077	0.192	0.013	0.034	0.205	0.513
Nickel	0.235	0.587	0.424	1.06	0.041	0.102
Zinc	0.29	0.725	0.309	0.772	0.299	0.746
Lead	0.084	0.209	0.066	0.166	0.14	0.35
WTI	0.06	0.151	0.1	0.251	0.036	0.089
Brent	0.164	0.411	0.118	0.295	0.193	0.482
Gasoil	0.239	0.598	0.158	0.394	0.299	0.748
Natural Gas	0.04	0.1	0.062	0.155	0.018	0.045
Heating Oil	0.241	0.603	0.206	0.515	0.272	0.68
Corn	0.052	0.129	−0.026	−0.064	0.149	0.372
Wheat	−0.009	−0.022	−0.072	−0.18	0.052	0.131
Coffee	0.083	0.209	0.21	0.524	−0.041	−0.103
Sugar	0.073	0.183	−0.006	−0.015	0.135	0.338
Cocoa	0.017	0.042	0.199	0.496	−0.163	−0.408
Cotton	−0.029	−0.071	0.116	0.29	−0.164	−0.411
Soybean	−0.119	−0.297	−0.054	−0.136	−0.145	−0.363
Rice	0.096	0.24	0.273	0.682	−0.043	−0.107
GSCI Agri.	0.082	0.205	0.178	0.444	−0.002	−0.004
GSCI Energy	0.232	0.58	0.384	0.961	0.089	0.222
GSCI Ind. Metals	0.211	0.529	0.136	0.34	0.316	0.79
GSCI Prec. Metals	0.263	0.657	0.085	0.212	0.436	1.09
DOW JONES INDUS. AVG	0.3	0.749	0.289	0.722	0.312	0.781
S&P 500 INDEX	0.375	0.938	0.502	1.255	0.254	0.635
NASDAQ COMPOSITE INDEX	0.306	0.766	0.391	0.978	0.214	0.536
TSX COMPOSITE INDEX	0.305	0.762	0.285	0.714	0.334	0.834
MEXICO IPC INDEX	0.434	1.085	0.318	0.796	0.588	1.469
BRAZIL BOVESPA INDEX	0.332	0.829	0.527	1.317	0.141	0.352
Euro Stoxx 50 Pr	0.399	0.997	0.678	1.696	0.135	0.339
FTSE 100 INDEX	0.293	0.733	0.349	0.873	0.263	0.657
CAC 40 INDEX	0.397	0.992	0.554	1.385	0.259	0.647
DAX INDEX	0.417	1.043	0.508	1.271	0.322	0.805
IBEX 35 INDEX	0.316	0.789	0.414	1.035	0.244	0.61
FTSE MIB INDEX	0.353	0.884	0.452	1.13	0.242	0.605
AEX-Index	0.406	1.015	0.59	1.475	0.228	0.569
OMX STOCKHOLM 30 INDEX	0.475	1.187	0.625	1.562	0.342	0.855
SWISS MARKET INDEX	0.302	0.755	0.448	1.121	0.165	0.413
NIKKEI 225	0.175	0.436	0.212	0.529	0.161	0.402
HANG SENG INDEX	0.238	0.596	0.247	0.617	0.247	0.618
ASX 200 INDEX	0.331	0.828	0.331	0.827	0.358	0.895
EUR-USD X-RATE	0.056	0.139	0.4	1.001	−0.294	−0.736
USD-CAD X-RATE	0.194	0.484	0.256	0.64	0.124	0.31
USD-JPY X-RATE	0.155	0.387	0.311	0.778	−0.033	−0.083
AUD-USD X-RATE	0.173	0.434	0.525	1.313	−0.17	−0.426

(continued)

Table 1.9   *(Continued)*

	1995–2012		1995–2003		2004–2012	
	Avg. Return	Sharpe Ratio	Avg. Return	Sharpe Ratio	Avg. Return	Sharpe Ratio
Hong Kong Dollar Spot	0.542	1.356	1.498	3.745	−0.429	−1.073
Singapore Dollar	0.264	0.66	0.298	0.746	0.229	0.573
New Zealand Dollar Spot	0.237	0.593	0.407	1.018	0.08	0.199
British Pound Spot	0.051	0.128	0.241	0.602	−0.123	−0.309
Swiss Franc Spot	0.113	0.283	0.355	0.888	−0.133	−0.332
Swedish Krona Spot	0.114	0.285	0.425	1.062	−0.196	−0.489
Norwegian Krone Spot	−0.013	−0.032	0.139	0.349	−0.167	−0.418
Indian Rupee Spot	0.605	1.5125	1.314	3.285	−0.104	−0.26
Vietnamese Dong Spot	3.681	9.2025	3.87	9.675	3.49	8.725
Brazilian Real Spot	2.359	5.8975	4.643	11.607	0.084	0.21
Mexican Peso Spot	0.068	0.169	0.26	0.651	−0.127	−0.317
Polish Zloty Spot	0.124	0.311	0.428	1.07	−0.168	−0.42
US Generic Govt 2 Year Yield*	0.413	1.033	0.427	1.067	0.384	0.959
US Generic Govt 5 Year Yield	0.264	0.66	0.309	0.773	0.206	0.515
US Generic Govt 10 Year Yield	0.117	0.292	0.215	0.539	0.008	0.02
US Generic Govt 30 Year Yield	−0.08	−0.201	0.088	0.22	−0.256	−0.64
German Government Bonds 2 Yr B	0.027	0.067	−0.034	−0.084	0.116	0.291
German Government Bonds 5 Yr O	0.085	0.214	0.05	0.125	0.106	0.266
German Government Bonds 10 Yr	0.057	0.143	0.212	0.531	−0.118	−0.294
German Government Bonds 30 Yr	0.105	0.261	0.104	0.259	0.09	0.225

*The profit and losses presented here in the case of rates are computed using the approximation that the return on a long bond position is equal to the duration of the bond times the variation in rates to which we added the monthly carry.

correlation between commodity sectors as presented earlier – must be playing a major role in this result.

However, the 2008 period has been a very difficult one for the trend-following industry, with the collapse of long-dated trends from September 2008 onwards.[18] The persistence of trends should indeed be an essential feature of markets from which trend-followers extract abnormal returns. To test such an hypothesis, we ran an OLS regression of the Sharpe ratios obtained previously on key metrics from the previous section:

– The number of regimes: the higher the number of regimes, the more difficult it should be for the trend-following investment strategy of Moskowitz *et al.* (2012) to generate a consistently positive return. What is more, when the number of regimes increases, the diagonal elements in the transition matrix can have a tendency to reduce, as cross-regime dependency increases, jeopardizing the potential profits obtained from a trend-following strategy. We denote $n(i)$ the number of regimes in the case of asset i.
– Hence, the persistence of regimes is also a key element: a stable and persistent regime should be a natural support to a trend-following strategy. Using the previously estimated regimes for each asset, we use as an independent variable the average of the diagonal elements of the estimated transition matrix. The higher this variable and the higher the Sharpe ratio

---

[18] Some market observers may argue that these events have happened before.

Table 1.10   Returns on the breakout strategy

	1995–2012		1995–2003		2004–2012	
	Avg. Return	Sharpe Ratio	Avg. Return	Sharpe Ratio	Avg. Return	Sharpe Ratio
Gold	0.41	1.026	0.245	0.614	0.566	1.416
Silver	0.118	0.294	−0.078	−0.196	0.232	0.579
Platinum	0.191	0.477	0.118	0.296	0.27	0.675
Aluminum	0.046	0.115	0.067	0.167	0.053	0.131
Copper	0.118	0.294	0.1	0.25	0.155	0.387
Nickel	0.178	0.445	0.378	0.946	−0.011	−0.028
Zinc	0.233	0.583	0.076	0.19	0.357	0.892
Lead	0.029	0.074	0.063	0.157	0.036	0.09
WTI	0.044	0.11	0.12	0.301	−0.046	−0.116
Brent	0.055	0.137	−0.085	−0.214	0.172	0.431
Gasoil	0.157	0.394	0.082	0.205	0.22	0.549
Natural Gas	−0.123	−0.308	−0.222	−0.556	−0.033	−0.083
Heating Oil	0.171	0.428	0.131	0.328	0.214	0.536
Corn	0.058	0.146	0.003	0.008	0.133	0.333
Wheat	0.167	0.419	0.2	0.501	0.125	0.313
Coffee	0.025	0.062	−0.138	−0.346	0.159	0.397
Sugar	−0.06	−0.149	−0.169	−0.422	0.024	0.061
Cocoa	−0.032	−0.079	0.066	0.165	−0.128	−0.32
Cotton	0.029	0.073	0.09	0.225	−0.048	−0.12
Soybean	−0.2	−0.5	−0.25	−0.625	−0.151	−0.377
Rice	0.107	0.268	0.282	0.704	−0.093	−0.232
GSCI Agri.	0.067	0.168	0.164	0.411	−0.03	−0.076
GSCI Energy	0.173	0.432	0.264	0.659	0.088	0.221
GSCI Ind. Metals	0.176	0.44	0.157	0.392	0.225	0.563
GSCI Prec. Metals	0.298	0.744	0.131	0.329	0.459	1.147
DOW JONES INDUS. AVG	0.315	0.788	0.416	1.039	0.22	0.549
S&P 500 INDEX	0.365	0.912	0.532	1.331	0.212	0.531
NASDAQ COMPOSITE INDEX	0.281	0.703	0.58	1.45	−0.004	−0.01
TSX COMPOSITE INDEX	0.375	0.937	0.426	1.064	0.35	0.876
MEXICO IPC INDEX	0.391	0.978	0.296	0.739	0.509	1.274
BRAZIL BOVESPA INDEX	0.314	0.784	0.393	0.982	0.238	0.595
Euro Stoxx 50 Pr	0.408	1.019	0.687	1.717	0.143	0.358
FTSE 100 INDEX	0.277	0.692	0.291	0.728	0.24	0.599
CAC 40 INDEX	0.367	0.918	0.621	1.551	0.135	0.336
DAX INDEX	0.428	1.07	0.545	1.363	0.307	0.767
IBEX 35 INDEX	0.466	1.165	0.591	1.476	0.353	0.884
FTSE MIB INDEX	0.311	0.778	0.462	1.155	0.198	0.495
AEX-Index	0.457	1.143	0.685	1.712	0.249	0.622
OMX STOCKHOLM 30 INDEX	0.39	0.975	0.442	1.106	0.355	0.889
SWISS MARKET INDEX	0.299	0.747	0.333	0.832	0.289	0.723
NIKKEI 225	0.177	0.443	0.179	0.447	0.173	0.432
HANG SENG INDEX	0.357	0.891	0.46	1.15	0.258	0.645
ASX 200 INDEX	0.153	0.383	0.024	0.06	0.271	0.678
EUR-USD X-RATE	0.032	0.081	0.211	0.527	−0.146	−0.364
USD-CAD X-RATE	0.07	0.176	0.205	0.512	−0.04	−0.101
USD-JPY X-RATE	0.252	0.629	0.401	1.002	0.121	0.301
AUD-USD X-RATE	0.237	0.592	0.445	1.112	0.037	0.092

(continued)

Table 1.10 (*Continued*)

	1995–2012		1995–2003		2004–2012	
	Avg. Return	Sharpe Ratio	Avg. Return	Sharpe Ratio	Avg. Return	Sharpe Ratio
Hong Kong Dollar Spot	0.478	1.196	1.431	3.578	−0.49	−1.225
Singapore Dollar	0.262	0.656	0.255	0.637	0.257	0.643
New Zealand Dollar Spot	0.308	0.77	0.516	1.289	0.113	0.282
British Pound Spot	0.018	0.044	0.144	0.36	−0.094	−0.235
Swiss Franc Spot	−0.064	−0.159	0.028	0.071	−0.151	−0.377
Swedish Krona Spot	0.176	0.441	0.449	1.121	−0.073	−0.182
Norwegian Krone Spot	0.025	0.063	0.22	0.55	−0.165	−0.411
Indian Rupee Spot	0.702	1.756	1.411	3.527	0.025	0.062
Vietnamese Dong Spot	3.648	9.12	3.971	9.927	3.287	8.217
Brazilian Real Spot	2.399	5.998	4.857	12.142	−0.046	−0.115
Mexican Peso Spot	0.019	0.046	0.134	0.335	−0.113	−0.282
Polish Zloty Spot	0.377	0.943	0.646	1.616	0.098	0.244
US Generic Govt 2 Year Yield*	0.336	0.84	0.359	0.897	0.311	0.776
US Generic Govt 5 Year Yield	0.224	0.559	0.28	0.7	0.159	0.398
US Generic Govt 10 Year Yield	−0.056	−0.14	−0.062	−0.154	−0.058	−0.146
US Generic Govt 30 Year Yield	−0.166	−0.416	−0.206	−0.516	−0.136	−0.339
German Government Bonds 2 Yr B	0.076	0.19	0.065	0.162	0.078	0.194
German Government Bonds 5 Yr O	−0.15	−0.374	−0.189	−0.473	−0.12	−0.301
German Government Bonds 10 Yr	−0.072	−0.18	0.039	0.096	−0.186	−0.465
German Government Bonds 30 Yr	0.012	0.03	−0.031	−0.077	0.053	0.133

*The profit and losses presented here in the case of rates are computed using the approximation that the return on a long bond position is equal to the duration of the bond times the variation in rates to which we added the monthly carry.

of a trend-following strategy we expect diagonal elements to grow when the anti-diagonal elements – that measure the probability of switches between regimes – decrease. We denote this variable $a(i)$ in the case of asset i.

- Then, very different trends in nature – that is in terms of expected return and volatility – can also endanger the profits obtained from a trend-following mechanism. When moving from a regime with a low volatility and a positive expected return to a regime with a high volatility and a negative expected return with the constant exposure of *ex ante* 40% of volatility, the realized return observed over such switches can destroy the performance of the investment strategy. We measure such heterogeneity through two variables: we denote respectively $m(i)$ and $v(i)$ the absolute difference between the minimum and the maximum expectation and volatility across the regimes of asset i. The larger this difference, the more difficult it should be for trend-following strategies to cope with such switches between regimes.
- Finally, to capture this negative premium observed in the previously mentioned plots, we add the variable $1_{commo}(i)$ that is a variable that is equal to 1 if the ith asset is a commodity and 0 if not. We add similar variables $1_{equity}(i)$ and $1_{currencies}(i)$ that are respectively equal to 1 if the ith asset belongs to the equity and currency asset classes.[19]

---

[19] For the OLS estimation to be performed, we need to discard one of the asset classes. Here, we refrain from introducing a variable for rates.

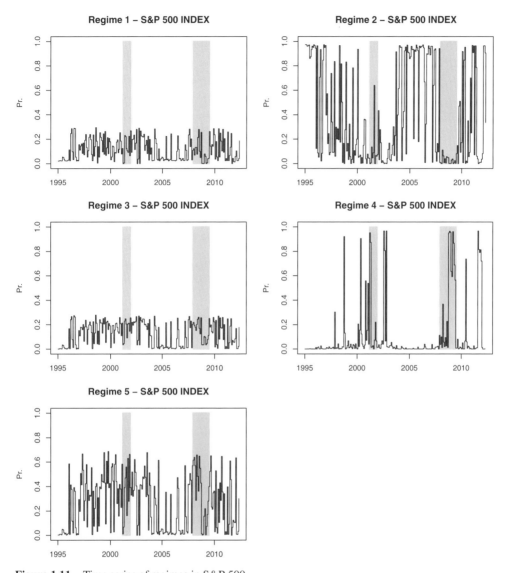

Figure 1.11   Time series of regimes in S&P 500

We ran the following regression:

$$SR(i) = \alpha + \beta_1 n(i) + \beta_2 a(i) + \beta_3 m(i) + \beta_4 v(i) + \beta_5 1_{\text{commo}}(i) + \beta_6 1_{\text{equity}}(i)$$
$$+ \beta_7 1_{\text{currencies}}(i) + \epsilon(i), \tag{1.17}$$

with $\epsilon(i)$ a centered disturbance. Results are available in Table 1.11. The results obtained in the momentum and in the breakout cases are different. In the time series momentum case, at a 5% risk level, there are three variables that explain statistically the Sharpe ratios obtained across strategies. The first of these variables is the number and the persistence of regimes that are positively related to the realized Sharpe ratio. Such statistical evidence supports the argument

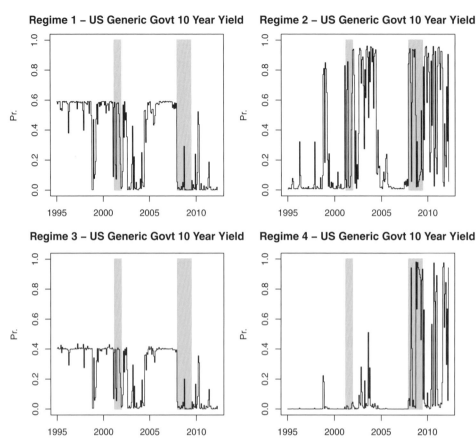

Figure 1.12   Time series of regimes in US 10Y rates

that a high number of regimes does not always threaten the performance of trend-following strategies, and that persistence of trends is essential to this industry. The third significant variable is the dummy variable for equity: equities seem to have generated an increase of the Sharpe ratio by 0.58 over the period. For the rest of the variables, we obtain the expected sign without finding statistically significant results: expectation and variance heterogeneity variables are negatively related to performance, and the persistence of regimes has a positive sign in the regression. Overall, we obtain an R^2 of 0.37, which is by usual standards quite high. Now, turning to the breakout strategy, we find three significant variables: persistence appears to have been a strong support to the performance of such a strategy. With a persistence equal to 1 – that is the maximum value for this average of probabilities – the expected Sharpe ratio from our regression should be equal to 2.13. The dummy variables for equities and currencies are significant as well, highlighting the interest of these assets for the trend-following industry. Signs of insignificant variables are also consistent with intuition, but again for the number of regimes that is positively related to the performance of the strategy.[20] The R^2 is lower than in the previous case and reaches a value of 0.19.

---

[20] This variable would be considered significant only at a 15% risk level.

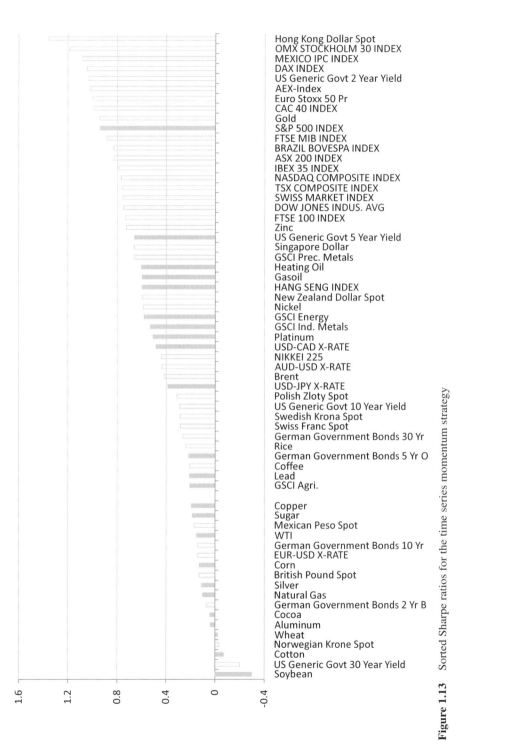

Figure 1.13 Sorted Sharpe ratios for the time series momentum strategy

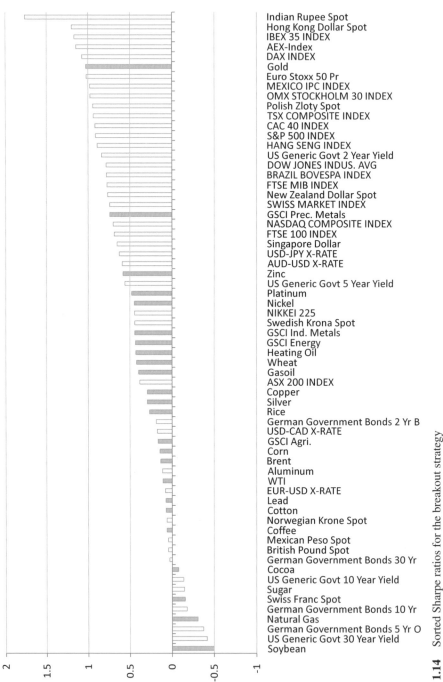

Figure 1.14 Sorted Sharpe ratios for the breakout strategy

Table 1.11   OLS regressions of the Sharpe ratio from the time series momentum strategy on explanatory factors

		Coef.	Std. Dev.	t-stat
Trend-following	Nb. of Regimes	0.14*	0.06	2.48
	Persistence	0.50	0.26	1.92
	Expectations heterogeneity	−0.01	0.02	−0.41
	Variance heterogeneity	−0.22	0.16	−1.31
	Is Commodity	0.11	0.14	0.77
	Is Equity	0.58*	0.14	4.04
	Is Currency	0.16	0.16	1.03
	R^2	0.37		
Breakout	Nb. of Regimes	0.2	0.13	1.53
	Persistence	2.13*	0.85	2.50
	Expectations heterogeneity	0.06	0.04	1.60
	Variance heterogeneity	−0.36	0.39	−0.93
	Is Commodity	0.38	0.34	1.14
	Is Equity	0.87*	0.34	2.57
	Is Currency	0.96*	0.36	2.62
	R^2	0.19		

Hence, the trend-following industry should be interested in commodities for the stability of the Sharpe ratio obtained with such strategies over such assets, and not for the stability of its trends. Still, as shown by the previous tables, the obtained Sharpe ratio can vary a lot depending on the considered commodity. The impact of the increasing use of commodities as investment tools by pension, hedge and mutual funds remains an open question: to what extent will those market participants increase the similarity between standard assets and commodities? This central question needs to be raised and answered by the CTA community. The impact of this economic phenomenon is also a potential explanation for the appearance of such trends. We will further discuss this point in Part II of the book. For now, we turn our attention toward risk patterns in commodities.

1.3   VOLATILITY TO RETURNS SPILLOVERS AND TAIL EVENTS IN COMMODITIES

As investors should be driven by Sharpe ratios, they should be both interested in expected returns and in the risk associated with these returns. This section investigates how risky commodities are. We first tackle the existence of returns to volatility spillovers – that is how the previously studied expected returns interact with volatility – in commodity markets before moving to the measurement of jumps in commodity markets.

1.3.1   Spillover Effects in Commodity Markets

1.3.1.1   *The Leverage Effect*

The relation between returns and volatility on most equity markets is known to be asymmetric: an increase in volatility that is subsequent to a negative return is larger than when a positive return occurs. This stylized fact for equities is now well documented, starting from the contribution of Black (1976). The main contributions in this respect are Christie (1982), Amihud and Mendelson (1987), Schwert (1989b), Cheung and Ng (1992), Campbell and Hentschel (1992), Damodaran (1993) and Koutmos (1998). In such markets, the usual explanation for such a pattern is related to the leverage of firms: when entering a crisis, the debt to equity ratio is high – and on average firms are leveraged – turning any negative return into an increasingly risky environment. This negative spillover effect of returns on subsequent volatilities is thus usually referred to as a leverage effect. Now, equity markets are not the only ones for which there is a positive or negative spillover from returns to volatility, and commodities are no exception. This section is dedicated to the measurement of these spillover effects across commodities.

Building on previous notation, r_t^i is the return on date t obtained from investing in asset i. r_t^i is a random variable, and follows some distribution L with expectation μ^i and a volatility that can change on every date t σ_t^i. Thus,

$$r_t^i \sim L\left(\mu^i, \sigma_t^i\right).\tag{1.18}$$

Following Gourieroux and Jasiak (2001),[21] there is a statistical spillover effect whenever the correlation between r_t^i and the variations of σ_t^i is different from zero; that is

$$\mathrm{cor}\left(r_t^i, \sigma_{t+1}^i - \sigma_t^i | \mathcal{F}_t\right),\tag{1.19}$$

where $\mathcal{F}_t$ is the filtration obtained from the information available at time t. For many of the time series models that are used in this book, $\mathcal{F}_t = \sigma\{r_{t-1}^i, r_{t-2}^i, \dots\}$. The available information is hence made of past returns on asset i. In the case of equities, this correlation is usually found to be negative.

1.3.1.2   Literature Review

The previously cited references on the equity market show consistent evidence that the previous correlation is negative, especially in the case of US equity. Is there any leverage effect in commodity markets? Giamouridis and Tamvakis (2001) assume that there is a non-zero correlation between past returns and volatility in such markets for two reasons:

1. First, for many commodities, the level of inventories is a key variable: any shortage should create abnormal positive returns, and boost the level of volatility in the meantime.
2. Second, there is a minimum price that makes producers break even: below such prices, producers are running their business making losses. Given the implications of dropping prices, such markets stand a good chance of having a limited downside risk.

Testing this intuition over commodity indices, the authors find evidence of a positive correlation between returns and volatility for both the GSCI and the JPMCI indices over the 1996–2000 period. They confirm that this relation is negative in the case of the S&P 500. As for many articles that will be quoted here, their approach relies on the Exponential GARCH (EGARCH) model presented initially in Nelson (1991). The empirical investigation presented

---

[21] They state this condition in terms of covariance, but as volatilities are non-zero and positive, it changes nothing about their conclusion when stating it in terms of correlation.

in this section will be based on the same type of modeling approach. Under Nelson's (1991) model, returns are driven by the following data-generating process:

$$r_t^i = \mu^i + \sigma_t^i \epsilon_t^i \tag{1.20}$$

$$\log \sigma_t^2 = \omega + \alpha \left| \epsilon_{t-1}^i \right| + \theta \epsilon_{t-1}^i + \beta \log \sigma_{t-1}^i, \tag{1.21}$$

where ϵ_t^i follows a distribution with an expectation equal to 0 and variance equal to 1. A negative correlation between returns and volatility is obtained when θ is negative: for such cases, a negative return increases the logarithm of the volatility by $\alpha + \theta$. There are different competing time series models to measure this phenomenon such as Ding *et al.*'s (1993) Asymmetric Power ARCH model or Glosten *et al.*'s (1993) GJR GARCH model. A large part of the literature still focuses on the EGARCH model, as it generates a leverage effect while maintaining the positivity of the conditional variance at all times. Grouping the empirical evidence obtained in the literature by commodity sector, we get the following insights from these empirical works: in the case of precious metals, consistent evidence shows that these commodities exhibit a positive leverage effect. Such findings have been uncovered in Batten and Lucey (2007), Tully and Lucey (2007), Batten *et al.* (2008) and Baur (2012) by using various samples and modeling approaches. Hammoudeh and Yuan (2008) and McKenzie *et al.* (2001) present more mixed evidence when it comes to industrial metals: Hammoudeh and Yuan (2008) find equity-like leverage effects in the case of copper, as well as insignificant leverage effects for gold and silver. McKenzie *et al.* (2001) estimated such time series models to the metals traded on the London Metal Exchange, and found no empirical evidence that there is some leverage effect for such commodities. The case of energy is maybe the case for which the highest number of estimations has been performed. Morana (2001) finds that the leverage effect helps the forecasting of oil prices. Hammoudeh *et al.* (2003), Lee and Zyren (2007), Chang *et al.* (2010), Singh *et al.* (2011) and Du *et al.* (2011) unanimously diagnose equity-like leverage effects. In the case of agricultural products, Zheng *et al.* (2008) find that returns on many food products are positively correlated to their volatility: the scarcity argument is here getting the upper hand. Finally, Brooks and Prokopczuk (2011) also find various signs for leverage effects, by using a continuous time model: they find a positive correlation between returns and volatility in the case of gold, silver and soybean. This correlation is negative in the case of the S&P 500, crude oil, gasoline and wheat. However, this correlation is statistically different from zero only in the cases of crude oil, gold, silver, soybeans and in the case of the S&P 500. Interestingly, when comparing the absolute value of these correlations, the highest value obtained in the case of commodities is only half of the S&P 500.

This question of leverage effects in commodities matters for several reasons, the first of which being risk management and the computation of Value-at-Risk (VaR). Forecasting the volatility of commodities is essential for such a purpose – and leverage effects are proved to make a difference. Then, the estimation of volatility is also very useful for the computation of hedge ratios, as illustrated in Kroner and Sultan (1993), Lien and Tse (2000) and Chen *et al.* (2001). Hedging a position requires correctly estimating the ratio of the hedging instrument's volatility to the asset to be hedged. The presence of leverage effects can have a marked impact here. Finally, Giamouridis and Tamvakis (2001) raise an interesting point: the addition to an equity portfolio – with a negative return to volatility spillover – of assets with positive leverage effect can increase the diversification of the final portfolio. Thus, having assets with opposite leverage effects can be a potential source of risk reduction.

1.3.1.3 The Modeling Approach

The previously quoted empirical evidence has been obtained by using various empirical approaches. Despite this fact, most of the conclusions listed above are consistent across academic contributions. We now turn our attention towards the estimation of the leverage effect in commodities. When doing so, the econometrician is faced with an essential issue: a negative (respectively positive) leverage effect creates negative (positive) skewness in financial return samples. In turn, it has been assumed that the presence of positive or negative skewness is a sign of the leverage effect. This is clearly an abusive shortcut: negative skewness can be generated by large negative jumps, triggering or not a rise in volatility. The leverage effect is often referred to as 'conditional skewness', given that it creates skewness from the dynamics of σ_t^i. Conversely, the portion of skewness that is not explained by the leverage effect is referred to as 'unconditional skewness', given that it is generated by a data-generating process whose parameters are not time dependent. By using the notation from Equation (1.21), ϵ_t^i captures this part of skewness that remains unexplained by the relay from past returns to the dynamics of volatility. For our empirical applications, we need to decide on a suitable distribution for ϵ_t^i. There are several candidates for such a purpose. Giot and Laurent (2003) have used a skewed Student distribution. Hung et al. (2008) make use of the heavy-tail distribution presented in Politis (2004). Ane and Labidi (2001) use a mixture of Gaussian distributions. A mixture of Gaussian distributions has been widely used and applied to other financial assets such as stocks and currencies in Kon (1984), Akgiray and Booth (1987), Tucker and Pond (1998), Lekkos (1999) and Alexander and Lazar (2006). An application to option pricing can be found in Monfort and Pegoraro (2006): beyond the empirical performance obtained when it comes to pricing options, they discuss the merit of the mixture of Gaussian distributions, emphasizing its connection to a non-parametric estimation of the conditional distribution of returns. A suitable competitor to the mixture of Gaussian distribution could be the Generalized Hyperbolic distribution (GH hereafter). The GH distribution was introduced by Barndorff-Nielsen and Blaesild (1981), and applied to finance in Eberlein and Prause (2002) and Chorro et al. (2010). These two distributions are interesting candidates as they encompass both fat tails and asymmetry of the conditional distribution of financial returns.

The difficulty that we are faced with now is a numerical one. When considering a model such that:

$$r_t^i = \mu^i + \sigma_t^i \epsilon_t^i, \tag{1.22}$$

where ϵ_t^i follows one of the previously mentioned distributions, the total skewness and kurtosis of the sample now has two sources of explanations σ_t^i and ϵ_t^i that appear in the equation in a multiplicative way. The usual estimation scheme here is to use the Quasi Maximum Likelihood (QML) approach. This amounts to first assuming that ϵ_t^i follows a centered Gaussian distribution to estimate the parameters driving the volatility process, and estimating the parameters characterizing ϵ_t^i in a second step by holding the estimated volatility parameters fixed. By using such an estimation approach, Chorro et al. (2010) have shown that the estimated parameters suffer from a strong bias, leading then to misleading conclusions concerning leverage effects in financial markets. Here, we will use the recursive estimation approach presented in Chorro et al. (2010), making it possible to disentangle both sources of skewness and kurtosis.[22] One

---

[22] See Chorro et al. (2010) for additional details regarding the recursive estimation methodology employed, and for additional references regarding this approach. Similar contributions are available in Song et al. (2005) and Fan et al. (2007). The intuition behind this estimation method is to perform multiple likelihood maximization by fixing either the volatility's or the conditional distribution's

key conclusion from their simulations and estimation strategy was that the GH and mixture of two Gaussian distributions delivered fairly comparable results in terms of their ability to capture the tails of the conditional distribution of financial returns. Given the numerical simplicity of the mixture of Gaussian distribution, we focus on this conditional distribution.

When ϵ_t^i follows a mixture of Gaussian distributions $MN(\phi, \mu_1, \sigma_1, \mu_2, \sigma_2)$, its density $f(.)$ is given by the following equation:

$$f\left(\epsilon_t^i\right) = \phi g\left(\epsilon_t^i; \mu_1, \sigma_1\right) + (1 - \phi)g\left(\epsilon_t^i; \mu_2, \sigma_2\right), \tag{1.23}$$

where $g(.; \mu, \sigma)$ is the density of Gaussian distribution with expectation μ and standard deviation σ; ϕ is a parameter taking its value between 0 and 1, mixing the two Gaussian distributions. As noted previously, despite the simplicity of this distribution, Monfort and Pegoraro (2006) showed its ability to replicate a wide range of empirical distributions, which is exactly what we need to disentangle these two sources of skewness and kurtosis. What is more, the mixture of Gaussian distributions has an appealing economic intuition: for example, with two Gaussian distributions, markets are implicitly viewed as being made of two types of different agents or two types of potential market configurations – bullish and bearish ones. The mixing parameter does the arbitrage between either the market power or the frequency of occurrence of each market episode. Interestingly, the unconditional distribution of a Markov switching with two regimes is a mixture of Gaussian distributions as well.

1.3.1.4 Empirical Findings

Now, we use again a dataset of commodities and more standard assets made of daily close-to-close returns from 1995 to 2012. We use the recursive estimation of Chorro *et al.* (2010), applied to the EGARCH model with a mixture of normal distributions (EGARCH-MN) defined by Equations (1.21) to (1.23). Estimated parameters are presented in Table 1.12, along with the standard deviations associated with each of these estimated parameters. Several key conclusions can be drawn from this table:

– First of all, the sign of the θ parameter that drives the leverage effect in the EGARCH model is globally consistent with the findings in the previous literature. It is found to be positive in the case of agricultural products and precious metals – both when considered individually and as an asset class through the GSCI indices. For example, in the case of gold it is found to be equal to 0.054, and in the case of the GSCI precious metals we obtain 0.0262. In the case of coffee it is equal to 0.0877, and for the GSCI agricultural sub-index we find 0.0425. It is consistently found to be negative in the case of energy and industrial metals. Again, this is consistent when considering the individual commodities and the two GSCI indices. In the case of Brent, we find $\theta = -0.029$ and in the case of GSCI Energy sub-index $\theta = -0.0353$. In the case of copper, this parameter is estimated to be equal to -0.027 and in the case of GSCI Industrial Metals -0.0524. In this respect, energy and industrial metals have a tendency to be characterized by equity-like leverage effects: the S&P 500 has a θ parameter estimated to be equal to -0.1637.

– Second, for most of the individual commodities, the leverage parameter is not found to be statistically different from zero. There are only four cases for which the leverage parameter

parameters each time, until this sequential optimization stops improving the value of the log-likelihood function. Monte Carlo results in Chorro *et al.* (2010) show that the convergence rate for such estimation is lower, but the estimation bias is strongly reduced and the efficiency of the estimates much higher than that of both the maximum or quasi maximum likelihood methods.

Table 1.12 EGARCH-MN parameters estimated

	Volatility Parameters					Conditional Distribution Parameters			
	ω	θ	α	β	ϕ	μ_1	σ_1	μ_2	σ_2
Gold	−0.2626 (0.0076)	0.054 (0.0262)	0.1588 (0.0095)	0.9729 (0.0015)	0.2678 (0.0539)	−0.0125 (0.0202)	0.7053 (0.0402)	0.0257 (0.0074)	0.3129 (0.0169)
Silver	−0.2063 (0.0065)	0.0387 (0.0232)	0.1771 (0.0101)	0.9775 (0.0016)	0.207 (0.0321)	−0.1178 (0.0342)	0.7501 (0.0362)	0.0449 (0.0071)	0.3214 (0.0105)
Platinum	−0.3781 (0.0115)	0.0267 (0.0237)	0.2301 (0.0149)	0.9581 (0.0025)	0.2587 (0.0394)	−0.0302 (0.0207)	0.6974 (0.0325)	0.0286 (0.0074)	0.3273 (0.0112)
Aluminum	−0.2432 (0.0094)	−0.0081 (0.0053)	0.1538 (0.0108)	0.9744 (0.0019)	0.8918 (0.0294)	0.0144 (0.007)	0.4029 (0.01)	−0.1167 (0.0635)	0.841 (0.0612)
Copper	−0.2617 (0.0081)	−0.027 (0.0205)	0.1841 (0.0116)	0.9706 (0.0019)	0.1902 (0.0414)	−0.0684 (0.0411)	0.7304 (0.0426)	0.0228 (0.0083)	0.351 (0.0122)
Nickel	−0.2633 (0.0082)	0.0135 (0.0329)	0.1472 (0.0125)	0.9658 (0.0022)	0.2143 (0.0425)	−0.0008 (3e-04)	0.7605 (0.0429)	0.0052 (0.0066)	0.3602 (0.0129)
Zinc	−0.1116 (0.0031)	0.0194 (0.014)	0.086 (0.0047)	0.9876 (8e-04)	0.2282 (0.0498)	−0.0296 (0.04)	0.7009 (0.0407)	0.0125 (0.0087)	0.3366 (0.014)
Lead	−0.1792 (0.0049)	0.0084 (0.007)	0.1508 (0.0078)	0.9803 (0.0012)	0.253 (0.0443)	−0.061 (0.0304)	0.6687 (0.0321)	0.0292 (0.0085)	0.3365 (0.0116)
WTI	−0.2178 (0.0098)	−0.0139 (0.0324)	0.1209 (0.0135)	0.9719 (0.0025)	0.1268 (0.0465)	−0.1277 (0.0607)	0.7751 (0.0655)	0.0296 (0.0094)	0.4102 (0.0132)
Brent	−0.3402 (0.0126)	−0.029 (0.0412)	0.1765 (0.0173)	0.956 (0.0032)	0.3032 (0.0846)	−0.0426 (0.0298)	0.657 (0.041)	0.0351 (0.0107)	0.3632 (0.0212)
Gasoil	−0.2423 (0.0112)	−0.0264 (0.0242)	0.1403 (0.0141)	0.9703 (0.0027)	0.2339 (0.1271)	−0.03 (0.0482)	0.6804 (0.0717)	0.026 (0.0141)	0.3997 (0.0284)
Natural Gas	−0.2366 (0.0075)	0.0204 (0.0219)	0.1594 (0.0141)	0.9664 (0.0025)	0.8507 (0.0358)	−0.009 (0.0087)	0.3813 (0.012)	0.0822 (0.0444)	0.8278 (0.0556)
Heating Oil	−0.1906 (0.0123)	−0.0192 (0.0526)	0.1136 (0.0149)	0.9762 (0.003)	0.0597 (0.0257)	−0.1763 (0.1089)	0.9197 (0.0991)	0.0227 (0.0085)	0.44 (0.01)
Corn	−0.3231 (0.0117)	0.0119 (0.0183)	0.2099 (0.0158)	0.9624 (0.0027)	0.1204 (0.0244)	0.1453 (0.0518)	0.9 (0.0565)	−0.0088 (0.0061)	0.3749 (0.0095)

Wheat	−0.0714 (0.0044)	0.0418 (0.0168)	0.0488 (0.0055)	0.9917 (0.001)	0.8575 (0.032)	−0.0241 (0.0089)	0.398 (0.0099)	0.1807 (0.0534)	0.8009 (0.049)
Coffee	−0.3771 (0.0118)	0.0877 (0.0361)	0.1492 (0.0186)	0.9464 (0.0032)	0.6869 (0.0526)	−0.0013 (0.0008)	0.3256 (0.0161)	0.0176 (0.029)	0.7047 (0.035)
Sugar	−0.156 (0.0061)	−0.0102 (0.0289)	0.1093 (0.0088)	0.9813 (0.0015)	0.9042 (0.0216)	0.0174 (0.0086)	0.3989 (0.0091)	−0.1491 (0.0698)	0.9647 (0.0673)
Cocoa	−0.1543 (0.0084)	0.0138 (0.0028)	0.1051 (0.0108)	0.9822 (0.0019)	0.1735 (0.0364)	0.0045 (0.0032)	0.8133 (0.0487)	0.004 (0.0069)	0.3861 (0.0115)
Cotton	−0.1724 (0.0063)	0.0188 (0.0155)	0.1195 (0.0087)	0.9801 (0.0015)	0.0601 (0.0189)	0.0842 (0.0728)	1.1023 (0.1094)	−0.0042 (0.0053)	0.4053 (0.0097)
Soybean	−0.3608 (0.0131)	−0.0008 (0.0005)	0.1926 (0.0164)	0.9578 (0.0028)	0.2874 (0.041)	−0.0388 (0.0274)	0.6946 (0.0299)	0.0274 (0.0093)	0.3405 (0.0115)
Rice	−1.1153 (0.0258)	−0.0121 (0.0104)	0.3449 (0.0364)	0.8516 (0.0063)	0.923 (0.0166)	−0.0098 (0.008)	0.3906 (0.0083)	0.2071 (0.0788)	1.0572 (0.0796)
GSCI Agri.	−0.283 (0.0108)	0.0425 (0.0188)	0.1651 (0.0121)	0.9699 (0.0021)	0.2146 (0.0668)	−0.0099 (0.0172)	0.6836 (0.0493)	−0.0006 (0.0011)	0.3879 (0.0146)
GSCI Energy	−0.3127 (0.013)	−0.0353 (0.0195)	0.1609 (0.0169)	0.9605 (0.0031)	0.2758 (0.1402)	−0.0525 (0.0401)	0.6488 (0.0589)	0.0337 (0.0125)	0.3953 (0.0301)
GSCI Ind. Metals	−0.3268 (0.0111)	−0.0524 (0.0239)	0.2037 (0.0137)	0.9642 (0.0023)	0.1284 (0.05)	−0.1093 (0.0662)	0.7515 (0.0633)	0.0233 (0.0084)	0.3933 (0.0142)
GSCI Prec. Metals	−0.1963 (0.0062)	0.0262 (0.0267)	0.1237 (0.0077)	0.9797 (0.0012)	0.1226 (0.0292)	−0.1081 (0.0504)	0.8599 (0.0606)	0.0342 (0.0073)	0.3615 (0.0108)
S&P 500	−0.2538 (0.0098)	−0.1637 (0.039)	0.12 (0.0123)	0.9706 (0.002)	0.4759 (0.088)	−0.0536 (0.0227)	0.5345 (0.0237)	0.0665 (0.0114)	0.2758 (0.0254)
10Y US	−0.1642 (0.0079)	−0.0361 (0.0284)	0.2176 (0.0104)	0.9869 (0.0017)	0.2131 (0.07)	0.0122 (0.024)	0.6543 (0.0477)	−0.0196 (0.0078)	0.3645 (0.0157)
US Dollar	−0.0982 (0.0107)	−0.01 (0.0107)	0.0759 (0.0083)	0.9923 (0.0015)	0.5026 (0.1339)	0.0203 (0.0142)	0.3249 (0.0424)	−0.0284 (0.0189)	0.6114 (0.0386)

is found to be significant: gold (0.054), wheat (0.0418), coffee (0.0877) and cocoa (0.0138). The rest of these parameters do not pass the significance test. On the contrary, each GSCI index but the precious metals one is found to have a statistically significant leverage effect of the previously mentioned sign. Hence, as an asset class – once individual patterns have been averaged out – commodity markets do exhibit leverage effects. The case of precious metals may be explained by the fact that precious metals are increasingly used as industrial metals, thus mixing two kinds of patterns.

– Finally, as presented in Figure 1.17, the magnitude of leverage effects in the commodity markets is less pronounced than those in the US equity market. Coffee set apart, the absolute maximum value for this parameter is around 0.05, when in the case of S&P 500 it is close to −0.15. Another way of analyzing these results and getting some sense from these estimation figures is to compute Engle and Ng's (1993) news impact curve. This curve represents how volatility responds to the magnitude and sign of past returns. Suppose that volatility is at its long-term level $\bar{\sigma}^i$. By following Equation (1.20), the increase in volatility given a past positive or negative shock in returns can be computed the following way:

$$\log \sigma^2_{t+1} = \omega + \alpha \left| \epsilon^i_{t-1} \right| + \theta \epsilon^i_{t-1} + \beta \log \bar{\sigma}^i_{t-1}. \tag{1.24}$$

This allows us to chart the potential variations of volatility depending on past realized returns. Such news impact curves are presented in Figure 1.15 by comparing the news impact curves of the GSCI commodity sectors to the one associated to the S&P 500, the 10-year rates and the dollar trade-weighted index. When negative (positive) leverage effects are observed on a market, this curve is asymmetric and skewed to the left (right). In the case of commodities – and consistent with our previous estimation results – the asymmetry of the news impact curve is far less pronounced than those associated with the S&P 500. As in the case of copper, the bulk of the asymmetry of returns on these commodities seems to come from the conditional distribution; that is, from ϵ^i_t.

The case of copper is very illustrative of the difficulties in disentangling leverage from unconditional skewness: Hammoudeh and Yuan (2008) and Brooks and Prokopczuk (2011) find evidence of statistically significant leverage effects for this commodity. When using a more robust estimation approach that makes it possible to discriminate between both sources of skewness, we conclude that most of this skewness comes from the unconditional skewness, as the leverage effect is not found to be statistically significant. For example, the bulk of the skewness in copper seems to come from the mixture of Gaussian distributions. The first Gaussian distribution has a negative expectation (−6.84%) and a volatility that is higher than the volatility of the second Gaussian distribution. The expectation of the second Gaussian distribution is positive, and of a lower absolute value than that of the first distribution. Hence, what has been diagnosed so far to be return to volatility spillovers in copper – thus generating skewness in market returns – is in fact an historical 19.02% chance that copper exhibits strong negative returns with higher volatility. This asymmetry in the conditional distribution is the primary contributor to the negative skewness found in the returns of copper.

Figure 1.16 presents the log-densities of ϵ^i_t estimated by using the EGARCH-MN model in the case of the four GSCI indices, compared with the results obtained in the case of S&P 500, the US 10-year rate and the trade-weighted US Dollar. Clearly, the main difference between all of these commodity indices and these more standard financial assets lies in the tails of their conditional distribution. In the case of commodities, tails are always decreasing at a slower rate

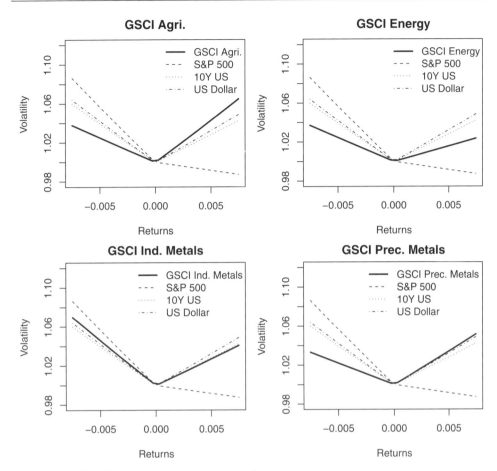

Figure 1.15   Volatility signature plots for commodity sectors

than in the S&P 500 case, for example: extreme returns have a higher frequency of occurrence in the case of commodities than in US equity.

Another way to consider this tail activity is to investigate the frequency and size of the jumps affecting the returns on commodities. In the next section, we investigate such an issue.

1.3.2   Twenty Years of Jumps in Commodity Markets

Given the great importance of tail events in commodities, investigating and measuring jump activity in such returns is an essential step toward understanding the dynamics of these markets. We have previously captured the tail behavior through the mixture of Gaussian distributions, by using a distribution flexible enough to capture tail patterns without having to understand what is at stake behind these extreme events. Now, we propose to measure more precisely what is happening in these tails: tail events in financial economics are usually modeled by jumps, i.e. extreme events – some market observers consider them as discontinuous events – that appear rarely in financial markets. Rarely here means that the number of jumps per year is lower than the number of trading days in a year. However, the scale of these extreme returns is such

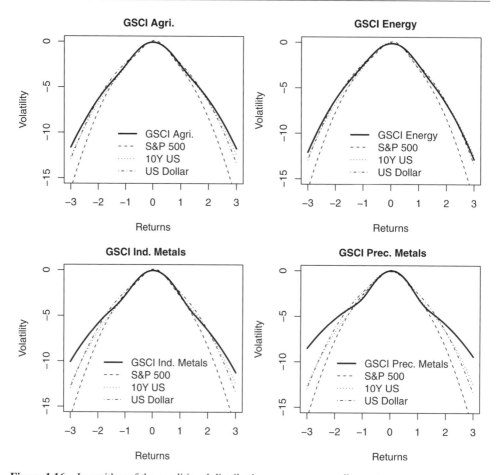

Figure 1.16 Logarithm of the conditional distributions across commodity sectors

that even though they occur rarely, they can change the direction of markets. The challenge (as in the case of volatility) is that these jumps are only a sort of concept that we use to put reality into equations. Indeed, jumps are not directly observable and their estimation is even more complex than volatility. As we will explain later, a full measurement of the jump activity in any market can only be done by computing three quantities that are increasingly difficult to estimate: the date for each jump, the sign of each jump and the absolute magnitude of each jump.

1.3.2.1 *Jumps in Commodities*

Jumps have helped financial economists to take decisive steps towards understanding the pricing mechanism implicit in financial markets. A wide literature has investigated the use of jump processes in equity markets, with a large part of it focusing on option pricing. Merton (1976) is often considered as one of the seminal contributions to this field: he proposed to add jumps to the pure Gaussian Black and Scholes (1973) model. By building on previous

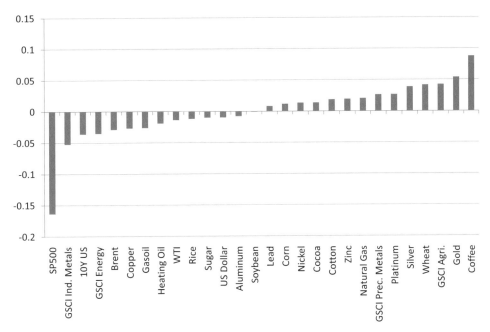

Figure 1.17   Estimated θ across commodities

notation,[23] r_t is again the close-to-close return obtained from investing in asset i on date t−1. A discrete time version of Merton's (1976) model could be written as follows:

$$r_t = \mu + \sigma\epsilon_t + \sum_{j=0}^{N_t} x_{j,t}, \qquad (1.25)$$

where μ is the returns' expectation before jumps, σ is the volatility of the Gaussian part of the data-generating process of returns, N_t is the number of jumps at time t and $x_{j,t}$ is the scale of the jth jump on date t. Various distributions can be considered here for ϵ_t, N_t and for $x_{j,t}$. However, ϵ_t is now usually assumed to follow a Gaussian distribution: tail events are captured by $\sum_{j=0}^{N_t} x_{j,t}$ while more normal days of trading are modeled through $\mu + \sigma\epsilon_t$. In a continuous time setting, $\mu + \sigma\epsilon_t$ is referred to as the continuous part of the process, while the jump part is the discontinuous one. Given that our focus here is set in discrete time, none of these components are continuous, but the spirit remains the same. Ball and Torous (1985) have presented early empirical results underlying the interest of adding jumps when it comes to option pricing. This jump-based framework has been extended to stochastic volatility in Bates (1996) and Backshi *et al.* (1997), based on the work of Heston (1993). Empirical estimates for the parameters of such models have been produced in Andersen *et al.* (2012), Chernov *et al.* (2003), Eraker *et al.* (2003) and Eraker (2004). In comparison to the dynamic research activity in equity markets, commodities have been subject to less attention. Early models were proposed in Brennan and Schwartz (1985), Gibson and Schwartz (1990), Schwartz (1997) and Schwartz and Smith (2000). These contributions focused on the Gaussian part of the

---

[23] We dropped the i indexation insofar as it simplifies the notation.

returns-generating process. Given that the previous contributions focused on the modeling of the term structure of futures, jumps have been set apart since the contribution of Hilliard and Reis (1998) showing that futures do not incorporate jump-related premia. In a more recent study, Deng (2005) details the merits of adding jumps for non-storable commodities such as electricity. Finally, Aravindhakshan and Brorsen (2011) and Brooks and Prokopczuk (2011) present the empirical interest of adding jumps to model the dynamics of various commodities. Brooks and Prokopczuk (2011) provide estimates to the jump parameters in Equation (1.25), by assuming that N_t follows a Poisson distribution driven by a jump intensity parameter λ, and that jump sizes $x_{j,t}$ are following a Gaussian distribution with expectation μ_x and variance σ_x^2. On average, they find that the jump intensity[24] for gold, silver, crude oil, gasoline, soybean and wheat is much more important than in the case of the S&P 500: for example, in the case of crude oil, they find that around 6.2 jumps occurred on average per year over the 1985–2010 period whereas in the S&P 500 case, only 1.8 jumps[25] were to be expected. They find significant differences as well between commodities, as, for example, silver prices are expected to jump about 22 times per year. On average, they also find that the expected size of a jump in the case of commodities is smaller than the expected size of a jump in the US equity case: silver has an expected jump equal to −46% whereas in the case of S&P 500 this parameter is estimated to be equal to −258%. Aravindhakshan and Brorsen (2011) have obtained similar figures in the case of wheat and the Commodities Research Bureau (CRB) index, disentangling positive from negative jumps. Ielpo and Sévi (2011) present empirical estimates of such quantities by using an intra-day dataset for crude oil prices: their estimates are model-free, in the sense that jumps are extracted directly from 5-minute returns by using the Huang and Tauchen (2005) method[26] that does not rely on a given specification of $\sum_{j=0}^{N_t} x_{j,t}$. While Brooks and Prokopczuk (2011) obtain around 6 jumps per year for the WTI, Ielpo and Sévi (2011) find around 37 jumps. The expected size of these jumps is, however, much smaller than those of Brooks and Prokopczuk (2011). Two elements can help explain these differences: the first one being the difficulty of disentangling the effects of volatility dynamics from the effects of jumps. Jumps create additional skewness and kurtosis in total returns, as does stochastic volatility. As presented in the previous section, the fact that these two components can have a similar impact on the final return makes their estimation complex. Second, it appears that daily data and intra-day datasets provide different figures when it comes to estimates of volatility parameters or jump components. The reason for this is that the definition of jumps from a daily perspective is somewhat different when considered from an intra-day point of view: intra-day datasets can show two jumps in one day that average each other out as they are of comparable size but of opposite sign. This type of jump will not be diagnosed as a jump in a daily dataset, as they will not appear in such datasets. Obtaining these daily and intra-day datasets is still an empirical challenge so far, as illustrated in Ielpo and Sévi (2012).

1.3.2.2 Estimating Jumps from Daily Returns

Even though such model-free intra-day datasets are, by essence, probably the best way to estimate and characterize the jump activity in any financial market, such intra-day datasets are

---

[24] The jump intensity measures the probability of observing at least one jump over a given period of time. With annual figures, if $\lambda = 10$, this means that the expected number of jumps over a year should be 10.

[25] A similar result is obtained in Eraker (2004).

[26] We do not provide much technical explanation regarding the extraction of jumps from intra-day datasets. The interested reader can find additional information in Huang and Tauchen (2005) and Ielpo and Sévi (2011).

costly and require an extensive cleaning process. Conversely, daily prices for futures or spot prices are much easier to obtain, and can offer interesting insights into the jump activity in commodity markets. Laurent *et al.* (2011) have proposed a test based on daily data making it possible to estimate the number of days over which a jump may have happened. The test is based on the standardization of returns: returns are scaled through the estimation of their expectation and volatility in a robust way. Their method is based on an improvement of the method presented in Franses and Ghijsels (1999). We briefly review the methodology before moving to the analysis of empirical results applied to our sample of commodities.

Returns are assumed to be accurately described by a combination of an ARMA-GARCH component r_t and an additive jump component $a_t I_t$, where $I_t = 1$ when day t includes jumps of a total size a_t:

$$r_t^* = r_t + a_t I_t \tag{1.26}$$

$$\phi(L)(r_t - \mu) = \theta(L)\sigma_t \epsilon_t \text{ where } \epsilon_t \overset{i.i.d.}{\sim} N(0,1) \tag{1.27}$$

$$\sigma_t^2 = \omega + \alpha \epsilon_{t-1}^2 \sigma_{t-1}^2 + \beta \sigma_{t-1}^2, \tag{1.28}$$

where $\phi(L)$ and $\theta(L)$ are polynomials of the lag operator with unit roots outside the unit circle. The jump detection rule is based on the fact that if ϵ_t begins Gaussian, ex-jump scaled returns should also be conditionally Gaussian. Rewriting the previous equations to have an explicit conditional drift μ_t and volatility σ_t, the model can be stated as follows:

$$r_t = \mu + \sigma_t \epsilon_t \tag{1.29}$$

$$\mu_t = \mu + \sum_{i=1}^{\infty} \lambda_i \sigma_{t-i} \epsilon_{t-i}. \tag{1.30}$$

When scaling the ex-jump return r_t as follows:

$$\tilde{J}_t = \frac{r_t - \mu_t}{\sigma_t}, \tag{1.31}$$

$\tilde{J}_t$ should evolve between two values that can be used as thresholds under the null hypothesis that no jump occurred on date t. Following Lee and Mykland (2008), Laurent *et al.* (2011) assume that $|\tilde{J}_t|$ follows a Gumbel distribution.[27] On the computations of the threshold at a given risk level, see Laurent *et al.* (2011), Equation (2.10). The key part of their approach is to disentangle r_t from $a_t I_t$. To do so, they use a robust estimation method inspired by Muler and Yohai (2008) and Muler *et al.* (2009).[28] Through Monte Carlo experiments, they show that their estimation methodology proved well enough behaved to conduct a jump analysis on the YENUSD currency, producing a list of dates for which jumps have occurred.

We intend to reproduce this analysis in the context of commodity markets.

1.3.2.3 Jumps in Commodity Markets

Figure 1.18 presents the time series of returns for the S&P 500, the 10-year rate and the US Dollar that will be used as a benchmark for analyzing the results obtained with commodities.

---

[27] Following the extreme value theory (EVT), the maximum of n i.i.d. realizations of the absolute value of a standard normal variable is asymptotically Gumbel distributed.

[28] For additional details on the methodology, see Laurent *et al.* (2011), pages 7–12.

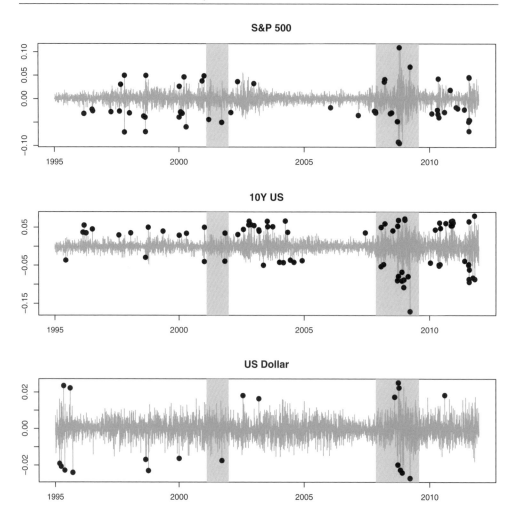

Figure 1.18 Estimated jumps for the S&P 500, the US Dollar and the US 10Y rate. Jumps are marked by black dots

Figure 1.19 presents similar graphics in the case of the GSCI indices. Table 1.13 presents various statistics obtained by applying Laurent *et al.*'s (2011) approach. We compute the total number of jumps obtained over the 1995–2012 period, as well as the average return observed over such days depending whether the return was positive or negative. In addition, we compute the average return of the 5 to 20 days following a jump. These statistics will help us understand how jumps are actually affecting the dynamics of returns on commodities. Three main conclusions can be drawn from our estimations:

– First of all, for most of the commodities, the total number of detected jumps is higher than those of the S&P 500, the US 10-year rate or the US Dollar. Platinum and lead seem to have the highest number of jumps across commodities, with respectively 109 and 101 jumps over the period, which is around 6 jumps a year. Hence, with this jump robust estimation method, the jump activity diagnosed in commodities is slightly below what was detected in Brooks

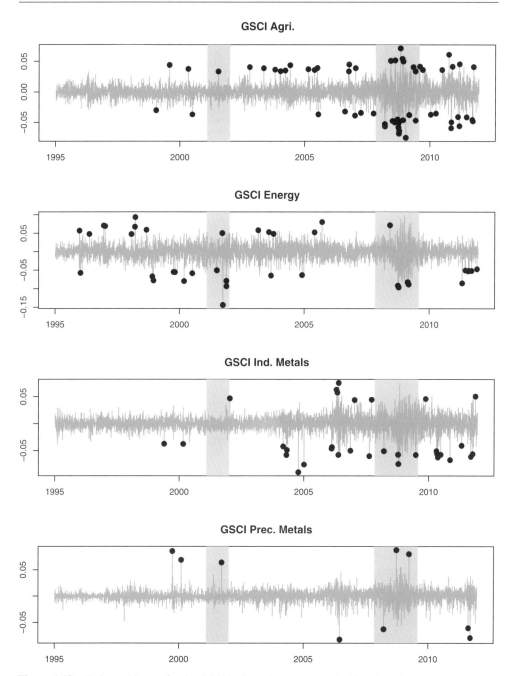

Figure 1.19   Estimated jumps for the GSCI indices. Jumps are marked by black dots

Table 1.13 Summary statistics from Laurent et al.'s (2011) jump estimation method

	Total Nb. Jumps	Positive jumps				Negative jumps				
		Nb. Pos. Jumps	Avg. Return	Next 5D	Next 10D	Next 20D	Nb. Neg. Jumps	Avg. Return	Next 5D	Next 10D	Next 20D
Gold	21	8	6.75	2.67	0.41	-0.17	13	-4.94	-0.54	0.26	1.29
Silver	91	31	6.02	0.73	1.13	0.05	60	-7.39	-0.42	-0.09	-0.98
Platinum	109	53	4.44	0.08	-0.32	-0.68	56	-5.07	-0.3	-1.26	-0.99
Aluminum	57	21	4.44	0.55	-0.56	-0.5	36	-5.03	0.04	-0.9	-1.5
Copper	86	30	5.7	-0.28	-0.55	0.78	56	-5.4	-0.1	-1.09	-1.67
Nickel	78	34	7.82	0.16	-2.9	-4.56	44	-8.12	-0.39	-0.63	0.84
Zinc	83	28	5.39	-1.02	-1.65	-2.95	55	-5.95	0.26	0.86	-0.15
Lead	101	39	6.71	0.74	1.28	0.9	62	-6.71	-0.29	0.4	-0.66
WTI	46	17	8.16	-3.05	-4.43	-6.41	29	-8.24	1.93	2.58	1.62
Brent	55	24	8.11	-3.4	-6.7	-6.92	31	-7.99	1.97	1.41	1.29
Gasoil	44	23	6.87	-3.62	-7.61	-8.12	21	-7.46	0.42	-0.59	-1.71
Natural Gas	52	30	13.72	-2.72	-4.61	-4.75	22	-12.42	2.81	-2.65	-5.4
Heating Oil	49	20	7.37	-1.01	-1.8	-2.08	29	-8.31	-0.02	0.51	0.33
Corn	80	56	5.38	-0.04	-0.42	-0.4	24	-6.93	0.1	1.69	2.61
Wheat	80	54	6.73	-0.43	-1.32	-1.58	26	-7.17	-1.28	0.68	-2.09
Coffee	88	45	8.25	-1.44	-1.55	-2.68	43	-8.67	-0.92	-0.12	-0.91
Sugar	55	17	8.45	1.38	0.34	1.11	38	-8.35	-0.32	0.15	1.53
Cocoa	81	37	6.55	0.31	-0.36	0.26	44	-6.83	-0.99	-1.01	-0.98
Cotton	84	47	5.7	0.36	0.58	-0.68	37	-6.59	-1.1	-1.44	-3.13
Soybean	72	36	4.46	0.06	0.73	1.19	36	-5.72	1.26	2.06	2.6
Rice	82	58	5.69	-0.3	0.38	0.8	24	-6.17	-0.33	0.42	-0.6
GSCI Agri.	59	29	4.24	0.66	0.12	0.61	30	-4.65	-0.62	-0.64	-2.1
GSCI Energy	38	15	6.2	-1.05	-3.24	-5.3	23	-7.12	0.72	0.11	-0.09
GSCI Ind. Metals	32	8	5.38	0.52	0.3	-2.46	24	-5.57	0.82	-0.27	-0.49
GSCI Prec. Metals	9	5	7.73	1.92	0.09	-5.65	4	-7.12	1.74	1.32	3.13
S&P 500	58	17	4.53	0.07	-1.51	-1.32	41	-3.9	0.99	0.13	-0.39
10Y US	76	44	5.13	-0.01	0.23	1.51	32	-6.27	-0.1	-1.73	-2.18
US Dollar	20	8	2.04	0.67	1.28	2.01	12	-2.12	0.33	0.88	0.61

and Prokopczuk (2011): they found an average of 7.5 jumps for the commodities considered. Note that we also find a large discrepancy between commodities: while we obtain 21 jumps for gold, silver has 91 jumps over the period. Similarly, wheat is characterized by 80 jumps whereas sugar has only 55 jumps. However, a common pattern appears from our estimates: the commodities displaying the highest number of jumps are agricultural commodities. Then energy and industrial metals also display an important number of jumps. The lowest number of jumps is obtained for precious metals: the GSCI sector index has only 9 jumps detected. This again is consistent with the fact that precious metals are fit for various uses. From gold to platinum we also observe discrepancies in terms of the number of jumps detected.

– Second, when comparing the number of positive and negative jumps, we cast light on a key difference between commodities and standard assets. Whereas the number of negative jumps in the case of S&P 500 is much higher (around two thirds) than the number of positive jumps, commodities exhibit a completely different story. Agricultural products have a tendency to have more positive than negative jumps – in line with Giamouridis and Tamvakis's (2001) hypothesis that there should be more positive than negative extreme returns. For the rest of commodities, it ranges from a pretty balanced situation, as in the case of platinum for which the number of positive (negative) days with jumps is equal to 53 (56). In the case of copper, we have 56 negative jumps vs. 30 positive jumps. This casts additional light on the origins of the diversification effect observed when adding commodities to a diversified portfolio. It also provides hints regarding which commodity offers the strongest relation to the worldwide business cycle: industrial metals and energy display a jump structure which is close to the S&P 500. This point will be further discussed in Part II of the book.

– Coming back to the origin of trends in commodity markets, a strong and negative/positive shock could create a long-lasting direction in markets through what is now called the 'jump to volatility channel' uncovered in a couple of recent contributions by Ait-Sahalia, Cacho-Diaz and Laeven (2011), Carr and Wu (2011) and Fulop, Li and Yu (2011). A negative (positive) jump in asset returns is passed on to market volatility when entering a bear (bull) market period. While this type of relationship exists on equity markets (and can be used to build investment strategies), there is currently no previous evidence of such patterns on commodity markets. To investigate this question, we present in Table 1.13 the average return following a positive or a negative jump. When a negative jump creates a prolonged negative trend on a given market, we obtain negative returns over the next 5 to 20 days. Conversely, when a negative (respectively positive) jump is followed by a mean reversion behavior, the upcoming returns following such a jump should be of an opposite sign. For example, in the case of soybean, a positive jump is usually followed by positive returns on soybeans in the following days. In the case of natural gas, when a negative jump occurs, a negative trend is observed over the next 20 trading days. Brent constitutes a fairly good example of a market which exhibits mean reversion after a shock: after either a positive or a negative shock, a return of the opposite sign is usually observed during the next few days. When considering the GSCI indices, we obtain results that are very consistent with the individual analyses: agricultural markets are typically affected by trends created by a positive or a negative shock. A positive shock to the energy or the industrial metals sector is usually followed by some mean reversion, while a negative shock triggers a pattern that is very similar to the equity case: after some mean-reversion, the average performance over 20 days is also negative. Finally, precious metals are typically affected by mean reverting

Table 1.14　Returns (in %) realized on common jump days on commodity indices, S&P 500, US Dollar and US 10Y rate

	GSCI Agri.	GSCI Energy	GSCI Ind. Metals	GSCI Prec. Metals	S&P 500	10Y US	US Dollar
08-Mar-96					−3.1	5.5	
05-Jul-96					−2.2	4.5	
27-Aug-98					−3.9	−2.9	
07-Oct-98						5	−2.3
03-Jan-00						2.9	−1.6
03-Jan-01					4.9	5	
14-Sep-01		5.1		6.4			
17-Sep-01					−5		−1.7
08-May-02					3.7	3.1	
15-Oct-02	4.1					5.7	
02-Jan-03					3.3	5.5	
13-Mar-03						4.3	1.6
17-Mar-08	−5.3		−5.1				
18-Mar-08					4.2	6	
19-Mar-08	−5.6			−6.3			
06-Jun-08		7.2			−3.1		
08-Aug-08	−5						1.7
15-Sep-08					−4.8	−9	
17-Sep-08				8.8	−4.8		
29-Sep-08	−5.8	−9.2			−9.2	−7.9	
30-Sep-08						6.9	2.5
06-Oct-08	−6.8		−5.7				
10-Oct-08	−6.4	−9.6	−7.4				2.2
29-Oct-08	7.2						−2.3
24-Nov-08	5.4						−2.4
17-Feb-09		−8.2				−7.9	
02-Mar-09	−3.7	−8.8					
18-Mar-09						−17.1	−2.7
12-Jan-10	−3.7					−4.3	
27-Apr-10			−5.1		−2.4		
20-May-10					−4	−5.1	
11-Aug-10					−2.9		1.8
12-Nov-10	−5.9					5.5	
16-Nov-10	−4.9		−6.7				
01-Dec-10	4.1					5.5	
22-Feb-11	−4.1				−2.1		
05-May-11		−8.5	−4.1				
01-Jun-11					−2.3	−3.8	
04-Aug-11		−5.2			−4.9	−8.6	
08-Aug-11		−5.1			−6.9	−9.4	
10-Aug-11					−4.5	−6.1	
22-Sep-11	−4.5	−5.2	−6.1				

patterns: a positive (negative) jump in precious metals should trigger a negative (positive) trend over the next 20 days.

– Finally, one last interesting question when it comes to jumps is assessing at what frequency jumps appear on several markets simultaneously. This question is also raised by Brooks and Prokopczuk (2011): they find a higher than expected probability of co-jumps between commodities belonging to different sectors, such as silver and soybean. Following our estimates, we find at least 40 days in our sample for which we observe a jump in at least two of the GSCI indices and the standard assets previously listed. Several conclusions are drawn from Table 1.14. First, standard assets and commodities exhibit a tendency to jump together. Second, this tendency seems to be more salient during crisis periods: most of the co-jumps found occur either during the 2001 or the 2008–2011 financial crisis. These jumps can be triggered by Central Bank actions, such as the Fed lowering its target rate following 9/11, triggering a positive jump in precious metals and a negative jump in the S&P 500. Negative jumps are then observed in the agricultural, energy and industrial metals' prices at the end of September 2001. Such a pattern is also observed in September 2008, following the collapse of Lehman Brothers. Finally, market crashes similar to the episode of August 2011 can be followed by a negative jump in the price of energy products.

Hence, several common patterns within commodities have been uncovered, and between commodities and more standard asset classes. The next chapter will document the relationship between these markets, both from a static and from a dynamic perspective.

REFERENCES

Aingworth, DD., Das, SR., Motwani, R., 2006. A Simple Approach for Pricing Equity Options With Markov Switching State Variables. *Quantitative Finance* 6(2):95–105

Ait-Sahalia, Y., Cacho-Diaz, J., Laeven, RJA. 2011. Modelling Financial Contagion Using Mutually Exciting Jump Processes. *NBER Working Paper* #15850, National Bureau of Economic Research, Boston, Massachusetts, USA

Akgiray, V., Booth, GG., 1987. Compound Distribution Models of Stock Returns: An Empirical Comparison. *The Journal of Financial Research* 10:269–280

Al-Anaswah, N., Wilfling, B., 2011. Identification of Speculative Bubbles using Statespace Models with Markov-switching. *Journal of Banking and Finance* 35:1073–1086

Alexander, C., Lazar, E. 2006. Normal Mixture Garch (1,1): Applications to Exchange Rate Modelling. *Journal of Applied Econometrics* 21(3):307–336

Alizadeh, A., Nomikos, N., Pouliasis, P. 2008. A Markov Regime Switching Approach for Hedging Energy Commodities. *Journal of Banking and Finance* 32:1970–1983

Amihud, Y., Mendelson, H. 1987. Trading Mechanisms and Stock Returns: An Empirical Investigation. *Journal of Finance* 42(3):533–553

Amisano, G., Giacomini, R. 2007. Comparing Density Forecasts via Weighted Likelihood Ratio Tests. *Journal of Business and Economic Statistics* 25:177–190

Andersen, TG., Dobrev, D., Schaumburg, E., 2012. Jump-robust Volatility Estimation Using Nearest Neighbor Truncation. *Journal of Econometrics* 169(1):75–93

Ane, T., Labidi, C. 2001. Revisiting the Finite Mixture of Gaussian Distributions with Applications to Futures Markets. *Journal of Futures Markets* 21(4):347–376

Ang, A., Bekaert, G. 2002. International Asset Allocation with Regime Shifts. *Review of Financial Studies* 15:1137–1187

Ang, A., Chen, J. 2002. Asymmetric Correlations of Equity Portfolios. *Journal of Financial Economics* 63:443–494

Ang, A., Timmermann, A. 2011. Regime Changes and Financial Markets. *NBER Working Paper* #17182, National Bureau of Economic Research, Boston, Massachusetts, USA

Anson, MJP. 2002. *Handbook of Alternative Assets*, Wiley Finance, Chichester, UK

Aravindhakshan, SC., Brorsen, BW. 2011. Identifying Jumps and Systematic Risk in Futures. *Proceedings of the NCCC-134 Conference on Applied Commodity Price Analysis*, Forecasting and Market Risk Management, USA

Ardeni, PG., Wright, B. 1992. The Prebisch–Singer Hypothesis: A Reappraisal Independent of Stationarity Hypotheses. *Economic Journal* 102:803–812

Asness, C. 1994. Variables That Explain Stock Returns. *Ph.D. Dissertation* University of Chicago, USA

Asness, C., Moskowitz, TJ., Pedersen, LH. 2010. Value and Momentum Everywhere. *AQR Capital*, University of Chicago and National Bureau of Economic Research, USA

Bakshi, G., Cao, C., Chen, Z. 1997. Empirical Performance of Alternative Option Pricing Models. *The Journal of Finance* 52(5):2003–2049

Ball, CA., Torous, WN. 1985. On Jumps in Common Stock Prices and Their Impact on Call Option Pricing. *The Journal of Finance* 40(1):155–173

Barndorff-Nielsen, OE., Blaesild, P. 1981. Hyperbolic Distributions and Ramifications: Contributions to Theory and Applications. In: Taillie, C., Patil, GP., Baldessari, BA. (Eds), *Statistical Distributions in Scientific Work*, Vol. 4., pages 19–44, Reidel, Dordrecht, The Netherlands

Barndorff-Nielsen, O., Shephard, N. 2002. Econometric Analysis of Realized Volatility and its Use in Estimating Stochastic Volatility Models. *Journal of the Royal Statistical Society, Series B* 64:253–280

Barndorff-Nielsen, O., Shephard, N. 2004. Power and Bipower Variation with Stochastic Volatility and Jumps. *Journal of Financial Econometrics* 2:1–37

Bates, DS. 1996. Jumps and Stochastic Volatility: Exchange Rate Processes Implicit in Deutsche Mark Options. *Review of Financial Studies* 9(1):69–107

Batten, JA., Ciner, C., Lucey, BM. 2008. The Macroeconomic Determinants of Volatility in Precious Metals Markets. *Resources Policy* 35(2):65–71

Batten, JA., Lucey, BM. 2007. Volatility in the Gold Futures Market. *Applied Economics Letters* 17(2):187–190

Baur, DG., 2012. The Asymmetric Volatility of Gold. *Journal of Alternative Investments*, 14(4):26–38

Bernard, JT., Khalaf, L., Kichian, M., McMahon, M. 2008. Forecasting Commodity Prices: GARCH, Jumps, and Mean Reversion. *Journal of Forecasting* 27(4):279–291

Bertholon, H., Monfort, A., Pegoraro, F. 2007. Pricing and Inference with Mixtures of Conditionally Normal Processes. *Banque de France Working Paper Series* #188, Paris, France

Bessembinder, H. 1992. Systematic Risk, Hedging Pressure and Risk Premiums in Futures Markets. *Review of Financial Studies* 5(4):637–667

Black, F. 1976. Studies of Stock Price Volatility Changes. *Proceedings of the 1976 Meetings of the American Statistical Association, Business and Economic Statistics*, USA

Black, F., Scholes, M. 1973. The Pricing of Options and Corporate Liabilities. *The Journal of Political Economy* 81(3):637–654

Bleaney, M., Greenaway, D. 1993. Long-run Trends in the Relative Price of Primary Commodities and in the Terms of Trade in Developing Countries. *Oxford Economic Papers* 45:349–363

Bodie, Z., Rosansky, VI. 1980. Risk and Return in Commodity Futures. *Financial Analysts Journal* 36(3):27–39

Bollerslev, T. 1986. Generalized Autoregressive Conditional Heteroskedasticity. *Journal of Econometrics* 31:307–327

Box, GEP., Jenkins, GM., Reinsel, GC. 2008. *Time Series Analysis: Forecasting and Control*, Wiley Series in Probability and Statistics, Chichester, UK

Brennan, MJ. 1991. The Price of Convenience and the Valuation of Commodity Contingent Claims. In: Land, D., Oeksendal, B. (Eds), *Stochastic Models and Options Values*, Elsevier

Brennan, M., Schwartz, E. 1985. Evaluating Natural Resource Investments. *Journal of Business* 58:135–157

Brooks, C., Prokopczuk, M. 2011. The Dynamics of Commodity Prices. *ICMA Centre Discussion Papers in Finance* #DP2011–09, USA

Campbell, JY., Hentschel, L. 1992. No News is Good News: An Asymmetric Model of Changing Volatility in Stock Returns. *Journal of Financial Economics* 31:281–318

Carr, P., Wu, X. 2011. Leverage Effect, Volatility Feedback, and Self-Exciting Market Disruptions: Disentangling the Multi-Dimensional Variations in S&P500 Index Options. *Bloomberg Portfolio Research Paper* #2009–03-Frontiers, New York, USA

Casassus, J., Collin-Dufresne, P. 2005. Stochastic Convenience Yield Implied from Commodity Futures and Interest Rates. *Journal of Finance* 60:2283–2331

Cashin, P., McDermott, JC. 2002. The Long-Run Behavior of Commodity Prices: Small Trends and Big Variability. *IMF Staff Papers* 49(2):175–199

Chang, CL., McAleer, M., Tansuchat, R. 2010. Analyzing and Forecasting Volatility Spillovers, Asymmetries and Hedging in Major Oil Markets. *Energy Economics* 32(6):1445–1455

Chauvet, M., Potter, S. 2000. Coincident and Leading Indicators of the Stock Market. *Journal of Empirical Finance* 7:87–111

Chen, SS., Lee, CF., Shrestha, K., 2001. On a Mean-Generalized Semivariance Approach to Determining the Hedge Ratio. *Journal of Futures Markets* 21:581–598

Chernov, M., Gallant, AR., Ghysels, E., Tauchen, G. 2003. Alternative Models for Stock Price Dynamics. *Journal of Econometrics* 116(1):225–257

Cheung, YW., Ng, LK. 1992. Stock Price Dynamics and Firm Size: An Empirical Investigation. *Journal of Finance* 47:1985–1997

Chevallier, J., Ding, W., Ielpo, F. 2012. Implementing a Simple Rule for Dynamic Stop-Loss Strategies. *Journal of Investing* Winter:1–4

Chorro, C., Guegan, D., Ielpo, F. 2010. Likelihood-Related Estimation Methods and Non-Gaussian GARCH Processes. Universite Paris 1 Pantheon-Sorbonne *HAL-SHS Working Papers* #00523371, Lyon, France

Chorro, C., Guegan, D., Ielpo, F. 2012. Option Pricing for GARCH-type Models with Generalized Hyperbolic Innovations. *Quantitative Finance* 12(7):1–50

Christie, AA. 1982. The Stochastic Behavior of Common Stock Variances – Value, Leverage and Interest Rate Effects. *Journal of Financial Economics* 3:145–166

Clare, A., Seaton, J., Smith, PN., Thomas, S. 2012. Breaking into the Blackbox: Trend Following, Stop Losses, and the Frequency of Trading: the case of the S&P500. *Discussion Papers*, Department of Economics, University of York, UK

Cochrane, J., Piazzesi, M. 2005. Bond Risk Premia. *American Economic Review* 95(1):138–160

Connor, G., Korajczyk, RA. 1993. A Test for the Number of Factors in an Approximate Factor Model. *Journal of Finance* 48(4):1263–1291

Cootner, PH. 1960. Returns to Speculators: Telser Versus Keynes. *The Journal of Political Economy* 68(4):396–404

Cuddington, J. 1992. Long-Run Trends in 26 Primary Commodity Prices. *Journal of Development Economics* 39:207–227

Cuddington, J., Urzua, C. 1989. Trends and Cycles in the Net Barter Terms of Trade: A New Approach. *Economic Journal* 99:426–442

Damodaran, A. 1993. A Simple Measure of Price Adjustment Coefficients. *Journal of Finance* 48(1):387–400

Deaton, A., Laroque, G. 1992. On the Behaviour of Commodity Prices. *Review of Economic Studies* 59:1–23

Deaves, R., Krinsky, I. 1995. Do Futures Prices For Commodities Embody Risk Premiums? *Journal of Futures Markets* 15(6):637–648

Dempster, MAH., Medova, E., Tang, K. 2010. Long and Short Term Jumps in Commodity Futures Prices. *SSRN Working Paper* #1107966, Social Science Research Network, USA

Deng, SJ. 1999. Stochastic Models of Energy Commodity Prices and Their Applications: Mean-reversion with Jumps and Spikes. *Proceedings of the Fourth Annual POWER Conference*, Berkeley, USA

Deng, SJ. 2005. Valuation of Investment and Opportunity-To-Invest in Power Generation Assets with Spikes in Electricity Price. *Managerial Finance* 31(6):95–115

Diebold, FX., Yilmaz, K. 2012. Better to Give than to Receive: Forecast-Based Measurement of Volatility Spillovers. *International Journal of Forecasting* 28(1):57–66

Ding, Z., Granger, CWJ., Engle, R., 1993. A Long Memory Property of Stock Market Returns and a New Model. *Journal of Empirical Finance* 1:83–106

Dionne, G., Gauthier, G., Hammami, K., Maurice, M., Simonato, JG. 2011. A Reduced Form Model of Default Spreads with Markov-Switching Macroeconomic Factors. *Journal of Banking and Finance* 35:1984–2000

Du, X., Yu, CL., Hayes, DJ., 2011. Speculation and Volatility Spillover in the Crude Oil and Agricultural Commodity Markets: A Bayesian analysis. *Energy Economics* 33(3):497–503

Duffie, D., Gray, S., Hoang, P. 1995. Volatility in Energy Prices. In: Pai, L., Field, P. (Eds) *Managing Energy Price Risk*, pages 273–290, Risk Publications, UK

Eberlein, E., Prause, K. 2002. The Generalized Hyperbolic Model: Financial Derivatives and Risk Measures. In: Geman, H., Madan, D., Pliska, S., Vorst, T. (Eds), *Mathematical Finance-Bachelier Congress 2000*, pages 245–267. Springer Verlag, Berlin, Germany

Engle, R. 1982. Autoregressive Conditional Heteroscedasticity with Estimates of the Variance of United Kingdom Inflation. *Econometrica* 50(4):987–1007

Engle, R., Ng, S. 1993. Measuring and Testing the Impact of News on Volatility. *Journal of Finance* 48(5):1749–1778

Eraker, B. 2004. Do Stock Prices and Volatility Jump? Reconciling Evidence from Spot and Option Prices. *The Journal of Finance* 59(3):1367–1404

Eraker, B., Johannes, M., Polson, N. 2003. The Impact of Jumps in Volatility and Returns. *The Journal of Finance* 58(3):1269–1300

Erb, CB., Campbell, RH. 2006. The Strategic and Tactical Value of Commodity Futures. *Financial Analysts Journal* 62(2):69–97

Fan, Y., Pastorello, S., Renault, E., 2007. Maximisation by Parts in Extremum Estimation. *Working Paper*, University of North Carolina, USA

Ferraro, D., Rogoff, K., Rossi, B. 2011. Can Oil Prices Forecast Exchange Rates? *Working Paper* #11–05, Duke University, Department of Economics, USA

Franses, P., Ghijsels, H. 1999. Additive Outliers, GARCH and Forecasting Volatility. *International Journal of Forecasting* 15:1–9

Fuertes, AM., Miffre, J., Rallis, G. 2008. Tactical Allocation in Commodity Futures Markets: Combining Momentum and Term Structure Signals. *EDHEC Business School Working Paper*, Lille, France

Fulop, A., Li, J., Yu, J. 2011. Bayesian Learning of Self-Exciting Return Dynamics. *SMU Economics and Statistics Working Paper Series* #03–2012, Singapore Management University, Singapore

Gatumel, M., Ielpo. F., 2011. The Number of Regimes Across Asset Returns: Identification and Economic Value. Universite Paris 1 Pantheon-Sorbonne *HAL-SHS Working Papers* #00658540, Lyon, France

Geman, H., Nguyen, VN. 2005. Soybean Inventory and Forward Curve Dynamics. *Management Science* 51:1076–1091

Ghoshray, A. 2011a. Underlying Trends and International Price Transmission of Agricultural Commodities. *Asian Development Bank Economics Working Paper Series* #257, Mandaluyong City, Philippines

Ghoshray, A. 2011b. A Reexamination of Trends in Primary Commodity Prices. *Journal of Development Economics* 95(2):242–251

Giamouridis, DG., Tamvakis, MN. 2001. The Relation Between Return and Volatility in the Commodity Markets. *Journal of Alternative Investments* 4(1):54–62

Gibson, R., Schwartz, E. 1990. Stochastic Convenience Yield and the Pricing of Oil Contingent Claims. *Journal of Finance* 45:959–976

Giot, P., Laurent, S. 2003. Market Risk in Commodity Markets: a VaR Approach. *Energy Economics* 25(5):435–457

Glosten, LR., Jagannathan, R., Runkle, DE. 1993. On the Relation between the Expected Value and the Volatility of the Nominal Excess Return on Stocks. *Journal of Finance* 48(5):1779–1801

Gorton, GB., Rouwenhorst, KG. 2005a. Facts and Fantasies about Commodity Futures. *Financial Analysts Journal* 62(2):47–68

Gorton, GB., Rouwenhorst, KG. 2005b. A Note on Erb and Harvey (2005). *Yale School of Management Working Paper* #2595, Yale School of Management, Yale, USA

Gorton, GB., Hayashi, F., Rouwenhorst, KG. 2012. The Fundamentals of Commodity Futures Returns. *Yale ICF Working Paper* #07–08, Yale ICF, Yale, USA

Gourieroux, C., Jasiak, J. 2001. *Financial Econometrics: Problems, Models, and Methods*. Princeton University Press, Princeton, USA

Grilli, E., Yang, M. 1988. Primary Commodity Prices, Manufactured Goods Prices, and the Terms of Trade of Developing Countries: What the Long Run Shows. *World Bank Economic Review* 2:1–47

Haigh, M., Holt, M. 2002. Crack Spread Hedging: Accounting for Time-Varying Volatility Spillovers in the Energy Futures Markets. *Journal of Applied Econometrics* 17(3):269–289

Hamilton, JD., 1989. A New Approach to the Economic Analysis of Nonstationary Time Series and the Business Cycle. *Econometrica* 57(2):357–384

Hammoudeh, S., Yuan, Y. 2008. Metal Volatility in Presence of Oil and Interest Rate Shocks. *Energy Economics* 30(2):606–620

Hammoudeh, S., Li, H., Jeon, BG. 2003. Causality and Volatility Spillovers among Petroleum Prices of WTI, Gasoline and Heating Oil in Different Locations. *The North American Journal of Economics and Finance* 14(1):89–114

Hansen, B.E. 1992. The Likelihood Ratio Test Under Nonstandard Conditions: Testing the Markov-Switching Model of GNP. *Journal of Applied Econometrics* 7:S61-S82

Helg, R. 1991. A Note on the Stationarity of the Primary Commodities Relative Price Index. *Economics Letters* 36:55–60

Henry, Ò., 2009. Regime Switching in the Relationship between Equity Returns and Short-Term Interest Rates in the UK. *Journal of Banking and Finance* 33:405–414

Heston, SL. 1993. A Closed-Form Solution for Options with Stochastic Volatility with Applications to Bond and Currency Options. *Review of Financial Studies* 6(2):327–343

Hilliard, J., Reis, J. 1998. Valuation of Commodity Futures and Options under Stochastic Convenience Yields, Interest Rates, and Jump Diffusions in the Spot. *Journal of Financial and Quantitative Analysis* 33:61–86

Hillier, D., Draper, P., Faff, R. 2006. Do Precious Metals Shine? An Investment Perspective. *Financial Analysts Journal* 62(2): 98–106

Huang, X., Tauchen, G. 2005. The Relative Price Contribution of Jumps to Total Price Variance. *Journal of Financial Econometrics* 3:456–499

Hung, JC., Lee, MC., Liu, HC. 2008. Estimation of Value-at-Risk for Energy Commodities via Fat-Tailed GARCH Models. *Energy Economics* 30:1173–1191

Ielpo, F., Sévi, B. 2011. Do Jumps Help in Forecasting the Density of Returns? *SSRN Working Paper*, Social Science Research Network, USA

Ielpo, F., Sévi, B. 2012. Empirical Bias in Intraday Volatility Measures. *Finance Research Letters* 9(4):231–237

Ilmanen, A. 2011. *Expected Returns: An Investor's Guide to Harvesting Market Rewards*. Wiley Finance, Chichester, UK

Irwin, SH., Zulauf, CR., Gerlow, ME., Tinker, JN. 1997. A Performance Comparison of a Technical Trading System with ARIMA models for Soybean Complex Prices. *Advances in Investment Analysis and Portfolio Management* 4:193–203

Jegadeesh, N., Titman, S. 1993. Returns to Buying Winners and Selling Losers: Implications for Stock Market Efficiency. *Journal of Finance* 48:65–91

Kaldor, N. 1939. Speculation and Economic Theory. *Review of Economic Studies* 7:1–27

Kat, HM., Oomen, RCA. 2007a. What Every Investor Should Know About Commodities, Part I: Univariate Return Analysis. *Journal of Investment Management* 5(1):1–25

Kat, HM., Oomen, RCA. 2007b. What Every Investor Should Know About Commodities, Part II: Multivariate Return Analysis. *Journal of Investment Management* 5(3):1–25

Kessler, S., Scherer, B. 2009. Varying Risk Premia in International Bond Markets. *Journal of Banking and Finance* 33(8):1361–1375

Keynes, JM. 1930. *A Treatise on Money*. MacMillan, London, UK

Kolb, RW. 1992. Is Normal Backwardation Normal? *Journal of Futures Markets* 12(1):75–90

Kon, SJ. 1984. Models of Stock Returns: A Comparison. *Journal of Finance* 39(1):147–165

Koutmos, G. 1998. Asymmetries in the Conditional Mean and the Conditional Variance: Evidence From Nine Stock Markets. *Journal of Economics and Business* 50(3):277–290

Kroner, KF., Sultan, J. 1993. Time-Varying Distributions and Dynamic Hedging with Foreign Currency Futures. *Journal of Financial and Quantitative Analysis* 28(4):535–551

Laurent, S., Lecourt, C., Palm, FC. 2011. Testing for Jumps in GARCH models: a Robust Approach. *Working Paper*, Maastricht University, Maastricht, Belgium

Lee, SS., Mykland, PA. 2008. Jumps in Financial Markets: a New Nonparametric Test and Jump Dynamics. *Review of Financial Studies* 21(6):2535–2563

Lee, T., Zyren, J. 2007. Volatility Relationship between Crude Oil and Petroleum Products. *Atlantic Economic Journal* 35(1):97–112

Lekkos, I. 1999. Distributional Properties of Spot and Forward Interest Rates: USD, DEM, GBP and JPY. *The Journal of Fixed Income* 8(4):35–54

Leon, J., Soto, R., 1997. Structural Breaks and Long Run Trends in Commodity Prices. *Journal of International Development* 9:347–366

Lien, D., Tse, YK., 2000. Hedging Downside Risk with Futures Contracts. *Applied Financial Economics* 10:163–170

Liu, P., Tang, K. 2011. The Stochastic Behavior of Commodity Prices with Heteroskedasticity in the Convenience Yield. *Journal of Empirical Finance* 18:211–224

Longin, F., Solnik, B. 2001. Extreme Correlation of International Equity Markets. *Journal of Finance* 56:649–676

Lukac, LP., Brorsen, BW., Irwin, SH. 1988. A Test of Futures Market Disequilibrium using Twelve Different Trading Systems. *Applied Economics* 20(5):623–639

Maheu, J., McCurdy, TH. 2000. Identifying Bull and Bear Markets in Stock Returns. *Journal of Business & Economic Statistics* 18(1):100–112

Maheu, J., McCurdy, TH., Song, Y. 2012. Components of Bull and Bear Markets: Bull Corrections and Bear Rallies. *Journal of Business and Economic Statistics* 30(3):391–403

Manoliu, M., Tompaidis, S. 2002. Energy Futures Prices: Term Structure Models with Kalman Filter Estimation. *Applied Mathematical Finance* 9:21–43

Marshall, BR., Cahan, RH., Cahan, JM. 2008. Can Commodity Futures be Profitably Traded with Quantitative Market Timing Strategies? *Journal of Banking and Finance* 32:1810–1819

McKenzie, M., Mitchell, H., Brooks, R., Faff, R. 2001. Power ARCH Modeling of Commodity Futures Data on the London Metal Exchange. *European Journal of Finance* 7:22–38

Merton, R. 1976. Option Pricing when Underlying Stock Returns are Discontinuous. *Journal of Financial Economics* 3:125–144

Miffre, J., Rallis, G. 2007. Momentum Strategies in Commodity Futures Markets. *Journal of Banking and Finance* 31(6):1863–1886

Monfort, A., Pegoraro, F. 2006. Option Pricing with Mixture of Gaussian Distributions. *Working Paper of the Banque de France*, Paris, France

Morana, C. 2001. A Semiparametric Approach to Short-Term Oil Price Forecasting. *Energy Economics* 23(3):325–338

Moskowitz, TJ., Ooi, YH., Pedersen, LH. 2012. Time Series Momentum. *Journal of Financial Economics* 104(2):228–250

Muler, N., Pena, D., Yohai, V. 2009. Robust Estimation for ARMA Models. *Annals of Statistics* 37:816–840

Muler, N., Yohai, V. 2008. Robust Estimates for GARCH Models. *Journal of Statistical Planning and Inference* 138:2918–2940

Nelson, DB. 1991. Conditional Heteroskedasticity in Asset Returns. *Econometrica* 59:347–370

Newbold, P., Pfaffenzeller, S., Rayner, A. 2005. How Well are Long-Run Commodity Price Series Characterized by Trend Components? *Journal of International Development* 17(4):479–494

Newey, WK., West, KD. 1987. A Simple, Positive Semidefinite, Heteroskedasticity and Autocorrelation Consistent Covariance Matrix. *Econometrica* 55:703–708

Ng, V., Pirrong, S. 1996. Price Dynamics in Refined Petroleum Spot and Futures Markets. *Journal of Empirical Finance* 2:359–388

Pindyck, R. 2001. The Dynamics of Commodity Spot and Futures Markets: A Primer. *The Energy Journal* 22(3):1–30

Pindyck, R. 2004. Volatility and Commodity Price Dynamics. *Journal of Futures Markets* 24:1029–1047

Politis, ND. 2004. A Heavy Tailed Distribution for ARCH Residuals with Application to Volatility Prediction. *Annals of Economics and Finance* 5:283–298

Prebisch, R. 1950. *The Economic Development of Latin America and its Principal Problems*. United Nations, New York, USA

Psaradakis, Z., Spagnolo, N. 2003. On the Determination of the Number of Regimes in Markov-Switching Autoregressive Models. *Journal of Time Series Analysis* 24(2):237–252

Sadorsky, P. 2006. Modeling and Forecasting Petroleum Futures Volatility. *Energy Economics* 28(4):467–488

Sapsford, D. 1985. The Statistical Debate on the Net Barter Terms of Trade Between Primary Commodities and Manufactures: A Comment and Some Additional Evidence. *Economic Journal* 95:781–788

Schwartz, E. 1997. The Stochastic Behavior of Commodity Prices: Implications for Valuation and Hedging. *Journal of Finance* 52:923–973

Schwartz, E., Smith, J. 2000. Short-Term Variations and Long-Term Dynamics in Commodity Prices. *Management Science* 46:893–911

Schwert, GW. 1988. Tests for Unit Roots: A Monte Carlo Investigation. *NBER Technical Working Papers* #0073, National Bureau of Economic Research, Boston, Massachusetts, USA

Schwert, GW. 1989a. Why does Stock Market Volatility Change Over Time? *Journal of Finance* 44:1115–1153

Schwert, GW. 1989b. Business Cycles, Financial Crises and Stock Volatility. *Carnegie–Rochester Conference Series on Public Policy* 31:83–125

Sekkel, R. 2011. International Evidence on Bond Risk Premia. *Journal of Banking and Finance* 35(1):174–181

Serletis, A. 1994. A Cointegration Analysis of Petroleum Futures Prices. *Energy Economics* 16:93–97

Singer, H. 1950. The Distribution of Gains Between Investing and Borrowing Countries. *American Economic Review: Papers and Proceedings* 11:473–485

Singh, A., Karali, B., Ramirez, OA. 2011. High Price Volatility And Spillover Effects In Energy Markets. *Proceedings of the 2011 Annual Meeting*, Agricultural and Applied Economics Association, Pittsburgh, Pennsylvania, USA

Smith, A., Naik, PA., Tsai, C. 2006. Markov-Switching Model Selection Using Kullback–Leibler Divergence. *Journal of Econometrics* 134(2):553–577

Song, PX., Fan, Y., Kalfeisch, D. 2005. Maximization by Parts in Likelihood Inference. *Journal of the American Statistical Association* 100:1145–1158

Sorensen, C. 2002. Modeling Seasonality in Agricultural Commodity Futures. *Journal of Futures Markets* 22(5):393–426

Szakmary, A., Shen, Q., Sharma, S. 2010. Trend Following Trading Strategies in Commodity Futures: a Reexamination. *Journal of Banking and Finance* 34: 409–426

Trolle, A., Schwartz, E. 2009. Unspanned Stochastic Volatility and the Pricing of Commodity Derivatives. *Review of Financial Studies* 22:4423–4461

Tucker, AL., Pond, L. 1998. The Probability Distribution of Foreign Exchange Price Changes: Tests of Candidate Processes. *Review of Economics and Statistics* 11:638–647

Tully, E., Lucey, BM. 2007. A Power GARCH Examination of the Gold Market. *Research in International Business and Finance* 21(2):316–325

Wang, C., Yu, M. 2004. Trading Activity and Price Reversals in Futures Markets. *Journal of Banking and Finance* 28:1337–1361

Wang, T., Wu, J., Yang, J. 2008. Realized Volatility and Correlation in Energy Futures Markets. *Journal of Futures Markets* 28:993–1011

Wickham, P., Reinhart, C. 1994. Commodity Prices – Cyclical Weakness or Secular Decline? *IMF Working Papers* #94/7, International Monetary Fund, Washington DC, USA

Zheng, Y., Kinnucan, H., Thompson, H. 2008. News and Volatility of Food Prices. *Applied Economics* 40(13):1629–1635

2

Cross-Asset Linkages

Beyond these individual analyses, another important aspect is the joint behavior of commodities – if any – and their relationship with other assets. We focus on these issues.

There exists a sparse literature concerning the statistical patterns observed either within commodities or between commodities and standard assets. The main references here are Kat and Oomen (2007b), Gorton and Rouwenhorst (2005) and Erb and Campbell (2006) that have been previously mentioned. Kat and Oomen (2007b) are of particular interest from this cross-asset perspective. They raise four main conclusions – most of them being consistent with the empirical findings in previous studies – that are relevant for the purposes of our chapter:

1. Correlations between groups of commodities are low, whereas correlations between commodities from the same group are larger.
2. Commodities exhibit a low long-term correlation with traditional asset classes. Gorton and Rouwenhorst (2005) have presented similar evidence: they even find negative correlation between equities and some of the commodities in the scope of their investigation.
3. There are limited joint extreme behaviors within commodities, and;
4. Between commodities and traditional asset classes. Extreme or tail events do not occur at the same time within commodity markets or between commodities and the rest of the assets investigated. Benchmarking these conclusions over the 1995–2012 period should help us understand how stable these findings are.

We have computed descriptive statistics that will be the basis of more advanced modeling efforts. Tables 2.1 and 2.2 present cross-commodity correlations. All of these correlations have been found to be significant at a 5% risk level: we find low but significant correlations. This conclusion is slightly different from Kat and Oomen (2007b). When investigating these estimates, three main conclusions can be reached:

– First, when considered globally, these correlations are rather low. They globally range around 0.3, with extremes between 0.07 for the correlation between natural gas and gold and 0.94 for the correlation between Brent and WTI. Over a long period of time, we find that the correlations between returns on commodities are rather low, with an important dispersion.
– Second, when considering the correlation within a group of commodities – such as energy commodities – we obtain the highest estimates. The previous example of Brent and WTI is not alone in our sample. For example, copper and aluminum are related through a correlation of 0.72. Gold and silver have a correlation equal to 0.71 over the period considered. The only exception to this picture is obtained with agricultural commodities: for example, corn has a low correlation with sugar (0.19) and cocoa (0.13). However, soybean and corn are still strongly related (0.62). The agricultural sector simply seems to display a higher degree of heterogeneity.
– Third, cross-sector correlations are weaker than correlations within commodities belonging to the same sector. This conclusion is obvious from the correlation between the GSCI

Table 2.1 Correlation between commodities 1995–2012 – Part 1

		Gold	Silver	Platinum	Aluminum	Copper	Nickel	Zinc	Lead	WTI	Brent	Gasoil	Natural Gas
Prec. Metals	Gold		0.71 *	0.44 *	0.25 *	0.31 *	0.19 *	0.27 *	0.2 *	0.2 *	0.22 *	0.14 *	0.07 *
	Silver	0.71		0.46 *	0.32 *	0.39 *	0.28 *	0.34 *	0.28 *	0.24 *	0.25 *	0.2 *	0.07 *
	Platinum	0.44	0.46		0.27 *	0.31 *	0.22 *	0.28 *	0.24 *	0.23 *	0.24 *	0.2 *	0.07 *
Ind. Metals	Aluminum	0.25	0.32	0.27		0.72 *	0.51 *	0.63 *	0.51 *	0.23 *	0.23 *	0.21 *	0.12 *
	Copper	0.31	0.39	0.31	0.72		0.6 *	0.71 *	0.59 *	0.29 *	0.3 *	0.24 *	0.12 *
	Nickel	0.19	0.28	0.22	0.51	0.6		0.55 *	0.49 *	0.22 *	0.21 *	0.19 *	0.07 *
	Zinc	0.27	0.34	0.28	0.63	0.71	0.55		0.62 *	0.23 *	0.22 *	0.21 *	0.09 *
	Lead	0.2	0.28	0.24	0.51	0.59	0.49	0.62		0.22 *	0.21 *	0.19 *	0.09 *
Energy	WTI	0.2	0.24	0.23	0.23	0.29	0.22	0.23	0.22		0.94 *	0.64 *	0.29 *
	Brent	0.22	0.25	0.24	0.23	0.3	0.21	0.22	0.21	0.94		0.66 *	0.28 *
	Gasoil	0.14	0.2	0.2	0.21	0.24	0.19	0.21	0.19	0.64	0.66		0.23 *
	Natural Gas	0.07	0.07	0.07	0.12	0.12	0.07	0.09	0.09	0.29	0.28	0.23	
	Heating Oil	0.19	0.22	0.21	0.21	0.26	0.18	0.2	0.19	0.86	0.86	0.7	0.34
Agriculture	Corn	0.21	0.24	0.21	0.19	0.24	0.14	0.19	0.14	0.24	0.25	0.17	0.11
	Wheat	0.17	0.19	0.15	0.15	0.2	0.11	0.14	0.12	0.2	0.21	0.14	0.06
	Coffee	0.11	0.15	0.14	0.14	0.15	0.13	0.14	0.12	0.11	0.12	0.12	0.04
	Sugar	0.12	0.16	0.15	0.14	0.18	0.12	0.12	0.14	0.16	0.17	0.13	0.06
	Cocoa	0.18	0.19	0.12	0.11	0.13	0.09	0.13	0.13	0.1	0.12	0.14	0.03
	Cotton	0.11	0.15	0.11	0.16	0.2	0.14	0.15	0.15	0.15	0.16	0.13	0.07
	Soybean	0.18	0.24	0.22	0.22	0.25	0.19	0.19	0.17	0.26	0.26	0.17	0.14
	Rice	0.07	0.09	0.09	0.09	0.12	0.12	0.1	0.11	0.08	0.08	0.04	0.04
Indices	GSCI Agri.	0.24	0.3	0.26	0.25	0.3	0.19	0.22	0.21	0.3	0.32	0.23	0.14
	GSCI Energy	0.21	0.25	0.23	0.24	0.3	0.21	0.23	0.22	0.94	0.93	0.69	0.48
	GSCI Ind. Metals	0.3	0.4	0.32	0.88	0.93	0.73	0.8	0.67	0.29	0.29	0.25	0.12
	GSCI Prec. Metals	0.93	0.74	0.48	0.3	0.34	0.23	0.31	0.23	0.21	0.23	0.18	0.07

Table 2.2 Correlation between commodities 1995–2012 – Part 2

		Heating Oil	Corn	Wheat	Coffee	Sugar	Cocoa	Cotton	Soybean	Rice	Agri.	Energy	Ind. Metals	Prec. Metals
Prec. Metals	Gold	0.19 *	0.21 *	0.17 *	0.11 *	0.12 *	0.18 *	0.11 *	0.18 *	0.07 *	0.24 *	0.21 *	0.3 *	0.93 *
	Silver	0.22 *	0.24 *	0.19 *	0.15 *	0.16 *	0.19 *	0.15 *	0.24 *	0.09 *	0.3 *	0.25 *	0.4 *	0.74 *
	Platinum	0.21 *	0.21 *	0.15 *	0.14 *	0.15 *	0.12 *	0.11 *	0.22 *	0.09 *	0.26 *	0.23 *	0.32 *	0.48 *
Ind. Metals	Aluminum	0.21 *	0.19 *	0.15 *	0.14 *	0.14 *	0.11 *	0.16 *	0.22 *	0.09 *	0.25 *	0.24 *	0.88 *	0.3 *
	Copper	0.26 *	0.24 *	0.2 *	0.15 *	0.18 *	0.13 *	0.2 *	0.25 *	0.12 *	0.3 *	0.3 *	0.93 *	0.34 *
	Nickel	0.18 *	0.14 *	0.11 *	0.13 *	0.12 *	0.09 *	0.14 *	0.19 *	0.12 *	0.19 *	0.21 *	0.73 *	0.23 *
	Zinc	0.2 *	0.19 *	0.14 *	0.14 *	0.12 *	0.13 *	0.15 *	0.19 *	0.1 *	0.22 *	0.23 *	0.8 *	0.31 *
	Lead	0.19 *	0.14 *	0.12 *	0.12 *	0.14 *	0.13 *	0.15 *	0.17 *	0.11 *	0.21 *	0.22 *	0.67 *	0.23 *
Energy	WTI	0.86 *	0.24 *	0.2 *	0.11 *	0.16 *	0.1 *	0.15 *	0.26 *	0.08 *	0.3 *	0.94 *	0.29 *	0.21 *
	Brent	0.86 *	0.25 *	0.21 *	0.12 *	0.17 *	0.12 *	0.16 *	0.26 *	0.08 *	0.32 *	0.93 *	0.29 *	0.23 *
	Gasoil	0.7 *	0.17 *	0.14 *	0.12 *	0.13 *	0.14 *	0.13 *	0.17 *	0.04	0.23 *	0.69 *	0.25 *	0.18 *
	Natural Gas	0.34 *	0.11 *	0.06 *	0.04	0.06 *	0.03	0.07 *	0.14 *	0.04	0.14 *	0.48 *	0.12 *	0.07 *
	Heating Oil		0.22 *	0.19 *	0.12 *	0.16 *	0.09 *	0.13 *	0.24 *	0.07 *	0.29 *	0.91 *	0.25 *	0.2 *
Agriculture	Corn	0.22		0.63 *	0.12 *	0.19 *	0.13 *	0.24 *	0.62 *	0.18 *	0.8 *	0.25 *	0.23 *	0.21 *
	Wheat	0.19	0.63		0.14 *	0.17 *	0.08 *	0.22 *	0.43 *	0.16 *	0.81 *	0.2 *	0.19 *	0.18 *
	Coffee	0.12	0.12	0.14		0.16 *	0.16 *	0.12 *	0.15 *	0.07 *	0.31 *	0.12 *	0.16 *	0.12 *
	Sugar	0.16	0.19	0.17	0.16		0.16 *	0.13 *	0.19 *	0.06 *	0.38 *	0.18 *	0.17 *	0.13 *
	Cocoa	0.09	0.13	0.08	0.16	0.13		0.1 *	0.11 *	0.07 *	0.19 *	0.11 *	0.13 *	0.19 *
	Cotton	0.13	0.24	0.22	0.12	0.19	0.1		0.29 *	0.13 *	0.41 *	0.16 *	0.2 *	0.12 *
	Soybean	0.24	0.62	0.43	0.15	0.19	0.11	0.29		0.24 *	0.7 *	0.27 *	0.26 *	0.19 *
	Rice	0.07	0.18	0.16	0.07	0.06	0.07	0.13	0.24		0.24 *	0.08 *	0.13 *	0.07 *
Indices	GSCI Agri.	0.29	0.8	0.81	0.31	0.38	0.19	0.41	0.7	0.24		0.32 *	0.29 *	0.26 *
	GSCI Energy	0.91	0.25	0.2	0.12	0.18	0.11	0.16	0.27	0.08	0.32		0.3 *	0.22 *
	GSCI Ind. Metals	0.25	0.23	0.19	0.16	0.17	0.13	0.2	0.26	0.13	0.29	0.3		0.35 *
	GSCI Prec. Metals	0.2	0.21	0.18	0.12	0.13	0.19	0.12	0.19	0.07	0.26	0.22	0.35	

sub-indices: they are, on average, close to 0.3. This is indeed quite important for investors interested in the diversifying power of commodities. By averaging performances across sectors, a portfolio constructed from commodities coming from different sectors would have enjoyed an interesting diversification during the period considered (1995–2012).

These results are highly consistent with the conclusions reached in the previously mentioned literature. Of course, these results are dependent on the selected period: a shorter or a longer dataset may lead to different conclusions. However, given the consistency of our results with longer-term studies (as in Kat and Oomen, 2007b), there is a good chance that such conclusions hold in the long run. When it comes to the shorter run stability, we will discuss how these diversification arguments hold across economic regimes in Part II of the book.

Tables 2.3 and 2.4 present a correlation analysis between returns on commodities and the returns on equities, currencies and the variation of interest rates. We detail selected elements commodity by commodity:

– The precious metals share the same type of long-term correlations: gold, silver and platinum have a low to very low correlation with equities – with gold even showing some slightly negative correlations as in the Dow Jones (−0.02) or in the Swiss Market Index (SMI) (−0.04) cases. They are also characterized by negative correlations with the US Dollar against all the other currencies considered here, with a correlation between gold and the Euro against Dollar equal to 0.42. Finally, when it comes to interest rates, we find a marked difference between gold and the other two precious metals of our dataset: gold is negatively correlated with interest rates whereas the other two are positively correlated with them. These correlations are, however, insignificant in the case of silver. Here again, commodities grouped by sector share some common characteristics but not all of them.
– In the case of industrial metals, the correlation of returns on commodities and equities is higher than in the case of precious metals: most of the correlations range between 0.2 and 0.3. This conclusion also holds when focusing on the GSCI Industrial Metals index. These correlations are lower than in the cross-equity case, but much higher than in previous studies. Beyond this point, industrial metals are negatively correlated with the US Dollar over the period considered here. As in the precious metals case, the sign and magnitude of the correlation between industrial metals and currencies can turn out to be quite asset specific. Consistent with the positive correlation with equity returns, industrial metals are positively correlated with interest rates.
– Energy commodities have correlations that are very similar to industrial metals, especially when it comes to their signs. The magnitude of the correlation is, however, somewhat weaker: for example, the WTI has a 10% correlation with the Dow Jones when copper's correlation is 27%. Heating oil, gasoil and natural gas show even weaker figures. The correlations with the variation of interest rates are also weaker than in the industrial metals case.
– Finally – and consistent with the findings by Kat and Oomen (2007b) – the weakest correlations with more traditional assets are obtained for agricultural commodities: in the case of equities and interest rates they revolve around 10%; that is, around half of what was obtained in the industrial metals case.

Beyond these asset by asset differences, we still find a common pattern in Tables 2.3 and 2.4: most of the returns on commodities exhibit to a large extent a higher correlation with currencies. This is, however, not surprising given that these currencies are taken against the US Dollar. Most commodity prices are labeled in US Dollars: any increase in the value of the

Table 2.3 Correlation between commodities and other markets – Part 1

		Prec. Metals			Ind. Metals					Energy				
		Gold	Silver	Platinum	Aluminum	Copper	Nickel	Zinc	Lead	WTI	Brent	Gasoil	Natural Gas	Heating Oil
Equities	Dow Jones	-0.02	0.12 *	0.1 *	0.18 *	0.27 *	0.18 *	0.18 *	0.19 *	0.1 *	0.1 *	0.04	0.03	0.08 *
	S&P 500	0	0.13 *	0.13 *	0.19 *	0.28 *	0.19 *	0.2 *	0.2 *	0.14 *	0.14 *	0.07 *	0.04	0.12 *
	Nasdaq	-0.01	0.09 *	0.1 *	0.15 *	0.21 *	0.14 *	0.15 *	0.14 *	0.11 *	0.11 *	0.04	0.01	0.08 *
	Canadian TSX	0.18 *	0.29 *	0.25 *	0.29 *	0.37 *	0.27 *	0.29 *	0.29 *	0.28 *	0.29 *	0.17 *	0.12 *	0.24 *
	Mexico IPC	0.08 *	0.19 *	0.13 *	0.2 *	0.28 *	0.22 *	0.22 *	0.22 *	0.18 *	0.18 *	0.1 *	0.06 *	0.13 *
	Brazil BOVESPA	0.08 *	0.2 *	0.17 *	0.21 *	0.28 *	0.21 *	0.23 *	0.22 *	0.16 *	0.14 *	0.09 *	0.03	0.1 *
	Euro Stoxx	-0.02	0.11 *	0.11 *	0.24 *	0.33 *	0.24 *	0.26 *	0.25 *	0.14 *	0.14 *	0.1 *	0.05 *	0.12 *
	FTSE	0.01	0.15 *	0.15 *	0.25 *	0.36 *	0.26 *	0.29 *	0.28 *	0.18 *	0.17 *	0.13 *	0.05 *	0.15 *
	CAC 40	-0.02	0.12 *	0.1 *	0.25 *	0.33 *	0.24 *	0.27 *	0.25 *	0.14 *	0.14 *	0.09 *	0.05 *	0.12 *
	DAX	-0.03	0.11 *	0.11 *	0.24 *	0.32 *	0.24 *	0.24 *	0.24 *	0.12 *	0.12 *	0.08 *	0.05 *	0.09 *
	IBEX	0.01	0.12 *	0.12 *	0.22 *	0.31 *	0.22 *	0.24 *	0.23 *	0.14 *	0.14 *	0.08 *	0.04	0.11 *
	MIB	-0.02	0.11 *	0.12 *	0.24 *	0.32 *	0.23 *	0.25 *	0.25 *	0.15 *	0.15 *	0.1 *	0.06 *	0.13 *
	AEX	-0.03	0.11 *	0.11 *	0.23 *	0.32 *	0.23 *	0.26 *	0.25 *	0.13 *	0.13 *	0.1 *	0.06 *	0.11 *
	OMX	0	0.12 *	0.13 *	0.23 *	0.3 *	0.21 *	0.25 *	0.22 *	0.12 *	0.11 *	0.07 *	0.03	0.09 *
	SMI	-0.04	0.1 *	0.09 *	0.19 *	0.28 *	0.19 *	0.22 *	0.23 *	0.1 *	0.1 *	0.06 *	0.04	0.09 *
	NIKKEI	0.08 *	0.17 *	0.19 *	0.19 *	0.26 *	0.18 *	0.21 *	0.19 *	0.09 *	0.09 *	0.08 *	0.05 *	0.08 *
	HANG SENG	0.04	0.16 *	0.18 *	0.18 *	0.26 *	0.21 *	0.21 *	0.23 *	0.14 *	0.13 *	0.09 *	0.08 *	0.09 *
	ASX	0.05 *	0.16 *	0.17 *	0.17 *	0.22 *	0.17 *	0.19 *	0.2 *	0.08 *	0.1 *	0.1 *	0.06 *	0.08 *

(continued)

Table 2.3 (Continued)

		Prec. Metals			Ind. Metals					Energy				
		Gold	Silver	Platinum	Aluminum	Copper	Nickel	Zinc	Lead	WTI	Brent	Gasoil	Natural Gas	Heating Oil
Currencies	Euro	0.42 *	0.35 *	0.26 *	0.24 *	0.24 *	0.16 *	0.2 *	0.2 *	0.13 *	0.15 *	0.13 *	0.06 *	0.13 *
	Canadian Dollar	-0.32 *	-0.39 *	-0.28 *	-0.31 *	-0.37 *	-0.29 *	-0.32 *	-0.33 *	-0.28 *	-0.27 *	-0.25 *	-0.09 *	-0.25 *
	Japanese Yen	-0.18 *	-0.12 *	-0.07 *	0	0.07 *	0.05 *	0.05 *	0.1 *	0.02	0.02	-0.01	-0.01	0.01
	Australian Dollar	0.32 *	0.39 *	0.33 *	0.34 *	0.44 *	0.3 *	0.36 *	0.35 *	0.26 *	0.25 *	0.23 *	0.13 *	0.24 *
	Hong Kong Dollar	-0.11 *	-0.07 *	-0.04	-0.06 *	-0.04	-0.05 *	-0.05 *	-0.03	0.01	0.01	0	-0.02	0.02
	Singapore Dollar	0.02	0.07 *	0.07 *	0.07 *	0.13 *	0.07 *	0.09 *	0.09 *	0.05 *	0.04	-0.01	0.03	0.04
	New Zealand Dollar	0.28 *	0.32 *	0.27 *	0.28 *	0.35 *	0.23 *	0.29 *	0.28 *	0.21 *	0.2 *	0.19 *	0.09 *	0.19 *
	British Pound	0.33 *	0.33 *	0.24 *	0.27 *	0.28 *	0.16 *	0.21 *	0.24 *	0.17 *	0.18 *	0.17 *	0.07 *	0.18 *
	Swiss Franc	-0.38 *	-0.29 *	-0.2 *	-0.18 *	-0.15 *	-0.09 *	-0.12 *	-0.12 *	-0.09 *	-0.11 *	-0.11 *	-0.05 *	-0.1 *
	Swedish Krona	-0.34 *	-0.34 *	-0.26 *	-0.31 *	-0.31 *	-0.22 *	-0.26 *	-0.26 *	-0.22 *	-0.22 *	-0.19 *	-0.07 *	-0.2 *
	Norwegian Krone	-0.38 *	-0.36 *	-0.29 *	-0.29 *	-0.32 *	-0.21 *	-0.26 *	-0.28 *	-0.27 *	-0.28 *	-0.25 *	-0.07 *	-0.24 *
	Indian Rupee	-0.12 *	-0.18 *	-0.18 *	-0.18 *	-0.21 *	-0.18 *	-0.19 *	-0.18 *	-0.13 *	-0.14 *	-0.1 *	-0.03	-0.11 *
	Vietnamese Dong	0.03	0	0.01	-0.07 *	0	-0.05 *	-0.04	-0.04	-0.01	-0.01	-0.04	0.03	-0.01
	Brazilian Real	-0.07 *	-0.16 *	-0.12 *	-0.24 *	-0.29 *	-0.22 *	-0.22 *	-0.24 *	-0.16 *	-0.16 *	-0.12 *	-0.07 *	-0.13 *
	Mexican Peso	-0.04	-0.14 *	-0.13 *	-0.24 *	-0.3 *	-0.24 *	-0.27 *	-0.27 *	-0.18 *	-0.18 *	-0.14 *	-0.06 *	-0.15 *
	Polish Zloty	-0.29 *	-0.3 *	-0.24 *	-0.3 *	-0.35 *	-0.24 *	-0.26 *	-0.27 *	-0.22 *	-0.23 *	-0.19 *	-0.09 *	-0.21 *
Rates	US 2 Year Yield	-0.14 *	-0.04	0.06 *	0.15 *	0.17 *	0.09 *	0.13 *	0.14 *	0.1 *	0.1 *	0.07 *	0.03	0.08 *
	US 5 Year Yield	-0.12 *	-0.01	0.08 *	0.16 *	0.18 *	0.13 *	0.14 *	0.16 *	0.14 *	0.14 *	0.09 *	0.04	0.1 *
	US 10 Year Yield	-0.12 *	0	0.09 *	0.15 *	0.18 *	0.14 *	0.14 *	0.15 *	0.16 *	0.14 *	0.1 *	0.04	0.11 *
	US 30 Year Yield	-0.08 *	0.03	0.11 *	0.16 *	0.19 *	0.14 *	0.14 *	0.16 *	0.19 *	0.16 *	0.12 *	0.04	0.13 *
	German 2 Year Yield	-0.11 *	-0.01	0.04	0.17 *	0.16 *	0.1 *	0.13 *	0.12 *	0.08 *	0.09 *	0.08 *	0.02	0.07 *
	German 5 Year Yield	-0.11 *	0.01	0.06 *	0.17 *	0.19 *	0.12 *	0.15 *	0.14 *	0.08 *	0.09 *	0.08 *	0.01	0.07 *
	German 10 Year Yield	-0.09 *	0.02	0.08 *	0.18 *	0.2 *	0.15 *	0.15 *	0.16 *	0.11 *	0.11 *	0.09 *	0.02	0.09 *
	German 30 Year Yield	-0.05 *	0.03	0.08 *	0.15 *	0.18 *	0.13 *	0.13 *	0.13 *	0.11 *	0.1 *	0.08 *	0.02	0.09 *

Table 2.4 Correlation between commodities and other markets – Part 2

	Agriculture								Indices			
	Corn	Wheat	Coffee	Sugar	Cocoa	Cotton	Soybean	Rice	GSCI Agri.	GSCI Energy	GSCI Ind. Metals	GSCI Prec. Metals
Dow Jones	0.11 *	0.1 *	0.08 *	0.06 *	0.07 *	0.1 *	0.14 *	0.09 *	0.16 *	0.1 *	0.25 *	-0.03
S&P 500	0.13 *	0.11 *	0.08 *	0.07 *	0.08 *	0.11 *	0.15 *	0.09 *	0.17 *	0.14 *	0.26 *	0
Nasdaq	0.08 *	0.06 *	0.05 *	0.05 *	0.04	0.08 *	0.11 *	0.06 *	0.11 *	0.1 *	0.2 *	-0.01
Canadian TSX	0.21 *	0.17 *	0.12 *	0.15 *	0.12 *	0.17 *	0.24 *	0.11 *	0.27 *	0.29 *	0.37 *	0.16 *
Mexico IPC	0.13 *	0.1 *	0.09 *	0.08 *	0.08 *	0.1 *	0.14 *	0.06 *	0.16 *	0.17 *	0.28 *	0.08 *
Brazil BOVESPA	0.15 *	0.09 *	0.1 *	0.08 *	0.08 *	0.11 *	0.16 *	0.05 *	0.16 *	0.15 *	0.28 *	0.08 *
Euro Stoxx	0.12 *	0.09 *	0.1 *	0.09 *	0.07 *	0.13 *	0.14 *	0.08 *	0.16 *	0.14 *	0.32 *	-0.02
FTSE	0.13 *	0.1 *	0.1 *	0.11 *	0.07 *	0.13 *	0.16 *	0.08 *	0.18 *	0.18 *	0.35 *	0.02
CAC 40	0.12 *	0.1 *	0.09 *	0.09 *	0.07 *	0.13 *	0.14 *	0.08 *	0.16 *	0.15 *	0.33 *	-0.02
DAX	0.11 *	0.1 *	0.1 *	0.09 *	0.06 *	0.11 *	0.14 *	0.1 *	0.16 *	0.12 *	0.31 *	-0.01
IBEX	0.11 *	0.1 *	0.09 *	0.08 *	0.07 *	0.12 *	0.13 *	0.09 *	0.15 *	0.13 *	0.3 *	0
MIB	0.12 *	0.09 *	0.1 *	0.09 *	0.06 *	0.15 *	0.14 *	0.08 *	0.16 *	0.15 *	0.31 *	-0.02
AEX	0.11 *	0.09 *	0.1 *	0.07 *	0.07 *	0.13 *	0.13 *	0.08 *	0.15 *	0.13 *	0.31 *	-0.02
OMX	0.1 *	0.06 *	0.09 *	0.07 *	0.06 *	0.13 *	0.13 *	0.07 *	0.14 *	0.11 *	0.3 *	0.01
SMI	0.1 *	0.08 *	0.09 *	0.08 *	0.07 *	0.11 *	0.12 *	0.08 *	0.14 *	0.11 *	0.27 *	-0.04
NIKKEI	0.11 *	0.09 *	0.07 *	0.08 *	0.07 *	0.06 *	0.1 *	0.05 *	0.13 *	0.1 *	0.25 *	0.09 *
HANG SENG	0.08 *	0.07 *	0.09 *	0.09 *	0.07 *	0.06 *	0.13 *	0.05 *	0.13 *	0.14 *	0.25 *	0.05 *
ASX	0.07 *	0.06 *	0.08 *	0.06 *	0.07 *	0.07 *	0.1 *	0.04	0.1 *	0.1 *	0.22 *	0.07 *
Euro	0.21 *	0.19 *	0.11 *	0.11 *	0.18 *	0.12 *	0.19 *	0.1 *	0.24 *	0.14 *	0.25 *	0.45 *
Canadian Dollar	-0.24 *	-0.19 *	-0.13 *	-0.15 *	-0.14 *	-0.18 *	-0.24 *	-0.09 *	-0.29 *	-0.28 *	-0.39 *	-0.35 *
Japanese Yen	0	-0.02	0	0.05 *	-0.01	0.04	-0.01	0.01	0.01	0.03	0.05 *	-0.21 *
Australian Dollar	0.25 *	0.21 *	0.14 *	0.2 *	0.21 *	0.16 *	0.25 *	0.1 *	0.31 *	0.27 *	0.43 *	0.36 *
Hong Kong Dollar	0	-0.01	-0.02	0	-0.02	0	-0.01	0.01	-0.01	0.01	-0.05 *	-0.11 *
Singapore Dollar	0.04	0.03	0.05 *	0.02	0.05 *	0.03	0.08 *	0.04	0.06 *	0.05 *	0.11 *	0.02

(continued)

Table 2.4 (*Continued*)

	Agriculture								Indices			
	Corn	Wheat	Coffee	Sugar	Cocoa	Cotton	Soybean	Rice	GSCI Agri.	GSCI Energy	GSCI Ind. Metals	GSCI Prec. Metals
New Zealand Dollar	0.21 *	0.21 *	0.13 *	0.17 *	0.17 *	0.12 *	0.2 *	0.1 *	0.28 *	0.22 *	0.35 *	0.33 *
British Pound	0.2 *	0.16 *	0.11 *	0.11 *	0.21 *	0.12 *	0.17 *	0.07 *	0.23 *	0.19 *	0.29 *	0.36 *
Swiss Franc	-0.16 *	-0.15 *	-0.08 *	-0.07 *	-0.13 *	-0.07 *	-0.15 *	-0.06 *	-0.18 *	-0.1 *	-0.17 *	-0.41 *
Swedish Krona	-0.23 *	-0.21 *	-0.14 *	-0.13 *	-0.18 *	-0.16 *	-0.23 *	-0.12 *	-0.29 *	-0.22 *	-0.33 *	-0.39 *
Norwegian Krone	-0.24 *	-0.23 *	-0.13 *	-0.15 *	-0.2 *	-0.16 *	-0.25 *	-0.11 *	-0.31 *	-0.27 *	-0.33 *	-0.43 *
Indian Rupee	-0.14 *	-0.15 *	-0.11 *	-0.07 *	-0.1 *	-0.1 *	-0.15 *	-0.09 *	-0.2 *	-0.13 *	-0.22 *	-0.16 *
Vietnamese Dong	0.02	0	-0.01	0.02	0	0.02	0.04	0.01	0.02	-0.01	-0.04	0.01
Brazilian Real	-0.13 *	-0.11 *	-0.16 *	-0.13 *	-0.08 *	-0.12 *	-0.15 *	-0.08 *	-0.19 *	-0.16 *	-0.29 *	-0.09 *
Mexican Peso	-0.12 *	-0.09 *	-0.1 *	-0.11 *	-0.08 *	-0.1 *	-0.14 *	-0.06 *	-0.17 *	-0.19 *	-0.31 *	-0.06 *
Polish Zloty	-0.22 *	-0.21 *	-0.14 *	-0.15 *	-0.17 *	-0.13 *	-0.23 *	-0.14 *	-0.28 *	-0.23 *	-0.35 *	-0.32 *
US 2 Year Yield	0.07 *	0.08 *	0.06 *	0.05 *	0.03	0.09 *	0.11 *	0.03	0.11 *	0.1 *	0.17 *	-0.11 *
US 5 Year Yield	0.09 *	0.09 *	0.07 *	0.06 *	0.05 *	0.1 *	0.13 *	0.03	0.14 *	0.13 *	0.19 *	-0.09 *
US 10 Year Yield	0.08 *	0.09 *	0.07 *	0.06 *	0.06 *	0.08 *	0.12 *	0.01	0.13 *	0.14 *	0.18 *	-0.07 *
US 30 Year Yield	0.09 *	0.09 *	0.06 *	0.07 *	0.07 *	0.07 *	0.13 *	0	0.14 *	0.16 *	0.19 *	-0.05 *
German 2 Year Yield	0.08 *	0.04	0.07 *	0.07 *	0.05 *	0.08 *	0.13 *	0.06 *	0.12 *	0.1 *	0.17 *	-0.12 *
German 5 Year Yield	0.1 *	0.05 *	0.07 *	0.08 *	0.06 *	0.1 *	0.14 *	0.05 *	0.13 *	0.09 *	0.19 *	-0.11 *
German 10 Year Yield	0.1 *	0.05 *	0.08 *	0.08 *	0.06 *	0.08 *	0.15 *	0.03	0.13 *	0.11 *	0.21 *	-0.09 *
German 30 Year Yield	0.08 *	0.05 *	0.07 *	0.05 *	0.03	0.05 *	0.12 *	0.01	0.11 *	0.1 *	0.18 *	-0.04

US Dollar should slow the worldwide demand for these raw materials whose price in local currencies increases. This is, however, only a part of the problem: since Chen and Rogoff (2003), a connection between commodities and a few currencies has been established, known as commodity currencies. The empirical relation – for example – between the Canadian, the Australian and the New Zealand Dollars and commodities has been uncovered by many academic articles. A large debate is still ongoing to prove whether commodities help forecasting commodity currencies, or whether the relationship works the other way around. Chen *et al.* (2010) find that currencies predict commodities, both in- and out-of-sample. In-sample studies of a similar kind are Amano and Van Norden (1998a and b), Issa (2008) and Cayen *et al.* (2010), all of them diagnosing an empirical relationship between commodities and these currencies. Chen and Rogoff (2003) find supporting evidence that commodities have a forecasting power over these real exchange rates. Ferraro *et al.* (2011) find a short-term relation between oil prices and several currencies. These empirical relations are usually explained through a terms of trade argument: these currencies are usually associated with commodity exporter countries. When the terms of trade of these countries improve, the associated currency appreciates due to the stronger worldwide demand for the country's currency. We will investigate empirically these spillovers from commodities to currencies at the end of this chapter.

Following the insights gained from the joint analysis of the academic literature and of the various tables presented here, two issues emerge:

1. How do commodities interact with each other, and with the rest of the financial assets from a static cross-sectional perspective?
2. How does a shock spread from commodities to other assets? The dynamics within commodities and with the rest of the assets is clearly a matter of interest.

We will discuss these cross-asset linkages in the second section of this cross-asset analysis.

2.1 COMMON RISK FACTORS IN COMMODITIES

This section[1] aims at establishing an understanding of the common risk factors priced in commodity markets as well as their interactions with equities, currencies and interest rates. The latter will reveal the relationship between the global macroeconomic environment and commodity markets. Since commodity markets often exhibit cross-sectional dependency, common risk factors exist and can be identified. These topics will help us understand the origin of the commodity diversification effect (Gorton and Rouwenhorst (2005)), which has motivated institutional investors to increase portfolio allocations to commodities (Daskalaki and Skiadopoulos (2011)). The operational significance of the results is to evaluate risk-adjusted performance of portfolios allocated to commodities, and to help build cross-asset strategies. Investors can then pinpoint the correlation between any two positions taken within commodity markets, and attempt to profitably exploit the common sources of risk. In turn, it should provide the reader with an increased understanding of the risks at work in the commodity world.

---

[1] We are thankful to Ling Ni Boon for helpful research assistance in the writing of this section.

2.1.1 Literature Review

The search for common components has been widely performed mainly for equities, for which the general consensus is that there are at least three factors (Fama and French (1993)):

1. market risk (i.e. excess return of the market),
2. size (i.e. market capitalization) and
3. value (i.e. book-to-market ratio).

Due to the claim that commodities are an alternative asset class, and given their heterogeneous structure (Erb and Campbell (2006), Kat and Oomen (2007a; 2007b)), these factors may not explain variances in commodities' returns. As for commodities, research has focused on a single commodity assets. Pricing of single commodity assets has been attempted under the stochastic discount factor (SDF) setting, i.e. using the Capital Asset Pricing Model (CAPM) (Dusak (1973)), Bodie and Rosansky (1980)) and Consumption CAPM (CCAPM) (Breeden (1980)). There are many studies that apply the CCAPM on multiple commodity assets, such as Jagannathan (1985) and de Roon and Szymanowska (2010), who find that validity of the model is dependent on the frequency of the data. Overall, such equity-like approaches have been disappointing, failing to cope with the uniqueness of commodities' features.

The alternative approach, closer to ours, is based on the underlying assumption that a commodity asset's expected return is influenced by commodity market-specific factors. This is consistent with the finding that correlation between commodities and more traditional assets appears limited in the long run. Yet, many studies, such as Stoll (1979), Hirschleifer (1988; 1989) and de Roon et al. (2000), consider the impact of systematic factors and hedging pressure on single commodity futures only. Drawing upon the theory of storage[2] (Working (1949)), Gorton et al. (2012) have investigated commodity inventory levels and commodity futures' expected returns. Acharya et al. (2011) have constructed an equilibrium model of commodity markets in which speculators are constrained by capital while producers face commodity futures hedging demands to find that limits in financial arbitrage cause limits to hedging by producers, which subsequently affect asset and goods prices. Despite the fairly extensive library of works on this topic, most of them focus on a single commodity asset only. This fact probably derives from the strong heterogeneity of commodities which limits the potential of interest in a cross-commodity perspective.

More recently, Daskalaki et al. (2012) have explored common components of a cross-section of commodity futures data by using asset-pricing models suited to equities, as well as Principle Component Analysis (PCA) factor models. The authors have implemented not only the CAPM and CCAPM models, but also Money-CAPM and Money-CCAPM (MCAPM, MCCAPM) which has real money growth as an additional factor (Balvers and Huang (2009)) due to evidence that individual commodity futures' returns are influenced by monetary policy (Barsky and Kilian (2004), Frankel (2006), Anzuini et al. (2010)). Motivated by broker-dealers' significant role in commodity futures markets, their leverage is tested as a state variable as well (Adrian et al. (2010)). Furthermore, the foreign exchange factor is tested by using an international-CAPM setting, since there is evidence that commodity futures are affected by exchange rate risk (Erb and Campbell (2006)). Yet, none of these studies succeeded in pricing the cross-section of commodity futures.

---

[2] The theory of storage states that when commodity inventory levels are high, commodity futures prices are likely to be in contango, and volatility and spot futures prices are typically low. The converse is also true.

Daskalaki *et al.* (2012) proceeded to investigate equity-motivated tradable factor models under the hypothesis that if markets are unsegmented, then these factors should price cross-section of commodity futures. This hypothesis is supported by the results by Bessembinder and Chan (1992) and Erb and Campbell (2006), who demonstrate that individual commodity futures returns are not driven by Fama and French (1993) factors. Low correlation between commodities and other asset classes in the long term could also be evidence for market segmentation. Yet, as we have seen, in the short run, commodities are highly correlated with other asset classes. Tang and Xiong (2010) claim that increased allocation of investment in commodity indices (i.e. the financialization of commodities) contributes to equity and commodity markets' integration, while Hong and Yogo (2011) even find common variables that could predict equity and commodity returns. However, Daskalaki *et al.* (2012) are cautious in pointing out that this is a necessary but not sufficient condition of market integration. Once again, none of these factor models price commodity futures, substantiating the claim that equity and commodity markets are segmented.

Since macro and equity-motivated-factor models have failed, attention is turned to commodity-specific factors. Two major theories on commodity returns, hedging pressure and theory of storage, are relied upon to construct these factors. Basu and Miffre (2012) have attempted to build factor-mimicking portfolios on hedging pressure, but find results that are dependent on the assumptions during construction. Gorton *et al.* (2012) find that inventory levels provide information on futures risk premiums but only in an individual commodities context. Daskalaki *et al.* (2012) find, unexpectedly, that commodity-specific factors are unsuccessful in pricing commodity futures, suggesting that the cross-section of commodity futures has no common risk factor structure. Thus, the authors conclude that commodity futures markets have a heterogeneous structure.

The alternative approach that Daskalaki *et al.* (2012) have adopted – the one which we eventually extend – consists in implementing principal components (PC) factor models. Factor models from one up to five factors are implemented and compared. Performance of the PC model is poor on various counts. For instance, the result is dependent on whether monthly or quarterly data is used. In monthly data, the first PC influences mainly only commodities from the same group. Besides that, risk premiums of PCs are mostly insignificant. For quarterly data, only the third factor is shown to price the returns, yet it explains only a minor fraction of the total variation (i.e. $\simeq 10\%$). The PC model is susceptible to robustness tests as it fails to respond to the rise in correlation across commodities during the 2004–2008 boom period. Moreover, the demonstrated heterogeneity is not attributable to any particular commodity category, but is a market-universal characteristic.

In the following sections, we extend the work by Daskalaki *et al.* (2012) on PC models by using a criterion to determine the number of factors to include, as opposed to progressively testing PC models with n factors, identifying the factors, and then analyzing their dynamics over time.

We find evidence that corroborates the heterogeneity of commodities. The explanatory power of the first factor of the commodity dataset is lower than other datasets comprised of equities, foreign exchange rates and interest rates. When a criterion is used to determine the number of factors, only one common component is estimated for commodities, suggesting that variances in commodity markets are largely due to idiosyncrasies that cannot be accounted for by common factors. Three factors are estimated for the equities market, two for interest rates and one factor for foreign exchange markets.

2.1.2   PCA and the Estimation of the Number of Common Components

The joint behavior of commodities is analyzed under the factor model specification. A factor model's formulaic appearance is identical to that of a simple regression model, but a different interpretation is attached to each element. The elements' familiar names under the simple regression setting are abused in this first introduction to factor models to obtain an intuitive grasp of the concept:

- The *dependent variable* is the returns data.
- The *independent variable(s)* is/are then the common component(s), also known as factors, which are assumed to be unobservable.
- The *error terms* capture the idiosyncrasies of the returns, i.e. asset-unique variables that explain variance in the returns.
- The *coefficients* associated with each factor are known as the loadings.

Thus, a factor model consists of returns data, factors (unobservable), their loadings and idiosyncratic terms.

An *r*-factor *approximate factor model* is represented as such:

$$X_{it} = \lambda_i' F_t + e_{it}$$
$$i = 1 \dots N \quad \text{and} \quad t = 1 \dots T \tag{2.1}$$

- X_{it} is the return of the *i*th asset at time *t*.
- F_t is the $r \times 1$ vector of unobservable common factors, $F_t = (F_{1t}, F_{2t}, \dots, F_{rt})$.
- λ_i is the $r \times 1$ vector of factor loadings.
- e_{it} is the idiosyncratic component.
- $'$ denotes the complex conjugate transpose of the matrix, and the following assumptions are imposed:
  1. F_t and e_t are uncorrelated.
  2. The matrix comprised of $cov(e_i, e_j)$ is not necessarily diagonal, allowing for serial correlation and heteroskedasticity, but the degree of correlation between the idiosyncratic components is limited, i.e. the largest eigenvalue of Ω, the $N \times N$ covariance matrix of the idiosyncratic component, is assumed to be bounded.

As in Daskalaki *et al.* (2012), a PC factor model approach is also adopted in our analysis, but the number of factors to include is decided upon by using the criteria proposed by Alessi *et al.* (2010). The task is outlined in three steps:

1. Selection of the number of common components to include.
2. Estimation of the components.
3. Identification of the components.

The explanation of steps 2 and 3 unfolds first.

Step 2 is accomplished via a dimension-reduction technique known as Principal Component Analysis (PCA), which aims to select the salient factors that explain variances in the data. The first *r* PCs are obtained by solving a minimization problem, set up to yield the least error-sum-squared:

$$V(r) = \frac{min}{\Lambda, F^r} \frac{1}{NT} \sum_{i=1}^{N} \sum_{t=1}^{T} (X_{it} - \lambda_i^r F_t^r)^2$$

with $\Lambda = (\lambda_1, \lambda_2, \ldots \lambda_N)'$, subject to either $\frac{F'F}{T} = I_r$ and $\Lambda'\Lambda$ is diagonal, or $\frac{\Lambda'\Lambda}{N} = I_r$ and $F'F$ is diagonal.

Some linear algebraic manipulation can demonstrate that the result of this minimization problem is essentially the ordered eigenvalues corresponding to the asset return's covariance matrix.[3]

To identify the factors in Step 3, the correlation between the estimated factors in Step 2 and the assets whose variances the factors are trying to explain is investigated. When the assets are too numerous, then selected assets are chosen such that when the factor is regressed upon the set of assets, at least 95% R^2 is attained. By interpreting the sign and magnitude of the correlations, an attempt to label the factors is made in order to establish economic sense.

As for Step 1, determining the number of factors to include, numerous criteria have been developed but arguably the most popular technique consists of using an information criterion. This approach is based on the idea that an $(r + 1)$-factor model can fit no worse than an r-factor model, but is less efficient. The balance between parsimony and explicability is evaluated via a loss function, and is defined as $V(r, F^r) + rg(N, T)$, or $log(V(r, \hat{F}^r)) + r\bar{\sigma}^2 g(N, T)$ whereby $V(r, F^r) = \frac{min}{\Lambda} \frac{1}{NT} \sum_{i=1}^{N} \sum_{t=1}^{T} (x_{it} - \lambda_i^{r'} F_t^r)^2$ is the value function, $g(N, T)$ is the penalty for overfitting, r is a constant, and $\bar{\sigma}^2$ is a consistent estimate of $\frac{1}{NT} \sum_{i=1}^{N} \sum_{t=1}^{T} E[e_{it}]^2$, which in practice can be replaced by $V(r_{max}, \hat{F}^{r_{max}})$.[4] N is the cross-section dimension while T is the time dimension. The estimated number of factors is then the r corresponding to the lowest value of the loss function among those considered.

The criterion adopted in our analysis is proposed by Alessi, Barigozzi and Capasso (ABC), which is a refinement of the one by Bai and Ng (2002). ABC defines a refined loss function and evaluates it over a range of the constant and random sub-samples of the data. The estimated number of factors is then the number that is insensitive to neighboring values of the constant, and has no dependence on the sub-samples. The purpose of the constant is to tune the penalizing power of $g(N, T)$, resulting in an estimate that is empirically more robust than when c is fixed. The results presented below are those obtained by using penalty functions $g_1(N, T) = \frac{N+T}{NT} ln(min(\sqrt{N}, \sqrt{T})^2)$ or $g_2(N, T) = (N + T - k)\frac{ln(NT)}{NT}$. g_1 is frequently used in empirical work due to its stability and g_2 has been shown to have good properties when errors are cross-correlated. The choice of ABC's criterion as opposed to various other methods, e.g. Bai and Ng (2002), Connor and Korajczyk (1993), Onatski (2009), is motivated by a Monte Carlo study implemented on financial data comprising equities, commodities, credit spreads, interest rates and currencies (Boon and Ielpo (2012)). The results demonstrate that ABC's criterion is superior in accuracy (overall best in the Monte Carlo study, even when cross-section and serial correlation exist in the data), and precision (less sensitive to whether linear

---

[3] While PCA and an alternate dimension-reduction technique called Factor Analysis are distinct methods, in this chapter, 'factor' and 'principal component' (PC) are used synonymously to refer to the vector F_t.

[4] There is no general guide in selecting r_{max} in panel data analysis. In time series analysis, Schwert's rule (1988) of $r_{max} = 8int[(\frac{T}{100})^{\frac{1}{4}}]$ is occasionally used.

dependencies exist in the financial data, yielding the same estimation regardless of whether the criterion is applied to the data, or the vector autoregressive residuals).

In subsequent analysis, the following transformation on the data is performed:

1. Equities as returns.
2. Foreign exchange (FX) as log returns.
3. Interest rates as differences.
4. Commodities as returns.

2.1.3 Empirical Findings

By using this empirical approach, we tackle this issue of the factors priced in commodity markets, relying on the dataset listed in Table 2.5. We do so by highlighting four different stylized facts:

1. We present evidence that the risk factors priced in other asset classes are only weakly priced in commodities.

Table 2.5   Composition and summary statistics of the global macro hedge fund dataset. Range: January 19 1994 to 24 August 2012

Data Composition (60 assets)				
Equities	Dow Jones Industrial Average, S&P 500, Nasdaq 100, S&P TSX, Mexico IPC, Brazil Bovespa,			
(15 assets)	Eurostoxx, FTSE, CAC 40, DAX, IBEX 35, Swiss Market Index, Nikkei 225, Hang Seng, S&P ASX 200.			
Interest rates	US 30Y, US 10Y, US 5Y, US 2Y,			
(8 assets)	GE 30Y, GE 10Y, GE 5Y, GE 2Y.			
Foreign exchange	EUR, CAD, YEN, AUD, NZD, GBP, CHF,			
(12 assets)	SEK, NOK, ZAR, MXN, TWD			
	Metals: Gold, silver, platinum, aluminum, copper, nickel, zinc, lead.			
Commodities	Fuel: WTI, Brent, Gasoil, Natural Gas, Heating Oil.			
(25 assets)	Softs: Coffee, Sugar, Cocoa, Cotton.			
	Grains: Corn, Wheat, Soybean, Rice.			
	Financials: GSCI Agriculture, Energy, Industrial Metals, Precious Metals.			

Summary statistics by asset category					
Category	Mean (Annualized Return)	Median	Standard Deviation (Annualized Return)	Min	Max
Equities return	11%	1.725×10^{-4}	42%	−0.158	0.334
Interest variation in rates	108%	-2.0×10^{-4}	0.6%	−0.533	0.473
Foreign exchange log return	25%	0	45%	−0.186	0.168
Commodities geometric return	5%	0	24%	−0.156	0.189

Table 2.6   Explanatory power of the first factor

	Equities	Interest Rates	FX	Commodities
Proportion of variance explained	49%	69%	45%	28%

2. The concentration of risk factors is much weaker in commodities: the first factor of commodities explains only a weak part of this investment universe.
3. By estimating the number of common factors over each dataset, we find a single common factor in commodities.
4. By identifying the number of common factors in a global dataset, we find that commodities are still contributing with other asset classes to the joint evolution of financial markets.

Prior to determining the number of factors using ABC's criterion, the explanatory power of the first factor in each dataset is analyzed. By doing so, we aim at analyzing the concentration of correlations in commodity markets and compare it to other markets. The decompositon of the amount of variance explained by each factor is obtained by taking the ratio of the eigenvalue associated with each factor and the sum of all eigenvalues of the entire return covariance matrix. A very concentrated market – that is a market for which correlations across asset variations are very high – should deliver a ratio that is very close to 100%. Conversely, when a market exhibits a low cross-asset correlation – as we suspect in the case of commodities since Gorton and Rouwenhorst (2005) – this ratio should be closer to 0%. Such results are presented in Table 2.6. As expected, this concentration is quite high in the case of interest rate variations for which the first factor obtained from the PCA explains 69% of the dataset. Equities are not far behind, as their first factor explains 49% of equities' variations. Next is the currency asset class, for which the first PCA factor explains 45% of the dataset. Finally, the first factor of commodities explains 28% of the returns on commodities. Thus, commodities obtain the weakest value of all in this first investigation of risk concentration. This finding is clearly in line with the past literature, underlining the diversification effects obtained within commodities.

To get a general idea about which assets are priced in individual commodity returns, each commodity's return is then regressed on each of the previously estimated first factors by using an OLS estimation to the following equation:

$$r_t^i = \alpha + \beta r_t^A + \varepsilon_t, \tag{2.2}$$

where r_t^i is the close-to-close return on the ith commodity, r_t^A is the return on the first factor of the asset class A and ε_t some disturbance with a zero-mean. α is a simple intercept and β is thus the slope of the regression.

In this CAPM-like framework, the higher the absolute value of β and the R^2 associated with the regression, the higher the explanatory power of the risk factor considered. The slope coefficient and R^2 are reported in Table 2.7. Low R^2 levels are observed when commodity assets are regressed on the first factor of equities and interest rates. Yet, the R^2 is, in general, higher when the regressions are done on the first factor of foreign exchange data and commodities. The former is likely because prices of commodities are often denominated in US Dollars; that is, usually the first factor found among G10 currencies. The latter suggests that despite the high heterogeneity, there exists some common component that is priced into commodity assets, which we are interested in uncovering. These findings are thus consistent

Table 2.7   Slope coefficient of commodity asset by first factor of each dataset

	Equities		Rates		Currencies		Commodities	
	β	R² (%)	β	R² (%)	β	R² (%)	β	R² (%)
Gold	0.01*	0.13	0*	0.38	−0.25*	16.68	0.09*	15.17
Silver	0.08*	3.1	0*	0.12	−0.45*	17.33	0.19*	21.9
Platinum	0.06*	3.31	0.01*	0.75	−0.26*	10.79	0.12*	14.66
Aluminum	0.09*	7.57	0.01*	2.14	−0.25*	11.62	0.14*	25
Copper	0.14*	11.94	0.02*	2.58	−0.36*	14.62	0.2*	31.91
Nickel	0.13*	5.88	0.02*	1.27	−0.34*	6.7	0.23*	22.89
Zinc	0.12*	8.24	0.02*	1.71	−0.33*	10.82	0.2*	26.92
Lead	0.13*	7.79	0.02*	1.84	−0.37*	10.82	0.21*	24.27
WTI	0.11*	3.82	0.02*	1.54	−0.33*	6.78	0.38*	64.23
Brent	0.1*	3.74	0.02*	1.22	−0.31*	6.43	0.36*	63.2
Gasoil	0.06*	1.65	0.01*	0.38	−0.27*	5.69	0.27*	38.87
Natural Gas	0.04*	0.2	0.01	0.05	−0.16*	0.67	0.37*	24.91
Heating Oil	0.08*	2.46	0.01*	0.72	−0.29*	5.46	0.36*	61.26
Corn	0.06*	1.96	0.01*	0.39	−0.21*	4.24	0.15*	15.6
Wheat	0.06*	1.76	0.01*	0.57	−0.22*	3.98	0.15*	13.3
Coffee	0.07*	1.48	0.01*	0.27	−0.2*	1.98	0.13*	5.37
Sugar	0.05*	1.07	0.01*	0.37	−0.2*	2.64	0.13*	7.82
Cocoa	0.05*	0.9	0.01*	0.59	−0.24*	4.77	0.1*	5.81
Cotton	0.06*	2.01	0.01*	0.92	−0.18*	2.86	0.11*	7.74
Soybean	0.06*	2.48	0.01*	0.93	−0.2*	4.97	0.13*	15.54
Rice	0.04*	1.05	0*	0.09	−0.13*	1.71	0.07*	3.52

with the idea that including commodities in a bond or an equity portfolio should yield an increased diversification, given that those three asset classes have been pricing different risk factors over the period considered here. Now, consistent with previous findings, commodities are pricing risk factors that are common to those priced in currency markets. These findings are consistent with the empirical conclusions obtained by Daskalaki and Skiadopoulos (2011): the usual risk factors are useless when it comes to explaining the returns on commodities. There are a couple of exceptions: copper exhibits a stronger sensitivity to equities, with an R^2 that is equal to 11.94%. Nickel, zinc and lead also exhibit an increased sensitivity to the equity factor over the period covered here. Hence, industrial metals partly price equity risk.

Now, focusing on the pure commodity dataset, we perform an identification of the first five factors driving commodities. Figures 2.1 and 2.2 present the correlations between commodity returns and the returns over each of the first five factors obtained from the PCA analysis. The correlation bar plots indicate that factor 1 is a global commodity factor, with a stronger exposure to energy commodities. Factor 2 is an industrial metals factor. Factor 3 is an oil vs. gas factor, as these two commodities have a strong and an opposite sign correlation with this factor. Factor 4 is an agricultural factor. Factor 5 is another agricultural factor, opposing coffee to grain commodities. Hence from this empirical analysis, we conclude that, analyzing commodities by sector makes sense over the period considered here: there are risk factors that are common to commodities sectors, such as industrial metals or agricultural products. As reassuring as this conclusion may be, it is still an interesting confirmation that, despite the fact that commodities from a given sector are used for various purposes,

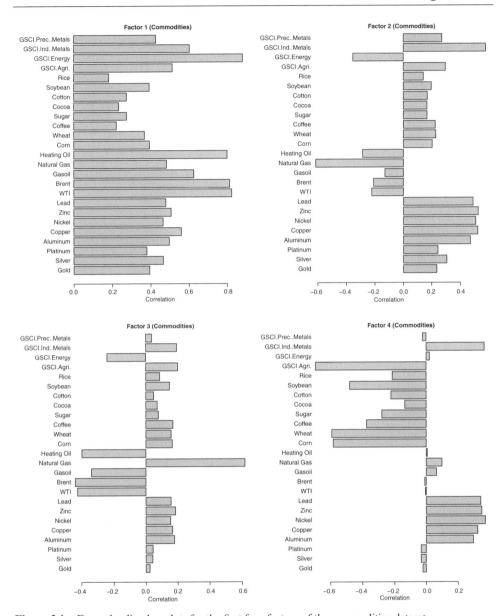

Figure 2.1   Factor loading bar plots for the first four factors of the commodities dataset

they still share some common risk factors. If commodities were driven by commodity-by-commodity specific factors, this correlation analysis should have yielded a single commodity that would have explained each of these first five factors. This is far from being the case here: beyond precious metals, we find factors that are built consistently with the way the sectors are built.

Next, we estimate the number of factors that explain the cross-section of each of the datasets considered here by using the ABC criterion. These results are presented in Table 2.8. Equities

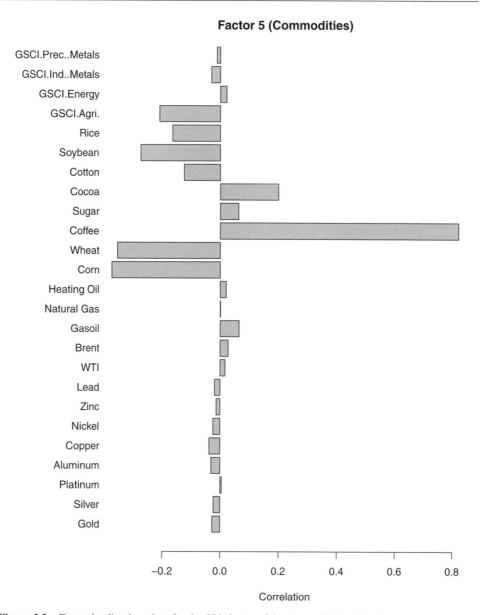

Figure 2.2 Factor loading bar plots for the fifth factor of the commodities dataset

Table 2.8 Estimated number of factors and proportion of variance explained by dataset

Dataset	Equities	Interest Rates	FX	Commodities
Estimated number of factors by ABC	3	2	1	1
Proportion of variance explained	75%	88%	45%	28%

Table 2.9 Result summary for global macro data

Factor	1	2	3	4	5	6	7
Label	Equities vs. Bond	US Dollar	Interest Rates	Euro vs, Energy	Industrial Metals	Agricultural	Euro Rates vs. US Rates
Proportion	54%	15%	7.4%	4.9%	2.9%	2.5%	1.6%
Cumulative	54%	69%	76.4%	81.3%	84.2%	86.7%	88.3%

- 'Proportion' indicates the proportion of variance explained by each principal component.
- 'Cumulative' is the proportion of variance explained by principal component(s) up to that order.

are estimated to have three factors, in line with Fama and French's (1993) model. These three factors explain up to 75% of equities' fluctuations. Interest rates are found to be driven by two factors that explain 88% of their variations, consistent with the findings in Litterman and Scheinkman (1991).[5] Hence, these two investment universes exhibit a strong concentration of risk around common risk factors. Only a weak part of their variations is explained by asset-specific factors that market observers would call alpha or idiosyncratic risk. When it comes to currencies or commodities, we get a very different picture: the estimation scheme only diagnoses a single common factor in the dataset, and this common factor explains less than half of the variations of these datasets. Here, asset-specific risk factors dominate the evolution of these markets. This finding is key to investment managers: these latter two investment universes have a strong bottom-up side and a more limited top-down one – even though we will show that they remain connected to global business cycles in Part II of the book.

Finally, in order to improve our understanding of the interactions of commodities with other asset classes, we now run the ABC criterion over the full dataset considered as a whole. Commodities are analyzed in an expanded investment universe consisting of other assets such as equities, currencies and interest rates by compiling the datasets analyzed above into a single dataset. The purpose is to reveal commodities' influence from a global perspective. If commodities are a driving force in financial markets, then they should be linked to the common factors of such a dataset. This could be evidence of integration of commodities into global financial markets. Furthermore, the decomposition of the percentage of the variance explained by commodity-linked factors divulges the extent of such integration, and could shed light on the observation that, in the long run, commodities are uncorrelated with other asset classes but are linked to them in the short run. Seven factors are estimated by using ABC's criterion, as detailed in Table 2.9. These factors are identified, as previously, through a correlation analysis, as presented in Figures 2.4 and 2.5. Factor 1 is a factor that opposes equity to bonds, and can be considered a risk appetite factor. During bullish periods, investors are more willing to take risks, and hence prefer to invest in risky assets – equities – than in riskless assets – bonds. Conversely, during bearish periods, investments are diverted from equities into bonds. Factor 2 is a factor that is strongly correlated to the US Dollar[6] and negatively with commodities – that are labeled in Dollars. Factor 3 is strongly related to interest rates, whereas factor 4 is

---

[5] They actually found three factors, but the last factor explains between 1 and 2% of interest rate variations – by using a dataset covering a different period from ours.

[6] Every currency considered here is against the US Dollar. For example, the Euro currency is, in fact, the Euro vs. the US Dollar cross.

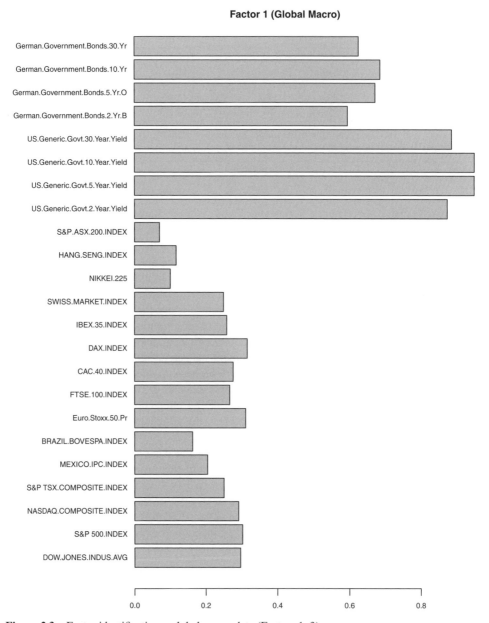

Factor 1 (Global Macro)

Figure 2.3   Factor identification – global macro data (Factors 1–3)

positively correlated to the Euro and negatively to the energy sector. Factor 5 is an industrial metals factor, factor 6 is an agricultural factor and factor 7 is a Euro vs. US rates factor. Three of the seven factors (i.e. factors 4 to 6) are linked to commodities and they explain about 10% of variances in the return, or about 12% of the total variances accounted for by all seven factors. This contribution is not limited to the negative relation between the US Dollar and the price of US-Dollar-labeled commodities: it includes additional cross-asset factors that jointly

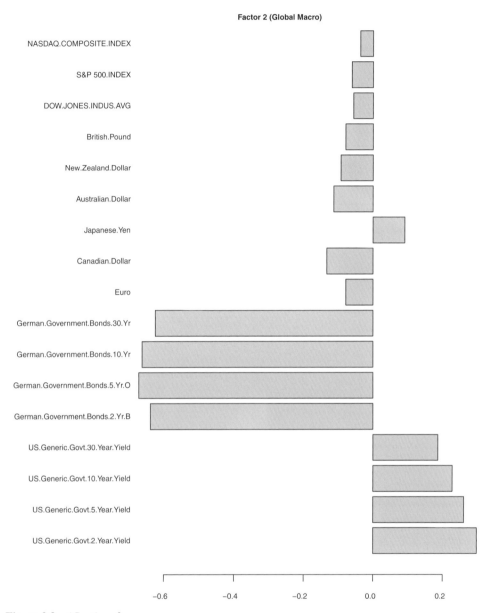

Figure 2.3 (*Continued*)

explain the evolution of financial assets. Thus, commodities are reasonably strong driving forces of a global macro investment universe, explaining a small part of the joint mechanics of worldwide financial markets.

Hence, our static analysis points toward the fact that commodities are somewhat integrated to financial markets, even though they price only weakly bond and equity risks. This is, however, only a static view: the next section will discuss how commodities and traditional assets actually interact from a dynamic perspective.

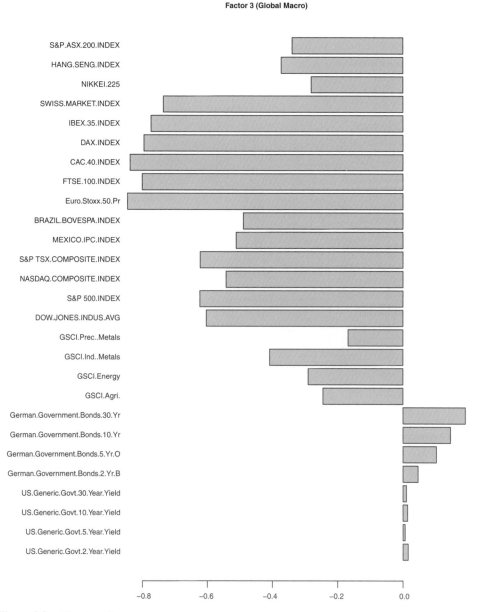

Figure 2.3   (*Continued*)

2.2   VOLATILITY SPILLOVERS IN COMMODITY MARKETS

Cross-sectional effects amongst financial and non-financial assets are clearly important in asset pricing. However, they say little about how markets interact: how does a shock from one market spread to others? Is there a commodity market that has a significant influence on the others? Observing a low correlation between commodity markets does not imply in return that

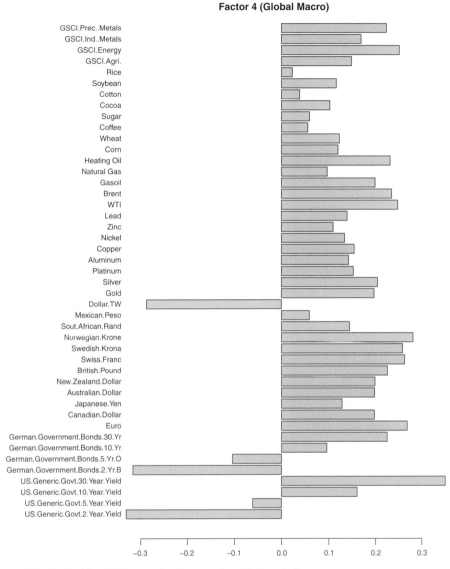

Figure 2.4   Factor identification – global macro data (Factors 4–5)

there are no dynamic cross-asset linkages. When commodity markets clearly price different risk factors from a linear asset-pricing perspective, extreme events can still trigger contagion effects across markets. This intuition would be consistent with what we obtained in Chapter 1: co-jumps across commodities and traditional assets have a tendency to occur right before or during economic crises. Consistent with these preliminary findings, this section explores the dynamic spillovers between markets by using a recent and simple econometrics tool designed for such purposes.

The literature covering these aspects in the case of commodities is sparse: systemic risk has only become a significant matter since 2008. Cross-asset linkages should be considered

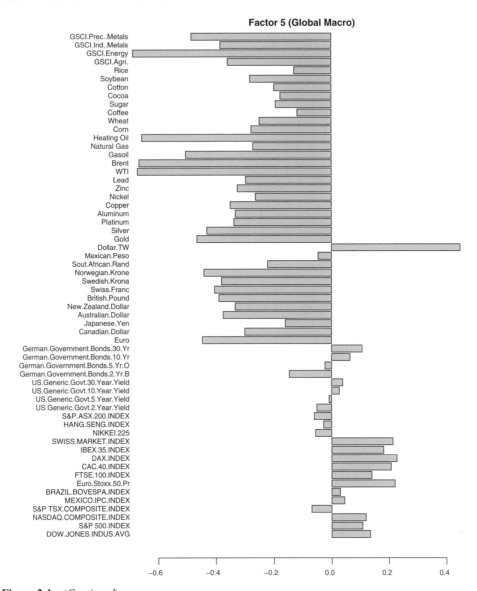

Figure 2.4   (*Continued*)

from two different perspectives: first, within a given asset class, how do shocks spread from one asset to another? Second, is this shock able to contaminate assets belonging to other asset classes? These are thus two different kinds of cross-asset spillover effects: inside an asset class and across asset classes.[7] Regarding the first topic – and consistent with our previous discussions – we should disentangle the influence from one sector on another from simple

---

[7] As pointed out in Briere *et al.* (2012), such spillovers actually encompass two different kinds of phenomena: directional shocks – as documented in Diebold and Yilmaz (2012) – and a contagion effect as defined by Forbes and Rigobon (2002). Contagion can be defined as a significant increase in cross-market linkages after a shock. Here, our focus is primarily on the directional effects that can be uncovered from the dataset we are about to investigate.

Factor 6 (Global Macro)

Figure 2.5 Factor identification – global macro data (Factors 6–7)

spillovers from one asset to another. This latter problem is closer to what the academic literature calls the price discovery process in markets. Different markets can trade assets that are either identical or very similar. Due to time-zones or to the nature of assets, some markets are more liquid than others, therefore incorporating information more rapidly than other markets. In the case of commodities, similar assets traded in different marketplaces are typically affected by non-synchronous trading, and a stronger contribution coming from the trading places located in developed markets. Booth and Ciner (1997) analyzed spillovers between corn traded on

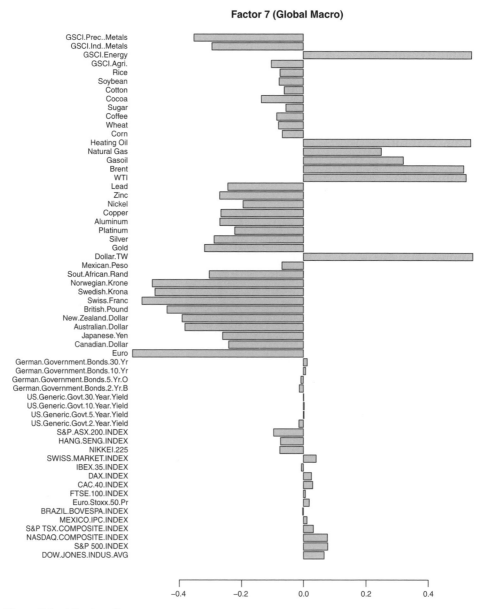

Figure 2.5 (*Continued*)

the CBOT and on the Tokyo Grain Exchange (TGE), finding return spillovers between them. Booth *et al.* (1998) performed a similar study in the case of wheat futures traded on the CBOT and on the Canadian Winnipeg Commodity Exchange (WCE), finding one-way information spillover from CBOT to WCE. Lin and Tamvakis (2001) investigated such linkages in the case of crude and refined oil prices traded on the NYMEX and on the International Petroleum Exchange (IPE) in London. Their empirical conclusions show how the closing of the NYMEX trading session influences the opening of IPE's. Other empirical contributions can be found, describing how developed and emerging markets influence each other. Low *et al.* (1999) focused on soybean and sugar, finding similar transmissions. Soybean is also investigated in Holder *et al.* (2002), along with corn. Precious metals are analyzed in Xu and Fung (2005), showing how the US market has a net contribution to other markets in terms of spillovers. Natural gas is analyzed in Kao and Wan (2009), finding again evidence of a net contribution of the US market. Kumar and Pandey (2011) have recently investigated these international linkages between commodity futures markets, finding that the Indian market has been in a position to receive more shocks than to be the source of them: shocks come from the NYMEX, the Chicago Board of Trade (CBOT) or from the London Metal Exchange (LME). Finally, a weak yet growing influence of Chinese markets is found in Fung *et al.* (2003), Hua and Chen (2007) and Ge *et al.* (2008) for various products such as copper, soybean and wheat.

While it is not surprising that similar products are affected by similar shocks given their potential substitution effects, cross-commodity spillovers are also reported in the academic literature. This point is of utmost interest for investors, as it could potentially jeopardize the celebrated commodity diversification effects found, among others, in Gorton and Rouwenhorst (2005) and Erb and Campbell (2006). The literature around this point is scarce: most of the attention of academics has been devoted to the potential spillovers coming from oil prices, following the large positive and negative shocks observed between 1979 and 2008. Baffes (2007) questions such spillover effects originated in oil prices by using a dataset of 35 commodities over the 1960–2005 period, finding directional linkages from oil to food prices. More recently, Kaltalioglu and Soytas (2011) have rejected such conclusions: by using a dataset of food and raw agricultural products over the 1980–2008 period, they conclude that there is no statistical evidence of an impact of oil shocks on agricultural prices. There are two main reasons why oil shocks could contaminate the price of agricultural products: first, processing crops involves a lot of mechanical activities where the price of oil is a cost. Second, the substitution of the use of agricultural products from food to biofuels creates a direct linkage between the price of energy and the price of corn, for example. These evolutions are, however, recent, preventing a dataset ending before 2005 from capturing this second effect. Turning to precious metals, Escribano and Granger (1998) find evidence of a simultaneous relation between silver and gold. By using a more recent dataset, Ciner (2001) finds that this relationship breaks after 1990. More recently, Khalifa *et al.* (2012) confirm the existence of simultaneous relations between commodities over the 1999–2012 period. Other linkages have been uncovered in Chng (2009), who finds strong linkages on the Tokyo Commodity Exchange (TOCOM) between the rubber, palladium and gasoline futures markets. More globally speaking, Tang and Xiong (2010) find that over the 2000s the correlation between commodities has been rising – especially for those belonging to the GSCI and the DJ-UBS indices.

Beyond cross-commodity dependencies, the final key point in this spillover analysis is the equity to commodity relationship: after the success of the paper by Gorton and Rouwenhorst (2005), investors have increasingly started to trust the diversification effect that commodities could bring to their portfolio. However, when there may be positive or negative spillovers from one to another, the expected improved risk-adjusted return could be dramatically lowered. There are actually a few spillover analyses around this commodity–equity linkage. Most of the literature is based on time-varying correlation analysis: Chong and Miffre (2010) find that the correlation between standard assets and commodities is lower during a period of crisis, i.e. when diversification effects are most sought after. Silvennoinen and Thorp (2010) find the exact opposite conclusion: over turbulent periods, these correlations are rising. Such disagreement may come from differences in terms of methodologies, or in terms of the periods covered in each dataset. Buyukshahin *et al.* (2010) find that such correlation increases after 2008, casting some doubt on the commodity diversification effect. Daskalaki and Skiadopoulos (2011), Bicchetti and Maystre (2012) and Delatte and Lopez (2012) find evidence consistent with these conclusions.

The literature around cross-commodities is spread over different types of academic journals, from pure commodity-oriented ones – that are usually closer to economic journals than financial ones – to generalist finance journals. Several reasons explain such a situation. First, there is a clear lack of agreement regarding the methodologies to be used to measure such dependency effects. Four types of methodologies are currently running in the academic literature:

1. Dynamic correlation models have been proposed, some following Engle's (2002)' Dynamic Conditional Correlation (DCC) model and its extensions. These approaches aim at measuring how correlations across markets can move together – which is usually regarded as a measure of contagion. Examples of this kind can be found in the models by Karolyi and Stulz (1996), Longin and Solnik (2001), Ang and Chen (2002) and Forbes and Rigobon (2002).
2. Copulas – a more general dependence structure than the underlying Gaussian model behind the dynamic correlation models – received increasing attention, as presented in Patton (2006), Jondeau and Rockinger (2006) and Rodriguez (2007) for standard assets and in Reboredo (2011) and Delatte and Lopez (2012) in the case of commodities. However, beyond their ability to measure tail dependence – i.e. joint extreme events – turning them into a dynamic measure of dependence proved difficult.
3. Multivariate Markov-switching models also encompass in a certain way the measurement of cross-time series dependence, as presented in Khalifa *et al.* (2012). Their ability to produce switches between two types of dependence structures led to interesting findings in financial markets (see, e.g. Ielpo, 2012). Their numerical complexity when the number of underlying variables is increased, however, is a massive drag to their use to measure cross-market dynamics. The estimation methodologies required to estimate sophisticated, and hence realistic, specifications of such models in the case of spillover measurement are rather involved – even to people who have mastered the field of financial econometrics. This limits their use on a daily basis.
4. Finally, Diebold and Yilmaz (2012) have presented a new approach based on Vector Autoregressive models (VAR), a time series model that is now widely spread and understood in the academic literature. They propose to measure cross-asset volatility spillovers from the historical cross-series mean reversion parameters. We base our investigation of spillovers on their methods. Their approach has been used in Yilmaz (2010), Kocenda *et al.* (2011) and da Fonseca and Gottschalk (2012), for example. The simplicity of the approach and the efficiency of the estimates obtained make this approach a very promising one.

2.2.1   The Volatility Spillover Index

Let x_t be a covariance stationary variable of dimension N that obeys a Vector Autoregressive model:

$$x_t = \sum_{i=1}^{p} \Phi_i x_{t-i} + \varepsilon_t, \tag{2.3}$$

where ε_t is an independent and identically distributed vector of size N that follows a Gaussian distribution with a zero mean and a variance matrix denoted Σ. Its moving average representation is $x_t = \sum_{i=0}^{+\infty} A_i \varepsilon_{t-i}$, where the $N \times N$ matrices A_i obey the following recursive equation:

$$A_i = \Phi_1 A_{i-1} + \Phi_2 A_{i-2} + \cdots + \Phi_p A_{i-p}, \tag{2.4}$$

with A_0 being the identity matrix of size N, and $A_i = 0$ whenever $i < 0$. Such a representation is usually used to perform an impulse response analysis or a variance decomposition. In both cases, their use aims at understanding how the estimated system is working: how shocks – i.e. the ε_t – spread from the ith element of the system to the others in a sequential order. Diebold and Yilmaz (2012) build their whole methodology on the variance decomposition[8] of the investigated system x_t: the variance decomposition makes it possible to decompose the variance of the forecast errors into element-by-element contributions. This computation is done for a given forecasting horizon h. The spillover index is based on a share-by-share decomposition of the variance of the forecasting error of the ith variable coming from the other elements $j \neq i$ in x_t.

The covariance matrix of ε_t being usually not diagonal, Diebold and Yilmaz (2012) proposed using the Koop et $al.$ (1996) generalized VAR framework that produces variance decomposition that is invariant to ordering, unlike its main competitor: the Cholesky decomposition.

We simply follow the presentation by Diebold and Yilmaz (2012) of their methodology, detailing the quantities of interest for our purposes:

– The h-step ahead forecast error variance decomposition is denoted $\theta_{ij}(H)$ and is computed as follows:

$$\theta_{ij}(H) = \sigma_{ij} \frac{\sum_{h=0}^{H-1} (e_i' A_h e_j)^2}{\sum_{h=0}^{H-1} e_i' A_h \Sigma A_h' e_j}, \tag{2.5}$$

where Σ is the covariance matrix of ε_t, σ_{ii} is the standard deviation of ith element in ε_t and e_i is a vector containing zeros but for its ith element that is equal to 1. Those $\theta_{ij}(H)$ are then rescaled as they range between 0 and 1. These rescaled quantities are denoted $\tilde{\theta}_{ij}(H)$:

$$\tilde{\theta}_{ij}(H) = \frac{\theta_{ij}(H)}{\sum_{j=1}^{N} \theta_{ij}(H)}, \tag{2.6}$$

where N is the total number of series that are considered here. Now, by construction $\sum_{j=1}^{N} \tilde{\theta}_{ij}(H) = 1$ and $\sum_{i,j=1}^{N} \tilde{\theta}_{ij}(H) = N$. These $\tilde{\theta}_{ij}(H) = 1$ quantities are called variance shares, as they measure the share of the total forecasting error variance for series i that is explained through series j.

– The spillover index – i.e. the measure of how much the series considered is receiving shocks that are not its – is thus measured by summing up the $\tilde{\theta}_{ij}(H)$ for all $i \neq j$:

$$S(H) = \frac{\sum_{i,j=1,i\neq j}^{N} \tilde{\theta}_{ij}(H)}{N} \times 100. \tag{2.7}$$

---

[8] Any reader interested in learning more about variance decomposition in the case of VAR(p) could refer to Lütkepohl (2005).

When a group of series has a strong exchange of spillovers, this spillover index should be high. Given the way it is computed, it should range between 0 and 100. This index is analogous to Diebold and Yilmaz (2012) in the case for which the Koop *et al.* (1996) approach to variance decomposition is used.

- A salient feature of this variance decomposition scheme is then to be able to measure where volatility spillovers usually come from and where they are going. Two kinds of directional spillover measures are proposed in Diebold and Yilmaz (2012). A first measure gauges the spillovers received by market i from all other markets j through the following quantity:

$$S_{i\leftarrow}(H) = \frac{\sum_{j=1,j\neq i}^{N} \tilde{\theta}_{ij}(H)}{\sum_{j=1}^{N} \tilde{\theta}_{ij}(H)} \times 100. \tag{2.8}$$

Then, the spillovers coming from asset i to the other assets are measured through the following quantity:

$$S_{i\rightarrow}(H) = \frac{\sum_{j=1,j\neq i}^{N} \tilde{\theta}_{ji}(H)}{\sum_{j=1}^{N} \tilde{\theta}_{ji}(H)} \times 100. \tag{2.9}$$

From these two measures, a net spillover coming from asset i and going to all the other assets considered is obtained as follows:

$$S_i(H) = S_{i\rightarrow}(H) - S_{i\leftarrow}(H). \tag{2.10}$$

This net spillover index is an interesting measure of the contribution of a given asset to the total number of shocks observed amongst a given group of assets.

- By using this framework, this concept of net spillover can be developed to measure pairwise spillover indices, thus measuring how assets interact with each other in a detailed way. The net spillover from asset i to asset j is computed as follows:

$$S_{ij}(H) = \left(\frac{\tilde{\theta}_{ij}(H)}{\sum_{k=1}^{N} \tilde{\theta}_{ik}(H)} - \frac{\tilde{\theta}_{ji}(H)}{\sum_{k=1}^{N} \tilde{\theta}_{jk}(H)} \right). \tag{2.11}$$

Additional explanations around the computations of these quantities are available in Diebold and Yilmaz (2012). We intend to make use of these measures to help the reader understand volatility spillovers in commodity markets. In the coming pages, we discuss three different problems by using these spillover indices: are there volatility spillovers between commodities? Between standard assets and commodities? Finally, we will focus on the spillovers between commodities and the commodity currencies that were previously mentioned.

2.2.2 Four Empirical Applications

We now use Diebold and Yilmaz's (2012) approach to measuring spillovers. We apply their approach to four types of datasets:

- A broad dataset of commodities, equities, currencies and interest rates starting in January 1995 and ending in July 2012. For this dataset, we use the daily highs and lows as advised in Diebold and Yilmaz (2012) to compute volatility. This dataset will simply be used to compare the different total spillover scores obtained by type of assets.

- A dataset made up of the individual commodities used in Chapter 1. Again, volatilities are measured through the high/low measure. With this dataset, we will assess the importance of cross-commodity spillovers.
- A dataset made up of the four GSCI indices along with the close-to-close returns on the S&P 500, the variations of the US 10-year rate and the returns on the US Dollar.[9] This dataset should help us understand how each asset from this asset allocation basket interacts with the others.
- Finally, a dataset combining the GSCI indices and a group of currencies known for their linkages with commodities is used to understand what kind of spillovers these currencies have with commodities.

The first step to understanding these spillovers is to build a comparison between the average level of spillovers observed from 1995 to 2012. To perform such an investigation, we use a dataset made of the four previously mentioned assets: each of these assets is listed in Tables 2.3 and 2.4. By dividing the full sample by asset type, we compute the total spillover score presented in Equation (2.7) by using a rolling window scheme, as advised in Diebold and Yilmaz (2012). We use rolling sub-periods of 250 days. The underlying VAR model has four lags, and the forecasting horizon is equal to ten days.[10] The results of such computations are presented in Figure 2.6. Several conclusions can be drawn from this figure and from the descriptive statistics presented in Table 2.10:

- First, the average level of total spillover across commodities is the lowest as one might expect: on top of the low correlation of these assets, weaker spillovers than in the case of standard assets are at work amongst commodities. Weak does not, however, mean non-existent: we still observe some variations of the commodity spillover index. This form of dependency in commodities cannot be measured through correlation: sequential shocks between commodities occur. Table 2.10 reports that the average level of these spillover indices is equal to 18.2% when the score obtained from rates is 46.7, i.e. the highest spillover index obtained.
- As for every other type of financial asset, the spillover index varies through time. A very interesting feature of this spillover index over the period considered here is the extent to which it increases over the two crisis periods covered in this dataset, consistent with the other assets. This effect is more pronounced in the case of the 2008 crisis, consistent with the idea that this crisis has been stronger. In this respect, commodities are just another type of financial asset, exhibiting increased spillovers over crisis periods.
- Then, as Table 2.10 makes very clear, the key difference of the commodity dataset is the apparent weaker variability of commodity spillovers. Whereas these spillovers in the case of rates can move from 31.4 to 61.0, the commodity spillover index varies between 10.4 and 28.5. The volatility of the spillover index is thus the lowest (4), when that for equities is the highest (9.3). This variability of the importance of spillovers is a key difference of commodities with respect to other standard assets.

Beyond this comparison, we now focus our attention on the dataset composed of pure commodities. These commodities are those listed in Tables 2.3 and 2.4. As for our previous

---

[9] We use a trade-weighted index.

[10] These settings are used as a benchmark because of Diebold and Yilmaz (2012): they perform comparisons with different specifications, highlighting the mild impact of close but different specifications of the VAR model on their results.

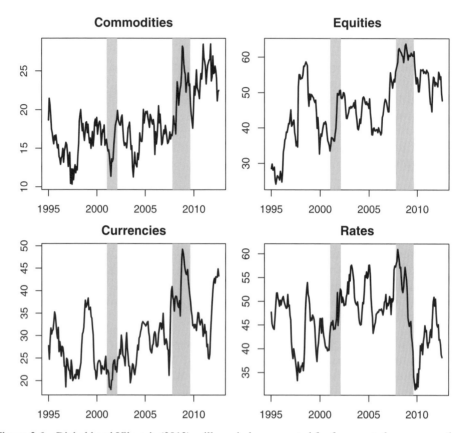

Figure 2.6   Diebold and Yilmaz's (2012) spillover index computed for four asset classes across time

empirical applications, this data includes different types of commodities: precious and industrial metals, energy commodities and agricultural products. For this specific case, we compute
the long-term directional spillover within commodities, as measured by using the full period
covered by our dataset. Results obtained from these computations are presented in Table 2.11.
The last line of this table presents the net spillover generated by each commodity, as computed
from Equation (2.10). Several conclusions can be reached:

- Even though correlation between these assets is low from a long-term perspective, this does
  not imply an absence of spillovers. From this table, we observe that some commodities

Table 2.10   Descriptive statistics for the spillover index
obtained from each type of asset

	Commodities	Equities	Currencies	Rates
Average	18.2	46.5	29.8	46.7
Std. Dev.	4.0	9.3	6.9	6.2
Min.	10.4	24.1	18.0	31.4
Max.	28.5	63.7	49.3	61.0

Table 2.11 Directional spillovers estimated from the pure commodity dataset

	Gold	Silver	Platinum	Aluminum	Copper	Nickel	Zinc	Lead	WTI	Brent	Gasoil	Natural Gas	Heating Oil	Corn	Wheat	Coffee	Sugar	Cocoa	Cotton	Soybean	Rice	Total Received
Gold	98.25	0.02	0.13	0.17	0	0.05	0.36	0.01	0	0.56	0.04	0.09	0	0.01	0	0.16	0	0.09	0	0.01	0.03	1.75
Silver	26.57	72.09	0.17	0.14	0.14	0.12	0.08	0.11	0.09	0.07	0.04	0	0.11	0.01	0	0.11	0	0.05	0.05	0.03	0.01	27.91
Platinum	9.54	1.95	87.43	0.12	0.11	0.01	0.06	0.11	0.01	0.29	0	0.01	0.04	0.01	0.07	0	0.12	0.02	0	0	0.1	12.57
Aluminum	1.58	2.01	0.79	94.99	0	0.19	0.02	0.01	0.05	0.04	0.01	0.08	0	0.01	0	0.01	0.02	0.08	0.09	0	0	5.01
Copper	3.95	4.13	0.45	20.51	69.78	0.02	0.12	0.24	0.06	0.21	0.1	0.01	0	0.07	0.01	0.03	0.13	0.13	0	0.04	0.15	30.22
Nickel	0.62	0.77	0.63	6.41	6.97	82.91	0	0.66	0.06	0.01	0.3	0.18	0.11	0.07	0.05	0.06	0.13	0.05	0.02	0.02	0.02	17.09
Zinc	2.34	1.72	0.63	14.24	9.2	2.09	68.29	0.7	0.05	0.04	0.07	0.04	0	0	0	0	0.19	0.3	0.01	0.01	0.01	31.71
Lead	1.59	1.42	0.17	8.43	3.05	0.99	3.57	79.91	0	0.02	0.08	0.04	0	0.1	0	0.04	0.19	0.01	0.01	0.29	0.09	20.09
WTI	3.69	1.2	0.31	0.34	0.81	0.33	0.04	0.32	90.15	2.43	0	0.03	0	0.05	0.03	0.01	0.08	0.02	0.1	0.06	0	9.85
Brent	3.9	1.15	0.81	0.19	0.53	0.31	0.02	0.1	56	36.52	0.09	0.15	0	0.01	0.01	0	0.12	0	0.08	0.02	0.03	63.48
Gasoil	2.39	0.3	0.14	0.71	0.58	0.54	0.03	0.13	21.5	9.14	63.29	0.21	0.87	0.03	0.05	0.01	0.02	0.05	0.01	0.01	0.03	36.71
Natural Gas	0.02	0.02	0.01	0.02	0.05	0.05	0.12	0.02	0.28	0.05	0.32	98.24	0.14	0.03	0.01	0	0	0.05	0	0.07	0.53	1.76
Heating Oil	3.09	0.6	0.26	0.33	0.47	0.19	0.07	0.09	45.63	6.95	2.27	0.48	39.28	0	0.06	0	0.06	0.05	0.09	0	0.02	60.72
Corn	0.18	0.29	0.05	0.16	1.93	0.14	0.02	0.01	0.79	0.29	0.06	0.01	0.15	94.93	0.03	0	0.8	0	0.05	0.12	0	5.07
Wheat	0.38	0.54	0.12	0.14	0.28	0.14	0.25	0.05	0.33	0.01	0.07	0.03	0.04	18.94	78.04	0.04	0.4	0.04	0.14	0.02	0	21.96
Coffee	0.04	0.05	0.37	0.05	0.11	0.25	0.35	0	0.15	0	0.03	0.02	0.04	0.27	0.4	96.93	0.12	0.14	0	0	0	3.07
Sugar	0.48	0.1	0.1	0.04	0.02	0.05	0.07	0.03	0.44	0.15	0.01	0.05	0.04	0.04	0.29	0.48	97.23	0.06	0.28	0	0.67	2.77
Cocoa	0.62	0.12	0.13	0.22	0.08	0.48	0.09	0.17	0.06	0.01	0.06	0.02	0.1	0.24	0.54	0.46	0.08	96.36	0.15	0	0.03	3.64
Cotton	0.11	0.29	0.57	0.05	0.01	0.2	0.01	0.02	0.05	0.02	0.02	0.01	0.05	0.18	0.21	0.18	0.35	0.08	97.5	0.04	0.03	2.5
Soybean	0.59	1.08	0.69	0.2	0.59	0.31	0.01	0.06	0.4	0.57	0.02	0.29	0.01	11.92	2.32	0.05	0.32	0.33	0.14	80.08	0.02	19.92
Rice	0.14	0.02	0.04	0	0.08	0.02	0.37	0.08	0.1	0.04	0.15	0.02	0.5	0.52	0.85	0.03	0.6	0.34	0.05	0.67	95.37	4.63
Total Given	38.63	19.77	6.98	35.58	26.37	7.25	7.63	3.53	58.3	36.4	5.57	1.79	5.49	25.45	5.95	1.7	3.58	1.92	1.29	1.75	1.8	Total Spillover: 18.21
Net Spillover	36.88	-8.14	-5.59	30.57	-3.85	-9.84	-24.08	-16.57	48.46	-27.08	-31.14	0.03	-55.23	20.38	-16.01	-1.37	0.81	-1.71	-1.21	-18.17	-2.83	

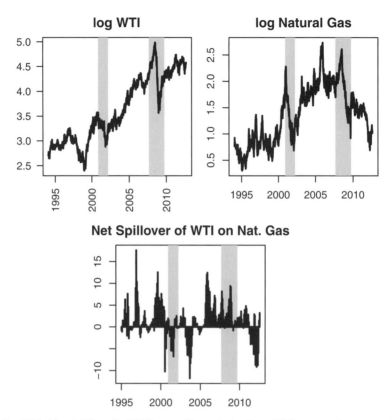

Figure 2.7   Diebold and Yilmaz's (2012) net spillover index from WTI to natural gas over time

are net givers: gold (36.88), aluminum (30.57), WTI (48.46) and corn (20.38) are the main givers amongst the set of commodities considered here. This analysis is probably specific to the period that we consider, even though this period is rather long. However, our results point at one net contributor for each of the commodity sectors considered here.

• Next, most of the spillovers of these net contributors are, in fact, given to other commodities belonging to the same sector. Gold has a net contribution to silver equal to 26.57 and a net contribution to platinum equal to 9.54, while its total net contribution across all assets is equal to 36.88. Hence, most of its contribution to spillovers goes to these two other precious metals that are net receivers in this respect. Very similar cases can be made for the role of WTI, aluminum and corn. Figure 2.7 shows the net spillover of the WTI on natural gas: the sign of the spillovers varies through time. While it is positive for most of the sample, it turns negative – i.e. natural gas became a net spillover giver to WTI a few months after the end of both crises considered in our sample. A similar case of intra-sector spillover can be made with aluminum and copper, as presented in Figure 2.9. Aluminum is a natural spillover giver to copper across our full sample, but for the 1998–1999 period during which copper became a net giver, though on a more limited scale. Finally, as presented in Figure 2.8, rice is a natural spillover giver to soybean. Here again, at the onset of both crises, soybean becomes a net spillover giver to rice.

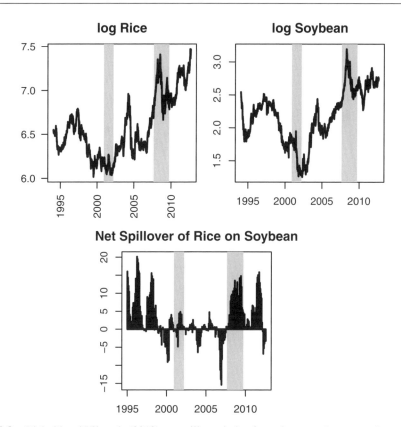

Figure 2.8   Diebold and Yilmaz's (2012) net spillover index from rice to soybean over time

- A couple of cross-sector spillovers can, however, be observed, as in the case of silver and copper. Silver has a net contribution to copper of around 4, which is not much when compared to the scores obtained by the four main contributors. However, those are long-term measures. Figure 2.10 charts the time series evolution of the rolling estimation of a pairwise net spillover index between these two commodities. Consistent with the intuition that the intensity of cross-asset spillovers varies through time, we observe that the spillovers given by silver to copper can vary over the period investigated. Another example of such cross-sector spillovers can be made with the spillovers of WTI on corn, as presented in Figure 2.11. As explained earlier in this section, two effects can explain such a relation. First, oil is a natural source of cost for the production of corn, thus raising its production price. Second, corn is increasingly used as a biofuel, being thus a direct substitute for oil. With these two factors in mind, Figure 2.11 clearly points to net spillovers from oil to corn after the end of the 2008 crisis.

A last remark around these cross-commodity spillovers must be made: when comparing the four sectors considered here, spillovers inside and outside each sector are found for all of them. However, the intensity of these spillovers varies across commodities. While metals – precious and industrial – and energy display large volatility spillovers, agricultural products have the weakest spillovers of our sample. This can be seen when considering the diagonal

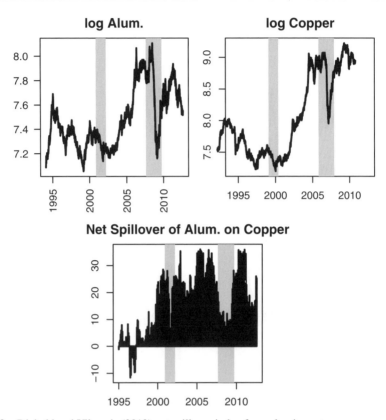

Figure 2.9   Diebold and Yilmaz's (2012) net spillover index from aluminum to copper over time

elements of Table 2.10. When those reach values ranging between 36.52 (Brent) and 97.50 (cotton), this range is much smaller in the case of agriculture: soybean (80.08) has the weakest value, and cotton reaches the maximum observed one. On average, no agricultural commodity displays the weakest cross-commodity spillovers, as the diagonal elements for those commodities in Table 2.10 are closer to 100 than in any other case. In this respect, it is most likely that agricultural commodities are driving a large part of the diversification obtained from a commodity portfolio, and should therefore not be overlooked.

Following this analysis of the interactions between commodities, we now turn to a different kind of dataset and perspective. Since Gorton and Rouwenhorst (2005), an increasing number of diversified portfolios are partly invested in standard assets such as equities or bonds and partly invested in alternative assets such as commodities. We now perform the volatility spillover analysis by mixing the data for the GSCI indices, the S&P 500, the US 10-year rate and the US Dollar. By analyzing these spillovers, we intend to improve our understanding of the interactions between those different types of assets across market phases. The total spillover index is presented in Figure 2.12: compared to the indices presented earlier in Figure 2.6, the average value is much lower than in the bonds or equity case. Volatility spillovers between these asset classes are thus lower than in the standard asset case. What is more, volatility spillovers over this dataset are lower than for any of the datasets considered separately. In

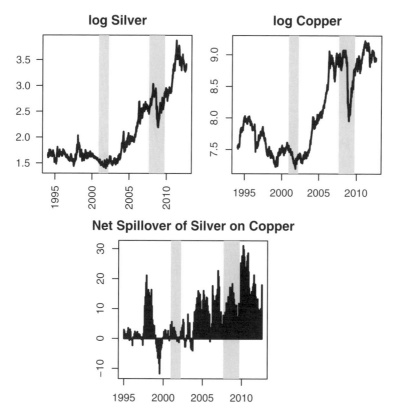

Figure 2.10   Diebold and Yilmaz's (2012) net spillover index from silver to copper over time

the case of commodities, this is related to the fact that we use indices that naturally diversify away individual commodity shocks. However, from this standpoint, adding commodities to a diversified portfolio is an interesting way to decrease the impact of cross-asset linkages. What is more, we also find that the volatility spillover index increases during crisis periods, with the index nearly reaching the value of 25% in 2012. Finally, as an interesting feature – and a warning for investors – the spillover index exhibits a linear trend over 1995–2012, thus indicating an increasing connection between asset classes that some will interpret as a financialization of commodity markets. Table 2.12 presents the full table of the decomposition of the volatility spillover index. According to this table, the agricultural, energy and precious metals sectors are net contributors to spillovers. Out of these three, only energy and precious metals are net contributors to the standard asset classes: the energy sector has a net contribution to S&P 500 equal to 2.44, and precious metals have a net contribution to interest rates equal to 4.62. These are the main commodities for standard asset class linkages. Industrial metals are net receivers of spillovers over the full sample. Overall, commodities are not receiving much spillover from standard assets; one more element that explains the appeal of this asset class for investors. Figures 2.13, 2.15 and 2.14 present the rolling estimation of volatility spillover coming from commodities towards respectively US equities, interest rates and the Dollar. Figures 2.13 and 2.15 confirm the net contribution of energy and precious metals to equities and interest rates. Figure 2.14 underlines the strongly unstable relation of spillovers between

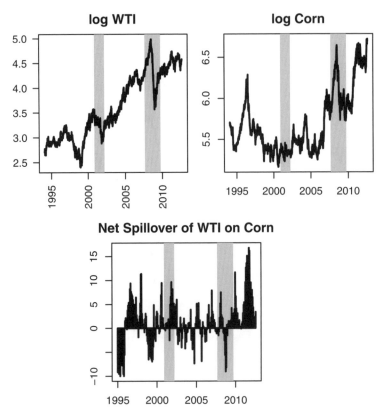

Figure 2.11   Diebold and Yilmaz's (2012) net spillover index from WTI to corn over time

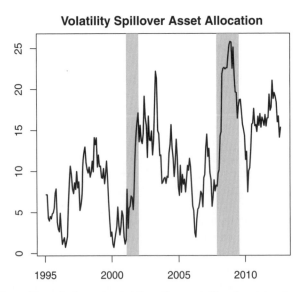

Figure 2.12   Rolling spillover index estimated from the asset allocation dataset

Table 2.12 Directional spillovers estimated from the asset allocation dataset

	Agriculture	Energy	Ind. Metals	Prec. Metals	SP500	10Y Rates	US Dollar	Total Received
Agriculture	98.90	0.06	0.17	0.66	0.01	0.04	0.17	1.11
Energy	0.58	98.19	0.02	0.53	0.64	0.03	0.00	1.81
Ind. Metals	1.41	0.90	95.79	0.99	0.51	0.31	0.10	4.21
Prec. Metals	0.44	1.91	1.45	95.31	0.64	0.01	0.24	4.69
SP500	0.62	3.08	0.35	0.77	95.08	0.00	0.10	4.92
10Y Rates	0.10	1.44	0.28	4.63	3.50	90.01	0.04	9.99
US Dollar	0.60	0.88	0.27	0.75	11.92	1.10	84.48	15.52
Total Given	3.65	7.77	2.59	8.03	15.33	1.63	0.76	6.03
Net Spillovers	2.55	5.97	−1.62	3.34	10.41	−8.36	−14.76	8.52

commodities and the US Dollar. This may result from these complex relations between them: as it is the currency in which commodities are labeled, an increase in the value of the Dollar should be transmitted to the value of commodities. In the meantime, the US Dollar being a flight-to-quality currency over the period, periods of drop in risk appetite coincide with drops in energy and industrial metals, as precious metals and the Dollar rise. This explains part of the time-varying behavior observed in Figure 2.14.

Finally, we turn to the relationship between currencies and commodities. By using the previous panel of currencies and GSCI indices, we run the volatility spillover analysis. Table

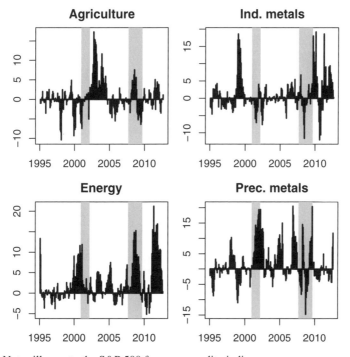

Figure 2.13 Net spillovers to the S&P 500 from commodity indices

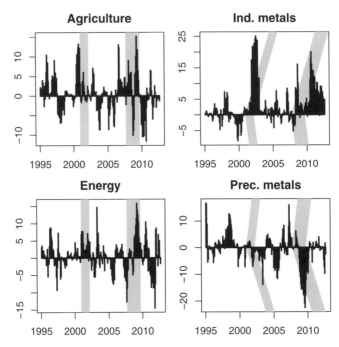

Figure 2.14   Net spillovers to the US Dollar from commodity indices

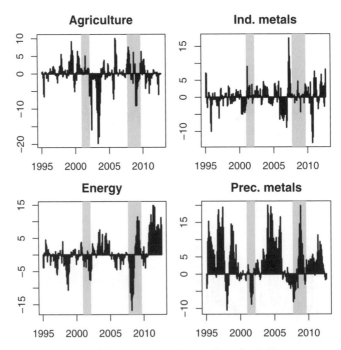

Figure 2.15   Net spillovers to the US 10-year rate from commodity indices

Table 2.13 Directional spillovers estimated from the asset allocation dataset

	GSCI Agri.	GSCI Energy	GSCI Ind. Metals	GSCI Prec. Metals	Euro	Can. Dollar	Jap. Yen	Austr. Dollar	N.Z. Dollar	Brit. Pound	Swiss Franc	Swedish Krona	Norwegian Krone	S. African Rand	Mexican Peso	Dollar TW	Spillover Received
GSCI Agri.	98.31	0.07	0.09	0.56	0.12	0.1	0.01	0.03	0.01	0.01	0	0.02	0.01	0.32	0.05	0.3	1.69
GSCI Energy	0.58	97.21	0	0.53	0.08	0.02	0.02	0.98	0.03	0.33	0.01	0.06	0.1	0.01	0.01	0.02	2.79
GSCI Ind. Metals	1.22	0.61	96.1	0.86	0.46	0.04	0.05	0.04	0.03	0.21	0.02	0.04	0.08	0.01	0.16	0.09	3.9
GSCI Prec. Metals	0.37	1.74	1.15	95.34	0.02	0.22	0.04	0.34	0.08	0.21	0.09	0.18	0.14	0.01	0.01	0.06	4.66
Euro	0.23	1.55	0.25	4.67	87.61	0.31	0.08	0.59	0.01	0.98	1.28	0.13	0.29	0.13	0.35	1.53	12.39
Canadian Dollar	0.97	1.19	0.86	1.63	0.46	91.84	0.1	0.22	0.06	0.09	0.01	1.28	0.51	0.04	0.39	0.34	8.15
Jap. Yen	0.21	0.79	0.26	2.43	3.22	0.53	90.9	0.22	0.17	0.56	0.28	0.01	0.01	0.05	0.07	0.29	9.1
Austr. Dollar	0.93	1.76	1.15	3.31	5.36	3.29	3.08	79.39	0.08	0.39	0.08	0.31	0.06	0.04	0.09	0.69	20.61
N.Z. Dollar	0.66	1.52	1.88	2.88	5.05	2.05	1.98	22.26	61.16	0.07	0.02	0.08	0.16	0.13	0	0.1	38.84
Brit. Pound	0.22	0.98	0.4	2.72	16.59	0.27	0.96	2.82	0.44	72.93	0.27	0.12	0.19	0	0.06	1.03	27.07
Swiss Franc	0.15	0.79	0.15	4.39	27.85	0.07	1.9	0.04	0.02	1.95	62.16	0.05	0.01	0.04	0.09	0.34	37.84
Swedish Krona	0.5	1.18	0.62	3.07	25.13	1.64	0.7	2.09	0.07	1.17	4.96	57.88	0.01	0.07	0.67	0.23	42.12
Norwegian Krone	0.86	1.63	0.25	5.11	22.07	1.35	1.55	1.19	0.14	3.46	9.72	6.77	45.24	0.02	0.23	0.41	54.76
S. African Rand	0.27	1.04	0.71	1.23	2.03	1.5	1.41	2.52	0.63	0.01	0.08	0.04	0.06	88.14	0.33	0.01	11.86
Mexican Peso	0.15	0.14	1.01	0.98	0.14	1.85	0.33	1.18	0.33	0.1	0.29	0.01	0.07	0.31	93.1	0.01	6.9
Dollar TW	0.16	1.54	0.17	4.34	39.29	1.11	3.5	0.29	0.06	3.31	10.03	1.96	2.13	0.07	0.27	31.76	68.24
Spillover Given	7.07	14.53	8.52	28.88	62.79	13.52	14.72	30.49	3.4	14.99	30.4	16.04	7.8	1.41	2.9	14.65	21.93
Net Spillovers	5.37	11.74	4.62	24.23	50.4	5.37	5.62	9.88	-35.45	-12.08	-7.44	-26.07	-46.95	-10.45	-4	-53.59	0

2.13 contains the results. First, the total overall spillover is equal to 21.93: we find 22% of volatility spillovers between currencies and commodities. However, without a more detailed analysis, it is difficult to state whether these spillovers come from cross-currency relationships, or from the impact of commodities on currencies. By focusing on the net contributions, we find that the four GSCI indices have a net contribution to the volatility spillovers of our sample. The strongest net contribution comes from precious metals, and energy ranks second. Moving to the currencies, only 4 out of the 12 currencies considered here have a positive net spillover contribution. The rest of them are negative, suggesting that most of the currencies considered here are net receivers. Digging into the table, it appears that agricultural commodities are not contributing much to the currencies in our sample. Consistent with the previous results, agricultural products have the weakest relation to other assets. Precious metals have a positive contribution to all currencies. Their biggest contribution is to the Euro, consistent with the idea that surges in risk aversion have jointly affected the Euro and precious metals over a significant part of our sample from 2008 onwards. What is usually called a commodity currency would be a currency driven by the fluctuations of cyclical commodities. Having discarded agriculture as a spillover contributor to currencies, all that remains is energy and industrial metals. Energy has a more pronounced contribution to the Euro, Canadian Dollar, Australian and New Zealand Dollars, Swedish Krona, Norwegian Krone and Mexican Peso. For all those cases, the net spillovers obtained are higher than 1. When considering the contributions of industrial metals, we find a net spillover higher than 1 in only three cases: the Australian and New Zealand Dollars and the Mexican Peso. The volatility spillovers of industrial metals are hence affecting the evolution of those three currencies. These findings are therefore consistent with the idea that these currencies are commodity currencies, as commodities – especially energy and industrial metals – have an impact over the evolution of their value.

Hence, both the cross-sectional analysis and the dynamic analysis point to a configuration of a weaker relation between commodities and standard assets as of 2012. Now, weaker – as we discussed already – does not mean non-existent. We have uncovered a certain time variation in these relations with clearly different patterns during economic crises. This leads us to our next topic: the analysis of the dependency between economic cycles and commodities.

Overall, this spillover analysis has helped us to uncover different stylized facts over the past 15 years. First, commodities exhibit weaker volatility spillovers than other asset classes. These have, however, been increasing over the period. Agricultural commodities are the commodities exhibiting the lowest spillovers, whereas precious metals and energy are the biggest net contributors. A diversified portfolio, including commodities – and especially agricultural products – helps decrease the total spillover index. This stylized fact has, however, been less and less valid over the years. Finally, some currencies are more responsive than others to commodity volatility spillovers: Nordic and Oceanic currencies are among the currencies with the highest sensitivity.

REFERENCES

Acharya, VV., Lochstoer, LA., Ramadorai, T. 2011. Limits to Arbitrage and Hedging: Evidence from Commodity Markets. *NBER Working Paper* #16875, National Bureau of Economic Research, Boston, Massachusetts, USA

Adrian, T., Etula, E., Muir, T. 2010. Financial Intermediaries and the Crosssection of Asset Returns. *Technical Report* #422, Federal Reserve Bank of New York Staff Report, USA

Alessi, L., Barigozzi, M., Capasso, M. 2010. Improved Penalization for Determining the Number of Factors in Approximate Factor Models. *Statistics and Probability Letters* 80(23–24):1806–1813

Amano, RA., van Norden, S. 1998. Oil Prices and the Rise and Fall of the US Real Exchange Rate. *Journal of International Money and Finance* 17(2):299–316

Amano, RA. van Norden, S. 1998. Exchange Rates and Oil Prices. *Review of International Economics* 6(4):683–694

Ang, A., Chen, J., 2002. Asymmetric Correlations of Equity Portfolios. *Journal of Financial Economics* 63:443–494

Anzuini, A., Lombardi, MJ., Pagano, P. 2010. The Impact of Monetary Policy Shocks on Commodity Prices. *Working Paper Series* #1232, European Central Bank, Germany.

Baffes, J. 2007. Oil Spills on Other Commodities. *Resources Policy* 32(3):126–134

Bai, J., Ng, S. 2002. Determining the Number of Factors in Approximate Factor Models. *Econometrica* 70(1):191–221

Bai, J., Ng, S. 2008. Large Dimensional Factor Analysis. *Foundations and Trends in Econometrics* 3(2):89–163

Balvers, RJ., Huang, D. 2009. Money and the C-CAPM. *Journal of Financial and Quantitative Analysis* 44(2):337–368

Barsky, RB., Kilian, L. 2004. Oil and the Macroeconomy since the 1970s. *Journal of Economic Perspectives* 18(4):115–134

Basu, D., Miffre, J. 2012. Capturing the Risk Premium of Commodity Futures: The Role of Hedging Pressure. *Technical report*, EDHEC Business School, Lille, France.

Bessembinder, H., Chan, K. 1992. Time-Varying Risk Premia and Forecastable Returns in Futures Markets. *Journal of Financial Economics* 32(2):169–193

Bichetti, D., Maystre, N. 2012. The Synchronized and Long-Lasting Structural Change on Commodity Markets: Evidence from High Frequency Data. *Munich Personal RePEc Archive Paper* #37486, Germany.

Bodie, Z., Rosansky, V. 1980. Diversification Returns And Asset Contributions. *Financial Analysts Journal* 48(3):26–32

Boon, LN., Ielpo, F. 2012. Determining the Maximum Number of Uncorrelated Strategies in a Global Portfolio. *SSRN Working Paper*, Social Science Research Network, USA

Booth, GG., Ciner, C. 1997. International Transmission of Information in Corn Futures Markets. *Journal of Multinational Financial Management* 7(3):175–187

Booth, GG., Brockman, P., Tse, Y. 1998. The Relationship between US and Canadian Wheat Futures. *Applied Financial Economics* 8(1):73–80

Breeden, DT. 1980. Consumption Risk in Futures Markets. *Journal of Finance* 35(2):503–520

Briere, M., Chapelle, A., Szafarz, A. 2012. No Contagion, Only Globalization and Flight to Quality. *Journal of International Money and Finance* 31(6):1729–1744

Buyukshahin, B., Haigh, M., Robe, M. 2010. Commodities and Equities: Ever A 'Market of One'? *Journal of Alternative Investments* 12(3):76–95

Cayen, JP., Coletti, D., Lalonde, R., Maier, P. 2010. What Drives Exchange Rates? New Evidence from a Panel of U.S. Dollar Bilateral Exchange Rates. *Working Paper* #10–5, Bank of Canada, Canada

Chen, YC., Rogoff, K. 2003. Commodity currencies. *Journal of International Economics* 60(1):133–160

Chen, YC., Rogoff, K., Rossi, B. 2010. Can Exchange Rates Forecast Commodity Prices? *Quarterly Journal of Economics* 125(3):1145–1194

Chng, MT. 2009. Economic Linkages across Commodity Futures: Hedging and Trading Implications. *Journal of Banking and Finance* 33:958–970

Chong, J., Miffre, J. 2010. Conditional Correlation and Volatility in Commodity Futures and Traditional Asset Markets. *Journal of Alternative Investment* 12:61–75

Ciner, C. 2001. On the Long Run Relationship between Gold and Silver Prices: a Note. *Global Finance Journal* 12(2):299–303

Connor, G., Korajczyk, RA. 1993. A Test for the Number of Factors in an Approximate Factor Model. *Journal of Finance* 48(4):1263–1291

da Fonseca, J., Gottschalk, K. 2012. The Co-movement of Credit Default Swap Spreads, Stock Market Returns and Volatilities: Evidence from Asia-Pacific Markets. *Working Paper AUT*, Australia.

Daskalaki, C., Skiadopoulos, G. 2011. Should Investors Include Commodities in their Portfolios After All? *Journal of Banking and Finance* 35(10):2606–2626

Daskalaki, C., Kostakis, A., Skiadopoulos, G. 2012. Are There Common Factors in Commodity Futures Returns? *SSRN Working Paper* #2056186, Social Science Research Network, USA

Delatte, AL., Lopez, C. 2012. Commodity and Equity Markets: Some Stylized Facts from a Copula Approach. *Working Paper Rouen Business School*, Rouen, France

de Roon, F., Nijman, T., Veld, C. 2000. Hedging Pressure Effects in Futures Markets. *Working Paper*, Tilburg University, The Netherlands.

de Roon, F., Szymanowska, M. 2010. The Cross-Section of Commodity Futures Returns. *SSRN Working Paper* #891073, Social Science Research Network, USA

Diebold, FX., Yilmaz, K. 2012. Better to Give than to Receive: Forecast-Based Measurement of Volatility Spillovers. *International Journal of Forecasting* 28(1):57–66

Dusak, K. 1973. Futures Trading and Investor Returns: An Investigation of Commodity Market Risk Premiums. *Journal of Political Economy* 81(6):1387–1406

Embrechts, P., McNeil, A., Straumann, D. 2002. Correlation and Dependence in Risk Management: Properties and Pitfalls. In: Dempstor, MAH. (Ed.), *Risk Management: Value at Risk and Beyond*, pages 176–223. Cambridge University Press, Cambridge, UK

Engle, R. 2002. Dynamic Conditional Correlation: A Simple Class of Multivariate Generalized Autoregressive Conditional Heteroskedasticity Models. *Journal of Business and Economic Statistics* 20(3):339–350

Erb, CB., Campbell, RH. 2006. The Strategic and Tactical Value of Commodity Futures. *Financial Analysts Journal* 62(2):69–97

Escribano, A., Granger, C. 1998. Investigating the Relationship between Gold and Silver Prices. *Journal of Forecasting* 17(2):81–107

Fama, EF., French, KR. 1993. Common Risk Factors in the Returns on Stocks and Bonds. *Journal of Financial Economics* 33(1):3–56

Ferraro, D., Rogoff, K., Rossi, B. 2011. *Can Oil Prices Forecast Exchange Rates?* Working Paper #11–05, Duke University, Department of Economics, USA

Forbes, K., Rigobon, R. 2002. No Contagion, only Interdependence: Measuring Stock Market Co-Movements. *Journal of Finance* 57:2223–2261

Frankel, JA. 2006. The Effect of Monetary Policy on Real Commodity Prices. *NBER Working Paper* #12713, National Bureau of Economic Research, Boston, Massachusetts, USA.

Fung, HG., Leung, WK., Xu, XE. 2003. Information Flows between the US and China Commodity Futures Trading. *Review of Quantitative Finance and Accounting* 21(3):267–285

Ge, Y., Wang, HH., Ahn, SK. 2008. Implication of Cotton Price Behavior on Market Integration. *Proceedings of the NCCC-134 Conference on Applied Commodity Price Analysis, Forecasting, and Market Risk Management*, St. Louis, USA.

Gorton, GB., Rouwenhorst, KG. 2005. Facts and Fantasies about Commodity Futures. *Financial Analysts Journal* 62(2):47–68

Gorton, GB., Hayashi, F., Rouwenhorst, KG. 2012. The Fundamentals of Commodity Futures Returns. *Yale ICF Working Paper* #07–08, Yale ICF, Yale, USA.

Hirshleifer, D. 1988. Residual Risk, Trading Costs, and Commodity Futures Risk Premia. *Review of Financial Studies* 1(2):173–193

Hirshleifer, D. 1989. Determinants of Hedging and Risk Premia in Commodity Futures Markets. *Journal of Financial and Quantitative Analysis* 24(3):313–331

Holder, ME., Pace, RD., Tomas III, MJ. 2002. Complements or Substitutes? Equivalent Futures Contract Markets – The Case of Corn and Soybean Futures on US and Japanese Exchanges. *Journal of Futures Markets* 22(4):355–370

Hong, H., Yogo, M. 2011. What Does Futures Market Interest Tell us About the Macroeconomy and Asset Prices? *NBER Working Paper* #16712, National Bureau of Economic Research, Boston, Massachusetts, USA.

Hua, R., Chen, B. 2007. International Linkages of the Chinese Futures Markets. *Applied Financial Economics* 17(6):1275–1287

Ielpo, F. 2012. Equity, Credit and the Business Cycle. *Applied Financial Economics* 22(12):939–954

Issa, R., Lafrance, R. 2008. The Turning Black Tide: Energy Prices and the Canadian Dollar. *Canadian Journal of Economics* 41(3):737–759

Jagannathan, R. 1985. An Investigation of Commodity Futures Prices Using the Consumption-based Intertemporal Capital Asset Pricing Model. *Journal of Finance* 40(1):175–191

Jondeau, E., Rockinger, M. 2006. The Copula-GARCH Model of Conditional Dependencies: An International Stock Market Application. *Journal of International Money and Finance* 25: 827–853

Kaltalioglu, M., Soytas, U. 2011. Volatility Spillover from Oil Food and Agricultural Raw Material Markets. *Modern Economy* 2:71–76

Kao, CW., Wan, JY. 2009. Information Transmission and Market Interactions across the Atlantic – An Empirical Study on the Natural Gas Market. *Energy Economics* 31(1):152–161

Karolyi, GA., Stulz, RM. 1996. Why Do Markets Move Together? An Investigation of U.S. – Japan Stock Return Comovements. *Journal of Finance* 51(3):951–986

Kat, HM., Oomen, RCA. 2007a. What Every Investor Should Know About Commodities, Part I: Univariate Return Analysis. *Journal of Investment Management* 5(1):1–25

Kat, HM., Oomen, RCA. 2007b. What Every Investor Should Know About Commodities, Part II: Multivariate Return Analysis. *Journal of Investment Management* 5(3):1–25

Khalifa, A., Hammoudeh, S., Otranto, E., Ramchander, S. 2012. Volatility Transmission across Currency, Commodity and Equity Markets under Multichain Regime Switching: Implications for Hedging and Portfolio Allocation. *Working Paper* #2012/14, Center for North South Economic Research, USA.

Kocenda, E., Bubak, V., Zikes, F. 2011. Volatility Transmission in Emerging European Foreign Exchange Markets. *Journal of Banking and Finance* 35(11):2829–2841

Koop, G., Pesaran, MH., Potter, SM. 1996. Impulse Response Analysis in Non-Linear Multivariate Models. *Journal of Econometrics* 62:901–933

Kumar, B., Pandey, A. 2011. International Linkages of the Indian Commodity Futures Markets. *Modern Economy* 2(3):213–227

Lin, SX., Tamvakis, MM. 2001. Spillover Effects in Energy Futures Markets. *Energy Economics* 23(1):43–56

Litterman, R., Scheinkman, J. 1991. Common Factors Affecting Bond Returns. *The Journal of Fixed Income* 1:54–61

Longin, F., Solnik, B. 2001. Extreme Correlation of International Equity Markets. *Journal of Finance* 56:649–676

Low, AHW., Muthuswamy, J., Wcbb, RI. 1999. Arbitrage, Cointegration, and the Joint Dynamics of Prices across Commodity Futures Auctions. *Journal of Futures Markets* 19(7):799–815

Lütkepohl, H. 2005. *New Introduction to Multiple Time Series Analysis.* Springer, UK

Onatski, A. 2009. Testing Hypotheses About the Number of Factors in Large Factor Models. *Econometrica* 77(5):1447–1479

Patton, AJ. 2006. Modelling Asymmetric Exchange Rate Dependence. *International Economic Review* 47(2):527–556

Reboredo, JC. 2011. How Do Crude Oil Prices Co-Move? *Energy Economics* 33:948–955

Rodriguez, JC. 2007. Measuring Financial Contagion: a Copula Approach. *Journal of Empirical Finance* 14:401–423

Schwert, GW. 1988. Tests for Unit Roots: A Monte Carlo Investigation. *NBER Technical Working Papers* #0073, National Bureau of Economic Research, Boston, Massachusetts, USA

Silvennoinen, A., Thorp, S. 2010. Financialization, Crisis and Commodity Correlation Dynamics. *Research Paper Series* #267, Quantitative Finance Research Center, University of Technology, Sydney, Australia

Stoll, HR. 1979. Commodity Futures and Spot Price Determination and Hedging in Capital Market Equilibrium. *Journal of Financial and Quantitative Analysis* 14(4):873–894

Tang, K., Xiong, W. 2010. Index Investment and Financialization of Commodities. *NBER Working Paper* #16385, National Bureau of Economic Research, USA.

Working, H. 1949. The theory of price of storage. *American Economic Review* 39(6):1254–1262

Xu, XE., Fung, HG. 2005. Cross-Market Linkages between US and Japanese Precious Metals Futures Trading. *International Finance Markets, Institution and Money* 15(2):107–124

Yilmaz, K. 2010. Return and Volatility Spillovers among the East Asian Equity Markets. *Journal of Asian Economics* 21(3):304–313

Part II
Commodities and the Business Cycle

From 2008 to 2011, commodity markets experienced growing attention from the banking industry for various reasons. First, the oil bubble that collapsed with the start of the financial crisis in September 2008 drew the attention of market participants to the energy sector. After this episode, the price of gold started to surge and reached all-time highs. The economic recovery observed from February 2009 until January 2010 – that has been fueled by the joint stimulation of various central banks around the world – ended up in a strong increase in agricultural prices, partly explaining the restrictive monetary policy imposed by the Public Bank of China in the subsequent months. Finally, the collapse of the gold bubble at the end of 2011 triggered various analyses of the relationship between commodity prices and the cyclical ups and downs of worldwide economic activity. If these recent events suggest that commodity markets are strongly related to the business cycle, this evidence nevertheless goes against the widespread intuition that commodity markets are a strong source of diversification in a standard cash-bond-equity portfolio.

Table II.1 presents the correlations between a subset of commodity returns and three classical investment vehicles for asset allocation funds: the S&P 500, the Russell 3000, and the returns on a US government bond index. These computations are performed for two different samples: while the long-term correlations are represented in the higher triangular matrix from January 1987 to December 2010, the short-term correlations are given in the lower triangular matrix from January 2008 to December 2010 as well. This table yields the following conclusions:

1. The correlation between commodities and more traditional assets appears limited from a long-term perspective: for example, the correlation between the WTI and the S&P 500 is around 3% on average. The correlation between gold and bonds can be rounded to 0%. This probably explains why the asset allocation industry (namely hedge funds, private wealth managers and asset managers) found a growing interest in the understanding of such an investment vehicle.
2. The correlations within commodities are rather low in the long run as well. For example, coffee and sugar are only related by a correlation coefficient of 8%. The largest correlation in this table can be found between WTI and gold – 22% – which is much lower than the highest correlation between the S&P 500 and the Russell 3000 indices (i.e. 85%).
3. However, in the short term, it appears that these correlations have changed dramatically. Whereas in the long term the correlation between WTI and the Russell 3000 index is close to 5%, from 2008 to 2010 this correlation reached 28% – and similar comments can be made for the S&P 500 index. Within commodities, instead of the 8% long-term correlation between sugar and WTI, we obtain a correlation coefficient close to 35%.

What happened to the attractive 'uncorrelation' of commodity markets with other asset classes? One possible answer is to assume some sort of a stronger integration of commodities into global financial markets: the growing inclusion of commodity futures in strategies built by hedge funds (or in the balanced mandates managed by asset managers) may have impacted the behavior of these futures with respect to other markets. Hence, the following research

Table II.1   Historical correlations between commodities: 1987–2010 (higher triangular matrix) and 2008–2010 (lower triangular matrix)

	WTI	Gold	Sugar	Coffee	Cotton	S&P500	Russell 3000	US Bonds
WTI		22%	8%	6%	9%	3%	5%	−9%
Gold	33%		9%	8%	10%	−7%	−3%	0%
Sugar	35%	24.6%		8%	7%	3%	4%	−2%
Coffee	40%	24.2%	40%		6%	5%	7%	−6%
Cotton	35%	20.6%	32%	42%		9%	9%	−6%
S&P 500	34%	−0.4%	18%	26%	27%		85%	−5%
Russell 3000	28%	−1.0%	16%	25%	26%	94%		−10%
Govt bond US	−23%	4.4%	−5%	−12%	−12%	−28%	−27%	

questions arise: how can we measure this integration phenomenon? Is it possible to assess how integrated commodity markets have become with equities and bonds? To delve more deeply into these questions, we will consider whether it is possible to link commodity markets to the macroeconomy (as the link between equity markets and the macroeconomy has been clearly documented). That is why we will also focus our research on the relationship between the global macroeconomic environment and commodity markets (e.g., agricultural, metals and energy products).

PLAN OF PART II

Part II aims at gathering different pieces of evidence to contribute to a better understanding of these key questions.

First, if an increasing integration between commodity and more traditional asset markets has been taking place over the past decade, this must be measurable by the reaction of these markets to economic news. That is why we develop a commodity-by-commodity analysis of the impact of news. We apply this methodology to all kinds of commodities (agricultural and energy products, precious and industrial metals) in Chapter 3.

Second, we study the relationship between the business cycle in various economic zones and the performance of commodities. Namely, we investigate whether commodity markets are related to a given economic zone or to the worldwide business cycle – mainly through the global demand for raw materials and energy. To do so, we consider how commodity prices evolve through the business cycle based on the class of Markov regime-switching models. We apply this methodology for the USA, the Eurozone and China in Chapter 4.

Next, we investigate how commodity markets perform depending on the type of economic regime of the worldwide economy – as proxied by US data. We question the relevance of a strong monitoring of the business cycle when investing in commodities, and conclude that a top-down macroeconomic analysis can create substantial value for commodity investors.

3

The Reaction of Commodity Markets to Economic News

This chapter investigates what kind of economic news impacts commodity prices, depending on the underlying state of the economy (e.g. expansion or recession). We also want to identify whether the amount of news impacting commodity markets has likely increased over the recent period.

The investigation of the reaction of commodity markets to economic news is based on the intuition that liquid financial markets integrate new information efficiently. For example, suppose that the WTI price is strongly based on the level of US GDP growth. If, on the release of the 2008 third quarter growth, the actual published figure is 2% below the market consensus, then the WTI price is very likely to plunge so as to reflect this new information.

3.1 MEASURING THE IMPACT OF PRICE DISCOVERY ON ASSET PRICES

One way to determine what is priced on a given market is to measure the impact of news on asset prices. Note $R_{i,t}$ the actual value for the release figure i at time t, and $F_{i,t}$ the market consensus for this figure.[1] The 'surprise' component in this economic news $S_{i,t}$ is given by:

$$S_{i,t} = R_{i,t} - F_{i,t}. \tag{3.1}$$

Given that various items of news may have different scales, it is very common to scale $S_{i,t}$ by its full sample standard deviation. By scaling the surprises by σ_i, we make the various announcements comparable and it will thus be possible to rank the main movers on commodity markets. Denote $s_{i,t}$ as the scaled variable:

$$s_{i,t} = \frac{R_{i,t} - F_{i,t}}{\sigma_i}. \tag{3.2}$$

For a given financial asset, the return on investment on day t is denoted r_t. This sampling frequency allows us to focus on the impact of surprises on the fundamental value of the asset studied.[2] Formally, the news analysis is performed by running the following sets of regressions:

$$r_t = \phi_0 + \phi_1 r_{t-1} + \sum_{i=1}^{n} \mathbb{1}_i \beta_i \times s_{i,t} + \sigma_t \epsilon_t \tag{3.3}$$

$$\log \sigma_t^2 = \omega + \alpha \epsilon_{t-1} + \theta |\epsilon_{t-1}| + \log \sigma_{t-1}^2 \tag{3.4}$$

---

[1] The series $F_{i,t}$ is taken from the Bloomberg survey dataset. It represents the median value of a survey of economists. Given that Bloomberg is one of the most widespread information services used by market participants, practitioners refer to such a measure as a market consensus or forecast.

[2] Although an approach based on a higher frequency can also be interesting to commodity investors, a price variation that would not last at least one day can hardly be regarded as a fundamental change in the value of the investigated asset.

with $\mathbb{1}_i$ a dummy variable equal to 1 whenever the news i is released at time t, and 0 otherwise. n is the total number of items of news. The analysis focuses mainly on the sensitivity of r_t to $s_{i,t}$; that is to say β_i. Note that:

- Whenever β_i is statistically different from 0, it seems reasonable to assume that this asset price incorporates the economic information associated with the surprise component $s_{i,t}$.
- The sign of β_i is essential to the market interpretation of the data.
- Equations (3.3)–(3.4) incorporate two types of robustness check: an autoregressive component through $\phi_0 + \phi_1 r_{t-1}$, and a time-varying volatility component through the dynamics of the Exponential GARCH (EGARCH) model.

Overall, this methodology corresponds to standard practice in order to gauge the impact of news on financial returns. We propose to apply it to the analysis of commodity markets in this chapter.

3.2   KEY INSIGHTS FROM THE ACADEMIC LITERATURE

In this section, we briefly review the main insights from previous academic literature, as the conclusions drawn from it cast some interesting light on the market reaction to economic news. From this analysis, we can understand how sensitive commodity markets are to unexpected news.

- In a seminal article, Frankel and Hardouvelis (1985) investigate the empirical relationship between commodities and economic news during 1980–1982. They find that inflation surprises are negatively interpreted on commodity markets, consistent with the negative reaction of these markets to the announcement of a tighter monetary policy.
- By using a dataset covering the period 1980–1984, Barnhart (1989) reveals that few economic announcements have a statistically significant impact on commodity markets. The gold price reacts negatively to M1 growth surprises, and positively to the Fed's increase of its target rate (consistent with its role as a hedge against inflation).
- Being the first to use a dataset covering a financial crisis, namely the 1985–1989 period, Ghura (1990) identifies that gold responds positively to unemployment surprises, but it loses its sensitivity to inflation or economic activity during that specific period of time.
- With a more recent dataset than previous studies (1992–1995), Christie-David *et al.* (2000) show that gold and silver prices have a limited number of market movers. They find that GDP, inflation and capacity utilization rates lead to higher precious metals prices.
- By focusing on the gold price during 1994–1997, Cai *et al.* (2001) establish that unemployment, GDP and inflation news have a statistically significant impact on gold prices. They conclude that fewer market movers impact commodities compared to T-bonds or currencies.
- Hess *et al.* (2008) propose a recent contribution concerning the impact of news on commodity markets. Based on a dataset from 1985 to 2005 for two commodity indices (CRB and GSCI), the authors are able to pinpoint that the impact of news actually depends on the phase of the business cycle. Periods of recession are characterized by a strong relationship between economic news and the returns of the two commodity indices considered. Conversely, during periods of expansion, commodity markets exhibit a weak link – if any – with economic news.
- With a similar dataset (1983–2008) and by focusing on the WTI and gasoline prices, Kilian and Vega (2011) did not find any statistically significant market mover.

- Finally, Roache and Rossi (2009) show evidence that the gold price reacts positively to inflation news, and negatively to unemployment news and the publication of leading surveys. Their study also reveals that commodity prices are increasingly reacting to macroeconomic news, as they are becoming more and more integrated in the sphere of financial markets.

From this survey of academic literature, the reader will gain the following two insights:

1. In the long run, commodity returns are expected to exhibit a weak relationship to economic information. This is consistent with the view that commodity futures are not standard financial assets, in the sense that their valuation cannot be performed by discounting future streams of payment (as would be the case for equites and bonds).
2. By using datasets that include a financial crisis, or by modeling explicitly the business cycle, we are able to find a strong reaction of various commodities to economic news.

In this chapter, we will test empirically these two working hypotheses with a full sample dataset of news, and with a sub-sample dataset composed of more recent observations.

3.3 DATABASE OF NEWS

In this section, we present the Bloomberg dataset of 16 series of economic surprises stemming from three geographical zones: the USA, the EMU and China. For the news associated with Europe and the USA, the dataset starts in 1999 and ends in 2011. For the news associated with China, the dataset starts in 2007 and ends in 2011.

The news items presented here have been selected based on two reasons. First, they are listed in the usual economic news provided by financial information providers such as Bloomberg or Reuters. Second, the academic empirical literature has listed the main 'market movers', i.e. news items which affect the financial markets (Balduzzi *et al.* (2001), Guegan and Ielpo (2009), Roache and Rossi (2009)). Some explanations for each type of news item are given below:

- *Non Farm Payroll*: number of jobs added or lost in the US economy over the last month, not including jobs relating to the farming industry. It includes goods-producing, construction and manufacturing companies.
- *ISM*: survey from the Institute for Supply Management based on comments from purchasing managers in the manufacturing sector. It provides the earliest clues of how the US economy has fared during the previous four weeks.
- *Jobless Claims*: the weekly number of new jobless applications in the US.
- *US CPI MoM*: Consumer Price Index Month on Month.
- *US Retail Sales*: Retail and Food Services Sales in million US Dollars.
- *Fed Target Rate*: interest rate at which depository institutions actively trade balances held at the Federal Reserve.
- *US GDP*: US Gross Domestic Product.
- *ZEW Eco. Sent.*: survey from the Mannheim Centre for European Economic Research (ZEW). Expectations from 350 financial experts for the Euro-zone, Japan, Great Britain and the USA.
- *IFO Expectations*: survey from the Munich Society for the Promotion of Economic Research (IFO). Monthly survey responses from 7,000 firms in manufacturing, construction, wholesaling and retailing. Firms are asked to give their assessments of the current business situation and their expectations for the next six months.

Table 3.1   Database of economic news from Bloomberg

	Type of Data	Geographical Zone	Correlation with US GDP
Non Farm Payroll	Employment	USA	77%
ISM	Economic survey	USA	84%
Jobless Claims	Employment	USA	−68%
US CPI MoM	Inflation	USA	22%
US Retail Sales	Economic activity	USA	27%
Fed Target Rate	Central bank rate	USA	3%
US GDP	Economic activity	USA	100%
ZEW Eco. Sent.	Economic survey	Germany	20%
IFO Expectations	Economic survey	Germany	75%
EMU CPI	Inflation	EMU	26%
EMU GDP	Economic activity	EMU	80%
FR Bus. Conf.	Economic survey	France	70%
ECB Ref. Rate	Central bank rate	EMU	−13%
China CPI YoY	Inflation	China	45%
China Ind. Prod.	Economic activity	China	73%
China PMI	Economic survey	China	41%

Note: Correlation with US GDP stands for the correlation between each time series (e.g., not the surprise component) and the quarterly variation of real GDP.

- *EMU CPI*: Euro Area Consumer Price Index from Eurostat.
- *EMU GDP*: Euro Area Gross Domestic Product from Eurostat.
- *FR Bus. Conf.*: France Business Confidence Index from INSEE.
- *ECB Ref. Rate*: minimum refinancing rate from the European Central Bank.
- *China CPI YoY*: China Consumer Price Index Year on Year
- *China Ind. Prod.*: China Industrial Production Index.
- *China PMI*: China Purchasing Managers' Index.

The news items cover different aspects of the business cycle: real activity with macroe-conomic data (such as industrial production) or surveys (such as the ISM from the Institute for Supply Management or the German IFO from the Munich Society for the Promotion of Economic Research), inflation dynamics with the Consumer Price Index (CPI), monetary variables with the Fed's target rate and the ECB's minimum refinancing rate.[3]

A detailed list of these news items is provided in Table 3.1, along with the correlation between the US GDP and each of these.

Except for the weekly jobless claims – i.e. the weekly number of new jobless applications in the US – and the ECB decision rate, the majority of economic news is found to have a positive correlation with the US business cycle (as measured by GDP growth).

The weakest positive correlation is obtained for the German ZEW from the Mannheim Centre for European Economic Research: this survey gathers the opinion of market partici-pants regarding the current state of the German economy. Another German survey – the IFO

---

[3] Note that the Chinese decision rate is not modified through a pre-scheduled decision meeting, as in the case of the Fed and the ECB. For this reason – and due also to the lack of consistency that it would introduce in the analysis – we have discarded the announcements by the Public Bank of China (PBOC).

survey – is computed in a very different way, by collecting the opinion of purchasing managers. In this respect, the IFO is closer in spirit to the famous US ISM survey, which may explain why we find a strong correlation with the US GDP in the latter case.

3.4 AN EXAMPLE: S&P 500, 10Y AND USD

Before dealing with the impact of news on commodity markets, we start first with a review of the impact of news on standard assets: the S&P 500 index, the US 10-year bond rate, and the trade-weighted value of the US Dollar. This preliminary step can be seen as a benchmark of comparison with standard assets. Table 3.2 contains the estimation analysis obtained with these three assets.

Out of the seven US economic indicators, the 10-year US bond rate responds to six of them, i.e. to all figures except the GDP itself. The US Dollar index also responds positively to the ISM, the Non Farm Payrolls and the Fed decision rate. The S&P 500 responds positively to the retail sales, and negatively to the Fed action. When strictly focusing on the US economy, the equity index is clearly less sensitive to economic indicators than the 10-year bond rate and the US Dollar. Besides, equity markets are also prone to react to economic news coming from other countries: the S&P 500 reacts positively to the ECB decision rate, and negatively to European news such as the ZEW survey (unlike the US Dollar which reacts negatively to good news coming from the ZEW survey). Finally, the US Dollar is found to react negatively to a positive surprise in the French Business Confidence index, and positively to an unexpected increase in the Chinese Consumer Price Index (CPI).

Next, we investigate in more detail the behavior of commodity indices.

Table 3.2 Impact of news on the S&P 500 index, the US 10-year rate, and the trade-weighted value of the US Dollar

	S&P 500	10Y US	US Dollar
Intercept	−7.15** (−4.68)	−6.35** (−4.21)	−1.25 (−0.82)
AR	0.02 (1.23)	−0.02 (−1.05)	0 (0.07)
Non Farm Payroll	−0.09 (−0.99)	**0.75** (6.31)**	**0.19** (5.07)**
ISM	0.1 (1.01)	**0.55** (4.62)**	**0.13** (3.29)**
Jobless Claims	−0.03 (−0.34)	**−0.33** (−2.82)**	−0.04 (−1.04)
US CPI MoM	−0.11 (−1.19)	**0.4** (3.3)**	0.04 (0.91)
US Retail Sales	**0.29** (2.59)**	**0.7** (4.92)**	0.07 (1.42)
Fed Target Rate	**−0.25* (−1.86)**	**0.4** (2.29)**	**0.19** (3.4)**
US GDP	0.06 (0.33)	−0.21 (−0.96)	−0.02 (−0.26)
ZEW Economic Sentiment	**−0.29** (−2.46)**	−0.04 (−0.24)	**0.08* (1.76)**
IFO Expectations	−0.03 (−0.22)	0.16 (0.96)	−0.04 (−0.85)
EMU CPI Flash Estimate	−0.11 (−0.9)	0 (0.01)	0.03 (0.73)
EMU GDP	0.13 (0.71)	−0.08 (−0.32)	0.03 (0.41)
France Business Confidence	0.05 (0.45)	0.21 (1.47)	**−0.09* (−1.84)**
ECB Refinancing Rate	**0.37** (3.32)**	−0.02 (−0.16)	0.03 (0.63)
China CPI YoY	0.02 (0.14)	−0.05 (−0.33)	**0.08* (1.7)**
China Industrial Production	−0.01 (−0.11)	0.03 (0.19)	−0.02 (−0.51)
China PMI	0.08 (0.51)	0.05 (0.27)	0.02 (0.4)

Note: T-stats are between brackets. Bold figures indicate statistically significant figures at a 10% risk level.

3.5 COMMODITY INDICES

Table 3.3 reports the long-term reaction of various Goldman Sachs Commodity Indices (GSCI) to economic news. The GSCI is a broadly diversified index designed for investors seeking to store value in commodity markets.

Two main conclusions can be drawn from this table:

1. The nature of the reaction of commodity markets to economic news is closer to that observed for equity or foreign exchange markets.
2. Commodity markets react to very different news items compared to these markets.

Some illustrations include the GSCI Agricultural sub-index reacting to an increase in the Fed target rate, or the GSCI Industrial Metals reacting to the EMU GDP. We may also remark that the US ISM impacts only the GSCI Industrial Metals sub-index.

In the long run, the various GSCI sub-indices exhibit a limited sensitivity to economic news, consistent with the findings by Hess *et al.* (2008) and Kilian and Vega (2011). For instance, the GSCI Energy sub-index is found to react only to the weekly jobless claims and the ECB refinancing rate. The GSCI Precious Metals sub-index offers a sensitivity only to the US Non Farm Payroll and the Chinese Purchasing Managers Index (PMI). Finally, the GSCI Agricultural and Industrial Metals sectors offer a stronger reaction to a greater number of economic news items, consistent with the intuition that these sectors are the most correlated with the worldwide business cycle. We shall investigate this question further in the next section.

Table 3.3 Impact of news on the main commodity indices

	GSCI Agri.	GSCI Energy	GSCI Ind. Metals	GSCI Prec. Metals
Intercept	2.46 (1.61)	−2.1 (−1.37)	−4.53** (−2.95)	1.52 (0.99)
AR	−0.01 (−0.27)	0.03 (1.15)	0.02 (1.07)	0.04** (2.19)
Non Farm Payroll	0.14 (1.56)	0.12 (0.79)	**0.19* (1.8)**	**−0.16* (−1.92)**
ISM	0.08 (0.84)	0.09 (0.6)	**0.21** (1.99)**	−0.03 (−0.32)
Jobless Claims	0.05 (0.52)	**−0.25* (−1.68)**	**−0.24** (−2.33)**	−0.05 (−0.57)
US CPI MoM	**0.18** (2)**	−0.04 (−0.27)	−0.06 (−0.61)	0.03 (0.38)
US Retail Sales	0.09 (0.79)	−0.25 (−1.4)	0 (−0.03)	−0.1 (−1.01)
Fed Target Rate	**−0.23* (−1.75)**	0.08 (0.36)	0.08 (0.51)	−0.02 (−0.19)
US GDP	0.15 (0.91)	0.22 (0.79)	0.24 (1.25)	−0.03 (−0.21)
ZEW Economic Sentiment	**−0.31** (−2.76)**	−0.21 (−1.15)	−0.2 (−1.56)	0.09 (0.86)
IFO Expectations	−0.06 (−0.5)	−0.03 (−0.15)	−0.2 (−1.41)	0.08 (0.72)
EMU CPI Flash Estimate	**−0.36** (−3.2)**	−0.21 (−1.11)	−0.14 (−1.06)	−0.09 (−0.85)
EMU GDP	0.05 (0.26)	0.1 (0.32)	**−0.39* (−1.84)**	−0.08 (−0.49)
France Business Confidence	**0.19* (1.69)**	0.19 (1.06)	0.2 (1.54)	0.13 (1.25)
ECB Refinancing Rate	**0.2* (1.88)**	**0.29* (1.66)**	**0.35** (2.88)**	−0.07 (−0.7)
China CPI YoY	−0.08 (−0.74)	0.06 (0.31)	0.06 (0.47)	−0.1 (−0.98)
China Industrial Production	0.03 (0.24)	−0.13 (−0.79)	−0.08 (−0.63)	0.05 (0.54)
China PMI	−0.19 (−1.36)	0.14 (0.6)	0.26 (1.6)	**−0.5** (−3.92)**

Note: T-stats are between brackets. Bold figures indicate statistically significant figures at a 10% risk level.

3.6 DEPENDENCE ON THE BUSINESS CYCLE: NBER RECESSIONS/EXPANSION PHASES

Beyond this long-term picture of commodity markets characterized by a rather low reaction to business cycle news, Hess *et al.* (2008) provide empirical evidence that this reaction depends strongly upon the *phase* of this cycle, i.e. boom or bust (Hamilton (1989)). To address this issue, we first split our data sample into sub-periods according to the US recessionary and expansionary periods as dated by the NBER Business Cycle Dating Committee.[4] Then, we run the regression presented in Equations (3.3)–(3.4). The estimation results are reproduced in Table 3.4.

The first striking result lies in the number of market movers that we can identify depending on the phase of the business cycle. During expansion periods, only 4 (out of 19) economic news releases are found to impact commodity markets across the various GSCI sub-indices: the IFO survey for the agricultural sector, the US ISM for the energy sector, the US Non Farm Payroll figure and the IFO survey for precious metals. During 1999–2011, expansion periods were characterized by a low reaction of commodities to additional economic news. Hence, we confirm the findings from previous literature concerning this lack of reaction of commodity markets to economic news.

During recession periods, eight news releases are found to impact significantly the agricultural, energy and industrial metals sectors. Precious metals react to three economic news releases – namely the US ISM, the French Business Confidence index and the Chinese PMI – whereas it reacts to two different news releases during expansion periods. Thus, we observe that the reaction of commodity markets to economic news is much stronger during recession periods.

Our finding implies that, during expansion periods, commodity markets are characterized by a low level of reaction to economic news. Conversely, during recession periods, we identify a strong reaction of commodities when compared to our benchmark of standard assets. Since expansions are relatively longer than recessions, this may contribute to give the impression that commodity markets are de-correlated from the business cycle.

Figure 3.1 presents the percentage of news releases with statistical significance (at a 10% risk level) on commodities for three samples: (i) the total sample (which we refer to as the long-term sample), (ii) the sample matching expansion periods, and (iii) the sample corresponding to recessions. This figure casts additional light on the fact that commodity markets are very close to equity markets in their reactions to economic news. During recession periods, the number of news releases impacting commodity markets ranges from 10 to 50% (which is even higher than the results obtained for the S&P 500). The strongest link to economic news is reached for copper, whereas the weakest reaction is found for rice. On energy markets, we remark on some discrepancies concerning the number of market movers that can be identified between expansion and recession periods. For instance, 5% of the news releases are found to trigger a reaction in the Brent price during recessions, whereas this percentage is closer to 45% for the remaining commodities studied. This result also has implications for portfolio managers concerning the potential diversification power expected from energy commodities.

---

[4] The NBER methodology of dating a business cycle is authoritative and well known, and widely used by financial practitioners.

Table 3.4 Impact of economic news on GSCI sub-indices of commodities according to the NBER Recessions/Expansion Phases

		GSCI Agri.	GSCI Energy	GSCI Ind. Metals	GSCI Prec. Metals
	Intercept	2.99* (1.94)	−1.78 (−1.16)	−4.67** (−3.03)	1.29 (0.84)
	AR	−0.01 (−0.39)	0.04 (1.19)	0.02 (1.17)	0.04** (2.2)
Recession	Non Farm Payroll	**0.45* (1.88)**	**0.8** (2.03)**	**0.76** (2.75)**	0.07 (0.33)
	ISM	0 (0.01)	−0.22 (−0.65)	−0.02 (−0.09)	**−0.41** (−2.19)**
	Jobless Claims	0.07 (0.43)	**−0.58** (−2.3)**	**−0.42** (−2.39)**	−0.01 (−0.04)
	US CPI MoM	**0.37** (2.18)**	0 (0.02)	0.02 (0.08)	−0.22 (−1.41)
	US Retail Sales	0.15 (1.06)	**−0.41* (−1.75)**	−0.02 (−0.15)	−0.1 (−0.78)
	Fed Target Rate	**−0.4** (−2.36)**	−0.01 (−0.03)	0.1 (0.52)	0.02 (0.1)
	US GDP	0.53 (1.08)	1.16 (1.45)	**1.1* (1.95)**	−0.05 (−0.11)
	ZEW Economic Sentiment	**−0.7** (−2.96)**	**−1.23** (−3.19)**	**−0.85** (−3.16)**	0.12 (0.58)
	IFO Expectations	**−0.73** (−3.35)**	**−0.88** (−2.46)**	**−0.82** (−3.28)**	**−0.36* (−1.81)**
	EMU CPI Flash Estimate	**−0.8** (−3.55)**	**−0.73** (−1.96)**	−0.14 (−0.54)	**−0.36* (−1.78)**
	EMU GDP	0.24 (0.39)	0.71 (0.71)	−1.05 (−1.5)	−0.48 (−0.88)
	France Business Confidence	**0.4** (2.12)**	**0.81** (2.64)**	**0.41** (1.89)**	**0.53** (3.11)**
	ECB Refinancing Rate	**0.29** (2.14)**	**0.48** (2.2)**	**0.54** (3.53)**	−0.05 (−0.4)
	China CPI YoY	−0.16 (−0.43)	−0.08 (−0.13)	0.17 (0.4)	−0.28 (−0.84)
	China Industrial Production	−0.37 (−1.4)	−0.64 (−1.48)	−0.04 (−0.14)	0.04 (0.19)
	China PMI	−0.22 (−1.46)	0.32 (1.28)	**0.29** (1.67)**	**−0.59** (−4.26)**
Expansion	Non Farm Payroll	0.09 (0.91)	0 (0.01)	0.09 (0.81)	**−0.2** (−2.29)**
	ISM	0.11 (1.05)	0.18 (1.11)	**0.28** (2.38)**	0.07 (0.77)
	Jobless Claims	0.04 (0.4)	−0.09 (−0.48)	−0.16 (−1.25)	−0.05 (−0.49)
	US CPI MoM	0.11 (1.05)	−0.05 (−0.29)	−0.1 (−0.8)	0.13 (1.37)
	US Retail Sales	−0.01 (−0.04)	−0.01 (−0.05)	0.03 (0.15)	−0.09 (−0.61)
	Fed Target Rate	−0.06 (−0.28)	0.18 (0.51)	0 (0.01)	0 (0.01)
	US GDP	0.1 (0.56)	0.1 (0.34)	0.12 (0.58)	−0.02 (−0.12)
	ZEW Economic Sentiment	−0.21 (−1.6)	0.09 (0.44)	0 (−0.02)	0.07 (0.6)
	IFO Expectations	**0.25* (1.65)**	0.36 (1.43)	0.09 (0.53)	**0.28** (2.01)**
	EMU CPI Flash Estimate	−0.2 (−1.51)	−0.04 (−0.17)	−0.13 (−0.86)	0.03 (0.27)
	EMU GDP	0.03 (0.15)	0.04 (0.12)	−0.33 (−1.47)	−0.04 (−0.22)
	France Business Confidence	0.1 (0.75)	−0.1 (−0.47)	0.11 (0.68)	−0.07 (−0.61)
	ECB Refinancing Rate	0.03 (0.19)	−0.03 (−0.12)	0.03 (0.16)	−0.14 (−0.91)
	China CPI YoY	−0.07 (−0.65)	0.06 (0.33)	0.05 (0.35)	−0.09 (−0.83)
	China Industrial Production	0.09 (0.84)	−0.05 (−0.26)	−0.08 (−0.64)	0.05 (0.48)
	China PMI	0.36 (0.88)	−0.33 (−0.5)	0.35 (0.75)	0.34 (0.92)

Note: Expansion and recession periods are taken from the NBER Business Cycle Dating Committee. T-stats are between brackets. Bold figures indicate statistically significant figures at a 10% risk level.

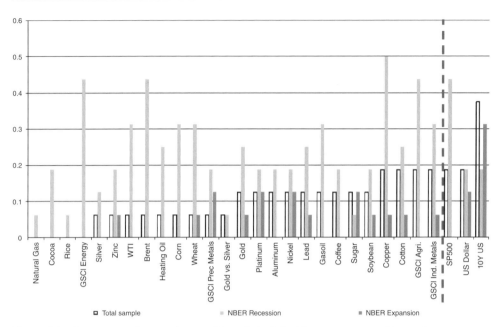

Figure 3.1   Percentage of news releases with statistical significance on commodity markets

3.7   ROLLING ANALYSIS

Before turning to a commodity-by-commodity analysis of the impact of news releases, this section investigates the following question: during 1999–2011, can we identify an increasing sensitivity of commodity markets to the business cycle? A positive reply would provide some empirical support to the view that commodities are characterized by an increased correlation with financial markets.

In what follows, we perform a rolling analysis, i.e. we run regressions similar to the previous section by using a rolling three-year sample. We are therefore able to compute the percentage of news releases having a statistical impact on commodity markets with a clearer view of how this evolves through time.

In addition, for each of the estimates obtained, we compute the average absolute of β as detailed in Equation (3.3). This provides us with a sensitivity index of the reaction of commodities to economic news.

Formally, we compute the number of news releases whose β has a t-statistic greater than 1.64 (in absolute value). This corresponds to the quantile of a scaled Gaussian distribution at the 10% risk level. The sensitivity index for a given market – consistent with Equation (3.3) – is given by:

$$B = \frac{1}{I} \sum_{i=1}^{I} |\hat{\beta}_i|, \tag{3.5}$$

with B the sensitivity index, $\hat{\beta}_i$ the estimated sensitivities to the individual news releases, and I the total number of news releases.

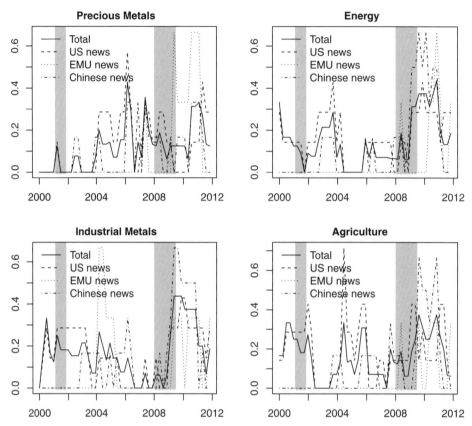

Figure 3.2 Percentage of news releases with a statistical impact over different sectors of the commodity market

Figure 3.2 shows the evolution of the percentage of market movers for the GSCI sub-indices. Figure 3.3 contains the evolution of the sensitivity scores. Several stylized facts can be listed:

1. Commodity markets exhibit a time-varying sensitivity to business cycle indicators. In Figures 3.2 and 3.3, the percentage of news releases to which commodity markets react and the cumulated sum of the absolute β vary strongly over time. For industrial metals and agricultural products, this time-varying pattern follows closely the phases of the US business cycle, according to the NBER. For energy markets, our results show a strong reaction to economic news during 2008–2009, especially concerning the sensitivity score. These markets display a high sensitivity to Chinese news in 2008, and then to US news in 2009. Sensitivity to Chinese news is also observable in 2009 for industrial metals and agricultural products. Finally, precious metals are characterized by an increased sensitivity to news during 2004–2006. This period corresponds to rising inflation and tighter monetary policy. Under such circumstances, commodity markets typically display an increased sensitivity to economic signals. Precious metals also show an increased sensitivity to European news after the 2008–2009 crisis, i.e. their price tends to rise with the level of risk aversion.

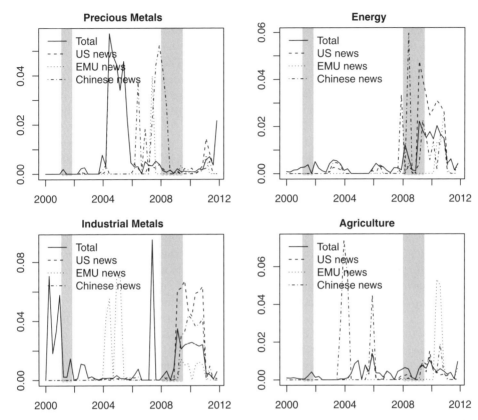

Figure 3.3 Rolling sensitivity index of news with a statistical impact over different sectors of the commodity market

2. The reaction of commodity markets to news depends on recession/expansion phases, but the picture globally looks more complex. In Figures 3.2 and 3.3, we notice that precious metals react to European news despite the end of the US economic crisis. The European sovereign crisis could therefore have led to a rising level of risk aversion that triggered a surge in the price of precious metals (through a flight-to-quality event). A similar comment can be made during the 2004–2005 US slowdown in leading indicators: agricultural prices have shown an increased sensitivity to economic news, both in terms of number and average market beta.

3. There is limited evidence of a 'financialization' of commodities (Tang and Xiong (2010), Dionne *et al.* (2011)). Tang and Xiong (2010) examine the financialization process of commodity markets precipitated by the rapid growth of commodity index funds since the 2000s. The authors highlight the relationship between the growing involvement of investors in such index funds and the shocks suffered by the commodity markets, with the oil market in the front line. The two most popular index funds, the Goldman Sachs Commodity Index (GSCI) and the Dow Jones AIG Commodity Index (DJ-AIG), are typical of these pronounced movements in commodity markets. Tang and Xiong (2010) show that the interactions between the financial markets and the commodity markets are gaining in

importance and that the recent financial crisis made a significant contribution[5] to increasing the price volatility of commodities in 2008. The authors use a linear regression model to show first that the exposure of an index like GSCI to share market shocks and the US Dollar exchange rate increased significantly after 2004. They then use a rolling regression model to verify that the growing exposure of energy sectors such as oil to these same shocks (share market, US$ exchange rate) is clearly linked statistically to the presence of commodity index funds. The authors subsequently analyze the relationship between the commodity prices and the investment flows in the index funds. Their analysis, based on a vector autoregressive model and the associated response impulse functions, demonstrates the very strong predictive capability of investment flows in index funds as a function of other variables linked to the financial and commodity markets. This latter result illustrates more accurately the growing integration of the two spheres. Lastly, the authors explain oil price volatility based on the activity of commodity index funds. The results of their regressions illustrate statistically the link between the strong growth in volatility in the commodity markets in 2008 (including the price of oil) and index fund activity, triggering contagion effects. Dionne *et al.* (2011) use the multivariate Markov-switching environment to estimate the default spread component of corporate yield spreads with observed macroeconomic factors. Such an increasing link between the spheres of commodities and asset markets should be observable in Figures 3.2 and 3.3. Indeed, the main asset classes are known to react strongly to economic news, insofar as financial asset prices incorporate a risk-adjusted forecast of the future economic development. Given the analysis in terms of β and in terms of percentage of news releases leading to market reactions, we lack an obvious trend in our empirical results. We clearly highlight the changing sensitivity of commodity markets depending on the nature of the economic regime that the world business cycle is going through. But it appears difficult to assess whether the heightened reaction of commodity markets to news in 2008 – when compared to 2001 – can be related to a growing inclusion of these asset classes in balanced portfolios in the asset management industry, or to a stronger than usual economic slowdown.

3.8   PRELIMINARY FINDINGS

Sections 3.4 to 3.7 have provided us with several stylized facts on the reaction of commodities to economic news during 1999–2011, which we attempt to summarize before turning to an asset-specific analysis:

1. In the long run, commodity markets display a weaker sensitivity to economic news than bond and equity markets. Energy markets illustrate this pattern, with only two economic news releases to which these commodities seem to be sensitive.
2. During recessions, the number of news releases to which commodity markets are responding is more important than during expansion periods. Again, energy markets provide the most striking example of such a stylized fact, with a statistical sensitivity to 8 (out of 19) economic news releases included in our study.
3. Agricultural products and industrial metals are the most sensitive commodities to economic news. They stand out as the most cyclical commodities of the GSCI sub-indices considered.

---

[5] This analysis is well documented. For example, Tang and Xiong (2010) reveal that the total value of commodity exchanges via index funds for institutional investors soared from $15 billion in 2003 to $200 billion mid-2008.

4. There is limited evidence of a growing financial integration of commodities: it is difficult to uncover a growing sensitivity of commodity markets to economic news over time.

Based on these preliminary findings, in the next section we develop a more detailed analysis of individual markets, which should provide us with a better understanding of the relationship between commodity markets and the business cycle.

3.9 MARKET-BY-MARKET ANALYSIS

In this section, we report the results obtained when estimating Equations (3.3)–(3.4) commodity by commodity.

3.9.1 Database for Commodity Prices

In what follows, all the data comes from Bloomberg with a monthly frequency:

- Gold is the Commodity Exchange (COMEX) Gold futures price traded in US Dollars per troy ounce.
- Silver is the COMEX Silver futures price traded in US Dollars per troy ounce.
- Platinum is the COMEX Platinum futures price in US Dollars per troy ounce.
- Aluminum is the London Metal Exchange (LME) futures price traded in US Dollars per tonne.
- Copper is the COMEX Copper futures price traded in US Dollars per pound.
- Nickel is the LME Nickel futures price traded in US Dollars per tonne.
- Zinc is the LME futures price traded in US Dollars per tonne.
- Lead is the LME futures price traded in US Dollars per tonne.
- WTI is the New York Mercantile Exchange (NYMEX) WTI Light Sweet Crude Oil futures price traded in US Dollars per barrel.
- Brent is the InterContinental Exchange (ICE) Brent Crude futures price traded in US Dollars per barrel.
- Gasoil is the Reformulated Regular Gasoline Blendstock (RBOB) Gasoline futures price traded in US Dollars per gallon.
- Natural Gas is the Henry Hub Natural Gas futures price traded in US Dollars per million British thermal units (mmBtu).
- Heating Oil is the NYMEX Heating Oil futures price traded in US Dollars per gallon.
- Corn is the Chicago Board of Trade (CBOT) Corn futures price traded in US Dollars per bushel.
- Wheat is the CBOT Wheat futures price traded in US Dollars per bushel.
- Coffee is the ICE Coffee 'C' futures price traded in US Dollars per pound.
- Sugar is the NYMEX Sugar #11 futures price traded in US Dollars per pound.
- Cocoa is the ICE Cocoa futures price traded in US Dollars per tonne.
- Cotton is the ICE Cotton No.2 futures price traded in US Dollars per pound.
- Soybean is the CBOT Soybean futures price traded in US Dollars per short ton.
- Rice is the Chicago Mercantile Exchange (CME) Rough Rice futures price traded in US Dollars per hundredweight.

Table 3.5   Estimation of the impact of economic news over selected precious metals

	Gold	Silver	Platinum	GSCI Prec. Metals
Intercept	−1.89 (−1.25)	−1.73 (−1.15)	4.11** (2.73)	1.52 (0.99)
AR	0.03** (2.16)	0.04 (1.59)	0.03 (1.2)	0.04** (2.19)
Non Farm Payroll	−0.17** (−2.16)	−0.18 (−1.32)	−0.18* (−1.7)	−0.16* (−1.92)
ISM	**−0.03 (−0.37)**	0.05 (0.39)	0.07 (0.7)	**−0.03 (−0.32)**
Jobless Claims	−0.05 (−0.59)	−0.27* (−1.91)	−0.1 (−0.96)	−0.05 (−0.57)
US CPI MoM	0.06 (0.71)	0.11 (0.75)	0.11 (1.06)	0.03 (0.38)
US Retail Sales	−0.03 (−0.31)	−0.04 (−0.23)	−0.02 (−0.13)	−0.1 (−1.01)
Fed Target Rate	−0.04 (−0.33)	−0.23 (−1.12)	−0.09 (−0.58)	−0.02 (−0.19)
US GDP	−0.01 (−0.04)	0.08 (0.29)	**0.38** (1.98)**	−0.03 (−0.21)
ZEW Eco. Sent.	0.07 (0.76)	0.03 (0.16)	−0.21 (−1.6)	0.09 (0.86)
IFO Expectations	0.13 (1.22)	0.18 (0.92)	0.2 (1.41)	**0.08 (0.72)**
EMU CPI	**−0.05 (−0.46)**	−0.2 (−1.14)	**−0.18 (−1.37)**	**−0.09 (−0.85)**
EMU GDP	−0.08 (−0.49)	−0.11 (−0.37)	−0.04 (−0.19)	−0.08 (−0.49)
FR Bus. Conf.	**0.12 (1.32)**	**0.02 (0.15)**	0.1 (0.8)	**0.13 (1.25)**
ECB Ref. Rate	−0.06 (−0.67)	0.14 (0.87)	0.12 (0.99)	−0.07 (−0.7)
China CPI YoY	−0.03 (−0.33)	0.04 (0.21)	−0.06 (−0.51)	−0.1 (−0.98)
China Ind. Prod.	0 (0.03)	0.01 (0.08)	0.26** (2.18)	0.05 (0.54)
China PMI	**−0.43** (−3.58)**	**−0.48** (−2.23)**	−0.23 (−1.45)	**−0.5** (−3.92)**

Note: T-stats are between brackets. Bold figures indicate statistically significant figures at a 10% risk level.

3.9.2   Precious Metals

Tables 3.5 and 3.6 present the results obtained with a subset of precious metals, i.e. gold, silver and platinum. When considering the full sample, we obtain the results reproduced in Table 3.5. When considering the potential reaction of precious metals depending on the phase of the business cycle – i.e. 'expansion' or 'recession' – as indicated by the NBER, we obtain the results reproduced in Table 3.6. In each table, the GSCI sub-index for precious metals is used as a benchmark.

The results may be summarized as follows:[6]

1. **Gold:** From a long-term perspective, gold reacts negatively to positive surprises in Non Farm Payrolls and the Chinese PMI. In this respect, sustained and accelerating growth regimes are thus likely to hinder the rise of gold prices. We do not find evidence of a reaction of gold prices to surprises concerning inflation news. When breaking down the phases of the business cycle (Table 3.6), we obtain a different picture. During recessions, gold reacts negatively to the US ISM, the EMU CPI and the Chinese PMI. Two out of the three figures having a statistical impact on gold are economic surveys. These surveys are to be monitored cautiously to anticipate periods of rising gold prices. During expansion periods, gold displays a negative sign with the Non Farm Payrolls, but a positive sign with the US CPI and the German IFO. Hence, during expansion, positive surprises concerning inflation – i.e. when the inflation index rises more than expected – should trigger a surge in gold prices. Overall, we identify that gold has a very different reaction to economic news depending on the underlying economic regime.

---

[6] We skip the results of the EGARCH model, which consistently exhibit statistically significant parameters in the variance equation.

Table 3.6   Estimation of the impact of economic news over selected precious metals depending on the NBER phase of the business cycle

		Gold	Silver	Platinum	GSCI Prec. Metals
	Intercept	−2.15 (−1.41)	−1.66 (−1.08)	4.38** (2.88)	1.29 (0.84)
	AR	0.03** (2.2)	0.05* (1.64)	0.03 (1.23)	0.04** (2.2)
REC	Non Farm Payroll	0.03 (0.17)	−0.32 (−0.86)	−0.42 (−1.51)	0.07 (0.33)
	ISM	**−0.36** (−2.04)**	−0.49 (−1.54)	−0.34 (−1.41)	**−0.41** (−2.19)**
	Jobless Claims	−0.06 (−0.45)	−0.24 (−1.02)	−0.18 (−1.01)	−0.01 (−0.04)
	US CPI MoM	−0.19 (−1.29)	−0.36 (−1.37)	−0.24 (−1.23)	−0.22 (−1.41)
	US Retail Sales	−0.02 (−0.15)	0.02 (0.08)	0.17 (1.03)	−0.1 (−0.78)
	Fed Target Rate	0.01 (0.05)	−0.17 (−0.66)	−0.12 (−0.6)	0.02 (0.1)
	US GDP	0.1 (0.24)	0.22 (0.3)	**1.98** (3.54)**	−0.05 (−0.11)
	ZEW Eco. Sent.	0.29 (1.44)	−0.26 (−0.73)	**−0.92** (−3.41)**	0.12 (0.58)
	IFO Expectations	−0.1 (−0.55)	−0.41 (−1.21)	0.15 (0.61)	**−0.36* (−1.81)**
	EMU CPI	**−0.39** (−1.99)**	−0.49 (−1.41)	**−0.71** (−2.75)**	**−0.36* (−1.78)**
	EMU GDP	−0.62 (−1.18)	−0.8 (−0.85)	−0.73 (−1.05)	−0.48 (−0.88)
	FR Bus. Conf.	**0.6** (3.72)**	**0.74** (2.58)**	0.3 (1.38)	**0.53** (3.11)**
	ECB Ref. Rate	−0.06 (−0.55)	0.09 (0.44)	0.15 (0.99)	−0.05 (−0.4)
	China CPI YoY	0.36 (1.14)	0.45 (0.79)	−0.01 (−0.03)	−0.28 (−0.84)
	China Ind. Prod.	−0.11 (−0.51)	0.25 (0.62)	0.09 (0.29)	0.04 (0.19)
	China PMI	**−0.51** (−3.88)**	**−0.66** (−2.82)**	−0.25 (−1.44)	**−0.59** (−4.26)**
EXP	Non Farm Payroll	**−0.21** (−2.49)**	−0.17 (−1.15)	−0.14 (−1.31)	**−0.2** (−2.29)**
	ISM	0.06 (0.67)	0.18 (1.19)	0.17 (1.51)	0.07 (0.77)
	Jobless Claims	−0.02 (−0.19)	−0.24 (−1.41)	−0.04 (−0.32)	−0.05 (−0.49)
	US CPI MoM	**0.16* (1.74)**	**0.31* (1.83)**	**0.26** (2.07)**	0.13 (1.37)
	US Retail Sales	−0.04 (−0.31)	−0.1 (−0.4)	−0.25 (−1.3)	−0.09 (−0.61)
	Fed Target Rate	−0.03 (−0.17)	−0.17 (−0.52)	0.05 (0.23)	0 (0.01)
	US GDP	0 (0)	0.08 (0.28)	0.18 (0.89)	−0.02 (−0.12)
	ZEW Eco. Sent.	0.01 (0.09)	0.11 (0.57)	0 (−0.02)	0.07 (0.6)
	IFO Expectations	**0.22* (1.68)**	**0.42* (1.81)**	0.23 (1.3)	**0.28** (2.01)**
	EMU CPI	0.1 (0.88)	−0.05 (−0.25)	0.03 (0.17)	0.03 (0.27)
	EMU GDP	−0.02 (−0.14)	−0.04 (−0.12)	0.03 (0.13)	−0.04 (−0.22)
	FR Bus. Conf.	−0.12 (−1.03)	−0.34 (−1.6)	0 (0.01)	−0.07 (−0.61)
	ECB Ref. Rate	−0.1 (−0.66)	0.16 (0.59)	0.06 (0.32)	−0.14 (−0.91)
	China CPI YoY	−0.07 (−0.75)	−0.02 (−0.12)	−0.1 (−0.74)	−0.09 (−0.83)
	China Ind. Prod.	0.02 (0.22)	−0.04 (−0.2)	**0.29** (2.24)**	0.05 (0.48)
	China PMI	0.38 (1.11)	**1.03* (1.66)**	0.4 (0.87)	0.34 (0.92)

Note: REC stands for 'Recession' and EXP for 'Expansion' according to the NBER Business Cycle Dating Committee. T-stats are between brackets. Bold figures indicate statistically significant figures at a 10% risk level.

2. **Silver:** From a long-term perspective, silver reacts negatively to positive surprises in the jobless claims and the Chinese PMI. The picture is more complex than for gold: the negative sign with the Chinese PMI underlines the 'safe haven' role of silver during recessions, whereas its negative reaction to an unexpected increase in the number of unemployed people in the USA tells us a different story. This effect comes from the key fact that many precious metals are used both as safe havens (Baur and McDermott (2010), Beaudry *et al.* (2011)) and for industrial purposes. During recession periods, silver reacts positively to negative surprises in the Chinese PMI, and negatively to positive surprises in the French Business Confidence index. During expansion periods, silver reacts positively to positive

surprises in the US CPI, the Chinese PMI and the IFO expectations. It has a weaker sensitivity to the weekly jobless claims.

3. **Platinum:** During the full sample (Table 3.5), platinum shows a negative sensitivity to Non Farm Payrolls, the German ZEW and the EMU CPI, and a positive reaction to the US GDP and Chinese industrial production. The most striking fact for platinum is that it features a stronger relationship to economic news than gold and silver: while gold only reacts to two news releases, platinum reacts to five of the news releases considered. We also clearly see the mix between the safe haven characteristic of the average precious metal, and the apparent use of such metal for industrial purposes. When considering only recession periods, the strongest sensitivity of platinum is obtained for the US GDP: an unexpected decrease in the US GDP would lead to a strong decline in the prices of platinum. Two minor effects come from the sign of the German ZEW and the EMU CPI, in a contra-cyclical way. Expansion periods are characterized by a rise in the platinum price, whenever the US CPI and the Chinese industrial production surprises are on the upside. Similarly to the GSCI benchmark for precious metals, platinum can be used for industrial purposes. Hence, it reacts positively to positive news about economic growth, and it is traditionally used as a hedge against inflation.

3.9.3   Industrial Metals

In the case of industrial metals, we use the following subset of markets: aluminum, copper, nickel, zinc and lead. As for precious metals, we report the estimation results obtained during the full sample (Table 3.7), and during expansion vs. recession periods (Table 3.8).

Our results can be summarized as follows:

1. **Aluminum:** Over the 1999–2011 period, the price of aluminum has been rising with Non Farm Payrolls, the US ISM and the ECB rates. Conversely, it reacted negatively to increases in the number of unemployed people in the US, as measured by the jobless claims. In the long run, the aluminum price seems to increase when unemployment and production perspectives are improving, and to decrease when these conditions deteriorate. In Table 3.8, we observe that recession periods lead to a heightened sensitivity of aluminum to the world business cycle: it decreases with declining payrolls and ECB rates but increases with German surveys. Conversely, during expansion periods, the aluminum price seems to react weakly to economic news (only to the US ISM).

2. **Copper:** The case of copper is very similar to aluminum, with a large discrepancy in terms of market reaction to economic news during recessions and expansions. During the full sample, the price of copper increases with the ISM, US unemployment and the ECB main refinancing rate, and decreases with the German surveys and the EMU CPI. During recession periods, the copper price drops with decreases in US surveys, US unemployment and US GDP, and with lowered ECB rate and Chinese PMI (surprisingly to the downside). Negative EMU GDP and German IFO lead to increases in the price of copper. This result may be explained by the fact that we focus on the NBER recession dates, whereas Europe effectively entered the financial crisis during late 2008 – i.e. almost one year after the USA. During expansion periods, the copper price is found to rise only with positive ISM surprises.

3. **Nickel:** During the full sample, the price of nickel displays a negative sensitivity to surprises in US retail sales, jobless claims, the EMU CPI and the EMU GDP. This surprising

Table 3.7 Estimation of the impact of economic news over selected industrial metals

	Aluminum	Copper	Nickel	Zinc	Lead	GSCI Ind. Metals
Intercept	-3.04** (-1.98)	-4.7** (-3.07)	0.71 (0.46)	-2.61* (-1.71)	5.39** (3.52)	-4.53** (-2.95)
AR	0 (0.21)	0.03 (1.13)	0.02 (0.64)	0.01 (0.5)	0.03 (0.86)	0.02 (1.07)
Non Farm Payroll	**0.22** (**2.32**)	0.15 (1.19)	0.16 (0.97)	0.2 (1.52)	0.09 (0.59)	**0.19*** (**1.8**)
ISM	**0.16*** (**1.65**)	**0.37** (**2.96**)	0.24 (1.39)	0.18 (1.37)	0.21 (1.48)	**0.21** (**1.99**)
Jobless Claims	**-0.18*** (**-1.89**)	**-0.28** (**-2.26**)	**-0.32*** (**-1.92**)	-0.21 (-1.59)	-0.2 (-1.38)	**-0.24** (**-2.33**)
US CPI MoM	-0.11 (-1.17)	0.04 (0.29)	-0.28 (-1.63)	-0.12 (-0.86)	0.03 (0.2)	-0.06 (-0.61)
US Retail Sales	0.16 (1.4)	-0.04 (-0.29)	**-0.53** (**-2.63**)	0.02 (0.12)	-0.22 (-1.24)	0 (-0.03)
Fed Target Rate	0.05 (0.33)	0.03 (0.16)	0.05 (0.2)	0.05 (0.26)	0.27 (1.28)	0.08 (0.51)
US GDP	0.12 (0.69)	0.37 (1.61)	0.02 (0.06)	**0.5** (**2.01**)	-0.05 (-0.17)	0.24 (1.25)
ZEW Eco. Sent.	-0.12 (-0.99)	**-0.27*** (**-1.73**)	-0.21 (-1)	0.16 (0.97)	-0.24 (-1.3)	-0.2 (-1.56)
IFO Expectations	-0.18 (-1.36)	-0.26 (-1.54)	-0.27 (-1.14)	0 (0)	-0.14 (-0.69)	-0.2 (-1.41)
EMU CPI	-0.06 (-0.53)	**-0.26*** (**-1.66**)	**-0.41*** (**-1.93**)	-0.11 (-0.67)	-0.16 (-0.9)	-0.14 (-1.06)
EMU GDP	-0.27 (-1.39)	-0.4 (-1.6)	**-0.78** (**-2.27**)	-0.35 (-1.3)	-0.46 (-1.58)	**-0.39*** (**-1.84**)
FR Bus. Conf.	0.08 (0.66)	0.21 (1.38)	0.19 (0.9)	-0.09 (-0.56)	0.26 (1.49)	0.2 (1.54)
ECB Ref. Rate	**0.27** (**2.42**)	**0.53** (**3.66**)	0.32 (1.63)	0.09 (0.59)	-0.08 (-0.45)	**0.35** (**2.88**)
China CPI YoY	0.07 (0.57)	0.03 (0.18)	-0.09 (-0.42)	-0.01 (-0.08)	0.09 (0.53)	0.06 (0.47)
China Ind. Prod.	0.06 (0.54)	-0.15 (-1.06)	-0.09 (-0.47)	-0.17 (-1.11)	**-0.41** (**-2.48**)	-0.08 (-0.63)
China PMI	0.05 (0.31)	0.23 (1.18)	0.05 (0.2)	0.28 (1.34)	**0.49** (**2.19**)	0.26 (1.6)

Note: T-stats are between brackets. Bold figures indicate statistically significant figures at a 10% risk level.

Table 3.8 Estimation of the impact of economic news over selected industrial metals depending on the NBER phase of the business cycle

		Aluminum	Copper	Nickel	Zinc	Lead	GSCI Ind. Metals
	Intercept	−3.06** (−1.98)	−4.47** (−2.9)	0.45 (0.29)	−2.78* (−1.8)	5.06** (3.27)	−4.67** (−3.03)
	AR	0.01 (0.3)	0.03 (1.23)	0.02 (0.64)	0.01 (0.47)	0.03 (0.93)	0.02 (1.17)
REC	Non Farm Payroll	**0.9** (3.54)**	**0.78** (2.37)**	0.47 (1.05)	**0.76** (2.15)**	0.22 (0.57)	**0.76** (2.75)**
	ISM	0.12 (0.54)	0.19 (0.69)	−0.48 (−1.24)	−0.37 (−1.22)	−0.02 (−0.05)	−0.02 (−0.09)
	Jobless Claims	−0.23 (−1.39)	**−0.49** (−2.32)**	**−0.89** (−3.1)**	**−0.41* (−1.79)**	−0.32 (−1.31)	**−0.42** (−2.39)**
	US CPI MoM	−0.21 (−1.16)	0.24 (1.04)	0.11 (0.35)	−0.12 (−0.47)	0.17 (0.61)	0.02 (0.08)
	US Retail Sales	0.22 (1.43)	−0.11 (−0.54)	**−0.95** (−3.57)**	0.04 (0.19)	−0.27 (−1.19)	−0.02 (−0.15)
	Fed Target Rate	0.05 (0.3)	**0 (0.01)**	0.31 (0.97)	0.06 (0.23)	0.37 (1.34)	0.1 (0.52)
	US GDP	0.63 (1.23)	**1.46** (2.19)**	0.36 (0.4)	**1.38* (1.92)**	**1.46* (1.87)**	**1.1* (1.95)**
	ZEW Eco. Sent.	**−0.46* (−1.87)**	**−1.06** (−3.31)**	−0.64 (−1.47)	0.51 (1.48)	**−0.78** (−2.09)**	**−0.85** (−3.16)**
	IFO Expectations	**−0.62** (−2.7)**	**−1.12** (−3.78)**	**−0.92** (−2.28)**	−0.39 (−1.22)	−0.47 (−1.35)	**−0.82** (−3.28)**
	EMU CPI	−0.14 (−0.59)	−0.29 (−0.93)	−0.63 (−1.51)	−0.24 (−0.73)	−0.57 (−1.59)	−0.14 (−0.54)
	EMU GDP	−0.72 (−1.12)	−0.7 (−0.85)	**−1.95* (−1.72)**	**−2.39** (−2.67)**	**−3.28** (−3.38)**	−1.05 (−1.5)
	FR Bus. Conf.	0.25 (1.27)	**0.6* (2.36)**	**0.59* (1.68)**	−0.19 (−0.7)	**0.94** (3.17)**	**0.41* (1.89)**
	ECB Ref. Rate	**0.37** (2.59)**	**0.81** (4.42)**	**0.48* (1.92)**	**0.42** (2.11)**	−0.17 (−0.79)	**0.54** (3.53)**
	China CPI YoY	0.18 (0.47)	0.09 (0.19)	−0.48 (−0.7)	**1.02* (1.88)**	0.55 (0.94)	0.17 (0.4)
	China Ind. Prod.	0.28 (1.02)	−0.29 (−0.82)	0.25 (0.5)	−0.63 (−1.62)	−0.67 (−1.59)	−0.04 (−0.14)
	China PMI	0.16 (0.98)	**0.41** (1.98)**	0.24 (0.83)	**0.39* (1.74)**	**0.61* (2.52)**	**0.29* (1.67)**
EXP	Non Farm Payroll	0.11 (1.06)	0.04 (0.31)	0.1 (0.56)	0.1 (0.7)	0.06 (0.37)	0.09 (0.81)
	ISM	**0.19* (1.81)**	**0.44** (3.19)**	**0.43** (2.28)**	**0.34** (2.26)**	**0.28* (1.77)**	**0.28** (2.38)**
	Jobless Claims	−0.17 (−1.47)	−0.2 (−1.35)	−0.03 (−0.17)	−0.14 (−0.83)	−0.13 (−0.72)	−0.16 (−1.25)
	US CPI MoM	−0.07 (−0.62)	−0.05 (−0.33)	**−0.46** (−2.28)**	−0.1 (−0.64)	−0.03 (−0.17)	−0.1 (−0.8)
	US Retail Sales	0.1 (0.54)	0.05 (0.22)	0.03 (0.09)	−0.03 (−0.11)	−0.14 (−0.52)	0.03 (0.15)
	Fed Target Rate	0.06 (0.26)	−0.01 (−0.03)	−0.49 (−1.26)	0.05 (0.15)	0.07 (0.2)	0 (0.01)
	US GDP	0.05 (0.26)	0.22 (0.89)	−0.02 (−0.07)	0.37 (1.39)	−0.23 (−0.8)	0.12 (0.58)
	ZEW Eco. Sent.	−0.02 (−0.12)	−0.02 (−0.13)	−0.06 (−0.23)	0.06 (0.32)	−0.06 (−0.29)	0 (−0.02)
	IFO Expectations	0.03 (0.19)	0.14 (0.69)	0.04 (0.14)	0.2 (0.91)	−0.01 (−0.02)	0.09 (0.53)
	EMU CPI	−0.06 (−0.41)	−0.27 (−1.52)	−0.32 (−1.33)	−0.07 (−0.37)	−0.03 (−0.17)	−0.13 (−0.86)
	EMU GDP	−0.22 (−1.1)	−0.38 (−1.43)	**−0.66* (−1.84)**	−0.15 (−0.53)	−0.18 (−0.6)	−0.33 (−1.47)
	FR Bus. Conf.	0 (0.01)	0.03 (0.15)	−0.01 (−0.03)	−0.03 (−0.15)	−0.08 (−0.35)	0.11 (0.68)
	ECB Ref. Rate	0.1 (0.56)	0.07 (0.27)	0.12 (0.37)	**−0.42* (−1.64)**	0.05 (0.17)	0.03 (0.16)
	China CPI YoY	0.05 (0.39)	0.02 (0.11)	−0.02 (−0.11)	−0.11 (−0.66)	0.04 (0.23)	0.05 (0.35)
	China Ind. Prod.	0.02 (0.15)	−0.12 (−0.81)	−0.15 (−0.72)	−0.08 (−0.47)	**−0.36** (−2)**	−0.08 (−0.64)
	China PMI	−0.64 (−1.49)	−0.75 (−1.37)	−0.35 (−0.46)	−0.07 (−0.11)	0.02 (0.03)	0.35 (0.75)

Note: REC stands for 'Recession' and EXP for 'Expansion' according to the NBER Business Cycle Dating Committee. T-stats are between brackets. Bold figures indicate statistically significant figures at a 10% risk level.

pattern features a clearly counter-cyclical reaction to economic news. When considering recession periods, we uncover again a negative sensitivity of the nickel price to the German IFO, US retail sales, jobless claims and the EMU GDP. This commodity records nonetheless a positive reaction to increases in the ECB main refinancing rate, and in the French Business Confidence index. During expansion periods, the price of nickel reacts positively to unexpected increases in the US ISM, and negatively to unexpected increases in the US CPI and the EMU GDP. This finding underlines the potential complexity of the relationship between industrial metals and the economic newsflow.

4. **Zinc:** During the full sample, the price of zinc only reacts positively to surprises in the US GDP. During recession periods, this sensitivity to the US GDP appears again, even with an increased importance. In addition, the price of zinc displays strongly pro-cyclical reactions to the ISM, US unemployment, the US GDP, the ECB rate and Chinese PMI. Conversely, during expansion periods, the price of zinc exhibits two kinds of reactions: one positive to the US ISM, and one negative to the ECB main refinancing rate. Hence, zinc prices are more likely to rise when US surveys are surprisingly to the upside, and when the ECB is in the process of lowering its main refinancing rate.

5. **Lead:** During the full sample, the lead price reacts positively to positive surprises in Chinese PMI, and to negative surprises in Chinese industrial production. When looking at the NBER business cycle phases, we find that this negative sensitivity to industrial production is only valid during expansion periods. This result may be related to the aggressive monetary policy conducted by the PBOC during the post-2008 period. During expansionary phases, we find a positive sensitivity of the lead price to the US ISM. During recession periods, this commodity displays a positive sensitivity to the Chinese PMI – as in the full sample case – and to the US GDP, and a negative reaction to the EMU GDP.

To sum up, we find common patterns across industrial metals: most of them display a pro-cyclical behavior during recessions, a weak reaction to news during expansion periods, and a significant sensitivity to Chinese news during recessions.

3.9.4   Energy

Tables 3.9 and 3.10 present the estimation results of Equations (3.3)–(3.4) in the case of energy commodities.

The main findings may be summarized as follows:

1. **WTI and Brent:** crude oil prices exhibit a weak long-term relationship to economic news. During the full sample, the only market mover on crude oil markets is US jobless claims, with a negative sign.[7] During recession periods, crude oil prices seem to be negatively related to US jobless claims, US retail sales, the German IFO, the German ZEW and the EMU CPI. In the meantime, these commodity prices also exhibit a positive reaction to increases in the ECB refinancing rate. This latter result illustrates that a rising ECB target rate is interpreted as good news on crude oil markets, as it reveals that the world economy is roaring. During expansion periods, we cannot identify any significant market mover on these markets.

2. **Gasoil:** The full sample analysis reveals two market movers for the gasoil price: US retail sales and the EMU CPI with negative signs. Hence, the gasoil market features an interesting

---

[7] Note that the Brent price also displays a positive sensitivity to the ECB refinancing rate.

Table 3.9 Estimation of the impact of economic news over selected energy markets

	WTI	Brent	Gasoil	Natural Gas	Heating Oil	GSCI Energy
Intercept	−0.95 (−0.61)	−4.46** (−2.92)	0.25 (0.16)	−1.27 (−0.82)	−3.4** (−2.21)	−2.1 (−1.37)
AR	0.05 (1.39)	0.05 (1.62)	0.05 (1.5)	0.01 (0.2)	0.05 (1.43)	0.03 (1.15)
Non Farm Payroll	0.15 (0.92)	0.09 (0.57)	0.19 (1.26)	0.31 (1.23)	0.16 (1.02)	0.12 (0.79)
ISM	0.2 (1.22)	0.04 (0.23)	0.09 (0.61)	0.29 (1.14)	0.13 (0.8)	0.09 (0.6)
Jobless Claims	−0.58** (−3.47)	−0.34** (−2.17)	0 (0.02)	0.16 (0.63)	−0.33** (−2.03)	−0.25* (−1.68)
US CPI MoM	−0.1 (−0.6)	−0.07 (−0.41)	−0.05 (−0.3)	0.02 (0.08)	0.01 (0.07)	−0.04 (−0.27)
US Retail Sales	−0.27 (−1.36)	−0.29 (−1.54)	−0.43** (−2.41)	−0.13 (−0.43)	−0.22 (−1.15)	−0.25 (−1.4)
Fed Target Rate	0 (0.01)	0.23 (1.02)	0.26 (1.22)	−0.21 (−0.57)	0.1 (0.42)	0.08 (0.36)
US GDP	0.21 (0.69)	0.1 (0.35)	0.04 (0.14)	0.24 (0.52)	0.19 (0.64)	0.22 (0.79)
ZEW Eco. Sent.	−0.19 (−0.93)	−0.13 (−0.65)	−0.08 (−0.41)	−0.39 (−1.23)	−0.27 (−1.31)	−0.21 (−1.15)
IFO Expectations	−0.06 (−0.24)	−0.07 (−0.3)	−0.25 (−1.23)	0.18 (0.51)	0.04 (0.18)	−0.03 (−0.15)
EMU CPI	−0.31 (−1.48)	−0.19 (−0.98)	−0.39** (−2.07)	0.25 (0.79)	−0.29 (−1.43)	−0.21 (−1.11)
EMU GDP	0.05 (0.14)	0.09 (0.27)	0.07 (0.23)	0.5 (0.96)	0.05 (0.15)	0.1 (0.32)
FR Bus. Conf.	0.16 (0.77)	0.22 (1.14)	0.15 (0.8)	0.44 (1.42)	0.21 (1.04)	0.19 (1.06)
ECB Ref. Rate	0.28 (1.43)	0.3* (1.64)	−0.06 (−0.33)	0.18 (0.61)	0.18 (0.96)	0.29* (1.66)
China CPI YoY	0.03 (0.13)	0.01 (0.07)	0.06 (0.36)	0.15 (0.48)	0.19 (1)	0.06 (0.31)
China Ind. Prod.	−0.09 (−0.49)	−0.1 (−0.53)	−0.1 (−0.6)	0 (−0.02)	−0.01 (−0.07)	−0.13 (−0.79)
China PMI	0.25 (0.97)	0.07 (0.27)	0.02 (0.07)	0.29 (0.74)	0.12 (0.46)	0.14 (0.6)

Note: T-stats are between brackets. Bold figures indicate statistically significant figures at a 10% risk level.

Table 3.10 Estimation of the impact of economic news over selected energy markets depending on the NBER phase of the business cycle

		WTI	Brent	Gasoil	Natural Gas	Heating Oil	GSCI Energy
	Intercept	-0.65 (-0.42)	-4.05** (-2.64)	0.62 (0.4)	-1.25 (-0.81)	-3.3** (-2.13)	-1.78 (-1.16)
	AR	0.05 (1.43)	0.05* (1.66)	0.05 (1.45)	0.02 (0.3)	0.05 (1.49)	0.04 (1.19)
REC	Non Farm Payroll	0.63 (1.44)	0.67 (1.59)	**0.82** (2.07)**	1.03 (1.52)	**0.77* (1.78)**	**0.8*** (2.03)**
	ISM	0.5 (1.3)	-0.02 (-0.04)	**-0.59* (-1.72)**	-0.65 (-1.12)	-0.36 (-0.98)	-0.22 (-0.65)
	Jobless Claims	**-1.31** (-4.63)**	**-0.71** (-2.62)**	-0.05 (-0.21)	0.26 (0.61)	**-0.61** (-2.23)**	**-0.58** (-2.3)**
	US CPI MoM	0.01 (0.04)	-0.09 (-0.31)	0.25 (0.89)	-0.26 (-0.53)	-0.04 (-0.15)	0 (0.02)
	US Retail Sales	**-0.48* (-1.82)**	**-0.51** (-2.01)**	**-0.59** (-2.49)**	-0.11 (-0.26)	-0.38 (-1.49)	**-0.41* (-1.75)**
	Fed Target Rate	-0.01 (-0.04)	0.26 (0.88)	0.23 (0.82)	-0.4 (-0.84)	0.04 (0.13)	-0.01 (-0.03)
	US GDP	1.31 (1.46)	**1.6* (1.87)**	0.23 (0.28)	0.3 (0.22)	0.82 (0.93)	1.16 (1.45)
	ZEW Eco. Sent.	**-1.21** (-2.81)**	**-0.93** (-2.25)**	-0.21 (-0.54)	**-1.44** (-2.18)**	**-1.35** (-3.22)**	**-1.23** (-3.19)**
	IFO Expectations	**-1.02** (-2.56)**	**-1.01** (-2.64)**	**-0.87** (-2.44)**	-0.51 (-0.84)	-0.51 (-1.32)	**-0.88** (-2.46)**
	EMU CPI	**-0.73* (-1.77)**	**-0.94** (-2.37)**	**-0.7* (-1.88)**	**1.11* (1.75)**	**-0.94** (-2.34)**	**-0.73** (-1.96)**
	EMU GDP	0.56 (0.5)	0.16 (0.15)	-0.16 (-0.16)	2.44 (1.42)	0.12 (0.11)	0.71 (0.71)
	FR Bus. Conf.	**0.91** (2.66)**	**0.96** (2.93)**	0.37 (1.22)	0.71 (1.36)	0.73** (2.18)	**0.81** (2.64)**
	ECB Ref. Rate	**0.55** (2.24)**	**0.54** (2.28)**	**-0.02 (-0.1)**	0.25 (0.66)	**0.29 (1.21)**	**0.48** (2.2)**
	China CPI YoY	-0.34 (-0.51)	0.26 (0.4)	**1.33** (2.19)**	0.12 (0.12)	0.6 (0.91)	-0.08 (-0.13)
	China Ind. Prod.	-0.61 (-1.27)	-0.61 (-1.34)	**-1.08** (-2.49)**	-0.41 (-0.56)	-0.53 (-1.13)	-0.64 (-1.48)
	China PMI	0.4 (1.42)	0.27 (1.02)	0.23 (0.93)	0.4 (0.93)	0.31 (1.15)	0.32 (1.28)
EXP	Non Farm Payroll	0.08 (0.46)	0 (-0.03)	0.07 (0.44)	0.17 (0.64)	0.06 (0.33)	0 (0.01)
	ISM	0.16 (0.87)	0.07 (0.4)	0.27 (1.6)	**0.52* (1.84)**	0.27 (1.48)	0.18 (1.11)
	Jobless Claims	-0.21 (-1.03)	-0.17 (-0.87)	0.02 (0.12)	0.08 (0.24)	-0.18 (-0.91)	-0.09 (-0.48)
	US CPI MoM	-0.15 (-0.74)	-0.05 (-0.26)	-0.15 (-0.84)	0.15 (0.5)	0.05 (0.24)	-0.05 (-0.29)
	US Retail Sales	0.02 (0.07)	0.01 (0.02)	-0.24 (-0.86)	-0.13 (-0.27)	0.01 (0.02)	-0.01 (-0.05)
	Fed Target Rate	-0.02 (-0.06)	0.18 (0.48)	0.23 (0.65)	0.2 (0.34)	0.19 (0.5)	0.18 (0.51)
	US GDP	0.08 (0.24)	-0.08 (-0.27)	0 (0.02)	0.21 (0.43)	0.12 (0.39)	0.1 (0.34)
	ZEW Eco. Sent.	0.12 (0.5)	0.12 (0.54)	-0.02 (-0.09)	-0.09 (-0.24)	0.06 (0.28)	0.09 (0.44)
	IFO Expectations	0.39 (1.38)	0.36 (1.36)	0.04 (0.17)	0.49 (1.15)	0.29 (1.05)	0.36 (1.43)
	EMU CPI	-0.15 (-0.64)	0.04 (0.2)	-0.3 (-1.4)	-0.08 (-0.21)	-0.08 (-0.33)	-0.04 (-0.17)
	EMU GDP	0 (-0.01)	0.08 (0.23)	0.09 (0.29)	0.31 (0.57)	0.04 (0.13)	0.04 (0.12)
	FR Bus. Conf.	-0.21 (-0.86)	-0.13 (-0.56)	0.05 (0.24)	0.32 (0.83)	-0.06 (-0.23)	-0.1 (-0.47)
	ECB Ref. Rate	-0.13 (-0.39)	-0.08 (-0.27)	-0.11 (-0.38)	0.04 (0.08)	0.01 (0.04)	-0.03 (-0.12)
	China CPI YoY	0.06 (0.29)	-0.02 (-0.1)	-0.06 (-0.3)	0.12 (0.38)	0.14 (0.7)	0.06 (0.33)
	China Ind. Prod.	-0.01 (-0.03)	0 (-0.01)	0.09 (0.48)	0.07 (0.22)	0.08 (0.4)	-0.05 (-0.26)
	China PMI	0.41 (0.55)	-0.44 (-0.62)	-1.2* (-1.81)	-1.04 (-0.92)	-0.47 (-0.65)	-0.33 (-0.5)

Note: REC stands for 'Recession' and EXP for 'Expansion' according to the NBER Business Cycle Dating Committee. T-stats are between brackets. Bold figures indicate statistically significant figures at a 10% risk level.

counter-cyclical behavior. During recession periods, we identify various market movers: the price of gasoil displays a negative reaction to US retail sales, the ISM, German surveys, the EMU CPI and Chinese industrial production. In addition, gasoil shows a positive reaction to the Chinese CPI and US Non Farm Payrolls. During expansionary phases, we cannot relate the gasoil price to economic news at statistically significant levels. This latter result conforms to what has been found for crude oil prices.

3. **Natural Gas:** The full sample analysis reveals no reaction of the natural gas market to economic news. Expansion periods are characterized by one market mover: the US ISM with a pro-cyclical pattern. During recession periods, the natural gas price shows a negative reaction to the German ZEW, and a positive reaction to the EMU CPI. Overall, natural gas seems to be the energy market with the weakest link to the economic newsflow, even when accounting for periods of recession.

4. **Heating Oil:** In line with the WTI and the Brent prices, the heating oil price reacts only to the ISM – positively – over the long run. During expansion periods, there is no reaction to economic news at statistically significant levels. During recession periods, the results are similar to crude oil prices. In addition, we uncover a positive sensitivity to the US Non Farm Payrolls.

To sum up, energy markets seem to share a common pattern, i.e. a weak reaction to economic news during periods of economic expansion. Over periods of recession, US unemployment news seems to play a leading role in the evolution of these markets.

3.9.5   Agricultural Commodities

In this section, we detail the results obtained with agricultural commodities in Tables 3.11, 3.12, 3.13 and 3.14.

The main empirical findings can be summarized as follows:

1. **Corn:** During the full sample, corn prices exhibit a negative relationship with the Fed target rate, the ZEW economic sentiment index and the Chinese PMI. According to this long-term perspective, corn prices seem to be contra-cyclical – fearing, for instance, a tighter monetary policy from the Fed. These negative sensitivities are also valid during periods of recession. However, we also find a positive reaction to the US Non Farm Payrolls and the US CPI. To sum up, corn prices are found to increase when the Fed lowers its target rate, and when the US payroll and inflation figures are rising. During expansion periods, this commodity market does not seem to react in a statistically significant manner to economic news.

2. **Wheat:** The price of wheat behaves similarly to corn, with two minor differences: (i) during recession periods, the wheat price does not react to the US Non Farm Payrolls figures, and (ii) during expansion periods, this commodity price exhibits some sensitivity to the German IFO, i.e. to European economic conditions.

3. **Coffee:** The price of coffee is found to react positively to US retail sales, and negatively to the German ZEW and the EMU CPI. By disentangling recession from expansion periods, we get the insight that the reaction to US retail sales and the EMU CPI occurs during recessions. Conversely, the negative reaction to surprises in the German ZEW is a feature of expansion periods. Moreover, during recession periods, we uncover the fact that the price of coffee exhibits a positive sensitivity to the ECB main refinancing rate.

4. **Sugar:** During the full sample, we find a positive reaction of the sugar price to the Chinese PMI and CPI, and to the French Business Confidence index. Conversely, our results

Table 3.11 Estimation of the impact of economic news over selected agricultural markets

	Corn	Wheat	Coffee	Sugar	Cocoa
Intercept	3.79** (2.48)	0.22 (0.14)	−0.91 (−0.59)	−0.13 (−0.08)	−0.6 (−0.39)
AR	0.03 (0.98)	0.02 (0.5)	0.01 (0.16)	0.01 (0.17)	0.01 (0.33)
Non Farm Payroll	0.15 (1.12)	0.22 (1.53)	0 (0.02)	−0.04 (−0.24)	0.03 (0.24)
ISM	−0.13 (−0.96)	0.2 (1.35)	−0.1 (−0.56)	0.16 (1.01)	0.05 (0.37)
Jobless Claims	0.09 (0.71)	0.16 (1.11)	−0.15 (−0.84)	−0.1 (−0.62)	0.02 (0.12)
US CPI MoM	0.18 (1.34)	0.23 (1.56)	0.27 (1.47)	0.16 (0.96)	0.09 (0.63)
US Retail Sales	0.12 (0.73)	0.03 (0.19)	**0.54** (2.51)	0.24 (1.23)	−0.04 (−0.25)
Fed Target Rate	**−0.38*** (−1.95)	−0.32 (−1.54)	−0.25 (−0.96)	−0.13 (−0.57)	0 (−0.01)
US GDP	0.19 (0.78)	0.18 (0.67)	0.3 (0.89)	0.13 (0.44)	−0.21 (−0.81)
ZEW Eco. Sent.	**−0.41** (−2.46)**	−0.29 (−1.62)	**−0.44** (−1.94)**	−0.32 (−1.57)	0.04 (0.23)
IFO Expectations	−0.14 (−0.75)	−0.04 (−0.18)	0.13 (0.51)	0.18 (0.81)	0.16 (0.81)
EMU CPI	−0.21 (−1.27)	**−0.4** (−2.22)**	**−0.48** (−2.16)**	**−0.52** (−2.57)**	**−0.32*** (−1.77)**
EMU GDP	0.14 (0.53)	0.11 (0.38)	0.24 (0.65)	0.29 (0.88)	−0.17 (−0.59)
FR Bus. Conf.	0.11 (0.71)	**0.31*** (1.73)	0.22 (1.01)	**0.32*** (1.64)	**0.31*** (1.79)**
ECB Ref. Rate	0.19 (1.19)	0.26 (1.54)	0.34 (1.6)	0.3 (1.59)	−0.15 (−0.92)
China CPI YoY	−0.22 (−1.35)	−0.24 (−1.36)	0.23 (1.09)	**0.59** (3.03)**	−0.28 (−1.6)
China Ind. Prod.	−0.05 (−0.35)	−0.04 (−0.25)	0.21 (1.02)	**0.33*** (1.8)**	0.02 (0.11)
China PMI	**−0.39*** (−1.86)**	**−0.39*** (−1.73)**	0.26 (0.94)	0.41 (1.63)	−0.06 (−0.25)

Note: T-stats are between brackets. Bold figures indicate statistically significant figures at a 10% risk level.

Table 3.12 Estimation of the impact of economic news over selected agricultural markets

	Cotton	Soybean	Rice	GSCI Agri.
Intercept	2.35 (1.53)	−0.87 (−0.57)	4.62** (3.01)	2.46 (1.61)
AR	0 (0.11)	0.02 (0.72)	0.02 (0.79)	−0.01 (−0.27)
Non Farm Payroll	0.18 (1.28)	0.16 (1.39)	−0.01 (−0.05)	0.14 (1.56)
ISM	0.11 (0.77)	0.1 (0.86)	0.11 (0.88)	0.08 (0.84)
Jobless Claims	−0.12 (−0.89)	0.12 (1.07)	0 (−0.01)	0.05 (0.52)
US CPI MoM	0.04 (0.32)	**0.22* (1.91)**	0.19 (1.43)	**0.18** (2)
US Retail Sales	0.22 (1.3)	0.01 (0.11)	0.08 (0.51)	0.09 (0.79)
Fed Target Rate	0.04 (0.19)	−0.12 (−0.72)	0.06 (0.29)	−0.23* (−1.75)
US GDP	0.18 (0.7)	0.11 (0.5)	0.24 (1.01)	0.15 (0.91)
ZEW Eco. Sent.	−0.21 (−1.22)	**−0.32** (−2.18)**	0.05 (0.33)	**−0.31** (−2.76)**
IFO Expectations	0 (0.01)	−0.09 (−0.54)	−0.1 (−0.59)	−0.06 (−0.5)
EMU CPI	**−0.37** (−2.15)**	**−0.38** (−2.62)**	−0.01 (−0.08)	**−0.36** (−3.2)**
EMU GDP	−0.41 (−1.46)	−0.05 (−0.2)	0.18 (0.68)	0.05 (0.26)
FR Bus. Conf.	**0.33** (1.98)**	0.13 (0.92)	0.25 (1.6)	0.19* (1.69)
ECB Ref. Rate	0.19 (1.16)	0.03 (0.19)	0.12 (0.8)	0.2* (1.88)
China CPI YoY	**0.36** (2.18)**	−0.12 (−0.87)	0.08 (0.5)	−0.08 (−0.74)
China Ind. Prod.	0.03 (0.19)	0.19 (1.46)	−0.05 (−0.32)	0.03 (0.24)
China PMI	0.04 (0.17)	−0.12 (−0.67)	−0.03 (−0.17)	−0.19 (−1.36)

Note: T-stats are between brackets. Bold figures indicate statistically significant figures at a 10% risk level.

highlight a negative reaction to the EMU CPI. During periods of recession, the sugar price shows a statistically significant and positive reaction to US Non Farm Payrolls and the French Business Confidence index. During expansion periods, this commodity price reacts negatively to positive surprises in the EMU CPI, and to negative surprises in the Chinese CPI.

5. **Cocoa:** Over the long term, the price of cocoa has a positive reaction to the French Business Confidence index, and a negative reaction to the EMU CPI. During recession periods, the cocoa price reacts positively to US Non Farm Payrolls, the French Business Confidence index and Chinese industrial production. However, we also record a negative reaction when it comes to positive surprises in the EMU CPI. During expansion periods, we cannot detect any statistically significant reaction of the cocoa price to economic news.

6. **Cotton:** The full sample analysis reveals that the cotton price reacts negatively to surprises in the EMU CPI, and positively to surprises in the French Business Confidence index and the Chinese CPI. During recession periods, the price of cotton shows a negative reaction to the German IFO and the EMU CPI. In addition, we uncover a positive reaction to the French Business Confidence index and the ECB refinancing rate. During expansionary phases, the price of cotton exhibits a positive reaction to surprises in the IFO index and the Chinese CPI.

7. **Soybean:** During the full sample, we record a positive sensitivity of the soybean price to surprises in the US CPI. In addition, we detect a negative reaction to surprises in the German ZEW and the EMU CPI. During recession periods, the price of soybean exhibits a negative relationship with surprises in the German ZEW, the German IFO and the EMU CPI. During expansion periods, we find one market mover for this commodity price at statistically significant levels, i.e. Chinese industrial production (with a positive sign).

Table 3.13 Estimation of the impact of economic news over selected agricultural markets depending on the NBER phase of the business cycle

		Corn	Wheat	Coffee	Sugar	Cocoa
	Intercept	4.01** (2.61)	0.62 (0.4)	−0.87 (−0.56)	−0.2 (−0.13)	−0.24 (−0.16)
	AR	0.03 (0.88)	0.01 (0.35)	0.01 (0.16)	0.01 (0.15)	0.01 (0.33)
REC	Non Farm Payroll	**0.66* (1.88)**	0.37 (0.97)	0.31 (0.64)	**0.72* (1.67)**	**0.7* (1.85)**
	ISM	−0.03 (−0.09)	0.25 (0.74)	−0.32 (−0.79)	−0.16 (−0.43)	−0.08 (−0.24)
	Jobless Claims	−0.02 (−0.08)	0.28 (1.12)	0.03 (0.1)	0 (0.01)	−0.08 (−0.31)
	US CPI MoM	**0.5** (1.97)**	**0.51** (1.86)**	0.29 (0.85)	0.1 (0.32)	0.22 (0.8)
	US Retail Sales	0.13 (0.61)	0.14 (0.6)	**0.88** (3.1)**	0.25 (0.96)	0.08 (0.33)
	Fed Target Rate	**−0.53** (−2.11)**	**−0.57** (−2.1)**	−0.39 (−1.16)	−0.2 (−0.65)	0.22 (0.8)
	US GDP	0.79 (1.1)	0.67 (0.86)	0.42 (0.44)	0.02 (0.02)	0.1 (0.13)
	ZEW Eco. Sent.	**−0.87** (−2.52)**	**−0.73* (−1.95)**	−0.39 (−0.84)	−0.35 (−0.83)	−0.24 (−0.63)
	IFO Expectations	**−1.1** (−3.44)**	**−1.19** (−3.42)**	−0.14 (−0.32)	−0.36 (−0.92)	−0.16 (−0.47)
	EMU CPI	−0.53 (−1.59)	**−0.9* (−2.5)**	**−0.95** (−2.12)**	−0.59 (−1.46)	**−0.82** (−2.29)**
	EMU GDP	0.91 (1.02)	0.7 (0.72)	0.4 (0.33)	−0.05 (−0.05)	−1.39 (−1.44)
	FR Bus. Conf.	0.37 (1.33)	0.38 (1.28)	0.26 (0.7)	**0.66** (1.98)**	**0.68** (2.31)**
	ECB Ref. Rate	0.23 (1.17)	**0.42** (1.96)**	**0.55** (2.05)**	0.36 (1.51)	−0.34 (−1.62)
	China CPI YoY	−0.24 (−0.45)	−0.02 (−0.03)	0.59 (0.8)	−0.32 (−0.48)	−0.94 (−1.61)
	China Ind. Prod.	−0.62 (−1.61)	−0.67 (−1.59)	0.12 (0.23)	0.31 (0.66)	**0.83** (1.98)**
	China PMI	**−0.45** (−2.01)**	**−0.5** (−2.04)**	0.25 (0.82)	0.38 (1.39)	0 (0)
EXP	Non Farm Payroll	0.07 (0.47)	0.19 (1.26)	−0.05 (−0.26)	−0.17 (−0.97)	−0.08 (−0.51)
	ISM	−0.14 (−0.92)	0.19 (1.18)	−0.04 (−0.22)	0.25 (1.41)	0.11 (0.66)
	Jobless Claims	0.16 (0.99)	0.11 (0.6)	−0.25 (−1.15)	−0.15 (−0.77)	0.09 (0.51)
	US CPI MoM	0.06 (0.36)	0.13 (0.74)	0.27 (1.23)	0.18 (0.91)	0.01 (0.04)
	US Retail Sales	0.1 (0.41)	−0.1 (−0.39)	0.08 (0.25)	0.24 (0.79)	−0.2 (−0.76)
	Fed Target Rate	−0.25 (−0.81)	−0.03 (−0.09)	−0.05 (−0.12)	0.02 (0.06)	−0.37 (−1.11)
	US GDP	0.1 (0.38)	0.09 (0.32)	0.28 (0.78)	0.15 (0.46)	−0.25 (−0.87)
	ZEW Eco. Sent.	−0.27 (−1.44)	−0.17 (−0.83)	**−0.46* (−1.8)**	−0.32 (−1.38)	0.13 (0.65)
	IFO Expectations	0.33 (1.46)	**0.54** (2.19)**	0.26 (0.84)	0.43 (1.57)	0.3 (1.25)
	EMU CPI	−0.08 (−0.43)	−0.21 (−1.01)	−0.32 (−1.24)	**−0.49** (−2.09)**	−0.14 (−0.7)
	EMU GDP	0.07 (0.24)	0.05 (0.17)	0.22 (0.58)	0.33 (0.95)	−0.05 (−0.16)
	FR Bus. Conf.	0.02 (0.12)	0.32 (1.45)	0.2 (0.74)	0.16 (0.66)	0.13 (0.63)
	ECB Ref. Rate	0.1 (0.41)	−0.04 (−0.15)	−0.06 (−0.16)	0.15 (0.47)	0.16 (0.57)
	China CPI YoY	−0.21 (−1.29)	−0.26 (−1.45)	0.19 (0.85)	**0.68** (3.32)**	−0.21 (−1.17)
	China Ind. Prod.	0.05 (0.31)	0.07 (0.42)	0.22 (1)	0.33 (1.63)	−0.14 (−0.77)
	China PMI	0.43 (0.73)	0.64 (1)	0.53 (0.66)	0.61 (0.84)	−0.07 (−0.11)

Note: REC stands for 'Recession' and EXP for 'Expansion' according to the NBER Business Cycle Dating Committee. T-stats are between brackets. Bold figures indicate statistically significant figures at a 10% risk level.

Table 3.14   Estimation of the impact of economic news over selected agricultural markets depending on the NBER cycles

		Cotton	Soybean	Rice	GSCI Agri.
	Intercept	2.34 (1.52)	−0.3 (−0.19)	4.65** (3.02)	2.99* (1.94)
	AR	0 (0.08)	0.01 (0.56)	0.02 (0.88)	−0.01 (−0.39)
REC	Non Farm Payroll	0.45 (1.23)	0.31 (1.02)	−0.25 (−0.72)	**0.45* (1.88)**
	ISM	−0.17 (−0.54)	−0.14 (−0.53)	0.42 (1.41)	0 (0.01)
	Jobless Claims	−0.14 (−0.59)	0 (−0.01)	0.27 (1.21)	0.07 (0.43)
	US CPI MoM	−0.06 (−0.23)	0.27 (1.23)	0.26 (1.05)	**0.37** (2.18)**
	US Retail Sales	0.18 (0.82)	0.11 (0.59)	0.21 (1.01)	0.15 (1.06)
	Fed Target Rate	0.11 (0.44)	−0.27 (−1.23)	−0.08 (−0.32)	**−0.4** (−2.36)**
	US GDP	0.7 (0.95)	−0.04 (−0.07)	0.87 (1.25)	0.53 (1.08)
	ZEW Eco. Sent.	−0.48 (−1.34)	**−0.76** (−2.52)**	−0.52 (−1.56)	**−0.7** (−2.96)**
	IFO Expectations	**−0.83** (−2.5)**	**−0.7** (−2.53)**	**−0.59* (−1.91)**	**−0.73** (−3.35)**
	EMU CPI	**−1.34** (−3.9)**	**−0.86** (−2.99)**	0.19 (0.59)	**−0.8** (−3.55)**
	EMU GDP	−0.79 (−0.86)	−0.39 (−0.5)	0.24 (0.27)	0.24 (0.39)
	FR Bus. Conf.	**0.76** (2.68)**	0.38 (1.61)	**0.75** (2.81)**	**0.4** (2.12)**
	ECB Ref. Rate	**0.43** (2.13)**	0 (−0.01)	−0.03 (−0.18)	**0.29** (2.14)**
	China CPI YoY	−0.03 (−0.06)	−0.36 (−0.77)	**0.93* (1.78)**	−0.16 (−0.43)
	China Ind. Prod.	0.38 (0.96)	−0.49 (−1.47)	−0.31 (−0.82)	−0.37 (−1.4)
	China PMI	0.07 (0.3)	0 (−0.02)	−0.18 (−0.83)	−0.22 (−1.46)
EXP	Non Farm Payroll	0.12 (0.84)	0.13 (1.06)	0.04 (0.27)	0.09 (0.91)
	ISM	0.19 (1.25)	0.17 (1.29)	0.03 (0.22)	0.11 (1.05)
	Jobless Claims	−0.11 (−0.68)	0.2 (1.39)	−0.12 (−0.78)	0.04 (0.4)
	US CPI MoM	0.08 (0.48)	0.21 (1.51)	0.18 (1.15)	0.11 (1.05)
	US Retail Sales	0.27 (1.08)	−0.1 (−0.48)	−0.08 (−0.35)	−0.01 (−0.04)
	Fed Target Rate	−0.04 (−0.13)	0.08 (0.31)	0.23 (0.78)	−0.06 (−0.28)
	US GDP	0.11 (0.42)	0.12 (0.54)	0.16 (0.63)	0.1 (0.56)
	ZEW Eco. Sent.	−0.13 (−0.65)	−0.19 (−1.17)	0.22 (1.21)	−0.21 (−1.6)
	IFO Expectations	**0.39* (1.69)**	0.2 (1.05)	0.11 (0.52)	**0.25* (1.65)**
	EMU CPI	−0.03 (−0.13)	−0.22 (−1.3)	−0.08 (−0.43)	−0.2 (−1.51)
	EMU GDP	−0.37 (−1.26)	−0.01 (−0.05)	0.17 (0.62)	0.03 (0.15)
	FR Bus. Conf.	0.13 (0.61)	0.02 (0.13)	0.02 (0.09)	0.1 (0.75)
	ECB Ref. Rate	−0.27 (−1.03)	0.08 (0.37)	0.3 (1.19)	0.03 (0.19)
	China CPI YoY	**0.4** (2.31)**	−0.11 (−0.77)	−0.02 (−0.1)	−0.07 (−0.65)
	China Ind. Prod.	−0.04 (−0.25)	**0.31** (2.2)**	0 (0.02)	0.09 (0.84)
	China PMI	0.56 (0.92)	−0.47 (−0.91)	0.48 (0.83)	0.36 (0.88)

Note: REC stands for 'Recession' and EXP for 'Expansion' according to the NBER Business Cycle Dating Committee. T-stats are between brackets. Bold figures indicate statistically significant figures at a 10% risk level.

8. **Rice:** During the full sample and expansionary phases, we are unable to detect any significant influence on the price of rice. During recession periods, we identify one negative relationship to the German IFO, and two positive reactions to the French business confidence index and the Chinese CPI.

Overall, agricultural products are characterized by a rather complicated pattern, as we find few similarities within that particular class of commodities. Finally, it is noteworthy that we find almost no market mover for this type of commodity during expansionary phases (as in the case of energy markets).

3.10   CONCLUDING REMARKS

Our results reveal an interesting pattern: the response of commodity prices to economic surprises is strong during global downturns and weak during expansion periods. In addition, by slicing the information available into two-year subsets, the results show very limited support for the 'financial integration' theory. Our results suggest that commodity markets have been over-reacting to economic news during the 2008–2009 crisis, similar to what happened in 2001. During 2009–2010, our estimations reveal indeed a decreased sensitivity of commodity markets to the economic newsflow.

Having detailed the reaction of each type of commodity to the economic newsflow, we investigate more closely in the next chapter how commodity prices vary along the business cycle in various geographical zones.

REFERENCES

Alizadeh, AH., Nomikos, NK., Pouliasis, PK. 2008. A Markov Regime Switching Approach for Hedging Energy Commodities. *Journal of Banking and Finance* 32(9):1970–1983

Andersen, L. 2010. Markov Models for Commodity Futures: Theory and Practice. *Quantitative Finance* 10(8):831–854

Balduzzi, P., Elton, EJ., Green, TC. 2001. Economic News and Bond Prices: Evidence from the U.S. Treasury Market. *The Journal of Financial and Quantitative Analysis* 36(4):523–543

Barnhart, SW. 1989. The Effects of Macroeconomic Announcements on Commodity Prices. *American Journal of Agricultural Economics* 17(2):389–403

Baur, DG., McDermott, TK. 2010. Is Gold a Safe Haven? International Evidence. *Journal of Banking and Finance* 34:1886–1898

Beaudry, P., Collard, F., Portier, F. 2011. Gold Rush Fever in Business Cycles. *Journal of Monetary Economics* 58:84–97

Caballero, RJ., Farhi, E., Gourinchas, PO. 2008. Financial Crash, Commodity Prices, and Global Imbalances. *Brookings Papers on Economic Activity* Fall 2008:1–54

Cai, J., Cheung YL., Wong, MCS. 2001. What Moves the Gold Market? *Journal of Futures Markets* 21(3):257–278

Chan, KF., Treepongkaruna, S., Brooks, R., Gray, S. 2011. Asset Market Linkages: Evidence from Financial, Commodity and Real Estate Assets. *Journal of Banking and Finance* 35(6):1415–1426

Chevallier, J. 2012. Global Imbalances, Cross-market Linkages, and the Financial Crisis: A Multivariate Markov-switching Analysis. *Economic Modelling* 29(3):943–973

Chng, MT. 2009. Economic Linkages Across Commodity Futures: Hedging and Trading Implications. *Journal of Banking and Finance* 33(5):958–970

Christie-David, R., Chaudhry, M., Koch, TW. 2000. Do Macroeconomics News Releases Affect Gold and Silver Prices? *Journal of Economics and Business* 52(5):405–421

Dionne, G., Gauthier, G., Hammami, K., Maurice, M., Simonato, JG. 2011. A Reduced Form Model of Default Spreads with Markov-switching Macroeconomic Factors. *Journal of Banking and Finance* 35:1984–2000

Elder, J., Miao, H., Ramchander, S. 2012. Impact of Macroeconomic News on Metal Futures. *Journal of Banking and Finance* 36(1):51–65

Frankel, JA., Hardouvelis, GA. 1985. Commodity Prices, Money Surprises and Fed Credibility. *Journal of Money, Credit and Banking* 17(4):425–438

Ghura, D. 1990. How Commodity Prices Respond to Macroeconomic News. *Policy Research Working Paper* #354, The World Bank, Washington DC, USA

Guegan, D., Ielpo, F. 2009. Further Evidence on the Impact of Economic News on Interest Rates. *Frontiers in Finance and Economics* 6(2):1–45

Hamilton, JD. 1989. A New Approach to the Economic Analysis of Nonstationary Time Series and the Business Cycle. *Econometrica* 57(2):357–384

Hess, D., Huang, H., Niessen, A. 2008. How Do Commodity Futures Respond to Macroeconomic News? *Financial Markets and Portfolio Management* 22(2):127–146

Kilian, L., Vega, C. 2011. Do Energy Prices Respond to U.S. Macroeconomic News? A Test of the Hypothesis of Predetermined Energy Prices. *The Review of Economics and Statistics* 93(2):660–671

Miltersen, KL. 2003. Commodity Price Modelling that Matches Current Observables: a New Approach. *Quantitative Finance* 3(1):51–58

Roache, SK., Rossi, M. 2009. The Effects of Economic News on Commodity Prices: Is Gold Just Another Commodity? *IMF Working Papers* #09/140, International Monetary Fund, Washington DC, USA

Tang, K. 2012. Time-varying Long-run Mean of Commodity Prices and the Modeling of Futures Term Structures. *Quantitative Finance*, forthcoming. DOI:10.1080/14697688.2010.488654

Tang, K., Xiong, W. 2010. Index Investing and the Financialization of Commodities. *NBER Working Paper* #16385, Cambridge, Massachusetts, USA

4

Economic Regimes and Commodity Markets as an Asset Class

This chapter is devoted to understanding the stylized behavior of commodity prices depending on various phases of worldwide business cycles. First, we detail the main conclusions stemming from the existing academic literature. Second, we present the structure of the Markov regime-switching model. Third, we investigate to which business cycle commodity markets seem most related. Fourth, we determine during which phase the commodity prices are more likely to rise or fall. Fifth, we develop a performance analysis from a portfolio management optimization viewpoint.

4.1 INDEX PERFORMANCES, THE FED AND THE NBER CRISES

Based on economic conditions, this section is devoted to understanding the stylized behavior of commodity prices depending on each phase of the world business cycle. For example, when considering the price of gold, can we relate inflationary periods to periods of rising gold prices?

There are numerous contributions in the academic literature regarding the dependence of commodity prices on business cycle conditions or the Fed monetary policy. Bjornson and Carter (1997) show that, when interest rates, inflation and economic growth are high, the returns on commodities are usually at low levels. Other empirical studies such as Lummer and Siegel (1993), Kaplan and Lummer (1998), Greer (2000), Jensen *et al.* (2000; 2002), Gorton and Rouwenhorst (2005), Erb and Campbell (2006) and Roache (2008) discuss the interest in including commodities in a diversified portfolio. These authors conclude that commodities can help increase the expected return and lower the volatility of the portfolio.

Most global studies about the role of commodity futures in a diversified portfolio deliver the same conclusion: when positions are set at the right period of time, a diversified portfolio benefits from investing in commodity futures both in terms of absolute returns and risk-adjusted returns (Gorton and Rouwenhorst (2005)). To determine when to include commodities in a portfolio (i.e. under which economic circumstances), Gorton and Rouwenhorst (2005) argue that commodities offer an interesting investment opportunity at the early stage of a recession and at the trough stage of an expansion period. This conclusion seems to hold empirically both in absolute terms and in relative returns when compared to equities and bonds during 1959–2004.

Beyond these questions of economic regime and their impact on the performances of commodities, Jensen *et al.* (2002) try to identify some stylized facts regarding the performances of commodities depending on the Fed monetary policy. When the Fed enters a tightening period – i.e. with an increase of the decision rate over several months – the returns on commodity indices are found to outperform the returns on equities and bonds. Conversely, during periods of quantitative easing, commodity returns are outperformed by the traditional asset

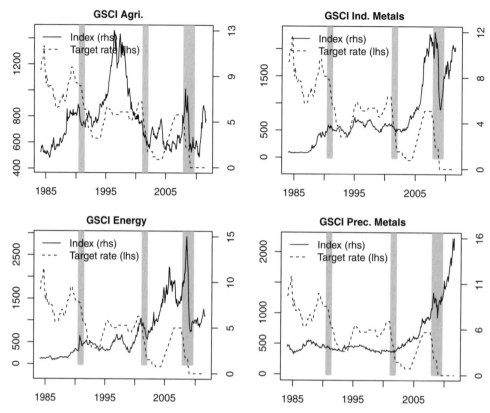

Figure 4.1 GSCI sub-indices' evolution over 1983–2011 along with NBER recession periods and the time series of the Fed target rate

allocation classes. The relationship between a rise in the Fed target rate and the performance of commodities is, however, complicated: the Fed usually raises its decision rate to slow the pace of the US economy. These inflationary worries are related to commodities, as the rise in the prices of raw products is more likely to be relayed by firms to the selling prices of final products.

These key facts can be observed in Figure 4.1 which displays the GSCI sub-indices, the NBER recession phases and the Fed target rate. The dataset starts in 1983 and ends in 2011, which provides a long-term perspective on the reaction of these indices to various economic conditions. Several observations can be made from this graph:

1. During the NBER recession periods, the GSCI sub-indices exhibit mostly negative performances. Empirical evidence therefore confirms that commodity prices are related to major changes in economic fundamentals.
2. During the NBER recovery periods – i.e. immediately after the end of a recession – when the Fed monetary policy remains on hold, commodity prices rise. This comment also holds for the GSCI Agricultural, Energy and Industrial Metals sub-indices when the Fed enters a tightening period. This effect may be explained by a lag before the increases in the Fed

decision rate actually trigger a collapse of commodity prices. Only the GSCI Precious Metals sub-index is characterized by a continuous rise following the increase in the Fed target rate in 2005. Before that, the global performance of precious metals was only slightly positive from 1985 to 2004.

In the next sections, we provide more stylized facts regarding the relationship between the economic regimes and the performances of commodity indices. Let us first detail how these regimes can be statistically measured.

4.2 MEASURING THE BUSINESS CYCLE

We recall here how to measure business cycles according to Hamilton's (1989) methodology. Let X_t be a vector of variables representing the position of a given economy in the business cycle at time t. This economy is composed of N states, which are defined by a different expectation and covariance of X_t such that for the state $i \in [1 : N]$:

$$X_t \sim N(\mu_i, \Sigma_i), \tag{4.1}$$

with μ_i the vector of expectations for the elements of X_t, and Σ_i the covariance matrix. When X_t is conditionally Gaussian, its unconditional distribution is a mixture of Gaussian distributions that can thus encompass non-normality. The probability at each time t for the economy to be assigned to state i is time varying. However the transition matrix – i.e. the matrix containing the unconditional probabilities to move from state 1 to state 2 – is fixed. Let us denote by P this transition matrix. The parameters driving the model are the first two moments for each state, the probabilities involved in the transition matrix, and the initial probabilities at time $t = 0$.

One of the main challenges for this model lies in the estimation of the parameters,[1] which are estimated by maximizing the log-likelihood function for a given time series. This log-likelihood function is given by:

$$L(\theta) = \sum_{t=1}^{T} \log f(X_t | \mathcal{F}_{t-1}, \theta), \tag{4.2}$$

with $f(.)$ the conditional density of X_t, T the total number of observations, and θ a vector containing the parameters to be estimated. $\mathcal{F}_{t-1}$ represents the information available at time t:

$$\mathcal{F}_{t-1} = \sigma\{X_{t-1}, X_{t-2}, \dots, X_1\}. \tag{4.3}$$

For a given θ, the conditional density at time t is:

$$f(X_t | \mathcal{F}_{t-1}, \theta) = \sum_{i=1}^{N} f(X_t | \mathcal{F}_{t-1}, \theta, S_t = i) P(S_t = i | \mathcal{F}_{t-1}), \tag{4.4}$$

with S_t the underlying state variable at time t. Intuitively, S_t is defined as the latent state of the economy, which is unknown to the econometrician but which can be inferred from the data by using a recursive filter in the spirit of the Kalman filter. Indeed, the central feature of the

---

[1] See Hamilton (1996) for a detailed presentation.

model is that the transition between regimes is governed by a Markov chain that assigns the probability of falling into the ith regime, according to the unobserved state variable.

$P(S_t = i | \mathcal{F}_{t-1})$ is the probability to be assigned the state i at time t, conditional upon the information available at time $t - 1$. The expression of $f(X_t | \mathcal{F}_{t-1}, \theta, S_t = i)$ is given by:

$$f(X_t | \mathcal{F}_{t-1}, \theta, S_t = i) = \frac{1}{(2\pi)^{\frac{k}{2}} |\Sigma_i|} \exp\left\{ -\frac{1}{2}(X_t - \mu_i)^{\top} \Sigma_i^{-1}(X_t - \mu_i) \right\}, \qquad (4.5)$$

with k the size of the vector X_t (i.e. the number of variables used to measure the phase of the business cycle). The parameters of the Markov-switching model are estimated by selecting θ such that:

$$\theta^* : \max_{\theta} L(\theta). \qquad (4.6)$$

As mentioned above, the estimation process requires the use of a recursive filter – known as the Expectation-Minimization (EM) algorithm – detailed in Hamilton's (1989) original article. As is standard practice in the literature, we use the EM filter to obtain explicitly the parameters of the Markov regime-switching model for a given θ.

4.3   TO WHICH BUSINESS CYCLE ARE THE COMMODITY MARKETS RELATED?

To the best of our knowledge, previous literature identifies the USA as being the leading business cycle for commodity markets (Barnhart (1989), Frankel and Hardouvelis (1985)). This view is justified by the fact that the US GDP is closely related to the worldwide business cycle, especially given the openness of this economy. Besides, most commodity prices are labeled in US Dollars, and the economic and monetary regimes under which the USA evolves are arguably of primary importance for commodity investors.

This hypothesis needs to be verified empirically. That is why we propose to conduct a formal statistical analysis of the performance of commodity markets through seven different domestic regimes in the USA, Europe, Germany, Canada, Australia, Brazil and China. These business cycles have been selected on the grounds of the potential interactions between these economies and commodity markets. For instance, Australia and Canada are well-known commodity producers, while China, Europe and the USA are mostly on the demand side of commodity markets. Brazil lies between the two categories, as both a producer and a consumer. Taken together, these various economic regimes will help us understand whether there is any region-specific behavior at stake in the price development of commodity markets, given that our sample includes various regions covering North and South America, Europe, Asia and Oceania.

During 1993–2011, we gathered for each of these countries seasonally adjusted measures of industrial production and consumer price indices.[2] This dataset is composed of monthly series. Then, we estimated Markov regime-switching models as detailed in Section 4.2. We set the number of regimes $N = 2$: regime 1 is characterized as 'expansion' (i.e. production and prices are rising together), while regime 2 is referred to as 'recession' (i.e. prices record a slightly negative variation and production sharply drops).

The estimation results are presented in Table 4.1 and Figure 4.2.

---

[2] Note that for Europe the sample starts in 1996.

Table 4.1 Descriptive statistics of the domestic cycles estimated with the Markov-switching model

			USA	Europe	Germany	Australia	Canada	China	Brazil
Expansion	Ind. Prod.	μ	3.949	3.101	3.696	4.512	2.977	15.291	4.179
		σ	0.661	0.91	1.012	0.806	1.116	1.636	1.922
	Inflation	μ	2.624	2.127	1.785	3.756	2.242	10.506	5.881
		σ	0.278	0.297	0.343	0.476	0.41	1.819	0.747
	Stat.	Pr. of expansion	0.984	0.981	0.969	0.936	0.963	0.978	0.988
		Freq. (months)	192	163	148	134	196	138	171
		Freq. (%)	0.828	0.901	0.818	0.59	0.856	0.603	0.747
Recession	Ind. Prod.	μ	−7.265	−12.28	−4.522	0.153	−4.561	12.153	−0.495
		σ	1.806	3.675	4.864	0.856	1.895	1.364	4.418
	Inflation	μ	1.827	0.234	0.351	1.78	0.104	0.557	41.933
		σ	0.994	0.371	0.347	0.358	0.617	0.53	13.333
	Stat.	Pr. of recession	0.92	0.849	0.878	0.918	0.821	0.967	0.947
		Freq. (months)	40	18	33	93	33	91	58
		Freq. (%)	0.172	0.099	0.182	0.41	0.144	0.397	0.253

According to Table 4.1, during expansion periods, US industrial production is expected to grow by 3.94%/month, while during recession periods it decreases by 7.27%/month. Similar comments arise for the different countries investigated here.[3] Another common feature of these different cycles consists in the duration of each regime: expansion periods typically last for a longer period of time than recessions. For instance, in Germany, the economy is expected to spend 18.2% of the sample in recession, with the remaining data points falling into expansionary phases.

Figure 4.2 shows the associated transition probabilities.[4] Figure 4.2 also displays in grey vertical lines the NBER business cycle reference dates, as published by the NBER Business Cycle Dating Committee.[5] Recessions start at the peak of a business cycle and end at the trough.

Visually, we observe that the estimates for the USA correspond most of the time to the NBER phases of the business cycle. In the rest of the world, the domestic cycles exhibit strong specificities. For instance, in 2008, the Eurozone entered a recessionary regime later than the USA, and also exited later. In 2011, Germany was impacted by a slowdown, without being followed by any other country.

Next, for each of these domestic cycles, we attempt to relate the performance of the S&P 500 (as a proxy of equity markets) compared to the GSCI and its sub-indices (Agriculture, Energy, Industrial Metals, Precious Metals). By doing so, we aim to evaluate how commodity markets behave along the business cycle, by explicitly taking into account country- and market-specific effects.

In essence, financial markets are forward-looking, i.e. they tend to anticipate the state of the economy for a given market depending on the phase of the business cycle. We are interested in the forecasting horizon that leads to the greatest discrimination between asset performances during expansionary and recessionary regimes. Thus, we need to find h such that excess

---

[3] It is worth remarking that in Brazil the recession was characterized by a surge in inflation during the so-called 'Tequila crisis' in the mid-1990s.

[4] The estimation routine generates one by-product in the form of the *transition* probability, which is the probability that state t will operate at t, conditional on information available up to $t-1$.

[5] See more on the NBER Business Cycle Expansions and Contractions at http://www.nber.org/cycles.html.

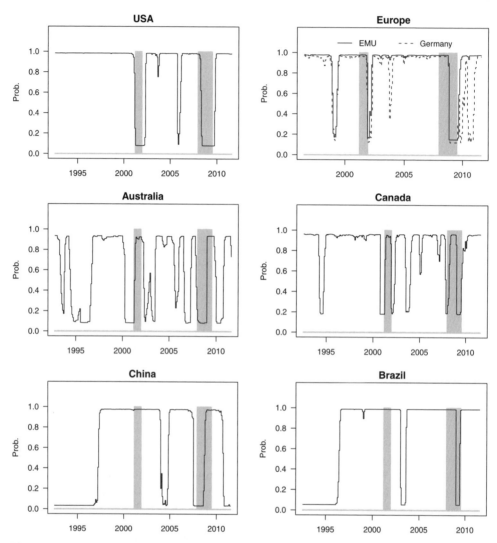

Figure 4.2   Business conditions during 1993–2011 estimated with the Markov-switching model.
Note: The transition probability is equal to 1 for expansion, and 0 for recession

returns – once adjusted for volatility – are as different as possible. Let $SR_h^{(i)}(m)$ be the Sharpe ratio obtained during state m for the asset i when considering that commodity markets are ahead of the business cycle by h months. We select h such that:

$$\max_h \sum_{j=1}^{N} \sum_{k=1,k\neq j,k>j}^{N} \left(SR_h^{(i)}(m_j) - SR_h^{(i)}(m_k)\right)^2, \tag{4.7}$$

with m_j the jth state of the economy, and N the total number of states. With $N = 2$, we have:

$$\max_h \left(SR_h^{(i)}(m_1) - SR_h^{(i)}(m_2)\right)^2. \tag{4.8}$$

This maximum spread between the Sharpe ratios can be used to measure the relation of a given phase of the business cycle with a given market. The results obtained are presented during the full sample (1993–2011) in Table 4.2, and during the sub-sample periods 1993–2003 and 2004–2011 in, respectively, Tables 4.3 and 4.4.

The following comments arise:

- During the full sample, the GSCI shows a strong connection to the business cycle located in the USA, Europe, Germany and Canada. The maximum score ranges from 0.23 in the USA to 0.42 in Europe. Therefore, we uncover that the US business cycle does not display the strongest relationship with commodity markets. This surprising finding is consistent across the GSCI sub-indices and during the sub-sample as well.
- The agricultural and energy sectors have the highest correlation with the business cycle measures. For instance, the maximum score is equal to 0.51 concerning the relationship betweeen the GSCI energy sub-index and the European business cycle.
- During the full sample, industrial metals are not found to be the most cyclical sector. However, during 2004–2011, industrial metals are characterized by the strongest connection with the business cycle measures (with a maximum score equal to 0.66 in China). This result illustrates the influence of sustained Chinese growth on the demand for raw materials in the industrial sector.
- In the long run, we find limited evidence of any connection between commodity markets and emerging countries such as China and Brazil, or with Australia. The bulk of the long-term relationship between macroeconomic conditions and commodity markets seems to occur in Europe and North America. For agricultural products, however, notice that the maximum score (equal to 0.19) is reached in China.
- During 1993–2003, the USA appears as the business cycle most correlated with commodity markets (before the 2008 financial crisis and the entry of China into the World Trade Organization (WTO)).
- During 2004–2011, the influence of Brazil and China grew: for industrial metals, the maximum score is obtained with the Chinese business cycle and a one-month forward-looking horizon. Similarly, the influence of the Brazilian business cycle is as strong as the USA for the energy and industrial metals sectors (with a maximum score close to 0.4). Late 2008, Europe entered the financial crisis as commodity prices decreased (especially with the evolution of the WTI crude oil futures price during July–October 2008). Recall that the USA had already been hit by the financial crisis since summer 2007 from the bailout of the Bear Stearns' hedge funds in June 2007 to the bankruptcy of Lehman Brothers in September 2008.
- Most of the commodities are found to be pro-cyclical: during expansion periods, commodity prices record a positive momentum. Conversely, recession periods are characterized by retreating prices. This behavior is very similar to the S&P 500.
- Precious metals stand out as the only exception. First, they display, on average, the weakest relationship to any business cycle. Second, they record negative to close to zero performances during periods of growth, and positive returns during periods of recession. This finding is consistent with the role of gold as a 'safe haven' to store value during recessions (Baur and McDermott (2010), Beaudry *et al.* (2011)), and as a hedge against inflation during expansion regimes.
- Finally, while the S&P 500 seems to be anticipating the business cycle by 5 to 6 months, commodities present a larger variety of forecasting horizons (ranging from 1 to 8). During

Table 4.2 Worldwide business cycles and commodity performances: 1993–2011

GSCI Agriculture						
	AU	BR	CA	CH	EU	GE	US
Recession	0.28%	−0.18%	−1.53%	1.22%	−4.20%	−3.10%	−2.77%
Expansion	−0.17%	0.11%	0.27%	−0.76%	0.10%	0.40%	0.49%
Lead	1	5	7	1	8	7	1
Score max.	0.04	0.03	0.14	0.19	0.25	0.25	0.24

GSCI Energy						
	AU	BR	CA	CH	EU	GE	US
Recession	1.15%	−1.85%	−3.56%	0.50%	−10.17%	−5.82%	−3.63%
Expansion	−0.19%	1.15%	1.08%	0.22%	1.72%	1.96%	1.08%
Lead	1	2	5	8	3	3	1
Score max.	0.07	0.16	0.2	0.03	0.51	0.37	0.22

GSCI Industrial Metals						
	AU	BR	CA	CH	EU	GE	US
Recession	−0.22%	−0.94%	−2.68%	0.52%	−6.10%	−2.76%	−2.80%
Expansion	1.07%	1.10%	1.15%	0.59%	1.40%	1.42%	1.23%
Lead	1	3	5	1	6	5	6
Score max.	0.11	0.17	0.29	0	0.51	0.3	0.3

GSCI Precious Metals						
	AU	BR	CA	CH	EU	GE	US
Recession	1.14%	0.98%	1.68%	1.04%	0.41%	1.74%	0.64%
Expansion	0.39%	0.64%	0.56%	0.46%	0.82%	0.63%	0.69%
Lead	8	1	1	6	5	2	8
Score max.	0.08	0.06	0.14	0.1	0.07	0.06	0.03

GSCI						
	AU	BR	CA	CH	EU	GE	US
Recession	0.57%	−1.04%	−2.99%	0.70%	−5.89%	−3.02%	−2.16%
Expansion	0.55%	1.18%	1.19%	0.38%	1.45%	1.55%	1.10%
Lead	1	3	5	8	3	3	5
Score max.	0.01	0.18	0.27	0.06	0.42	0.31	0.23

S&P 500						
	AU	BR	CA	CH	EU	GE	US
Recession	−0.14%	−0.39%	−1.48%	0.75%	−4.74%	−1.68%	−2.71%
Expansion	0.95%	0.79%	0.87%	0.34%	0.98%	0.87%	1.11%
Lead	1	6	3	5	5	5	6
Score max.	0.13	0.13	0.23	0.09	0.45	0.23	0.38

Note: AU stands for Australia, BR for Brazil, CA for Canada, CH for China, EU for Europe, GE for Germany, US for USA. The leading score is provided in months.

Table 4.3   Worldwide business cycles and commodity performances: 1993–2003

GSCI Agriculture						
AU	BR	CA	CH	EU	GE	US

	AU	BR	CA	CH	EU	GE	US
Recession	−0.08%	0.28%	−0.78%	0.74%	−1.02%	−2.97%	−1.97%
Expansion	−0.07%	−0.20%	0.05%	−0.73%	−0.65%	−0.53%	0.06%
Lead	2	2	5	8	8	7	3
Score max.	0	0.07	0.11	0.21	0.06	0.32	0.27

GSCI Energy						

	AU	BR	CA	CH	EU	GE	US
Recession	−1.10%	−1.21%	−2.12%	−0.62%	−1.12%	−5.09%	−4.42%
Expansion	0.84%	0.99%	1.56%	1.25%	2.87%	1.56%	1.12%
Lead	7	7	8	8	6	1	2
Score max.	0.13	0.16	0.24	0.11	0.21	0.28	0.33

GSCI Industrial Metals						

	AU	BR	CA	CH	EU	GE	US
Recession	−1.07%	−0.66%	−0.27%	0.29%	−0.93%	−2.73%	−2.25%
Expansion	0.36%	0.10%	0.11%	−0.07%	0.60%	0.26%	0.29%
Lead	1	8	7	2	3	2	3
Score max.	0.17	0.09	0.04	0.04	0.18	0.56	0.35

GSCI Precious Metals						

	AU	BR	CA	CH	EU	GE	US
Recession	0.36%	0.60%	0.95%	0.45%	0.60%	1.63%	0.61%
Expansion	0.14%	0.01%	−0.11%	−0.03%	−0.60%	−0.02%	0.09%
Lead	5	6	4	6	8	1	5
Score max.	0.03	0.07	0.15	0.07	0.17	0.19	0.08

GSCI						

	AU	BR	CA	CH	EU	GE	US
Recession	−0.74%	−0.22%	−1.25%	−0.15%	−0.65%	−3.07%	−3.97%
Expansion	0.38%	0.33%	0.67%	0.37%	0.95%	0.56%	0.66%
Lead	1	1	8	8	6	2	2
Score max.	0.1	0.07	0.21	0.05	0.13	0.22	0.37

S&P 500						

	AU	BR	CA	CH	EU	GE	US
Recession	0.78%	0.26%	−0.93%	0.91%	−1.14%	−3.21%	−2.41%
Expansion	0.57%	0.73%	1.22%	0.51%	1.84%	0.92%	0.99%
Lead	8	3	3	1	8	4	4
Score max.	0.01	0.02	0.25	0.14	0.32	0.38	0.38

Note: AU stands for Australia, BR for Brazil, CA for Canada, CH for China, EU for Europe, GE for Germany, US for USA. The leading score is provided in months.

Table 4.4   Worldwide business cycles and commodity performances: 2004–2011

	AU	BR	CA	CH	EU	GE	US
				GSCI Agriculture			
Recession	−1.61%	−3.83%	−4.67%	−5.02%	−5.44%	−6.62%	−2.76%
Expansion	1.38%	0.90%	1.11%	0.80%	1.06%	1.05%	1.06%
Lead	8	8	4	1	3	3	2
Score max.	0.22	0.29	0.37	0.33	0.37	0.48	0.25
				GSCI Energy			
Recession	−2.54%	−8.20%	−6.42%	−10.54%	−9.47%	−13.94%	−5.78%
Expansion	1.99%	1.42%	1.24%	1.34%	1.20%	1.66%	1.53%
Lead	8	8	3	1	1	3	2
Score max.	0.24	0.39	0.32	0.41	0.41	0.65	0.31
				GSCI Industrial Metals			
Recession	−1.42%	−5.10%	−4.49%	−8.90%	−7.87%	−9.01%	−4.83%
Expansion	3.37%	2.61%	2.22%	2.44%	2.64%	2.43%	2.95%
Lead	8	8	8	1	3	4	5
Score max.	0.36	0.47	0.4	0.66	0.64	0.61	0.5
				GSCI Precious Metals			
Recession	1.97%	2.06%	1.88%	2.91%	0.97%	1.67%	1.70%
Expansion	1.12%	1.33%	1.36%	1.22%	1.53%	1.42%	1.42%
Lead	1	1	1	8	8	1	7
Score max.	0.11	0	0.02	0.09	0.07	0.04	0.06
				GSCI			
Recession	−1.43%	−5.47%	−4.58%	−8.92%	−5.87%	−10.38%	−3.40%
Expansion	2.88%	2.08%	2.04%	2.13%	1.98%	2.32%	2.11%
Lead	8	8	3	1	3	3	2
Score max.	0.33	0.42	0.37	0.53	0.4	0.67	0.34
				S&P 500			
Recession	−0.85%	−2.10%	−2.78%	−5.96%	−4.95%	−5.06%	−3.51%
Expansion	1.28%	0.88%	0.99%	1.16%	1.25%	1.05%	1.44%
Lead	6	8	5	1	3	5	4
Score max.	0.28	0.27	0.38	0.66	0.54	0.51	0.51

Note: AU stands for Australia, BR for Brazil, CA for Canada, CH for China, EU for Europe, GE for Germany, US for USA. The leading score is provided in months.

the full sample, these horizons are closer to 3 to 5 when focusing only on the highest maximum score. Hence, it seems that commodity markets contain less anticipation from market agents than equity markets.

Having detailed the relationship between commodity prices and the business cycle in emerging and developed countries, we move in the next section to a more qualitative question: during what kind of phase of the business cycle are commodity prices more likely to rise or fall?

4.4 COMMODITY PERFORMANCES DEPENDING ON THE NATURE OF EACH ECONOMIC REGIME

In this section, we use a large dataset of US economic time series during 1984–2011. Indeed, the US business cycle offers the advantage of being well synchronized with the world business cycle in the long term. The key economic indicators retained are: industrial production, the consumer price index, consumer goods inventories, durable goods inventories, the unemployment rate and the Fed target rate. Hence, we capture various characteristics of the US business cycle, going from inventory to inflation cycles. The dataset is composed of monthly series and comes from Bloomberg.

Concerning the number of regimes necessary to model the US economy, previous literature focused on two states (Hamilton (1989), Kim and Nelson (1999), Birchenhall et al. (1999), Artis and Zhang (1998)) or more (Sichel (1994), Boldin (1996), Clements and Krolzig (1998, 2003), Artis et al. (2004)), typically capturing expansion/recession periods and additionally growth with/without limited inflation.

As pointed out by Hamilton (1996), the assumption that the process describing the data presents a given number N of regimes cannot be tested by using the usual likelihood ratio (LR) test, as specific regularity conditions are not fulfilled.[6]

To test explicitly whether a Markov-switching model with two states is superior to another model with three states, for instance, we use Vuong's (1989) test based on the distributional goodness-of-fit that the model is able to provide.[7] This approach draws on Amisano and Giacomini (2007), and it has been applied recently to US equity and credit markets by Ielpo (2012). Formally, to compare a Markov-switching model with N_i states to another model with N_j states, we need to compute the following test statistics:

$$t_{N_i,N_j} = \frac{1}{T} \sum_{t=1}^{T} \left(\log f_{\hat{\theta}_{N_i}} \left(X_t | \mathcal{F}_{t-1} \right) - \log f_{\hat{\theta}_{N_j}} \left(X_t | \mathcal{F}_{t-1} \right) \right), \tag{4.9}$$

Under the null hypothesis that the Markov-switching model with N_i states provides an equivalent fit to the model with N_j states, this statistic is distributed as:

$$\frac{t_{N_i,N_j}}{\hat{\sigma}_T} \sqrt{T} \sim N(0, 1), \tag{4.10}$$

with σ_T the standard deviation associated with the statistic t_{N_i,N_j}. The alternative hypothesis is that the test statistic is different from 0, and that the forecasting ability of both models is not

---

[6] Nonetheless, Hamilton (1996) presents a variety of tests to determine whether an additional state is required to model the dynamics of the data.

[7] Other penalized likelihood tests based on Psaradakis and Spagnolo (2003) or Smith et al. (2005, with the notion of Kullback–Leibler divergence) can be found in Gatumel and Ielpo (2012), along with Monte Carlo testing of the respective power of each test.

Table 4.5 Vuong's (1989) test to select the appropriate number of regimes

	1 state	2 states	3 states	4 states	5 states	6 states
1 state		−7.4	−10.05	−11.4	−13.31	−12.7
2 states			−6.48	−10.62	−13.49	−13.3
3 states				−5.01	−10.22	−8.47
4 states					−5.16	−4.86
5 states						−1.72
6 states						

the same. The standard deviation $\hat{\sigma}_T$ is estimated by using the Newey–West long-run variance Heteroskedasticity and Autocorrelation Consistent (HAC) estimator.

The best model is selected so that it is preferred to models with a lower number of states, but equivalent to models with a higher number of states. The resulting model specification should be parsimonious to avoid the problem of overfitting (Bradley and Jansen (2004)), while being as consistent as possible with the joint distribution of returns.

When performing Vuong's (1989) test, we find that $N = 5$ as shown in Table 4.5. We obtain two expansion regimes, two recession regimes and one 'stalling regime'. These regimes are displayed in Figure 4.3, with descriptive statistics given in Table 4.6. The following comments arise:

- Regimes 1 and 5 are *expansionary* regimes:
    1. Regime 5 is characterized by a 3.6%/month increase in industrial production, rising inflation, receding unemployment, but still – on average – decreasing Fed decision rates. Inventories are weakly evolving.
    2. Regime 1 is very similar to Regime 5. As we observe strongly building inventories, and an increasing Fed target rate, we label this regime as 'strong growth'.

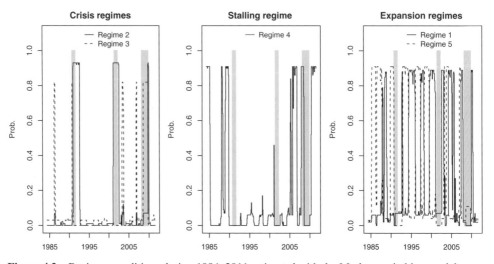

Figure 4.3 Business conditions during 1984–2011 estimated with the Markov-switching model

Table 4.6   Descriptive statistics of the estimated economic regimes

		Strong Exp.	Slowdown	Strong Crisis	Stalling	Medium Expans.
		Reg. 1	Reg. 2	Reg. 3	Reg. 4	Reg. 5
Indus. Prod.	μ	0.041	0	−0.076	0.021	0.036
	σ	0.009	0.017	0.024	0.011	0.007
CPI	μ	0.029	0.025	0.007	0.036	0.031
	σ	0.003	0.004	0.017	0.006	0.004
Good Inv.	μ	0.055	−0.065	−0.048	0.095	0.005
	σ	0.008	0.016	0.027	0.011	0.008
Dur. Good Inv.	μ	0.048	−0.079	−0.041	0.099	0.006
	σ	0.009	0.016	0.023	0.011	0.01
Unempl. rate	μ	−0.382	1.172	2.276	−0.307	−0.411
	σ	0.18	0.213	0.527	0.265	0.199
Fed TR	μ	0.971	−2.629	−1.379	−0.348	−0.399
	σ	0.407	0.565	0.513	1.042	0.358
	Freq. (months)	92	40	27	67	102
	Freq. (%)	0.28	0.122	0.082	0.204	0.311

Note: μ is for the expected performance of each of the listed figures, whereas σ stands for the volatility of these figures across economic regimes.

- Regimes 2 and 3 are *recessionary* regimes:
  1. Regime 2 is characterized by a strong decline in industrial production, with the unemployment rate rising rapidly and lowered Fed decision rates. By looking at Figure 4.3, we can understand that this regime corresponds to the burst of an economic crisis.
  2. Regime 3 is a typical slowdown period: industrial production decreases – but not as much as for Regime 2 – and the Fed decreases its decision rate, even more aggressively so as to limit as much as possible the building of unemployment. When examining the transition matrix presented in Table 4.7, the persistence of this regime is weaker than the persistence of Regime 2.
- Regime 4 is a 'stalling' regime, i.e. between expansion and recession. Industrial production grows by 2%/month, whereas goods and durable goods inventories are building up quickly, underlining the weak underlying consumer demand.

Table 4.8 presents the optimal forecasting horizon that should be retained to link the five regimes to the performances of commodities. We use the same metric as presented in Equation (4.8) which we refer to as the 'maximum score'. Based on these results, we can describe the stylized performances of commodity sectors, depending on the phase of the business cycle.

Table 4.7   Estimated transition matrix between regimes

	Reg. 1	Reg. 2	Reg. 3	Reg. 4	Reg. 5
Reg. 1	89%	1%	0%	6%	4%
Reg. 2	7%	93%	0%	0%	0%
Reg. 3	0%	7%	82%	0%	11%
Reg. 4	2%	0%	3%	91%	3%
Reg. 5	6%	0%	3%	0%	91%

Table 4.8 Optimal forecasting horizon for the various asset classes

	GSCI Agri.	GSCI Energy	GSCI Ind. Metals	GSCI Prec. Metals	GSCI Total	S&P 500	10Y US	US Dollar
Leading +0	0.16	0.25	0.2	0.07	0.24	0.12	0.09	0.14
Leading +1	0.14	0.27	0.2	0.11	0.29	0.21	0.05	0.08
Leading +2	0.26	0.27	0.24	0.11	0.3	0.24	0.09	0.06
Leading +3	0.25	0.26	0.22	0.13	0.29	0.24	0.08	0.1
Leading +4	**0.31**	**0.3**	0.32	0.14	**0.32**	0.25	0.08	0.06
Leading +5	0.22	0.26	**0.35**	**0.18**	0.3	0.29	0.16	0.07
Leading +6	0.19	0.21	0.31	0.11	0.26	0.31	0.17	0.1
Leading +7	0.17	0.18	0.29	0.21	0.26	0.36	0.22	0.1
Leading +8	0.22	0.19	0.36	0.15	0.28	**0.41**	**0.3**	**0.13**
Leading +9	0.19	0.13	0.37	0.14	0.24	0.4	0.24	0.11
Leading +10	0.11	0.05	0.34	0.08	0.18	0.39	0.18	0.15
Leading +11	0.17	0.12	0.34	0.18	0.22	0.36	0.33	0.18
Leading +12	0.27	0.16	0.27	0.2	0.27	0.37	0.31	0.27

Table 4.9 presents the performance by regime for each of the assets considered. The main findings can be summarized as follows:

- When entering the crisis, all commodities deliver strongly negative returns, except precious metals (with an increase by 1.29%/month on average). Hence, we verify the role of 'safe haven' for precious metals when entering a recession. Other commodity markets logically underperform compared to the S&P 500. For instance, the energy sector records a drop of −4.14%/month vs. −2.43%/month for equities.
- During the prolonged slowdown period, central banks are stimulating the economy. As a consequence, we find that energy and industrial metals commodities are improving on average by, respectively, 0.32%/month and 0.21%/month. Other cyclical commodities exhibit decreasing prices.
- During the medium expansion regime, agricultural prices are rising by 0.27%/month. Conversely, energy and industrial metals prices are decreasing by, respectively, −0.18%/month and −0.45%/month. More importantly, the S&P 500 outperforms all commodities. Investors should therefore not increase their exposure to commodity markets during periods of medium growth.

Table 4.9 Performance of various indices depending on each of the economic regimes

	Strong Exp.	Slowdown	Strong Crisis	Stalling	Medium Expans.
	State 1	State 2	State 3	State 4	State 5
GSCI Agri.	0.47%	−0.72%	−2.87%	1.27%	0.27%
GSCI Energy	2.63%	0.32%	−4.14%	1.60%	−0.18%
GSCI Ind. Metals	2.11%	0.21%	−2.12%	3.44%	−0.45%
GSCI Prec. Metals	0.55%	−0.51%	1.29%	1.25%	0.05%
GSCI Total	1.76%	−0.34%	−2.63%	1.36%	−0.37%
S&P 500	1.37%	−0.80%	−2.43%	0.84%	1.20%
10Y US	1.36%	−0.91%	−2.58%	−0.03%	−1.66%
US Dollar	−0.31%	0.11%	−0.29%	0.24%	−0.30%

- During strong expansions, energy and industrial metals prices show positive returns, and even outperfom equity returns. This strong expansionary phase is typically a period of 'commodity boom' for investors.
- During the stalling regime, all commodity prices are rising and outperform the returns on the S&P 500. With roaring inflation, even the precious metals deliver positive returns, consistent with the idea that these metals are also used as a hedge against inflation. Industrial metals are found to outperform all commodity indices.

By decomposing the business cycle into five regimes, our empirical results suggest that (long) investors should invest in commodities especially during the stalling regime, i.e. at the end of the economic cycle (before the recession). According to our estimates, the stalling regime corresponds to 20% of the data sample.

Finally, Table 4.10 provides a unique picture of the time-varying correlation levels during the expansion/recession (and even stalling) regimes, and of the extent to which the asset

Table 4.10 Correlations between assets across regimes

Regimes 1 and 5								
	Agri.	Energy	Ind. Metals	Prec. Metals	Total	S&P 500	10Y US	US Dollar
Agri.		−0.17	0.01	−0.02	−0.02	0.06	−0.17	0.11
Energy	**0.10**		0.06	0.02	0.94	0.00	0.03	−0.11
Ind. Metals	**0.14**	**−0.02**		0.31	0.17	0.18	0.10	−0.17
Prec. Metals	**0.26**	**0.25**	**0.01**		0.08	0.00	−0.11	−0.39
Total	**0.39**	**0.84**	**0.06**	**0.30**		−0.01	0.02	−0.14
S&P 500	**0.05**	**0.04**	**0.21**	**−0.06**	**0.08**		−0.22	0.11
10Y US	**0.09**	**−0.08**	**0.18**	**−0.04**	**−0.18**	**0.03**		0.07
US Dollar	**−0.01**	**−0.23**	**0.01**	**−0.31**	**−0.23**	**0.04**	**0.30**	

Regimes 2 and 3								
	Agri.	Energy	Ind. Metals	Prec. Metals	Total	S&P 500	10Y US	US Dollar
Agri.		0.19	0.11	0.23	0.33	0.49	0.11	−0.39
Energy	**0.28**		0.16	0.41	0.95	−0.27	0.31	−0.07
Ind. Metals	**0.55**	**0.58**		0.23	0.26	0.25	0.40	−0.11
Prec. Metals	**0.34**	**0.13**	**0.30**		0.48	−0.18	0.30	−0.23
Total	**0.47**	**0.94**	**0.71**	**0.28**		−0.16	0.38	−0.15
S&P 500	**0.45**	**0.30**	**0.60**	**0.02**	**0.36**		0.14	−0.16
10Y US	**−0.18**	**0.11**	**0.14**	**−0.30**	**0.13**	**−0.05**		0.24
US Dollar	**−0.44**	**−0.38**	**−0.53**	**−0.48**	**−0.42**	**−0.52**	**0.44**	

Regime 4								
	Agri.	Energy	Ind. Metals	Prec. Metals	Total	S&P 500	10Y US	US Dollar
Agri.		0.11	0.29	0.25	0.33	0.09	0.09	−0.47
Energy			0.13	0.31	0.90	0.17	0.25	−0.23
Ind. Metals				0.25	0.26	0.15	0.30	−0.60
Prec. Metals					0.43	−0.05	0.05	−0.36
Total						0.23	0.29	−0.39
S&P 500							0.34	0.01
10Y US								−0.06
US Dollar								

Note: The figures in bold contain the correlations between Regimes 1 and 5, then Regimes 2 and 3, in the same matrix.

correlations vary between them. As mentioned in the introduction, the correlation between regimes can change significantly. For instance, the correlation between industrial metals and agricultural products ranges from 0.01 to 0.29 depending on the phase of the business cycle. A similar conclusion can be reached for the correlation between energy commodities and the S&P 500, which oscillates between −0.27 and 0.17. From these empirical measures, we get the idea that commodity investors should handle with caution the 'low correlation' investment argument for commodities taken as a whole.

4.5   PERFORMANCE ANALYSIS

This section aims at understanding what kind of investor the information drawn from business cycles is useful to by comparing three different strategies (Geman and Ohana (2008), Daskalaki and Skiadopoulos (2011)):

1. **A pure commodity investment strategy:** for such a strategy, the investor can only invest in the four GSCI sub-indices (i.e., agricultural products, industrial metals, precious metals, and energy commodities). This type of portfolio is built for pure commodity investors, who are interested in the extra value that cyclical information has to offer.
2. **A pure equity–bonds investment strategy:** this strategy invests in both the S&P 500 and a 10-year US bond (as proxied by US government benchmarks taken from Merrill Lynch indices whose average maturity is 10 years). This type of portfolio is designed to mimic an asset allocation strategy that is supposed to overweigh risky assets vs. riskless assets during periods of strong growth (and conversely during downturns).
3. **A mixed equity–bonds–commodities strategy:** this third strategy is a mix of the two previous strategies. It aims at gauging the potential benefits of adding commodities to a classical asset allocation portfolio in the context of business cycle variations.

The central question arising from the availability of more than 20 years of data for commodities is: what is the value of following business cycles given the sharp trends observed in Figure 4.1? To answer this question, we use the following investment scheme: assuming that we know that the US economy is at time t in regime i, we get from Table 4.9 and Table 4.10 each asset's expected return μ_i and the corresponding covariance matrix Σ_i. The optimal Markowitz portfolio loadings are given by:

$$\omega_i = \frac{1}{2}\mu_i\Sigma_i^{-1} \tag{4.11}$$

Thus, we obtain one vector of portfolio loadings for each of the regimes impacting the US economy. These loadings are re-scaled for every strategy to have a comparable risk budget of 10%, i.e. each portfolio has an *ex ante* volatility of 10%.

Hence, when investing along the business cycle, investors can switch from one ω_i to another ω_j depending on the economic regime.[8] Note that we are not interested here in explaining how to make profits by investing in financial markets. Instead, our focus lies in evaluating the value of cyclical information for investors and fund managers.

In what follows, we compare the extra return of investing based on the knowledge of the various phases of the business cycle vs. the investment strategy depending only on a structural

---

[8] Of course, this stylized exercise represents only an attempt to measure the value of cyclical information. In practice, having this information when deciding on an investment strategy requires forecasting the US business cycle at least three quarters in advance.

view (i.e., the long run expected returns and covariance of the different assets considered here). This is simply done by replacing:

$$\omega_i = \bar{\omega} = \frac{1}{2}\bar{\mu}\bar{\Sigma}^{-1} \qquad (4.12)$$

where $\bar{\mu}$ and $\bar{\Sigma}$ are the total estimates of expected returns and covariance. Indeed, comparing our dynamic investment strategy dependent on the business cycle to a standard buy-and-hold strategy (or to a money market investment) would not allow us to operate such a comparison between cyclical and structural information. The most likely consequence would be that the former strategy outperforms the latter.

The loadings for the pure commodity strategy are presented in Table 4.11. The long-term loadings lead to a long position in industrial and precious metals, and in energy commodities as well. A short position in agricultural products is also recommended by the Markowitz optimal loadings. Such a portfolio typically invests in commodities with the strongest trends, weighted by their relative volatilities and correlations. When the investment strategy depends on cyclical information, the results look more complex. Consistent with what has been detailed in the previous section, during periods of strong and medium expansion, a long position in precious metals is turned into a long position in industrial metals. Given the alternance between these phases, most of the value in the diversified commodity portfolio comes from the regime-switching mechanism. When entering a stalling regime, the optimal portfolio goes long in every sector, as the surge in inflation triggers rising prices of precious metals. This long position in precious metals is maintained when entering the strong crisis period, but a short position in the three other categories of commodities is recommended. The slowdown phase should come with a short position in each sector, except energy which is the first rallying sector at the end of the crisis.

When comparing the returns on the two strategies at the bottom of Table 4.11, this cyclical positioning yields an average return increased by 4.12% for an equivalent risk budget.

Table 4.11 Performance analysis – pure commodity

Loadings		Agri.	Energy	Ind. Metals	Prec. Metals
	Static	−0.11	0.07	0.32	0.30
Strong Exp.	Reg. 1	0.12	0.09	0.39	−0.07
Slowdown	Reg. 2	−0.75	0.10	−0.19	−0.30
Strong Crisis	Reg. 3	−0.07	−0.06	−0.22	0.28
Stalling	Reg. 4	0.02	0.12	0.29	0.27
Medium Expans.	Reg. 5	0.06	0.15	−0.47	0.38

PnL		Cmdty Static	Cmdty Dynamic
	Avg. Return	5.85%	9.97%
	Volatility	10.01%	10.95%
	Sharpe Ratio	0.58	0.91

Note: PnL stands for profits and losses, Cmdty Static for the structural view of investing strategy in commodities, and Cmdty Dynamic for the regime-switching view of investing strategy in commodities.

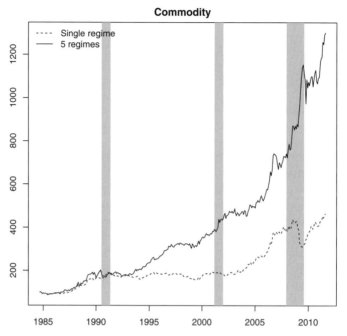

Figure 4.4   Commodity allocation

This result is also obvious by looking at Figure 4.4: when managing a pure commodity fund, the cyclical information offers an interesting value to an investor, even when reliable forecasts for long-term trends are available for commodity markets.

Table 4.12 and Figure 4.5 show similar results in the case of a balanced equity–bond portfolio. In the long run, the usual long bonds–long equity position is found to be the optimal

Table 4.12   Performance analysis – balanced portfolio

Loadings		S&P 500	US Bonds
	Static	0.26	1.03
Strong Exp.	Reg. 1	0.62	−0.13
Slowdown	Reg. 2	−0.31	1.48
Strong Crisis	Reg. 3	−0.38	0.45
Stalling	Reg. 4	0.77	0.52
Medium Expans.	Reg. 5	0.23	0.98

	Eq.–Bds Static	Eq.–Bds Dynamic
Avg. Return	11.43%	10.46%
Volatility	10.06%	10.49%
Sharpe Ratio	1.14	1.00

Note: Eq.–Bds Static stands for the structural view of investing strategy in equities/bonds, and Eq.–Bds Dynamic for the regime-switching view of investing strategy in equities/bonds.

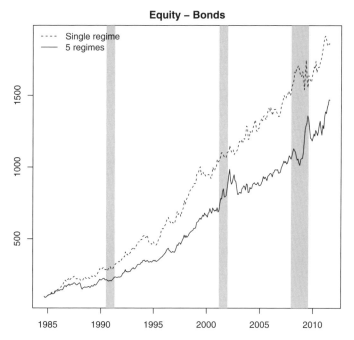

Figure 4.5   Equity–bonds allocation

allocation strategy. The cyclical information points toward a long position in equity and bonds during the stalling and medium expansion regimes. A short position in equity is recommended during the crisis period, and a short bond position looks optimal during strong expansion periods. Unlike the pure commodity case, the dynamic allocation does not overperform the static allocation. Indeed, we observe that the static allocation delivers a Sharpe ratio of 1.14, whereas the dynamic one is equal to 1. Hence, we uncover that the amount of cyclical information is not useful to the investor in that specific investment strategy.

Our third allocation strategy is based on a mix that brings together equities, bonds and commodities. Loadings and performances are reproduced in Table 4.13 and Figure 4.6. The long-term loadings are similar to the two previous portfolios: long positions are recommended, except for the GSCI agricultural sub-index. While the long bonds position is hardly changed when comparing the balanced strategy with the equities–bonds–commodities mix, the equity position has clearly been diminished in the latter portfolio. It has been partly replaced by long exposures in energy markets, industrial and precious metals.

Turning to the dynamic loadings, we obtain a more balanced picture. First, a positive to neutral exposure is maintained for energy, precious metals and bonds throughout the regimes. During slowdown and strong crisis periods, a negative to muted investment in commodities is recommended. The major short positions during such periods are to be found for equities and agricultural products, whereas the allocation in bonds makes it possible to benefit from rises in risk aversion. During medium expansion periods, the allocation is mainly driven by a long equity–long bonds exposure. Conversely, strong expansion periods require building a long exposure to industrial metals which is more important than the exposure to the S&P 500. Finally, the stalling regime – as highlighted previously – is the regime during which

Table 4.13   Performance analysis – balanced portfolio with commodities

Loadings		Agri.	Energy	Ind. Metals	Prec. Metals	S&P 500	US Bonds
	Static	−0.10	0.05	0.19	0.14	0.17	0.98
Strong Exp.	Reg. 1	0.05	0.08	0.29	0.04	0.42	0.08
Slowdown	Reg. 2	−0.28	0.04	−0.08	0.03	−0.18	1.37
Strong Crisis	Reg. 3	−0.13	0.00	0.07	0.03	−0.38	0.51
Stalling	Reg. 4	0.02	0.15	0.25	0.24	0.12	0.46
Medium Expans.	Reg. 5	−0.07	0.04	−0.06	0.09	0.22	0.98

	Eq.–Bds–Comdty Static	Eq.–Bds–Comdty Dynamic
Avg. Return	13.71%	17.02%
Volatility	10.03%	10.46%
Sharpe Ratio	1.37	1.63

Note: Eq.–Bds–Comdty Static stands for the structural view of investing strategy in equities/bonds/commodities, and Eq.–Bds–Comdty Dynamic for the regime-switching view of investing strategy in equities/bonds/commodities.

we observe the strongest pick-up in commodities: a positive investment in each of the four GSCI sub-indices is recommended, with a stronger weight in industrial and precious metals. The performance obtained in this setting is largely increased through the use of cyclical information: not only is the Sharpe ratio of the dynamic allocation strategy (1.63) higher than the static one (1.37), but it is also the highest Sharpe ratio recorded over the three investment strategies considered in our stylized exercise. Hence, we reach the conclusion that adding

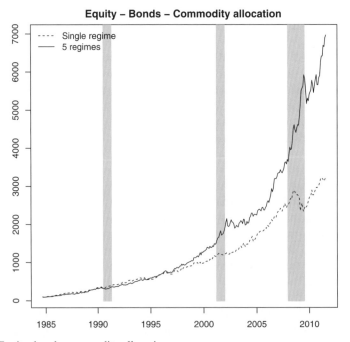

Figure 4.6   Equity–bonds–commodity allocation

Table 4.14   Sharpe ratios depending on the number of regimes

Nb. of reg.	Comdty S.	Comdty D.	Eq.–Bds–Cmdty S.	Eq.–Bds–Cmdty D.	Eq.–Bds S.	Eq.–Bds D.
2	0.58	0.88	1.47	1.63	1.24	1.34
3	0.58	0.76	1.47	1.51	1.24	1.23
4	0.58	0.84	1.47	1.74	1.24	**1.44**
5	0.58	**0.91**	1.47	**1.68**	1.24	1.02
6	0.58	0.99	1.47	1.31	1.24	0.93
7	0.58	0.56	1.47	1.59	1.24	1.30
8	0.58	0.84	1.47	1.72	1.24	1.35
9	0.58	0.67	1.47	0.96	1.24	1.13
10	0.58	0.74	1.47	1.22	1.24	1.02

Note: Nb. of reg. stands for Number of Regimes, Comdty S. for Commodity Static Strategy, Comdty D. for Commodity Dynamic Strategy, Eq.–Bds–Cmdty S. for Equities-Bonds-Commodities Static Strategy, Eq.–Bds–Cmdty D. for Equities-Bonds-Commodities Dynamic Strategy, Eq.–Bds S. for Equities–Bond Static Strategy, and Eq.–Bds D. for Equities-Bonds Dynamic Strategy.

commodities to a balanced portfolio appears to be the best possible use of commodities as an investment vehicle, especially when the investment strategy makes use of cyclical information.

By allowing us to compare directly the results obtained for the three competing strategies, our performance analysis reveals that:

- The **pure commodity allocation** profits from the additional business cycle information.
- The **balanced equity–bond** allocation profits more from structural information.
- The **mix of the two** benefits from the business cycle information.

Two additional questions need to be discussed before closing this chapter. First, we need to check whether our results depend on the number of selected regimes. Indeed, the problem of overfitting may arise when we work with five different economic regimes. The main idea is the following: the higher the number of regimes, the higher the possibility of achieving higher returns from an investment strategy based on them. That is why we present in Table 4.14 the Sharpe ratios obtained for each investment strategy depending on the number of regimes selected to model the US business cycle. We allow the number of regimes N to go from 2 (i.e. classic expansion–contraction setting) to 10 (as a higher number of regimes would be difficult to estimate for computational purposes).

The results reproduced in Table 4.14 globally discard the intuition that the higher the number of regimes, the higher the PnL (profits and losses). For the pure dynamic commodity case, the Sharpe ratio is equal to 0.91 when $N = 5$. It could be slightly increased when choosing $N = 6$, but this does not translate into higher returns. A similar comment can be made for the balanced equity–bond portfolio, and the mix of commodies–bonds–equities: an increased number of regimes does not systematically translate into a higher Sharpe ratio.

Moreover, in Table 4.14, we notice that when commodities are included in the investment universe, it is beneficial to increase the number of regimes. For a balanced equities–bonds portfolio, the highest Sharpe ratio is obtained for $N = 4$. In the pure commodity case, the best result is achieved for $N = 6$. When bringing these two strategies together, the maximum Sharpe ratio (1.72) is recorded with $N = 8$. Thus, it appears that investing in commodities benefits from cyclical information even more than the traditional assets upon which most asset allocation strategies are built.

Table 4.15 Measuring the value of economic information based on Hwang *et al.* (2007)

γ	2	3	5	10	20	30	50	100	300
Cmdty Portf.	5.3%	3.7%	2.3%	1.2%	0.6%	0.4%	0.2%	0.1%	0.0%
Equity–Bonds–Cmdty	2.2%	1.6%	1.0%	0.5%	0.3%	0.2%	0.1%	0.1%	0.0%
Equity–Bonds	−1.9%	−1.3%	−0.8%	−0.4%	−0.2%	−0.1%	−0.1%	0.0%	0.0%

Second, we investigate what the maximum management fees are that investors would be willing to pay to have their wealth managed according to this type of cyclical information. To do this, we consider an exponential utility function and various values for the risk aversion parameter. Then, we search for the fees that would make the investor indifferent between two information sets. This methodoloy is based on Hwang *et al.*'s (2007) analytic result:

$$
p_0 = w_0 \left(1 - \frac{\dfrac{1}{1-\gamma} + \dfrac{1}{2\gamma}\dfrac{SR_b}{1+SR_b}}{\dfrac{1}{1-\gamma} + \dfrac{1}{2\gamma}\dfrac{SR_a}{1+SR_a}} \right)
\tag{4.13}
$$

where p_0 measures the value of the extra information in the investment process a vs. b. w_0 is the initial wealth. $\frac{p_0}{w_0}$ measures the management fees. SR_a and SR_b stand for the Sharpe ratios of the strategies a and b, respectively.

In Table 4.15, by looking at the results from Huang and Satchell's (2007) approach with $\gamma = 3$, the following comments arise:

1. An investor would accept paying around **3.7%** per year to benefit from this business cycle information in the **pure commodity case**.
2. An investor would accept paying around **1.6%** per year to benefit from this business cycle information in the **equity–bonds–commodity case**.
3. An investor **would not accept** having his money managed using this information in **the equity–bonds portfolio**.

The bottom line of our analysis is that cyclical information is of strong interest to investment managers who are fully or partially investing their funds in commodities. For each regime, the main findings may be summarized as follows:

1. **Entering into a crisis:** commodities deliver strongly negative returns, except for the precious metals. The correlations are high, even between commodities.
2. **Prolonged slowdown period:** the energy and the industrial metals sectors are improving on average, whereas the S&P 500 is still lagging.
3. **Medium expansion regime:** agricultural prices are up by 0.27%/month, whereas the energy and industrial metals sectors are down by respectively 0.18% and 0.45%. The S&P 500 outperforms all commodity sectors.
4. **Strong expansions:** the energy and the industrial metals sectors outperfom equity returns.
5. **Stalling regime:** all commodity sectors are increasing and outperform the S&P 500 returns. Industrial metals outperform the rest of the commodity indices.

On top of these conclusions, it appears that, when investing in commodities, tracking cyclical information may be of strong interest to investors.

4.6 CONCLUDING REMARKS

This chapter documents the growing 'financialization' of commodities (Tang and Xiong (2010), Dionne *et al.* (2011)) as an asset class, and the extent to which they are related to the underlying business cycle. The main contribution of the chapter is to study the evolution of commodity prices along the business cycle in different geographic regions based on the class of Markov regime-switching models. Our results cast some light on the strong relationship that appears between commodity markets and the underlying business cycle. More particularly, we are able to detect an increased sensitivity to economic activity in China. Additionally, we perform a more qualitative analysis of the evolution of commodity markets through the US business cycle. By decomposing the phases of this cycle based on the joint behavior of production growth, inflation, unemployment and retail sales, we identify during which periods commodity markets are the most likely to grow or fall into recession.

From an investment point of view, the main results may be summarized as follows. First, investors should not add commodities to their portfolio on the grounds of a low correlation of the commodity with standard financial assets (such as bonds and equities). Indeed, we uncover a strong correlation of commodity markets with risky assets during economic downturns. Second, the economic influences on commodity prices are rather complex: the patterns detected for each type of commodity sub-index vary greatly between the geographical zones in Europe, the US, China, etc. Third, there is a cyclical rotation amongst commodity markets: during periods of strong growth, investors should overweigh industrial metals and energy vs. agricultural products and precious metals. Finally, 'stalling' economic regimes correspond to periods during which commodities outperform equities.

REFERENCES

Amisano, G., Giacomini, R. 2007. Comparing Density Forecasts via Weighted Likelihood Ratio Tests. *Journal of Business and Economic Statistics* 25:177–190

Artis, MJ., Krolzig, HM., Toro, J. 2004. The European Business Cycle. *Oxford Economic Papers* 56(1): 1–44

Artis, MJ., Zhang, W. 1998. International Business Cycles and the ERM: Is There a European Business Cycle? *International Journal of Finance and Economics* 2(1):1–16

Barnhart, SW. 1989. The Effects of Macroeconomic Announcements on Commodity Prices. *American Journal of Agricultural Economics* 17(2):389–403

Baur, DG., McDermott, TK. 2010. Is Gold a Safe Haven? International Evidence. *Journal of Banking and Finance* 34:1886–1898

Beaudry, P., Collard, F., Portier, F. 2011. Gold Rush Fever in Business Cycles. *Journal of Monetary Economics* 58:84–97

Birchenhall, CR., Jessen, H., Osborn, DR., Simpson, P. 1999. Predicting U.S. Business-Cycle Regimes. *Journal of Business and Economic Statistics* 17:313–323

Bjornson, B., Carter, CA. 1997. New Evidence on Agricultural Commodity Return Performance under Time-Varying Risk. *American Journal of Agricultural Economics* 79:918–930

Boldin, MD. 1996. A Check on the Robustness of Hamilton's Markov Switching Model Approach to the Economic Analysis of the Business Cycle. *Studies in Nonlinear Dynamics and Econometrics* 1:35–46

Bradley, MD., Jansen, DW. 2004. Forecasting with a Nonlinear Dynamic Model of Stock Returns and Industrial Production. *International Journal of Forecasting* 20(2):321–342

Clements, MP., Krolzig, HM. 1998. A Comparison of the Forecast Performance of Markov-switching and Threshold Autoregressive Models of US GNP. *The Econometrics Journal* 1(1):47–75

Clements, MP., Krolzig, HM. 2003. Business Cycle Asymmetries: Characterization and Testing Based on Markov-Switching Autoregressions. *Journal of Business and Economic Statistics* 21(1):196–211

Daskalaki, C., Skiadopoulos, G. 2011. Should Investors Include Commodities in their Portfolios After All? New Evidence. *Journal of Banking and Finance* 35(10):2606–2626

Dionne, G., Gauthier, G., Hammami, K., Maurice, M., Simonato, JG. 2011. A Reduced Form Model of Default Spreads with Markov-switching Macroeconomic Factors. *Journal of Banking and Finance* 35, 1984–2000

Erb, CB., Campbell, CR. 2006. The Strategic and Tactical Value of Commodity Futures. *Financial Analysts Journal* 62(2):69–97

Frankel, JA., Hardouvelis, GA. 1985. Commodity Prices, Money Surprises and Fed Credibility. *Journal of Money, Credit and Banking* 17(4):425–438

Gatumel, M., Ielpo, F. 2012. The Number of Regimes Across Asset Returns: Identification and Economic Value. *SSRN Working Paper* #1925058, Social Science Research Network, USA

Geman, H., Ohana, S. 2008. Time-consistency in Managing a Commodity Portfolio: A Dynamic Risk Measure Approach. *Journal of Banking and Finance* 32(10):1991–2005

Gorton, G., Rouwenhorst, KG. 2005. Facts and Fantasies about Commodity Futures. *Financial Analysts Journal* 62(2):47–68

Greer, RJ. 2000. The Nature of Commodity Index Returns. *The Journal of Alternative Investments* 3(1):45–52

Hamilton, J. 1989. A New Approach to the Economic Analysis of Nonstationary Time Series and the Business Cycle. *Econometrica* 57(2):357–384

Hamilton, J. 1996. *Time Series Analysis*, 2nd Edition, Princeton, Princeton University Press, USA

Hwang, S., Bond, S., Satchell, S., Mitchell, P. 2007. Will Private Equity and Hedge Funds Replace Real Estate in Mixed-Asset Portfolios? *Journal of Portfolio Management* 33(5):74–84

Ielpo, F. 2012. Equity, Credit and the Business Cycle. *Applied Financial Economics* 22(12):939–954

Jensen, GR., Johnson, RR., Mercer, JM. 2000. Efficient Use of Commodity Futures in Diversified Portfolios. *Journal of Futures Markets* 20(5):489–506

Jensen, GR., Johnson, RR., Mercer, JM. 2002. Tactical Asset Allocation and Commodity Futures. *Journal of Portfolio Management* 28(4):100–111

Kaplan, P., Lummer, SL. 1998. Update: GSCI Collateralized Futures as a Hedging Diversification Tool for Institutional Portfolios. *The Journal of Investing* 7(4):11–18

Kim, CJ., Nelson, C. 1999. Has the U.S. Economy Become More Stable? A Bayesian Approach Based on a Markov-Switching Model of the Business Cycle. *The Review of Economics and Statistics* 81(4): 608–616

Lummer, SL., Siegel, LB. 1993. GSCI Collateralized Futures: A Hedging and Diversification Tool for Institutional Portfolios. *The Journal of Investing* 2(2):75–82

Psaradakis, Z., Spagnolo, N. 2003. On the Determination of the Number of Regimes in Markov-Switching Autoregressive Models. *Journal of Time Series Analysis* 24(2):237–252

Roache, SK. 2008. Commodities and the Market Price of Risk. *IMF Working Papers* #08/221, International Monetary Fund, Washington DC, USA

Sichel, D. 1994. Inventories and the Three Phases of the Business Cycle. *Journal of Business and Economic Statistics* 12:269–277

Smith, A., Naik, PA., Tsai, C. 2005. Markov-Switching Model Selection Using Kullback–Leibler Divergence. *Working Paper* #05-001, Department of Agricultural and Resource Economics, University of California Davis, USA

Tang, K., Xiong, W. 2010. Index Investing and the Financialization of Commodities. *NBER Working Paper* #16385, Cambridge, Massachusetts, USA

Vuong, QH. 1989. Likelihood Ratio Tests for Model Selection and non-nested Hypotheses. *Econometrica* 57(2):307–333

Part III
Commodities and Fundamental Value

How do commodity markets value common factors? What factors should be used to construct a model capturing the fundamental value of commodity prices? Part III aims at addressing such questions related to the factors that are common to various segments of commodity markets, as well as the ability of the econometrician to build models incorporating such factors.

Cross-commodity relationships imply that two or several commodities share an equilibrium that links prices in the long run. These long-term connections – or inter-commodity equilibrium as denoted by Casassus *et al.* (2009) – include production relationships[1] where an upstream commodity and a downstream commodity are tied in a production process, and substitute/complementary relationships where two commodities serve as substitutes[2] or complements[3] in consumption and/or production. The existence of inter-commodity equilibrium usually indicates long-term co-movement among commodity prices. Temporary deviations from this equilibrium (because of demand and supply imbalances caused by macroeconomic factors and inventory shocks, etc.) will be corrected over the long run.

RATIONALE BEHIND COINTEGRATION

One of the most popular economic models that analyzes long-term relationships among variables is the cointegration model or Error Correction Model (ECM). This model allows the researcher to analyze the balance of long-period relationships. Cointegration is interpreted as a long-term relationship because cointegrated variables are tied to each other to keep certain linear combinations stationary, and hence they tend to move together. Nakajima and Ohashi (2011) interpret cointegration among commodity prices to reflect underlying production technologies and firms' activities. The idea behind cointegration is that there is a meaningful reason for commodity prices to move together in the long run, despite non-stationary departures from this equilibrium relationship in the short run. A major advantage of cointegration analysis is that it allows for the possibility that commodity prices in two different markets may respond differently to new market information in the short run, but would return to a long-run equilibrium if both are efficient. There are several reasons to explain why one might expect asymmetric responses from different markets in the short run. One is that the markets may have different access times to the information being delivered. Another is that the information

---

[1] One commodity can be produced from another commodity when the former is the output of a production process that uses the other commodity as an input factor. For example, the petroleum refining process cracks crude oil into its constituent products, among which heating oil and gasoline are actively traded commodities on the NYMEX. Another example can be found in the soybean complex, where soybeans can be crushed into soybean meal and soybean oil. These three commodities are traded separately on the CBOT.

[2] A substitute relationship exists when two traded commodities are substitutes in consumption. Crude oil and natural gas are commonly viewed as substitute goods. Competition between natural gas and petroleum products occurs principally in the industrial and electricity generation sectors. Similarly, ethanol and petroleum products are potentially competitive products. Corn and soybean meal can also serve as substitute cattle feeds.

[3] A complementary relationship exists when two commodities share a balanced supply or are complementary in consumption and/or production. Consider for instance the case of industrial metals, which are seldom used in pure form. Most applications can be found in the form of alloys: bronze (tin and copper), soft solder (tin and lead) or pewter (tin and lead). Nickel stocks are used in stainless steel, an alloy of steel. Zinc is often applied as zinc coatings, jointly used with aluminum.

may be interpreted differently initially. However, because the commodities trade on common trends, arbitrage opportunities between the markets will eventually result in a multi-market consensus concerning the value of new information.

Many studies have documented empirically cointegrating relationships in commodity markets. Malliaris and Urrutia (1996) document the long-term cointegration among prices of agricultural commodity futures contracts from the CBOT. Girma and Paulson (1999) find a cointegration relationship in petroleum futures markets. Ai *et al.* (2006) document that the market-level indicators such as inventory and harvest size explain a strikingly large portion of commodity prices in the long run. Cortazar *et al.* (2008) have studied the statistical relationship among commodities in a multi-commodity framework using futures prices. Akram (2009) reveals that different pairs of commodity prices may be cointegrated. However, none of these papers have provided a thorough analysis of cointegrating relationships within specific groups of commodities (agricultural products, metals, energy markets).

EQUILIBRIUM RELATIONSHIPS: ECONOMIC AND MARKET-SPECIFIC FACTORS

Commodity markets do not only display wide price fluctuations reflecting demand and supply disequilibria, they also support trading in futures and options whose prices fluctuate as much as stock prices. In turn, commodity prices can be affected by changes in macroeconomic fundamentals. This bi-directional relationship is of crucial importance, since it can play a major role in the determination of successful economic policies.

When commodity demand rises or declines, for example, changes in business cycles can serve as a causal factor. During an expansion, commodity prices may rise and, in response, consumers will require more income to purchase a given commodity. Given the (in)elasticity for a given commodity, consumers will have less income to spend on other commodities. The demand, and consequently the prices, for the other commodities will decline, presuming the interactions take place in a market economy in which the money supply is controlled. If a particular market responds slowly to demand and supply changes, a temporary imbalance(s) between supply and demand will occur and consequently be met by variations in production, inventory levels and backlogs of orders.

The most direct link concerning business cycle influences on commodity markets is that between GDP and commodity prices. Assuming the income elasticity of commodity demand to be nearly 1, increases in GDP – or in industrial production taken as a proxy – would cause the demand for a commodity to increase. Conversely, declines in GDP would cause commodity demand to decline.

An increase in commodity demand will either cause an increase in production to meet these demands, or an increase in commodity prices to curb demand. The first most likely will lead to a surplus, while the latter can lead to inflation.

Economic activity can be generally considered as a major factor of commodities demand. For instance, an increase of industrial production will raise directly the demands for metals, minerals and agricultural raw materials as intermediate inputs, and raise indirectly the demands for final goods through the resulting increases in incomes.

Macroeconomic events have long been recognized as playing a role in the pricing of primary commodities. The direction and stance of macroeconomic conditions and policies are signaled to commodity markets via the news contained in important information variables like rates of inflation, depreciation, unemployment, growth, budget deficits and interest rates.

Ramanujam and Vines (1990) study the interconnection between financial markets and four groups of commodities: food, beverages, agricultural products and metals. The authors show the effects of world interest rates on commodity prices, as speculators equate risk-adjusted returns between commodities and financial assets.

The relationship between commodity prices and macroeconomic variables under the influence of authorities is of potential interest to central bankers. Garner (1989), Marquis and Cunningham (1990) and Sephton (1991) have examined the extent to which commodity price inflation was linearly related to inflation in consumer prices over the long run, based on US data. If commodity price inflation is controllable, i.e. if it is possible for the central bank to exercise some discretion over the evolution of primary price inflation, the task of achieving general price stability may be somewhat simpler.[4]

Market-specific factors such as climate and geography, or global demand shocks due to government policies, can also contribute to explaining why commodity prices are expected to fluctuate together, at least in the long term (Stevens (1991)). Most famously, weather is often advanced in the literature as one of the main driving forces behind the long-term relationship among commodities. In this literature, the paper by Roll (1984) was one of the first empirical studies to document how weather persistence may affect agricultural commodity prices.[5] In addition, Reinhart and Wickham (1994) enumerate how world commodity prices respond to effects related mainly to policy issues such as stabilization funds, agricultural boards, international commodity agreements, external compensatory finance, etc.

At the same time, energy impacts commodity production in some very important ways. The use of chemical and petroleum derived inputs has increased in agriculture over time. The prices of these critical inputs, then, would be expected to alter supply, and, therefore, the prices of commodities using these inputs. Also, agricultural commodities have been increasingly used to produce energy, thereby leading to an expectation of a linkage between energy and commodity markets.

INTERACTIONS WITH ASSET MARKETS

Amid sharp rises in both commodity prices and commodity investing, many commentators have wondered whether commodities nowadays move in sync with equities. Previous literature on this topic, however, was unable to document a clear econometric link between the returns on passive commodity and equity investments over the course of the last decades. For instance, Chong and Miffre (2010) studied how returns on commodity markets (agricultural products, energy markets, livestock products, metals) co-vary over time with those of traditional asset classes (as proxied by global stock and bond indices). They found that the conditional return correlations between the S&P 500 and commodity futures fell over time, which suggests that commodities and equities have become more segmented. Commodity prices, however, behave differently from stock prices. They are strongly affected by production and inventory conditions, and tend to deviate temporarily from the prices that would exist without those effects. Since the contributions by Kaldor (1939) and Working (1949) under the form of the

---

[4] Indeed, it can be suggested that a central bank concerned with restraining general price inflation might target commodity price inflation, since inflation in primary commodities will most likely be passed on to consumers through higher final goods prices. Through stabilizing commodity price inflation, *ex ante* consumer prices will be less volatile and the misallocation of real resources will be reduced.

[5] In that specific paper, the price of oranges was the particular concern.

theory of storage,[6] commodity markets are known to adjust with lagged responses by economic agents. Suppliers of coffee, cocoa and copper, for example, take several years to react fully to price changes. Consumer delays arise from the derived demand for raw materials and for basic, pre-processed foods, from the filtering of price changes to the final demand for commodities. Hence, the lack of instantaneous adjustment in production and consumption can give rise to temporary states of disequilibria in commodity markets (Lord (1991)).

Commodity prices are argued to be leading indicators of inflation through two basic channels. One is that they respond more quickly to general economic shocks, such as an increase in demand. The second is that some changes in commodity prices reflect idiosyncratic shocks, such as a flood that decimates the supply of certain agricultural products, which are subsequently passed through to overall prices. Depending on the type of the shock, the observed link between commodity prices and inflation would be expected to be different. Moreover, changes over time in the mix of shocks in the economy could affect the stability of a bi-variate link between commodity prices and inflation. Commodity prices generally are set in highly competitive auction markets, and consequently tend to be more flexible than prices overall. As a result, movements in commodity prices would be expected to lead and be positively related to changes in aggregate price inflation in response to aggregate demand shocks. To the extent that demand shocks are not sector-specific, the levels of commodity prices and overall prices could therefore be linked.

Any commodity, however, is also subject to idiosyncratic shocks. This complicates the empirical relation between commodity prices and inflation. In the case of a direct shock to the supply of a commodity, movements in the price of the commodity could be positively related to overall prices. The observed effect would depend on the relative importance of the commodity being shocked and the flexibility of other prices. Poor weather conditions, for example, could reduce the supply of agricultural commodities and push up their prices. The higher prices would eventually be reflected in the price of the related final food products bought by consumers. To the extent that the shock affects aggregate supply and that the stickiness in the prices of other consumer goods limits their adjustment, the net effect would be higher overall prices. The rise in the prices of the affected agricultural commodities would be larger than the effect on overall prices, which means the relationship of the level of prices of the affected commodities to overall prices would be affected. One complication, however, is that a shift in relative demand for a commodity might dampen an otherwise positive correlation between the change in the price of a commodity and overall inflation. Take, for example, the case in which an increase in aggregate demand coincides with an increase in demand for manufactured goods or services relative to agricultural products. While this could lead to a rise in overall prices, prices of agricultural commodities might fall. In the short run, changes in commodity prices would not be positively related to inflation, and the levels of prices of the affected commodities and overall prices would drift apart. These examples do not exhaust the possible permutations of shocks affecting commodity price and inflation. However, they do indicate that the relationship between the movements in commodity prices and inflation depends on what is driving commodity price changes. Given the alternative links between

---

[6] Futures markets play an important role in setting the price for storage facilities, as has been demonstrated especially in these early works. Generally, the price of a commodity in the future is equal to its spot (cash) price plus the cost of storing it into the future. If futures prices are too high, arbitrageurs sell the nearby futures, buy the cash commodity, and store it against their futures contract. If futures prices are too low, arbitrageurs buy the nearby futures, take delivery, and sell the commodity in the cash market. All these actions tend to bring the spot and futures prices closer together, and lead to the convergence of the two as the futures contract comes nearer to expiry, becoming, in effect, the cash market.

commodity prices and overall prices, two characteristics of empirical patterns are of interest. The first is whether commodity prices and overall prices are tied together in the long run. The second is the nature of the short-run relationship between changes in commodity prices and inflation.

Another conventional piece of wisdom in the relationship between financial and commodity markets is that gold provides an effective inflation hedge. Because commodities are physical assets, they are the best way to hedge against rising prices. However, unlike most commodities, gold is durable, relatively transportable, universally acceptable and easily authenticated.

A real appreciation of the US Dollar with respect to currencies of other countries may lead immediately to an increase in local relative prices of commodities in other countries if the purchasing power parities are not maintained in concerned countries. Foreign demand for commodities may, therefore, reduce and foreign supply may rise. This may lead to a decrease of commodity prices in world commodity markets. Conversely, a real depreciation of the US Dollar may result in an increase of world commodity prices.

Other explanations for the link between commodity and asset markets can be put forth. For instance, Chng (2009) investigates the cross-market trading dynamics present in natural rubber, palladium and gasoline futures from the Tokyo Commodity Exchange (TOCOM) during 2000–2008. The empirical results show that a common industry exposure (i.e. the Japanese automobile market), and not a commodity market factor, is driving cross-market trading dynamics in these related commodity futures.

RELATED ISSUES

There are three related issues to the idea of cointegration in commodity markets that have been deliberately left out of the analysis in the following chapters.

Co-movement

First, Pindyck and Rotemberg (1990) offer numerous statistical tests confirming that the prices of several commodities (such as wheat, cotton, copper, gold, crude oil, lumber and cocoa) have a persistent tendency to move together. As one potential explanation for these excess co-movements,[7] they point out that commodity price movements are partly the result of herd behavior, i.e. traders who are alternatively bullish or bearish across all commodity markets without justification from economic fundamentals.[8]

Law of One Price

Second, the Law of One Price (LOP) – which postulates the existence of a representative price – has been the subject of considerable attention in the literature on commodity markets. According to the LOP, abstracting from tariffs and transportation costs, prices of identical goods, expressed in common currency, should be equalized in international trade. Equalization of prices is brought about by goods market arbitrage. The LOP exemplifies a long-run equilibrium relationship; that is, in the long-run exchange rate and prices are expected to be

---

[7] Co-movement between futures prices exists when two or more prices move together in the long run. Its existence implies that the discovery of one price will provide valuable information about others.

[8] More recent results on this topic can be found in Chunrong *et al.* (2006).

proportional even though short-run deviations from the equilibrium may occur. Lags due to contracts, imperfect information, long-term customer–seller relationships, inertia in consumer habits, etc. may cause short-term deviations from the LOP, but in the long run any deviations should be eliminated. By relying on the cointegration methodology, Ardeni (1989) finds that the LOP fails, and that deviations from the long-run relationship are permanent for a group of commodities composed of wheat, tea, beef, sugar, wool, zinc and tin. Baffes (1991) contradicts this statement by showing empirical evidence that the LOP cannot be rejected for the same group of commodities in several countries (Australia, Canada, UK, USA) during 1966–1986.

Booth *et al.* (1998) investigate the relationship between US and Canadian wheat futures prices during 1980–1994. Their results show that the two series are cointegrated, with evidence of an equilibrium relationship in the long run. Vataja (2000) also argues that the LOP should be seen as a long-term equilibrium concept, by means of cointegration analysis. The author finds that the LOP is supported about 75% of the time based on the IMF International Financial Statistics during 1960–1995. The LOP is supported fully in six groups: newsprint, rice, rubber, sugar, wool and zinc. The hypothesis is partially supported for wheat and tin, while no support is detected for lead and maize. Pynnonen and Vataja (2002) resort to bootstrapping techniques for testing cointegration in cocoa beans, lead, maize, newsprint, rice, rubber, sugar, tin and zinc prices during 1960–1995. They find that in 13 out of the 21 investigated bi-variate commodity price series, the no cointegration null hypothesis could be rejected in favor of the LOP hypothesis. Five of the remaining eight no cointegration cases could be explained by trade policy. Aruga and Managi (2011) identify that the LOP holds for the Japanese and US palladium markets, but it is rejected for platinum. Ultimately, Pippenger and Phillips (2008) highlight four pitfalls in testing the LOP in commodity markets: (i) the use of retail prices, (ii) omitting transportation costs, (iii) commodity arbitrage takes time and (iv) the failure to use identical products. As a result of the prevalence of these pitfalls in the literature, the authors cannot find empirical evidence that would lead to rejection of the LOP in commodity markets.

Market Efficiency

Third, the investigation of market efficiency[9] through the spot–futures relationship is often approached in a cointegrating framework. Market efficiency implies cointegration between the same factors that determine the future spot price are reflected in the current futures price, so the two price series should not drift apart. Cointegration between the spot and futures price series of commodities can therefore be used to test for this lack of bias.

Bessler and Covey (1991) show marginal support for the cointegration hypothesis in US cattle prices during 1985–1986. The authors find slight evidence of cointegration between nearby futures (i.e., those closest to expiration) and cash prices (meaning there was weak evidence that cash and futures were maintaining a long-run equilibrium relationship with respect to pricing new information), but no evidence of cointegration when more distant futures contracts were considered. Hence, they concluded that cash markets for live cattle are inefficient. Their findings have been complemented in two contributions by Goodwin and Schroeder (1991) and Schroeder and Goodwin (1991) who identify market characteristics (e.g.,

---

[9] Market efficiency implies that the current futures price of a commodity futures contract expiring in $t + 1$ should equal the commodity spot price expected to prevail in $t + 1$, i.e. that the current futures price incorporates all relevant information including past spot and futures prices.

distances between markets, industry concentration, market volumes, market types) as having significant influences on cointegration relationships between US regional cattle markets.

Fortenbery and Zapata (1993) have suggested that a possible reason for the latter result might be the lack of an explicit storage relationship between cash and futures markets for livestock. They applied cointegration analysis to cash and futures markets for corn and soybean, which showed evidence of cointegration for nearly all cash and futures market pairs considered. The authors argued that during years with high inventory costs (either because of high interest rates or large carrying charges between delivery dates), a more appropriate specification of the relationship between cash and futures prices would explicitly include interest rates. That is why Zapata and Fortenbery (1996) introduced interest rates as an explicit argument in the cointegration model, and found that interest rates can be important in describing the price discovery relationship between futures and cash markets for storable commodities. In the same spirit, Fortenbery and Zapata (1997) have investigated whether the US cheddar cheese futures market serves as a price discovery center for the spot market on the National Cheese Exchange (NCE). In this study, the authors cannot find evidence of a stable long-run relationship between cash and futures markets for cheddar cheese. A potential explanation lies in the fact that these commodity markets may not have gained enough trading experience to establish a long-run equilibrium relationship. Finally, this strand of literature has been examined by Foster (1999), who cannot rule out the presence of common trends within live cattle prices (by modeling multiple market linkages for many geographical regions).

Among other studies, Baillie and Myers (1991) conclude that the hypothesis of no cointegration between cash and futures prices cannot be rejected for the following commodities: beef, coffee, corn, cotton, gold and soybeans. Other studies in commodity markets include, to list few, non-ferrous metal (Chowdhury (1991)), and gold–silver spot and futures spread (Wahab *et al.* (1994)). Beck (1994) concludes that commodity markets are sometimes inefficient, but that no market can be found to be always inefficient among cattle, orange juice, hogs, corn, copper, cocoa and soybean. Crowder and Hamed (1993) study cointegration in oil spot and futures prices during 1983–1990. They find that crude oil spot and futures prices are indeed cointegrated. Moreover, there is no evidence of a risk premium, or that past forecast errors are useful in predicting the future spot price. Their results were confirmed by Moosa and A-Loughani (1995). Similarly, Schwarz and Szakmary (1994), using daily crude oil, heating oil and unleaded gasoline futures and spot prices, find that the petroleum spot prices are cointegrated with their respective futures prices. Their results were confirmed by Ng and Pirrong (1996). Aulton *et al.* (1997) found evidence of long-run market efficiency in the UK futures for wheat and pigmeat, but not for potatoes. Similarly, Kellard *et al.* (1999) found that the US markets for soybeans, live hogs and live cattle are efficient in the long run, but short-run inefficiencies were observed (particularly in the live cattle market). McKenzie and Holt (2002) indicate that live cattle, hogs, corn and soybean meal are both efficient and unbiased in the long run.

Finally, let us note that cointegration is not the only econometric tool designed to capture equilibrium relationships in commodity markets. For instance, Lombardi *et al.* (2011) examine the linkages across non-energy commodity prices during 2003–2008 based on a Factor-Augmented VAR (FAVAR) model. Exchange rates and economic activity are found to affect individual non-energy commodity prices, but there are no spillovers from oil to non-oil commodity prices (or an impact of the interest rate). In addition, the authors show that individual commodity prices are affected by common trends captured by the food and metals factors. Nonetheless, cointegration requires a strong economic rationale to attempt to relate two (or more) variables together over time. Hence, we prefer to focus solely on this approach in Part III.

PLAN OF PART III

Part III focuses on the core of the long-run relationship within commodities, as well as between commodity markets and financial markets, which we label as fundamental value. That is why we are neither focusing here on the LOP, nor on the relationship between the spot and futures commodity price series. Henceforth, the analysis proceeds in three separate settings of econometric estimates. Chapter 5 studies cointegration within specific groups of commodity markets (agricultural products, industrial and precious metals, energy commodities). Chapter 6 provides a broader picture on the cointegrating relationship between Goldman Sachs Commodity Indices (GSCI) and traditional asset markets (equities, bonds, exchange rates). Chapter 7 tests the link with the macroeconomic and monetary environments through relationships with industrial production and inflation.

5

Cross-Commodity Linkages

This chapter deals with a cointegration analysis commodity by commodity in their respective sub-category, i.e. agricultural products, industrial metals, precious metals, and energy markets. The main focus lies in the determination of the long-term relationship – if any – between these specific categories of commodities, and the identification of the common factors that could explain the convergence of the price series towards a fundamental value. First, we recall the main econometric steps to proceed with a cointegration analysis. Then, we carry out our investigation for each sub-category.

5.1 A PRIMER ON GRANGER CAUSALITY TESTING AND COINTEGRATION

5.1.1 Granger Causality Testing

In conjunction with the analysis of the matrix of cross-correlations, the econometrician may resort to Granger causality tests as well. These tests allow us to infer causality 'in the Granger sense' between a set of dependent and independent variables selected by the user, and may be useful in econometric modeling prior to the regression analysis. When applied to commodity markets, Granger causality tests will tell us the nature of the inter-relationships between the various markets and categories of commodities.

Recall that a process P_t^1 Granger causes P_t^2 at the order p if, in the linear regression of P_t^2 on lagged prices $P_{t-1}^1, \ldots, P_{t-p}^1, P_{t-1}^2, \ldots, P_{t-p}^2$, at least one of the regression coefficients of P_t^1 on the lagged prices $P_{t-1}^2, \ldots, P_{t-p}^2$ is significantly different from 0. The intuition behind Granger causality is that the information on past prices $P_{t-1}^2, \ldots, P_{t-p}^2$ is relevant to forecasting P_t^1 at future time t.

Granger causality is examined using the Granger causality test testing the null hypothesis H_0 that all regression coefficients of P_t^1 on the lagged prices $P_{t-1}^2, \ldots, P_{t-p}^2$ are null. A p-value lower than 0.05 means that H_0 can be rejected (and causality accepted) with 95% confidence level.

5.1.2 Cointegration without Structural Breaks

Cointegration can be seen as a useful econometric tool to decompose the long-term trend between pairs (or groups) of variables, and the short-term departures from the trend. In the context of commodity markets, a cointegration relationship will tell us whether a pair (or a group) of individual commodities are tied together in the long run (which means that there exists a strong economic rationale to link these variables in the economic analysis), and to what extent exogenous perturbations from this equilibrium can occur.

5.1.2.1 Preliminary Conditions

As a pre-requisite condition for cointegration, the time series need to be integrated of the same order. For instance, the econometrician can check, based on standard stationarity tests, that the prices of the raw time series considered are non-stationary and integrated of order one ($I(1)$). This amounts to checking that they are difference stationary, i.e. Δx_t^e and $\Delta x_t^{e'}$ are stationary.[1]

Before estimating any time series model, it is indeed necessary to test for the stationarity of the dependent variable (and independent variables as well in ARMAX models). Dickey and Fuller (1979) test the nullity of the coefficient α in the following regression:

$$\Delta x_t = x_{t+1} - x_t = \alpha x_t + \beta + e_t \tag{5.1}$$

– if α is significantly negative, then we say that the process x_t has no unit root[2], or that it is stationary, inducing a mean-reverting behavior for the prices;
– if α is not significantly different from 0, then we say that the process x_t 'has a unit root', inducing a random walk behavior for the prices.

In practice, the Augmented-Dickey–Fuller (1981, ADF) or Phillips–Peron (1988, PP) tests are used rather than Dickey–Fuller. These tests are based on the same principle but correct for potential serial autocorrelation and time trend in Δx_t through a more complicated regression:

$$\Delta x_t = \sum_{i=1}^{L} \beta_i \Delta x_{t-i} + \alpha x_t + \beta_1 t + \beta_2 + e_t \tag{5.2}$$

The ADF tests the null hypothesis H_0 that $\alpha = 0$ (the alternative hypothesis H_1 being that $\alpha < 0$) by computing the Ordinary Least Squares (OLS) estimate of α in the previous equation and its t-statistic $\hat{t}$; then, the statistic of the test is the t-statistic $\hat{t}_\alpha$ of coefficient α, which follows under H_0 a known law (studied by Fuller and here denoted Ful). The test computes the p-value p, which is the probability of $Ful \leq \hat{t}$ under H_0. If $p < 0.05$, H_0 can be safely rejected and H_1 accepted: we conclude that the series 'x_t has no unit root'. Extensions of these stationarity tests were also developed by Kwiatkowski, Phillips, Schmidt and Shin (1992, KPSS).

5.1.2.2 Johansen Cointegration Tests

To keep the notation parsimonious, let us consider here the cointegration setting with only two variables.[3] As is standard in a linear cointegration exercise, the econometrican needs to check first if the variables are cointegrated, i.e. if β exists such that $R_t = X_t^e - \beta X_t^{e'}$ is stationary. This can be done by performing an OLS regression of X_t^e on $X_t^{e'}$, or more rigorously by using the Johansen cointegration test (Johansen and Juselius (1990), Johansen (1991)).

Let X_t be a vector of N variables, all $I(1)$:

$$X_t = \Phi_1 X_{t-1} + \cdots + \Phi_p X_{t-p} + \epsilon_t \tag{5.3}$$

---

[1] Stationarity is a central concern in time series analysis, which implies that the mean of the variable shall be time invariant (in the weak sense of stationarity). See Hamilton (1996) for further reference.
[2] The concept of presence of unit root is similar to the concept of non-stationarity for a given time series variable.
[3] Note, however, that the Johansen cointegration framework can be generalized to k variables.

with $\epsilon_t \sim WGN(0, \Omega)$, WGN denotes White Gaussian Noise, Ω denotes the variance covariance matrix and Φ_i $(i = 1, \ldots, p)$ are parameter matrices of size $(N \times N)$.

Under the null H_0, there exist r cointegration relationships between N variables, i.e. X_t is cointegrated with rank r.

Note that the Johansen cointegration tests can be performed on the logarithmic transformation of the time series under consideration.

For a financial modeling viewpoint, if we find that commodities are cointegrated, i.e. that there exists a stationary combination of these variables in the long term, the direct implication would be that they share at least one common risk factor in the long term. Hence, their joint analysis can bring fruitful results to the econometrician.

5.1.2.3 Error-correction Model

The next step of the cointegration model consists in describing the dynamics of the variables in terms of the residuals of the long-term relation (Johansen (1988)). We want to introduce an error-correction mechanism on the levels and on the slopes between the variables e and e':

$$\begin{pmatrix} \Delta X_t^e \\ \Delta X_t^{e'} \end{pmatrix} = \begin{pmatrix} \mu_e \\ \mu_{e'} \end{pmatrix} + \sum_{k=1}^{p} \Gamma_k \begin{pmatrix} \Delta X_{t-k}^e \\ \Delta X_{t-k}^{e'} \end{pmatrix} + \begin{pmatrix} \Pi_e \\ \Pi_{e'} \end{pmatrix} R_t + \begin{pmatrix} \epsilon_t^e \\ \epsilon_t^{e'} \end{pmatrix} \quad (5.4)$$

where

- e stands for the first variable and e' stands for the second variable.
- X_t^e is the log price of variable e at time t.
- The 2×1 vector process $\Delta Z_t = (\Delta X_t^e = X_{t+1}^e - X_t^e, \Delta X_t^{e'} = X_{t+1}^{e'} - X_t^{e'})'$ is the vector of the variables' price returns.
- $\mu = (\mu_{X,e}, \mu_{X,e'})$ is the 1×2 vector composed of the constant part of the drifts.
- Γ_k are 2×2 matrices of real-valued parameters expressing dependence on lagged returns.
- $(R_t = X_t^e - \beta X_t^{e'})$ is the process composed of the deviations to the long-term relation between the variables' log prices.
- Π is a 2×1 vector matrix expressing the sensitivity to the deviations to the long-term relation between the variables' prices.
- The residual shocks $(\epsilon_t^e, \epsilon_t^{e'})$ are assumed to be i.i.d with a centered bi-variate normal distribution $N(0, \Sigma)$.

However, by considering a purely linear model, it is possible that the econometrician will either misspecify the model, or ignore a valid cointegration relationship. That is why we detail below the cointegration methodology with an unknown structural break.

5.1.3 Cointegration with Structural Breaks

In this section, we explore the possibility of wrongly accepting a cointegration relationship, when some of the underlying time series are contaminated by a structural break. For instance, sharp deviations from the long-term trend can occur between a group of commodities, which would imply that the cointegration relationship is not valid any more during specific sub-samples. The structural breakpoint detection allows us to take into account these events in the cointegration analysis, instead of simply ignoring them.

We present the procedure for estimating a vector error-correction model (VECM) with a structural shift in the level of the process, as developed by Lütkepohl *et al.* (2004). By doing so, we draw on the notation by Pfaff (2008).

Let $\vec{y}_t$ be a $K \times 1$ vector process generated by a constant, a linear trend, and level shift terms:[4]

$$\vec{y}_t = \vec{\mu}_0 + \vec{\mu}_1 t + \vec{\delta} d_{t\tau} + \vec{x}_t \tag{5.5}$$

with $d_{t\tau}$ a dummy variable which takes the value of 1 when $t \geq \tau$, and 0 otherwise. The shift point τ is unknown and is expressed as a fixed fraction of the sample size:

$$\tau = [T\lambda], \quad 0 < \underline{\lambda} \leq \lambda \leq \overline{\lambda} < 1 \tag{5.6}$$

where $\underline{\lambda}$ and $\overline{\lambda}$ define real numbers, and $[\cdot]$ the integer part. Therefore, the shift cannot occur at the very beginning or the very end of the sample. The estimation of the structural shift is based on the regressions:

$$\vec{y}_t = \vec{v}_0 + \vec{v}_1 t + \vec{\delta} d_{t\tau} + \vec{A}_1 \vec{y}_{t-1} + \cdots + \vec{A}_1 \vec{y}_{t-p} + \epsilon_{t\tau}, \quad t = p+1, \dots, T \tag{5.7}$$

with $\vec{A}_i, i = 1, \dots, p$ the $K \times K$ coefficient matrices, and ϵ_t the white noise K-dimensional error process. The estimator for the breakpoint is defined as:

$$\hat{\tau} = \arg \min_{\tau \in \mathcal{T}} \det \left(\sum_{t=p+1}^{T} \vec{\hat{e}}_{t\tau} \vec{\hat{e}}_{t\tau}' \right) \tag{5.8}$$

with $\mathcal{T} = [T\underline{\lambda}, T\overline{\lambda}]$, and $\vec{\hat{e}}_{t\tau}$ the least squares residuals of Equation (5.7). Once the breakpoint $\hat{\tau}$ has been estimated, the data are adjusted as follows:

$$\vec{\hat{x}}_t = \vec{y}_t - \vec{\hat{\mu}}_0 - \vec{\hat{\mu}}_1 t + \vec{\hat{\delta}} d_{t\hat{\tau}} \tag{5.9}$$

The test statistic can be written:

$$LR(r) = T \sum_{j=r+1}^{N} \ln(1 + \hat{\lambda}_j) \tag{5.10}$$

with corresponding critical values found in Trenkler (2003).

5.1.3.1 Estimation of the VECM

The error-correction model (ECM) can be written:

$$\Delta X_t = \Pi_1 \Delta X_{t-1} + \cdots + \Pi_{p-1} \Delta X_{t-p+1} + \Pi_p X_{t-p} + \epsilon_t \tag{5.11}$$

where the matrices Π_i ($i = 1, \dots, p$) are of size $(N \times N)$. All variables are $I(0)$, except X_{t-p} which is $I(1)$. For all variables to be $I(0)$, $\Pi_p X_{t-p}$ needs to be $I(0)$ as well.

Let $\Pi_p = -\beta \alpha'$, where α' is an (r, N) matrix which contains r cointegration vectors, and β is an (N, r) matrix which contains the weights associated with each vector. If there exist r

---

[4] Note that Lütkepohl *et al.* (2004) develop their analysis in the context where $\vec{x}_t$ can be represented as a VAR(p), whose components are at most $I(1)$ and cointegrated with rank r.

cointegration relationships, then $Rk(\Pi_p) = r$. Johansen's cointegration tests are based on this condition. We can thus rewrite Equation (5.11):

$$\Delta X_t = \Pi_1 \Delta X_{t-1} + \cdots + \Pi_{p-1} \Delta X_{t-p+1} - \beta \alpha' X_{t-p} + \epsilon_t \qquad (5.12)$$

The estimation of the corresponding vector error-correction model (VECM) is performed through maximum likelihood methods (Johansen and Juselius (1990), Johansen (1991)).

Before proceeding to the empirical cointegration analysis commodity by commodity, we report in the next section the results of the standard unit root tests. Indeed, it is important to verify that the series are integrated of the same order before proceeding with the formal cointegration analysis.

5.2 DATASET AND UNIT ROOT TEST RESULTS

Table 5.1 presents descriptive statistics on the dataset used in Section 5.1.1, i.e. agricultural products, metals and energy prices. All the data comes from Bloomberg in daily frequency. The descriptive statistics concern the variables transformed to log-returns. We can notice departure from normality with excess kurtosis and a skewness coefficient different from 3. This comment is further confirmed by the value of the Jarque Bera test statistic.

The time series used are shown in logarithmic form in Figure 5.1 for agricultural products, in Figure 5.2 for industrial metals, in Figure 5.3 for precious metals and in Figure 5.4 for energy commodities. While the prices of precious metals seem to rise together in the long run, industrial metals, agricultural products and energy markets display homogeneous behavior

Table 5.1 Descriptive statistics for agricultural products, metals and energy prices

	Min	Max	Mean	Std. Dev.	Skew.	Kurt.	JB
Gold	5.5324	7.5483	6.2847	0.5795	0.5762	5.1608	268.6936
Silver	1.2733	3.8803	2.1765	0.6662	0.7072	8.0458	287.2413
Platinum	5.8141	7.7189	6.6733	0.5767	0.0201	6.3994	241.9912
Aluminum	6.9475	8.1068	7.5065	0.2654	0.2760	2.6170	160.6329
Copper	7.2145	9.2262	8.1567	0.6461	0.1949	2.6544	291.6874
Nickel	8.2441	10.8513	9.4000	0.6158	0.1708	3.0440	141.9007
Zinc	6.6107	8.4152	7.2859	0.4437	0.5765	2.4534	219.4487
Lead	5.9269	8.2662	6.8975	0.6528	0.3162	3.0693	261.9778
WTI	2.3997	4.9826	3.7166	0.6623	-0.0490	4.5999	217.7409
Brent	2.2773	4.9877	3.6916	0.7118	-0.0020	4.4380	212.5636
Gasoil	4.5136	7.1894	5.8695	0.6970	0.0109	3.9951	216.4479
Natural Gas	0.1266	2.7361	1.4199	0.5385	0.0168	6.8089	93.4769
Heating Oil	3.4049	6.0190	4.7411	0.6827	-0.0068	3.1474	216.5013
Corn	5.1662	6.6682	5.7370	0.3862	0.7557	9.6851	297.2383
Wheat	5.4543	7.1566	6.0516	0.3725	0.5315	3.4023	183.1143
Coffee	3.7612	5.7241	4.7279	0.4223	-0.0448	12.0047	14.8688
Sugar	1.4061	3.5316	2.4378	0.4535	0.4387	4.2244	108.2157
Cocoa	6.5511	8.2250	7.4332	0.3865	0.0362	4.0128	70.5652
Cotton	3.3506	5.3666	4.1774	0.3182	0.9274	10.0467	697.2411
Soybean	6.0162	7.4079	6.6163	0.3465	0.3901	2.7788	183.1288
Rice	1.2641	3.1970	2.2312	0.4033	-0.2993	11.8919	66.8263

Note: The number of observations is equal to 2,757. Std. Dev. stands for Standard Deviation, Kurt. for Kurtosis, Skew. for Skewness, and JB for the Jarque Bera test statistic.

Logarithm of Agricultural Commodity Prices

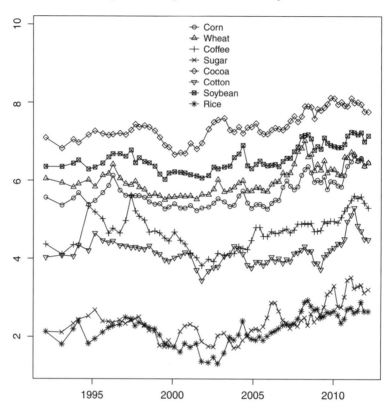

Figure 5.1   Logarithm of time series for agricultural products

across the time period, with similar price movements during periods of expansion / recession (except perhaps for natural gas). Hence, by means of this preliminary visual inspection, we validate intuitively the need to resort to cointegration to analyze in more detail the behavior of the respective groups of commodities included in this chapter.

Table 5.2 reports the usual unit root tests (Augmented Dickey–Fuller (ADF), Phillips–Perron (PP), Kwiatkowski–Phillips–Schmidt–Shin (KPSS)) results for the subset of agricultural products, metals and energy markets. These tests are meant to check formally the stationarity of the time series under consideration, in addition to the preliminary investigation of the plot for each time series. All tests have been conducted on raw data and then on log-returns. The results reproduced concern the log-returns, which are all shown to be stationary. Indeed, the test statistics reproduced for the ADF and PP tests are far smaller than the corresponding critical values (which can be found in Greene (2003) for instance, and are mentioned at the bottom of the table). The conclusion is that we can safely reject the null hypothesis of unit root for these two tests. For the KPSS test, the test statistics are smaller than the critical values (see again Greene (2003)), which leads us to accept the null hypothesis of stationarity. Hence, we verify that all series are integrated of the same order ($I(1)$), which is a pre-condition for cointegration.

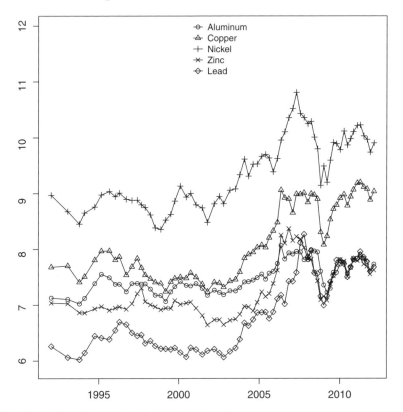

Figure 5.2   Logarithm of time series for industrial metals

5.3   COINTEGRATION IN AGRICULTURAL MARKETS

Linkages between agricultural commodities can be of two types: substitutability and/or complementarity (Malliaris and Urrutia (1996)). For instance, both corn and soybean meal are used for animal and chicken feed. While substitutability exists between the two, some degree of complementarity is also at play. While soybean meal is high in protein, corn is big in nutrients and vitamins. Soybean meal and corn are usually mixed in certain proportions which are determined by economic and nutritional considerations. Oats and wheat can be used along with soybean meal and corn in various proportions. Thus, substitutability and complementarity are not strictly mutually exclusive among soybean meal, corn, oats and wheat.

Beyond the supply and demand considerations that affect the interdependence of agricultural commodities, one should mention exogenous weather and macroeconomic shocks (Stevens (1991), Reinhart and Wickham (1994)). Furthermore, in the long term, technological advances and population growth also affect agricultural prices.

Prior to the econometric analysis, we review some of the main results from previous academic literature on the topic of cointegration in agricultural markets.

Logarithm of Precious Metals Commodity Prices

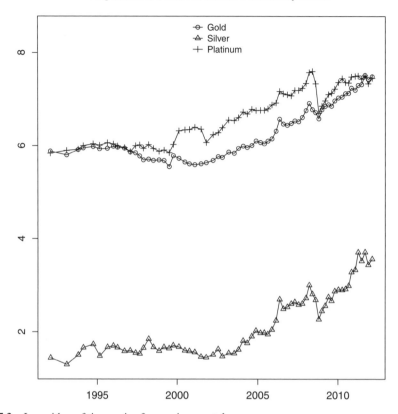

Figure 5.3   Logarithm of time series for precious metals

5.3.1   Literature Review

In what follows, we restrict our review of cointegration studies[5] dedicated to agricultural markets to two categories: (i) grains (e.g. soybeans, corn, wheat, etc.) and soft commodities (e.g. cocoa, coffee, sugar, cotton, etc.), and (ii) dairy products.

In addition, we mention the recent debate regarding the agriculture–energy linkage, whereby biofuels can be seen as alternative energy sources in a world of high oil prices.

5.3.1.1   Grains and Soft Commodities

- One important contribution in this literature stems from Malliaris and Urrutia (1996), who examine the linkages between the price of corn, wheat, oats, soybean, soybean meal and soybean oil futures traded on the Chicago Board of Trade (CBOT) during 1981–1991. By using residual-based cointegration tests and rollover prices, their empirical findings show the existence of a significant long-run bi-variate relationship among these commodity futures. Thus, futures contracts are interdependent and the price discovery of one provides

---

[5] For an extensive review, see Garcia and Leuthold (2004).

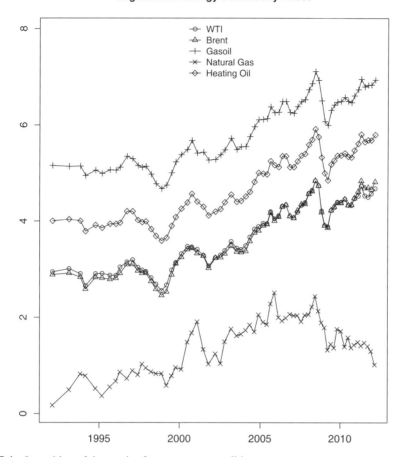

Figure 5.4   Logarithm of time series for energy commodities

information about others. The economic rationale for this long-term interdependence can be found in the substitutability and complementarity of agricultural commodities, geographical and climatological factors, global demand shocks due to government policies both at home and abroad, and the excess co-movement hypothesis.

- To complement their findings, Dawson and White (2002) study the interdependencies between various commodities futures contracts (barley, cocoa, coffee, sugar and wheat) on the London International Financial Futures Exchange (LIFFE) during 1991–2000. Whereas barley and wheat are substitutes in demand and supply and are expected to be related, other pairwise combinations are expected to be unrelated because they are neither complements nor substitutes in either production or consumption. By applying Johansen cointegration tests between all pairwise price combinations, the authors cannot identify any long-run relationship. Hence, their results imply that there is no interdependence between agricultural futures prices on the LIFFE, including between the intuitively related commodities of barley and wheat. Interestingly, the results also imply that traders assess the macroeconomic effects on commodity prices in relation to a commodity taken in isolation.

Table 5.2   Unit root test results for agricultural products, metals and energy markets

	ADF None	ADF Drift	ADF Trend	PP Constant	PP Trend	KPSS
Gold	−37.1056	−37.1925	−37.2477	−52.9168	−52.9698	0.0524
Silver	−37.3650	−37.4052	−37.4082	−55.1757	−55.1768	0.0279
Platinum	−38.4727	−38.5155	−38.5097	−53.1674	−53.1589	0.0525
Aluminum	−37.5246	−37.5248	−37.5216	−53.6836	−53.6768	0.0499
Copper	−37.9764	−37.9995	−38.0015	−54.2472	−54.2451	0.0973
Nickel	−36.5636	−36.5627	−36.5561	−52.6028	−52.5934	0.0804
Zinc	−37.5732	−37.5711	−37.5647	−54.2649	−54.2554	0.0906
Lead	−36.8914	−36.9064	−36.9001	−50.4940	−50.4850	0.0709
WTI	−38.6010	−38.6222	−38.6159	−54.7841	−54.7748	0.0434
Brent	−38.0714	−38.1020	−38.0977	−55.5461	−55.5393	0.0465
Gasoil	−36.7820	−36.8087	−36.8045	−52.6444	−52.6380	0.0542
Natural Gas	−37.0949	−37.0898	−37.1216	−54.3157	−54.3509	0.0222
Heating Oil	−37.6437	−37.6683	−37.6633	−54.6559	−54.6487	0.0482
Corn	−37.0523	−37.0558	−37.0612	−52.5560	−52.5574	0.0307
Wheat	−37.3575	−37.3526	−37.3527	−51.9992	−51.9967	0.0435
Coffee	−36.7885	−36.7870	−36.7804	−51.2554	−51.2458	0.0482
Sugar	−37.3943	−37.3956	−37.3908	−54.1424	−54.1354	0.0404
Cocoa	−37.7738	−37.7712	−37.7645	−54.0468	−54.0370	0.0423
Cotton	−36.6808	−36.6773	−36.6712	−51.7301	−51.7213	0.0498
Soybean	−35.7077	−35.7165	−35.7193	−51.8726	−51.8715	0.0332
Rice	−37.0520	−37.0498	−37.0473	−50.1294	−50.1241	0.0478

Note: Test statistics are given. ADF stands for the Augmented Dickey–Fuller unit root test, PP for the Phillips–Perron unit root test, and KPSS for the Kwiatkowski–Phillips–Schmidt–Shin unit root test. Corresponding critical values (at 5% level) can be found in Greene (2003): −1.9409 for ADF None, −2.8623 for ADF Drift, −3.4114 for ADF Trend, −2.8623 for PP Constant, −3.4114 for PP Trend and 0.4630 for KPSS.

- Several explanations can be suggested to explain the sharp differences with the previous paper. First, Dawson and White (2002) examine agricultural futures contracts for commodities whose cross-price elasticities of supply and demand are expected to be close to zero, whereas Malliaris and Urrutia (1996) examine closely related commodities. Second, futures contracts on a different exchange (LIFFE vs. CBOT) are used. Third, the contracts are for soft (feed) wheat and feed barley, whose demand patterns are sufficiently different to suggest that they are not close substitutes.[6] Fourth, these findings might be explained by the fact that market participants on the LIFFE tend to specialize in a commodity with a relatively small amount of trading across all commodities.
- Among other studies, Labys and Lord (1992) examine the cointegration of consumption and production in cocoa, coffee, copper, cotton, maize, soybean, sugar and wheat during 1960– 1989. They establish that commodity inventories have a long-term equilibrium, and that deviations from that equilibrium represent temporary deviations that fundamental market forces will eventually correct.
- Karbuz and Jumah (1995) use the concept of cointegration to examine long-run relationships between cocoa and coffee futures traded on New York's Coffee, Sugar, and Cocoa Exchange (CSCE) and London's Future and Options Exchange (London Fox) during 1980–1991. Their

---

[6] Wheat has a higher nutritional value in feed milling, but some animals, notably sheep, are restricted to a barley-based diet, and thus, the feed barley price can move independently of the wheat price if demand from sheep producers becomes out of step with feed demand from other livestock sectors.

empirical results show that, in general, the prices of cocoa and coffee tend to move together in the long run.

• Booth and Ciner (2001) investigate whether the prices of commodity futures traded on the Tokyo Grain Exchange (TGE) – i.e. corn, redbean, soybean and sugar – evolved together in the long run during 1993–1998. They cannot conclude in favor of the presence of cointegration, except for the pair of corn and soybean prices. Further on this issue, Bhar and Hamori (2006) have shown that a cointegrating relationship may be found between the TGE commodities from 2000 to 2003, but not earlier during the 1990s. Hence, this latter study clearly illustrates the interest of considering sub-samples when performing cointegration analyses.

5.3.1.2 Dairy Products

• Chavas and Kim (2005) investigate the existence of cointegration relationships among selected US dairy commodities (i.e. American cheese, butter and non-fat dry milk) during 1970–1999. The authors provide evidence of long-term price relationships among dairy commodities. This evidence is present whether the government intervenes in domestic markets or not.

5.3.1.3 Agriculture–Energy Linkage

• Nazlioglu (2011) assesses in a cointegration framework the price transmission from world oil prices to agricultural commodity prices (i.e. corn, soybeans and wheat) during 1994–2010. The results are twofold. First, corn and soybean prices are not cointegrated with oil prices. This finding is consistent with the increasing importance of corn and soybean as a consequence of the significant expansion of biofuels in the last few years. Indeed, increasing oil prices results in the growth of corn- and soybean-based biofuels production (which in turn drives up the demand for these agricultural commodities). Second, the null hypothesis of no cointegration between wheat and oil prices is rejected. This result is expected since wheat requires an energy-intensive production process.

• Natanelov et al. (2011) develop a comprehensive study on the interaction between crude oil futures and cocoa, coffee, corn, soybeans, soybean oil, wheat, rice, sugar and gold futures during 1989–2010. The results indicate strong linkages between the crude oil price and the cocoa, wheat and gold markets. Coffee is also found to exhibit a cointegrating relationship with crude oil after the liberalization of the coffee markets. In the case of soybeans, soybean oil and corn, the results indicate that biofuel policy has buffered the price relationship between those markets and crude oil futures, i.e. until crude oil prices surpass a certain threshold level.

The results from cointegration studies on various categories of agricultural commodities are conveniently summarized in Table 5.3.

Overall, agricultural commodities appear to belong to economically linked markets, which incorporate the information relative to several possible factors, such as substitutability, complementarity, weather and climatological factors, world agricultural demand and supply shocks, even herd trends.

These findings also have consequences in terms of cross-hedging agricultural commodities. For instance, if corn and soybeans are economically linked, a soybean position could be hedged

Table 5.3 Agricultural markets: cointegrating relationships

Authors	Period	Cointegration Relationship	SS	SB
Grains and soft commodities				
Malliaris and Urrutia (1996)	1981–1991	Corn ↔ Wheat ↔ Oat ↔ Soybean	No	No
Dawson and White (2002)	1991–2000	Barley Ø Cocoa Ø Coffee Ø Sugar Ø Wheat	No	No
Labys and Lord (1992)	1960–1989	Coffee, Cocoa, Wheat, Maize, Soybeans, Cotton, Sugar, Copper ↔ Inventories	No	No
Karbuz and Jumah (1995)	1980–1991	Cocoa ↔ Coffee	No	No
Booth and Ciner (2001)	1993–1998	Corn Ø Redbean Ø Soybean Ø Sugar Corn ↔ Soybean	No	No
Bhar and Hamori (2006)	1994–2003	Corn ↔ Redbean ↔ Soybean ↔ Sugar	Yes	No
Dairy products				
Chavas and Kim (2005)	1970–1999	American Cheese ↔ Butter ↔ Non-Fat Dry Milk	No	No
Agriculture–energy linkage				
Nazlioglu (2011)	1994–2010	Oil Ø Corn Oil Ø Soybean Oil ↔ Wheat	Yes	Yes
Natanelov *et al.* (2011)	1989–2010	Oil ↔ Cocoa Oil ↔ Wheat Oil ↔ Gold Oil Ø Soybean Oil Ø Soybean Oil Oil Ø Corn	Yes	No

Note: ↔ indicates the presence of a cointegration relationship. Ø indicates the absence of a cointegration relationship. SS stands for 'Sub Sample' analysis in the paper considered. SB stands for 'Structural Break' analysis in the paper considered.

in the much more liquid corn futures market for market participants holding physical positions on these markets.

Based on these rich results from past academic research, we report in what follows the estimation results on the Granger causality tests, as well as cointegration tests with/without structural breaks for corn, wheat, coffee, sugar, cocoa, cotton, soybean and rice based on an extended dataset from 1998 to 2011.

5.3.2 Results of Granger Causality Tests for Agricultural Products

Tables 5.4 and 5.5 display the results of pairwise Granger causality tests (with one lag) across agricultural commodities. The main results may be summarized as follows. Corn is found to Granger cause cocoa (at the 5% level). Wheat exhibits a Granger causality link with coffee (at the 5% level) and cocoa (at the 10% level). Interestingly, coffee has a reverse Granger causality link with cocoa (at the 5% level). Sugar is also linked with cocoa in the Granger sense (at the 5% level). Cotton is characterized by Granger causalities with wheat and cocoa. Soybean is linked to wheat and cocoa in the Granger sense. Finally, rice shows Granger causalities with corn and cotton (at the 5% level). Overall, we remark on the stability of the relationships with cocoa, which stands out as a key commodity in terms of linkages among agricultural products. These insights can therefore be tested more formally in the subsequent cointegration analysis.

Table 5.4 Pairwise Granger causality tests for agricultural products: corn, wheat, coffee, sugar

From	To	*p*-value	*F*-statistic
Corn	Wheat	0.3026	1.0627
Corn	Coffee	0.1455	2.1191
Corn	Sugar	0.7258	0.1230
Corn	Cocoa	0.0040	8.3107
Corn	Cotton	0.7155	0.1328
Corn	Soybean	0.8287	0.0468
Corn	Rice	0.7988	0.0650
Wheat	Corn	0.2403	1.3793
Wheat	Coffee	0.0140	6.0480
Wheat	Sugar	0.4013	0.7044
Wheat	Cocoa	0.0767	3.1343
Wheat	Cotton	0.5835	0.3007
Wheat	Soybean	0.7913	0.0700
Wheat	Rice	0.2609	1.2642
Coffee	Corn	0.6535	0.2015
Coffee	Wheat	0.9812	0.0006
Coffee	Sugar	0.6233	0.2414
Coffee	Cocoa	0.0140	6.0435
Coffee	Cotton	0.9530	0.0035
Coffee	Soybean	0.4256	0.6349
Coffee	Rice	0.9255	0.0087
Sugar	Corn	0.2946	1.0989
Sugar	Wheat	0.6023	0.2715
Sugar	Coffee	0.3727	0.7948
Sugar	Cocoa	0.0562	3.6465
Sugar	Cotton	0.1573	2.0009
Sugar	Soybean	0.7291	0.1200
Sugar	Rice	0.1289	2.3060

Note: The *p*-value and the *F*-statistic of the pairwise Granger causality tests between X and Y are given. The null hypothesis is that X does not Granger cause Y.

5.3.3 Cointegration Analyses for Agricultural Products

Based on the dataset gathered in Section 5.2, we have investigated the main results from previous literature which are summarized in Table 5.3. In what follows, we present the bulk of the results obtained (i.e. whether a cointegration relationship could be identified between the variables of interest). We detail only some particular cases where the cointegration relationship identified is stable over time, and is robust to the estimation of the VECM model.

Compared to previous literature, we consider systematically various sub-periods and test explicitly for the presence of structural breaks in the cointegration relationships under scrutiny. Note that we cannot possibly replicate all the results from previous literature, or run cointegration tests on every possible pair of commodities. That is why we choose to focus on a limited number of specifications, and compare extensively our results with previous authors given that a more recent dataset is used in this chapter.

Table 5.6 contains the summary of our main results for agricultural products.

Table 5.5   Pairwise Granger causality tests for agricultural products: cocoa, cotton, soybean, rice

From	To	p-value	F-statistic
Cocoa	Corn	0.6569	0.1973
Cocoa	Wheat	0.7828	0.0760
Cocoa	Coffee	0.4901	0.4764
Cocoa	Sugar	0.1942	1.6862
Cocoa	Cotton	0.3638	0.8250
Cocoa	Soybean	0.5402	0.3753
Cocoa	Rice	0.1121	2.5255
Cotton	Corn	0.2745	1.1945
Cotton	Wheat	0.0328	4.5584
Cotton	Coffee	0.1642	1.9353
Cotton	Sugar	0.1569	2.0042
Cotton	Cocoa	0.0009	10.9513
Cotton	Soybean	0.8994	0.0160
Cotton	Rice	0.2585	1.2770
Soybean	Corn	0.9542	0.0033
Soybean	Wheat	0.0571	3.6223
Soybean	Coffee	0.7409	0.1094
Soybean	Sugar	0.3757	0.7848
Soybean	Cocoa	0.0504	3.8308
Soybean	Cotton	0.7815	0.0770
Soybean	Rice	0.3750	0.7873
Rice	Corn	0.0564	3.6432
Rice	Wheat	0.4036	0.6976
Rice	Coffee	0.1874	1.7384
Rice	Sugar	0.1182	2.4412
Rice	Cocoa	0.7908	0.0703
Rice	Cotton	0.3734	0.7923
Rice	Soybean	0.0260	4.9564

Note: The p-value and the F-statistic of the pairwise Granger causality tests between X and Y are given. The null hypothesis is that X does not Granger cause Y.

5.3.4   Grains and Soft Commodities

5.3.4.1   Corn, Wheat and Soybean

In the first category composed of grains and soft commodities, we start our investigation with the relationship between corn, wheat and soybean. Based on Johansen's maximum eigenvalue test statistic,[7] one cointegration relationship can be identified during the full period (1993–2011), however the estimation of the VECM could not be validated.[8] The sub-periods decomposition (1993–2000 and 2000–2011) did not suceed in identifying any cointegration relationship. When examining the occurence of one structural break in the cointegration relationship between corn, wheat and soybean, we obtain significant results: we accept the fact that the rank of the cointegration r is at least equal to 1. This result is shown in Table 5.7.

---

[7] Note that the trace test statistic yields the same results. This comment applies in the remainder of Part III.
[8] Hence, we do not report these results, which are available upon request.

Table 5.6 Cointegration analyses of agricultural markets: summary of the main results

Period	Cointegration Relationship	SB
Grains and soft commodities		
1993–2011	Corn ↔ Wheat ↔ Soybean	No
1993–2000	Corn Ø Wheat Ø Soybean	No
2000–2011	Corn Ø Wheat Ø Soybean	No
1993–2011	Corn ↔ Wheat ↔ Soybean	Yes
1993–2011	Cocoa Ø Coffee Ø Sugar Ø Wheat	No
1993–2000	Cocoa Ø Coffee Ø Sugar Ø Wheat	No
2000–2011	Cocoa Ø Coffee Ø Sugar Ø Wheat	No
1993–2011	Cocoa ↔ Coffee ↔ Sugar ↔ Wheat	Yes
1993–2011	Cocoa Ø Coffee	No
1993–2000	Cocoa Ø Coffee	No
2000–2011	Cocoa Ø Coffee	No
1993–2011	Cocoa ↔ Coffee	Yes
1993–2011	Corn ↔ Soybean ↔ Sugar	No
1993–2000	Corn Ø Soybean Ø Sugar	No
2000–2011	Corn Ø Soybean Ø Sugar	No
1993–2011	Corn ↔ Soybean ↔ Sugar	Yes
1993–2011	Corn ↔ Soybean	No
1993–2000	Corn Ø Soybean	No
2000–2011	Corn Ø Soybean	No
1993–2011	Corn ↔ Soybean	Yes
Agriculture–energy linkage		
1993–2011	Oil Ø Corn	No
1993–2000	Oil Ø Corn	No
2000–2011	Oil Ø Corn	No
1993–2011	Oil ↔ Corn	Yes
1993–2011	Oil Ø Soybean	No
1993–2000	Oil Ø Soybean	No
2000–2011	Oil Ø Soybean	No
1993–2011	Oil ↔ Soybean	Yes
1993–2011	Oil Ø Wheat	No
1993–2000	Oil Ø Wheat	No
2000–2011	Oil Ø Wheat	No
1993–2011	Oil ↔ Wheat	Yes
1993–2011	Oil Ø Cocoa	No
1993–2000	Oil Ø Cocoa	No
2000–2011	Oil Ø Cocoa	No
1993–2011	Oil ↔ Cocoa	Yes

Note: ↔ indicates the presence of a cointegration relationship. Ø indicates the absence of a cointegration relationship. SB stands for 'Structural Break' analysis.

Table 5.7 Lütkepohl *et al.* (2004) cointegration test results with structural break for corn, wheat and soybean

1993–2011	Max. Eigen.	10%	5%	1%
$r \leq 2$	6.88	5.42	6.79	10.04
$r \leq 1$	26.57	13.78	15.83	19.85
$r = 0$	56.45	25.93	28.45	33.76

Table 5.8   VECM results with structural break (1993–2011) for corn, wheat and soybean

Error-Correction Term			
Corn	1		
Wheat	−3.540		
Soybean	2.945		

VECM	Δ Corn	Δ Wheat	Δ Soybean
ECT	−0.003	0.001	−0.003
(*t*.stat)	(−3.2)	(0.67)	(−4.25)
ΔCorn(−1)	−0.016	0.007	−0.008
(*t*.stat)	(−0.58)	(0.23)	(−0.33)
ΔWheat(−1)	0.025	0.027	−0.006
(*t*.stat)	(1.07)	(1.14)	(−0.31)
ΔSoybean(−1)	0.001	−0.049	0.019
(*t*.stat)	(−0.01)	(−1.61)	(0.79)

The next step consists in the estimation of the VECM (with one lag),[9] whose results are reproduced in Table 5.8. The estimation of this model is quite satisfactory, since two error-correction terms (ECTs) are negative and highly statistically significant for corn and soybean. Hence, we can conclude that these two time series are leaders in the price discovery process, and that they push back the system to its long-term equilibrium following short-term deviations.

Lastly, the cointegration relationship is pictured in Figure 5.5. We remark that this graph has the desirable properties of any cointegration analysis, as the joint evolution of Corn, Wheat and Soybean results in a stationary combination over time. The relationship is remarkably stable, with few departures from the long-run equilibrium, which are immediately corrected thanks to the strong error-correction mechanisms identified previously from corn and soybean. Finally, the procedure of detecting one structural break results in the following date (shown with a vertical dotted line on the graph): August 12, 2010. Overall, we have been able to confirm partially the results by Malliaris and Urrutia (1996), with a more recent dataset (but without the oat time series).

5.3.4.2   Cocoa, Coffee, Sugar and Wheat

Next, Table 5.6 contains the estimation results of the cointegration between cocoa, coffee, sugar and wheat. No cointegration relationship could be found during the full period or the corresponding sub-periods. By allowing the occurrence of one structural break, we find that the rank of the cointegration *r* is equal to 1. This result is reproduced in Table 5.9.

The corresponding VECM model estimated also produces satisfactory results, as shown in Table 5.10. We verify that the two strongest error-correction mechanisms come from cocoa and coffee, whose coefficients are strongly significant and negative (they are respectively equal

---

[9] To determine the lag order of the VECM, we seek to minimize the value of information criteria similarly to the approach for standard VAR models. We find that the specification with one lag provides the best fit to the data, while validating diagnostic tests regarding the non-autocorrelation of the residuals (Box–Pierce test). This specification also offers the advantage of being parsimonious to estimate and interpret. In addition, the VECM models are consistently estimated with a Trend component in the cointegration relationship, and an Intercept in the data. These comments apply in the remainder of Part III.

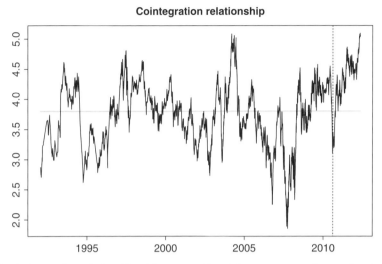

Figure 5.5   Cointegration relationship with structural break between corn, wheat and soybean

Table 5.9   Lütkepohl *et al.* (2004) cointegration test results with structural break for cocoa, coffee, sugar and wheat

1993–2011	Max. Eigen.	10%	5%	1%
$r \leq 3$	3.89	5.42	6.79	10.04
$r \leq 2$	11.66	13.78	15.83	19.85
$r \leq 1$	26.18	25.93	28.45	33.76
$r = 0$	46.39	42.08	45.2	51.6

Table 5.10   VECM results with structural break (1993–2011) for cocoa, coffee, sugar and wheat

Error-Correction Term	
Cocoa	1
Coffee	0.995
Sugar	−0.744
Wheat	−1.136

VECM	ΔCocoa	ΔCoffee	ΔSugar	ΔWheat
ECT	−0.005	−0.004	0.001	0.002
(*t*.stat)	(−3.78)	(−2.18)	(0.05)	(1.33)
ΔCocoa(−1)	−0.048	−0.001	−0.053	−0.043
(*t*.stat)	(−2.44)	(−0.06)	(−2.39)	(−2.19)
ΔCoffee(−1)	0.026	0.024	0.007	−0.001
(*t*.stat)	(1.7)	(1.24)	(0.42)	(−0.61)
ΔSugar(−1)	0.032	0.001	−0.020	0.017
(*t*.stat)	(1.85)	(0.06)	(−0.99)	(0.98)
ΔWheat(−1)	0.039	0.073	0.007	−0.004
(*t*.stat)	(2.04)	(3.05)	(0.32)	(−0.21)

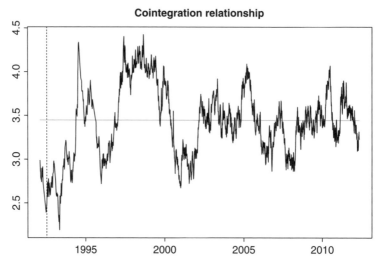

Figure 5.6   Cointegration relationship with structural break between cocoa, coffee, sugar and wheat

to −0.005 and −0.004). Hence, the departures from the long-run equilibrium from any of the four variables of interest will be corrected by either cocoa or coffee in this system.

The cointegration relationship is pictured in Figure 5.6. Starting from the structural break date on June 29, 1992, the relationship also exhibits the remarkable characteristics of being stationary around the mean in the long term. This graph therefore shows that the cointegration exercise between the time series of cocoa, coffee, sugar and wheat has been successful over 1993–2011 and the inclusion of one structural break. These results therefore extend the previous findings by Dawson and White (2002).

5.3.4.3   Cocoa and Coffee

We now consider the pair of agricultural commodities composed of cocoa and coffee. Contrary to previous literature, we are not able to identify any cointegration relationship, neither during the full period nor during the corresponding sub-periods. Only with the inclusion of one structural break are we able to confirm the existence of one cointegration relationship ($r=1$) between these two time series. The results of the cointegration test with one structural break are shown in Table 5.11.

The VECM model output can be found in Table 5.12. While both error-correction terms are found to be significant, only the coefficient for cocoa is negative. Hence, cocoa is the

Table 5.11   Lütkepohl *et al.* (2004) cointegration test results with structural break for cocoa and coffee

1993–2011	Max. Eigen.	10%	5%	1%
$r \leq 1$	6.81	5.42	6.79	10.04
$r = 0$	18.15	13.78	15.83	19.85

Table 5.12   VECM results with structural
break (1993–2011) for cocoa and coffee

Error-Correction Term		
Cocoa	1	
Coffee	−0.329	

VECM	ΔCocoa	ΔCoffee
ECT	−0.005	0.006
(*t*.stat)	(−2.14)	(2.21)
ΔCocoa(−1)	−0.035	0.003
(*t*.stat)	(−1.8)	(0.12)
ΔCoffee(−1)	0.028	0.025
(*t*.stat)	(1.83)	(1.31)

leader in the price discovery process among the two time series, as it leads back to the long-term equilibrium following short-term deviations (i.e. idiosyncratic shocks on one of the two agricultural markets).

Figure 5.7 represents the corresponding cointegration relationship. Following the identification of the structural break on June 29, 1992 we cannot be entirely satisfied with this graph compared to our previous analyses. Indeed, some departures from stationarity are visible, and the possibility remains that more than one structural break has occurred during the period when analyzing jointly the time series of cocoa and coffee. Our overall conclusion errs towards a prudent approach: we cannot confirm the results by Karbuz and Jumah (1995) who unambiguously concluded in favor of the existence of a cointegration relationship between cocoa and coffee. Therefore, it cannot be said from our empirical application that the prices of cocoa and coffee are determined by the same factors.

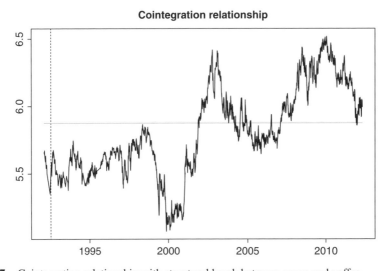

Figure 5.7   Cointegration relationship with structural break between cocoa and coffee

5.3.4.4 Corn, Soybean and Sugar

During 1993–2011, we are able to find one cointegrating relationship between corn, soybean and sugar (at the 10% significance level). While the relationship appears quite stable over time, the estimation of the VECM is not successful (i.e. the error-correction terms are not significantly negative). That is why we do not reproduce these results here. This first set of results is not robust to the sub-period decomposition. When detecting a structural break on February 11, 1998 it is possible again to find a cointegration relationship between corn, soybean and sugar during the full period (at the 1% level). In that latter case, the estimation of the VECM was not sucessful either, and the cointegration relationship does not appear to be stable. Hence, in our framework, we cannot confirm the findings by Booth and Ciner (2001) and Bhar and Hamori (2006) without the redbean time series.

5.3.4.5 Corn and Soybean

When restricting our investigation to the pair of agricultural commodities corn and soybean, we get very similar results. During the full period without break, it is possible to detect one cointegrating relationship, but the estimation of the VECM cannot be validated. The sub-periods' decomposition does not change qualitatively the results obtained. When running the breakpoint detection routine, we identify one structural change on July 2, 1996. The rank of the cointegration relationship r can be confirmed to be at least 1 (at the 1% level), and the graph of the long-term equilibrium between the two time series is stationary. Nevertheless, we are unable to estimate satisfactorily the VECM (i.e. to meet the required conditions on the sign and the significance of the ECT). Thus, these results are not reproduced either and they do not confirm the previous findings by Booth and Ciner (2001).

In our setting, we cannot seek to reproduce the results from previous literature concerning dairy products, since these time series are not included in the database presented in Section 5.2. That is why we jump directly to the results obtained for the agriculture–energy linkage (as introduced in the discussion of Section 5.3.1).

5.3.5 Agriculture–Energy Linkage

The main results from this section are also summarized in Table 5.6.

5.3.5.1 Oil and Corn

During the full period and the corresponding sub-periods, it is not possible to find statistically a cointegration relationship between the time series of WTI crude oil and corn. When allowing for the presence of one structural break, the picture changes completely. As shown in Table 5.13, it is indeed possible to establish the presence of one cointegrating relationship within this pair of agricultural commodities (at the 1% level).

Table 5.13   Lütkepohl *et al.* (2004) cointegration test results with structural break for oil and corn

1993–2011	Max. Eigen.	10%	5%	1%
$r \leq 1$	7.14	5.42	6.79	10.04
$r = 0$	24.05	13.78	15.83	19.85

Table 5.14 VECM results with structural break (1993–2011) for oil and corn

Error-Correction Term		
WTI	1	
Corn	−0.448	

VECM	ΔWTI	ΔCorn
ECT	−0.010	−0.002
(*t*.stat)	(−4.08)	(−1.05)
ΔWTI(−1)	−0.038	−0.053
(*t*.stat)	(−1.96)	(−3.37)
ΔCorn(−1)	0.037	0.007
(*t*.stat)	(1.60)	(0.37)

Next, the estimation of the VECM appears successful in Table 5.14. Indeed, both error-correction terms are negative. Only the ECT for WTI is significant (at the 1% level), which implies that the WTI futures price is the leader in the price discovery process between oil and corn. Any short-term deviations from the long-run equilibrium will be corrected with the WTI variable in this system. To put it simply, any deviation from the long-term equilibrium would be corrected by a variation of the WTI price.

Finally, we can observe in Figure 5.8 that the structural break has been detected on July 7, 2008. This result is not surprising given the oil price swing which occurred during the summer of 2008. After this event (and the feedback effect from the WTI price to the long-term equilibrium), we could assess, based on Figure 5.8, that the cointegration relationship is stable. However, this is clearly not the case before the break, which makes the relationship

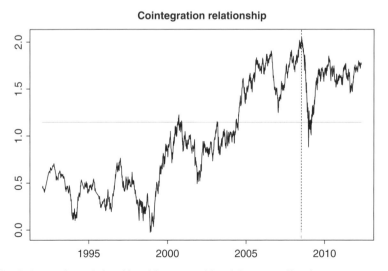

Figure 5.8 Cointegration relationship with structural break between oil and corn

Table 5.15   Lütkepohl *et al.* (2004) cointegration
test results with structural break for soybean and WTI

1993–2011	Max. Eigen.	10%	5%	1%
$r \leq 1$	6.50	5.42	6.79	10.04
$r = 0$	23.69	13.78	15.83	19.85

non-stationary. Hence, we agree here with the conclusions by Nazlioglu (2011) and Natanelov *et al.* (2011) who found evidence against the presence of cointegration between oil and corn.

5.3.5.2   Oil and Soybean

The relationship between oil and soybean is especially interesting to study, since both commodities can be seen as substitutes in the production of fuel for engines (at least in the vast majority of South American countries). Hence, their price series can be expected to be tied together in the long run, as they reflect various demands for food, transportation and energy needs. In Table 5.6, our main results yield to the rejection of a cointegration relationship between oil and soybean during the full and sub-periods, but this result changes with the introduction of one structural break.

As shown in Table 5.15, the rank of the cointegration r between oil and soybean is equal to 1 (at the 1% level) in the structural break framework by Lütkepohl *et al.* (2004).

The identification of such a cointegration relationship yields the estimation of the VECM model, as reproduced in Table 5.16. We can observe that both error-correction terms are negative, while only the ECT term for the WTI variable appears to be statistically significant (at the 1% level). Similarly to the previous case for oil and corn, we can assess that the WTI variable is the leader in the price discovery process between oil and soybean. That is to say, if there are strong deviations from the long-term relationship between the two variables (because the price of oil is driven by macroeconomic factors for instance, or if the production of soybean is hit by production difficulties), the fluctuations of the oil price will make most

Table 5.16   VECM results with structural break (1993–2011) for soybean and WTI

Error-Correction Term		
WTI	1	
Soybean	−0.609	

VECM	ΔWTI	ΔSoybean
ECT	−0.011	−0.001
(*t*.stat)	(−4.16)	(−0.67)
ΔWTI(−1)	−0.048	−0.055
(*t*.stat)	(−2.52)	(−3.99)
ΔSoybean(−1)	0.069	0.03
(*t*.stat)	(2.59)	(1.55)

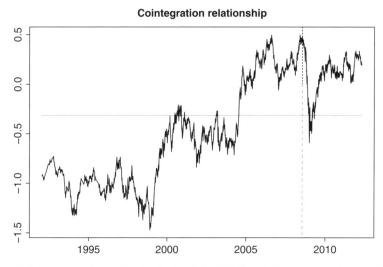

Figure 5.9   Cointegration relationship for the 1993–2011 full period between soybean and WTI

of the adjustment towards the recovery of a stable relationship over time between oil and soybean.

When looking at the cointegration relationship in Figure 5.9, we notice that the structural break occurred on July 15, 2008. Similarly to the previous pair of commodities, the cointegration relationship is disrupted by the events of the summer of 2008, when the crude oil futures price recorded an all-time high at \$147 per barrel on July 3, 2008 and then collapsed to below \$30 per barrel on December 23, 2008. The inspection of Figure 5.9 reveals clearly two regimes, before and after the structural break, while only the second regime appears as stationary. Therefore, we cannot conclude in favor of a stable cointegration relationship between oil and soybean in our setting. Our results thus conform to the previous studies by Nazlioglu (2011) and Natanelov *et al.* (2011). The collapse of the Asian demand for oil, rice and soybean in 2008 may contribute to explaining these empirical results.

5.3.5.3   Oil and Wheat

The next pair of agricultural commodities that we include in our cointegration analysis is composed of oil and wheat. As shown in Table 5.6, we could not find any cointegrating relationship between the two time series, neither during the full nor sub-periods. With the inclusion of one structural break, we obtain the results displayed in Table 5.17.

Table 5.17   Lütkepohl *et al.* (2004) cointegration test results with structural break for wheat and WTI

1993–2011	Max. Eigen.	10%	5%	1%
$r \leq 1$	8.05	5.42	6.79	10.04
$r = 0$	25.25	13.78	15.83	19.85

Table 5.18   VECM results with structural break (1993–2011) for wheat and WTI

Error-Correction Term		
WTI	1	
Wheat	−0.546	

VECM	ΔWTI	ΔWheat
ECT	−0.011	−0.001
(t.stat)	(−4.16)	(−0.32)
ΔWTI(−1)	−0.048	−0.047
(t.stat)	(−2.52)	(−2.83)
ΔWheat(−1)	0.055	0.016
(t.stat)	(2.50)	(0.85)

Following Lütkepohl *et al.* (2004), the results of the cointegration test with one structural break yields acceptance of the fact that the rank of the cointegration r is equal to 1. Hence, we are able to find one cointegrating relationship between oil and wheat during the full period.

In Table 5.18, the VECM estimates are very close to the results obtained for the previous pair of oil and soybean. While both error-correction terms are found to be negative, only the ECT for the WTI variable is statistically significant. Therefore, the same comments as in our previous analysis apply.

In Figure 5.10, the structural break date corresponds to July 15, 2008. Again, the same comments arise regarding the non-stationarity of the cointegrating relationship prior to the break. Our results differ on this point from the previous findings by Nazlioglu (2011) and Natanelov *et al.* (2011), who both found unequivocal evidence in favor of cointegration between oil and wheat.

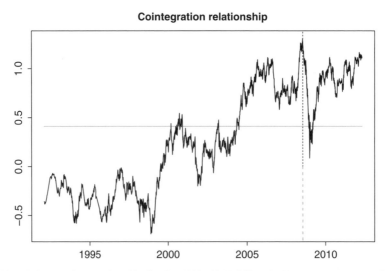

Figure 5.10   Cointegration relationship for the 1993–2011 full period between wheat and WTI

Table 5.19 Lütkepohl *et al.* (2004) cointegration test
results with structural break for cocoa and WTI

1993–2011	Max. Eigen.	10%	5%	1%
$r \leq 1$	7.14	5.42	6.79	10.04
$r = 0$	17.26	13.78	15.83	19.85

5.3.5.4 Oil and Cocoa

The last pair of agricultural commodities investigated consists of oil and cocoa. It is remarkable to notice in Table 5.6 that for the fourth case in a row in the agriculture and energy category, only one cointegrating relationship could be identified during the full period with a structural break.

This result is reproduced in Table 5.19, where it is readily observable that the rank of the cointegration r between oil and cocoa is equal to 1 (at the 5% level).

The VECM estimated is more satisfactory than in the previous two cases (oil and soybean on the one hand; oil and wheat on the other hand). Indeed, in Table 5.20, both error-correction terms are negative and significant (at the 1% level for WTI; at the 10% level for cocoa). It seems therefore that the combination of the two time series operates in a better fashion than in the two preceding cases, and that the WTI variable is not the only force pushing back the system towards its long-term equilibrium (following a short-term shock). Hence, the VECM passes most of the tests and can be readily considered valid.

In Figure 5.11, the visual investigation of the cointegrating relationship also brings new results compared to the previous pairs of agricultural commodities. In our current setting with oil and cocoa, the structural break date is June 29, 1992 (and not the summer of 2008). Nevertheless, the cointegrating relationship does not appear stationary overall, and there may be room for improvement by allowing more than one structural break in the data during the period 1993–2011. Unlike Nazlioglu (2011), we cannot conclude that a stable cointegration relationship exists between oil and cocoa.

Table 5.20 VECM results with structural break
(1993–2011) for cocoa and WTI

Error-Correction Term		
WTI	1	
Cocoa	0.923	

VECM	ΔWTI	ΔCocoa
ECT	−0.005	−0.003
(*t*.stat)	(−2.89)	(−1.67)
ΔWTI(−1)	−0.016	0.025
(*t*.stat)	(−0.82)	(1.47)
ΔCocoa(−1)	−0.052	−0.033
(*t*.stat)	(−2.42)	(−1.74)

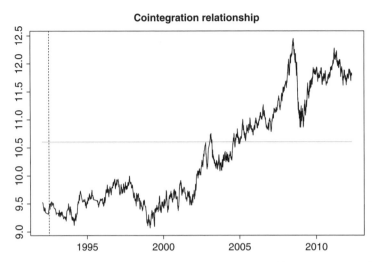

Figure 5.11   Cointegration relationship for the 1993–2011 full period between cocoa and WTI

5.3.5.5   *Summary and Discussion on Cointegration Analyses for Agricultural Products*

The main results regarding the investigation of cross-commodity linkages among agricultural products can be summarized as follows. First, there seems to be a robust cointegration relationship between corn, wheat and soybean during 1993–2011, with a rather stable cointegration relationship in the presence of one structural break, and a valid VECM. Second, the cointegration between cocoa, coffee, sugar and wheat also proved to be a successful exercise, with cocoa and coffee being the drivers in the adjustment towards the long-term equilibrium. Third, the examination of the pair of cocoa and coffee alone is not as successful as in the preceding case: it is not possible to conclude that the cointegration relationship is stable over time. Fourth, additional attempts with corn, soybean and sugar or corn and soybean also failed to detect meaningful cointegration relationships. Therefore, we are only able to confirm a fraction of the results highlighted in previous literature concerning grains and soft commodities, thereby highlighting that those results are dependent on the period under scrutiny. Fifth, the results concerning the agriculture–energy linkage do not always conform to the findings from previous authors. Most of the time, a cointegration relationship can only be detected in the presence of one structural break, which typically occurs during the summer of 2008 with the oil price swing. Whenever the structural break occurs at another date, it seems that the processes would have a better fit with an additional number of breaks (i.e. at least two). Overall, the interest of practicing cointegration analysis with at least one structural break is clear, and can bring fruitful results as in the first two attempts. However, it appears difficult to verify all the results from previous studies in our framework given the recent instability in the oil market.

Next, let us consider the cointegration relationships that exist among industrial metals.

5.4   COINTEGRATION IN INDUSTRIAL METALS MARKETS

Cointegration between the main industrial metals can be of interest to researchers and practitioners, since some metals have a substitutive character, while others may be seen as complementary. Let us review briefly the main results from the academic literature on this topic.

5.4.1 Literature Review

- MacDonald and Taylor (1988) investigate the cointegration between the prices of tin, zinc and lead on the London Metal Exchange (LME) during 1976–1985. The authors report overwhelming evidence of no cointegration for any of the metal prices considered in their study.
- By using data from 1900 to 1986, von Hagen (1989) shows that primary and manufactured goods prices are cointegrated, i.e. that the hypothesis of stationarity for the long-run relative price movements cannot be rejected.
- Franses and Kofman (1991) consider equilibrium relationships among aluminum, copper, lead, nickel and zinc prices on the LME in 1981. The authors are able to find one cointegrating relationship, with the copper price reacting rapidly to disequilibrium errors (and in this respect being less exogenous than other metals).
- Labson and Crompton (1993) examine whether a long-run stationary equilibrium relationship holds between aggregate income and consumption of various primary industrial metals, e.g. aluminum, copper, lead, steel, tin, zinc, during 1960–1992. They find little evidence to support the presence of a long-run equilibrium relationship between income and metals consumption.
- Chen and Lin (2004) examine the dynamic relation between the LME lead price and its possible predictors during 1964–1995. Their results highlight the presence of one cointegration relationship between lead prices, inventories and UK treasury bill rates.
- Cerda (2007) identifies a cointegration relationship between the price of copper, exchange rates and wholesale price indices during 1994–2003. The author identifies that the demand from large economic blocs (especially Asia) significantly affects the price of copper.

The main insights from these studies have been summarized in Table 5.21.

Table 5.21 Industrial metals: cointegrating relationships

Authors	Period	Cointegration Relationship	SS	SB
MacDonald and Taylor (1988)	1976–1985	Tin Ø Zinc Ø Lead	No	No
von Hagen (1989)	1900–1986	Primary Goods ↔ Manufactured Goods	No	No
Franses and Kofman (1991)	1981	Aluminum ↔ Copper ↔ Lead ↔ Nickel ↔ Zinc	No	No
Labson and Crompton (1993)	1960–1992	Aluminum Ø Copper Ø Lead Ø Steel Ø Tin Ø ↔ Zinc	No	No
Chen and Lin (2004)	1964–1995	Lead ↔ Inventories ↔ UK Treasury Bill	No	No
Cerda (2007)	1994–2003	Copper ↔ Exchange Rate ↔ Price Indices	No	No

Note: ↔ indicates the presence of a cointegration relationship. Ø indicates the absence of a cointegration relationship. SS stands for 'Sub Sample' analysis in the paper considered. SB stands for 'Structural Break' analysis in the paper considered.

Table 5.22   Pairwise Granger causality tests for industrial metals

From	To	p-value	F-statistic
Aluminum	Copper	0.5118	0.4305
Aluminum	Nickel	0.1989	1.6509
Aluminum	Zinc	0.6568	0.1975
Aluminum	Lead	0.0318	4.6104
Copper	Aluminum	0.2980	1.0834
Copper	Nickel	0.0414	4.1631
Copper	Zinc	0.4157	0.6624
Copper	Lead	0.0534	3.7332
Nickel	Aluminum	0.3498	0.8743
Nickel	Copper	0.7418	0.1086
Nickel	Zinc	0.7688	0.0864
Nickel	Lead	0.2040	1.6138
Zinc	Aluminum	0.0745	3.1819
Zinc	Copper	0.2179	1.5187
Zinc	Nickel	0.1109	2.5426
Zinc	Lead	0.1287	2.3084
Lead	Aluminum	0.8061	0.0603
Lead	Copper	0.5445	0.3673
Lead	Nickel	0.7522	0.0997
Lead	Zinc	0.0077	7.1105

Note: The p-value and the F-statistic of the pairwise Granger causality tests between X and Y are given. The null hypothesis is that X does not Granger cause Y.

It seems that the academic research has focused little attention on the cointegration relationships between industrial metals, due to the fact that each metal market is very dependent upon its own supply and demand fundamentals. Therefore, cointegration analyses cannot detect common price movements, except perhaps due to the influence of a common factor such as macroeconomic shocks. Nonetheless, we pursue our analysis by investigating the cointegration issue between aluminum, copper, nickel, zinc and lead prices in the next section.

5.4.2   Results of Granger Causality Tests for Industrial Metals

Table 5.22 displays the results of the pairwise Granger causality tests among industrial metals (with one lag). Aluminum is found to Granger cause lead. Copper causes, in the Granger sense, nickel and lead (at the 5% level). Nickel does not display significant Granger causalities. Zinc is found to Granger cause aluminum (at the 10% level). Finally, lead displays a significant Granger causality with zinc. Thus, there may be some inter-relationships at stake between industrial metals. That is why we resort to a cointegration analysis in the next section.

5.4.3   Cointegration Analyses for Industrial Metals

Concerning industrial metals, the main results from our cointegration analyses are summarized in Table 5.23. We comment on these results in more detail below. Note that we did not wish to replicate here the results by Chen and Lin (2004) or Cerda (2007), who made use of bonds and exchange rate data. The interested reader is invited to refer to Chapter 6 for further developments using that kind of data. Here, we focus more specifically on the relationships within commodities.

Table 5.23   Cointegration analyses of industrial metals: summary of the main results

Period	Cointegration Relationship	SB
1993–2011	Aluminum Ø Copper Ø Nickel Ø Zinc Ø Lead	No
1993–2000	Aluminum Ø Copper Ø Nickel Ø Zinc Ø Lead	No
2000–2011	Aluminum Ø Copper Ø Nickel Ø Zinc Ø Lead	No
1993–2011	Aluminum ↔ Copper ↔ Nickel ↔ Zinc ↔ Lead	Yes
1993–2011	Zinc Ø Lead	No
1993–2000	Zinc Ø Lead	No
2000–2011	Zinc Ø Lead	No
1993–2011	Zinc ↔ Lead	Yes

Note: ↔ indicates the presence of a cointegration relationship. Ø indicates the absence of a cointegration relationship. SB stands for 'Structural Break' analysis.

5.4.3.1   *Aluminum, Copper, Nickel, Zinc and Lead*

Our first cointegration exercise concerns the five time series of industrial metals contained in our database, i.e. aluminum, copper, nickel, zinc and lead. While no cointegration relationship could be found during either the full period or the corresponding sub-periods, Table 5.24 reports the results obtained when allowing for the presence of one structural break.

From this table, we learn that the rank of the cointegration r is at least equal to 1, i.e. we are able to find at least one stationary combination between the variables of interest in the industrial metals category.

The estimation of the VECM returns the results given in Table 5.25. Four out of five error-correction terms turn out to be negative. Three ECTs are significant at the 5% level (nickel and zinc) and at the 1% level (aluminum). Therefore, the results are quite satisfactory, and the VECM can be considered valid. When interpreting the size of the coefficients of the ECTs, we remark that they are roughly equal (around -0.008), but that aluminum stands out as having the highest significance level. Hence, in this system composed of five industrial metals, any short-term deviation from the long-run equilibrium can be corrected by aluminum as the driving force, followed by nickel and zinc. It is very interesting to be able to find such a strong error-correction mechanism between these markets, which are often judged as being separate markets operating based on their own demand and supply fundamentals, and whose trading is

Table 5.24   Lütkepohl *et al.* (2004) cointegration test results with structural break for aluminum, copper, nickel, zinc and lead

1993–2011	Max. Eigen.	10%	5%	1%
$r \leq 4$	5.65	5.42	6.79	10.04
$r \leq 3$	14.16	13.78	15.83	19.85
$r \leq 2$	29.35	25.93	28.45	33.76
$r \leq 1$	53.63	42.08	45.2	51.6
$r = 0$	82.02	61.92	65.66	73.12

Table 5.25 VECM results with structural break (1993–2011) for aluminum, copper, nickel, zinc and lead

Error-Correction Term					
Aluminum	1				
Copper	−0.288				
Nickel	0.318				
Zinc	0.169				
Lead	−0.898				

VECM	ΔAluminum	ΔCopper	ΔNickel	ΔZinc	ΔLead
ECT	−0.008	−0.004	−0.009	−0.008	0.003
(*t*.stat)	(−3.73)	(−1.4)	(−2.36)	(−2.79)	(0.96)
ΔAluminum(−1)	0.014	0.032	0.004	0.031	−0.053
(*t*.stat)	(0.52)	(0.89)	(0.09)	(0.83)	(−1.2)
ΔCopper(−1)	−0.015	−0.029	−0.071	−0.057	−0.028
(*t*.stat)	(−0.66)	(−0.98)	(−1.85)	(−1.88)	(−0.77)
ΔNickel(−1)	−0.002	−0.002	0.032	−0.006	0.001
(*t*.stat)	(−0.12)	(−0.13)	(1.36)	(−0.31)	(0.03)
ΔZinc(−1)	−0.032	−0.044	−0.028	−0.054	0.001
(*t*.stat)	(−1.55)	(−1.59)	(−0.77)	(−1.87)	(0.04)
ΔLead(−1)	0.006	0.013	0.018	0.063	0.055
(*t*.stat)	(0.38)	(0.61)	(0.65)	(2.88)	(2.12)

predominantly based on expert opinion (as in the LME). Contrary to this view, we highlight that there is a common variation trend among these industrial metals, which cannot be priced purely independently.

The cointegration relationship pictured in Figure 5.12 reveals the presence of a structural break on May 14, 2007. Before and after that date, the cointegration relationship appears rather stationary during each of the two regimes. These results confirm the findings by Franses and

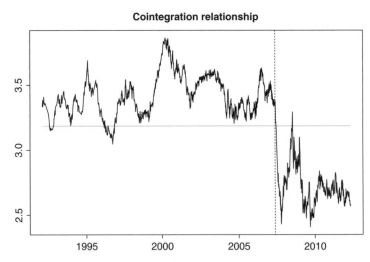

Cointegration relationship

Figure 5.12 Cointegration relationship for the 1993–2011 full period between aluminum, copper, nickel, zinc and lead

Table 5.26 Lütkepohl *et al.* (2004) cointegration test results with structural break for zinc and lead

1993–2011	Max. Eigen.	10%	5%	1%
$r \leq 1$	4.02	5.42	6.79	10.04
$r = 0$	15.64	13.78	15.83	19.85

Table 5.27 VECM results with structural break (1993–2011) for zinc and lead

Error-Correction Term	
Zinc	1
Lead	−2.10

VECM	ΔZinc	ΔLead
ECT	0	0.003
(*t*.stat)	(−0.14)	(2.44)
ΔZinc(−1)	−0.081	−0.051
(*t*.stat)	(−3.15)	(−1.66)
ΔLead(−1)	0.059	0.048
(*t*.stat)	(2.74)	(1.87)

Kofman (1991), and are more optimistic than the ones by Labson and Crompton (1993).[10] To conclude this section, the cointegration relationship between industrial metals seems robust, once we control for the presence of a structural break. The driving force behind these common trends could be understood as being economic activity, which fosters the need for industrial metals as an input to production goods. This insight will be further studied in Chapter 6.

5.4.3.2 *Zinc and Lead*

In our second cointegration exercise with industrial metals, we choose to focus on the pair of commodities composed of zinc and lead. Similarly to the previous case, we could identify one cointegration relationship only during the full period and by modeling explicitly one structural break.

These results are shown in Table 5.26: at the 10% level, we reject the null hypothesis that $r = 0$ in favor of one linear stationary combination of the two time series considered here.

However, the VECM estimation results are not as satisfactory as in the preceding case: none of the error-correction terms is significantly negative in Table 5.27.

The inspection of Figure 5.13 reveals that – before and after the structural break dated November 28, 2006 – the two regimes are not stationary and are impacted by ample fluctuations coming from either zinc or lead. Therefore, our results confirm the findings by MacDonald

---

[10] These latter authors considered a subset of industrial metals composed of aluminum, copper, lead, steel, tin and zinc, but failed to identify any cointegration relationship.

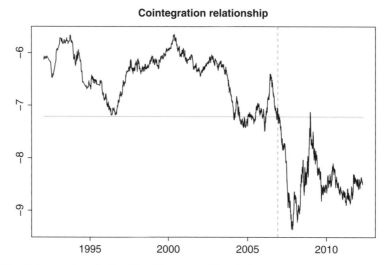

Figure 5.13   Cointegration relationship with structural break between zinc and lead

and Taylor (1988) who could not identify a robust cointegration relationship between zinc and lead.[11]

5.4.3.3   Summary and Discussion on Cointegration Analyses for Industrial Metals

To sum up the main findings from our cointegration analyses applied to the case of industrial metals, we find, in line with Franses and Kofman (1991), that there exist common variations between aluminum, copper, nickel, zinc and lead which gear toward a linear stationary combination in the long run. This result is obtained by including one structural break in the model. However, the same conclusion could not be reached for the pair zinc and lead. Overall, these results are quite optimistic for two main reasons. First, unlike most of the wisdom coming from trading experts in the LME, industrial metals need not necessarily be considered separate markets. Second, these findings teach us that industrial metals could be traded based on a common information signal. This signal could be the extent to which an economy is booming (or entering recession), which is reflected in the need for industrial metals as necessary inputs to production processes.

In what follows, we turn our attention to the case of precious metals.

5.5   COINTEGRATION IN PRECIOUS METALS MARKETS

Gold and silver have historically been seen as close substitutes for one another, both being precious metals that can be used to back currency and both having been used as currency. Moreover, Adrangi *et al.* (2003) document that these metals can play a useful role in diversifying risk, as well as being an attractive investment in their own right. Therefore, one might expect that gold and silver prices share similar dynamics.

---

[11] Note that their analysis also included tin.

However, there are also economic fundamentals that may act to drive the prices of gold and silver apart. While both are used extensively in industrial processes, there are significant differences between these uses. Silver is extremely reflective, a good conductor of electricity and has extensive use in optics and photography. Gold's industrial uses are fewer, with the majority of demand coming from the jewellery and dental markets, as well as being driven by the demand from Central Banks.

Besides gold and silver, palladium and platinum are considered attractive assets for portfolio investment, especially during times of rising inflation and global economic and political instability. Their price fluctuations seem to follow closely the price path of gold over the last two decades (Kearney and Lombra (2009)).

Gold, palladium and platinum can follow different price paths during specific time periods. Their respective price fundamentals can differ widely, as industrial use occupies approximately two-thirds of the total demand for palladium and platinum. Gold can also be traded independently as a refuge for value during periods of bearish markets.

Given their relative scarcity and high economic value, gold, silver, palladium and platinum are therefore considered together as precious metals in cointegration analyses.

5.5.1   Literature Review

In this section, we explore the main findings from the academic literature on cointegration among precious metals. Our review is carried out by analyzing together (i) gold and silver prices, (ii) gold, palladium and platinum prices and (iii) gold and crude oil prices.

5.5.1.1   *Gold and Silver Prices*

- Wahab *et al.* (1994) first identified a cointegrating relationship between gold and silver during 1982–1992. Escribano and Granger (1998) pursue this analysis based on monthly data during 1971–1990, and identify the influence of a large bubble from September 1979 to March 1980. The authors demonstrate that the bubble period had a lasting influence on cointegration, on the short-run dynamics, and possibly on the non-linearity of the relationship.
- Ciner (2001) examines the long-run trend between the prices of gold and silver futures contracts traded on the Tokyo Commodity Exchange (TOCOM) during 1992–1998. Contrary to previous studies, the cointegration tests do not support a stable long-run relationship between gold and silver prices in the futures markets. This finding indicates that these two markets should be approached as separate markets, and that changes in the gold-to-silver ratio should not be used to predict prices in the future. Another implication is that these two markets should not be regarded as substitutes to hedge against similar types of risks. This view is consistent with the understanding that these two commodities have different economic uses, and consequently that they are affected by different economic fundamentals.
- Lucey and Tully (2006) examine the dynamic relationship between gold and silver during 1978–2002. A stable, long-run relationship exists between gold and silver returns over the period examined. The authors conclude that the stable relationship between gold and silver found to prevail historically appears to have continued during their sample period. There are also significant periods during which the cointegrating relationship is weakened or broken. This may indicate that the results of Ciner (2001) are driven by the period under analysis. For portfolio managers and investors, the overall message is that while gold and silver,

in general, offer few diversification advantages when included together in a portfolio, this relationship is not stable. Thus, there may be potential to include both precious metals at certain times.

5.5.1.2 Gold, Palladium and Platinum Prices

- Kearney and Lombra (2009) attempt to explain the behavior of gold prices relative to platinum prices during 1985–2006. They do not reject the null of no cointegration between gold and platinum prices over the full sample period. However, the authors detect a sub-sample from 1996 through 2006 during which the two time series seem to behave differently. Kearney and Lombra (2009) uncover that forward sales are negatively related to gold prices and equilibrium errors during this period. Hence, the increase in forward sales in the 1990s adversely affected gold prices and therefore altered the return on gold, its relationship with platinum prices and, by extension, other assets considered to be close substitutes in investors' portfolios.
- Tsuchiya (2010) investigates whether the TOCOM gold, silver, palladium and platinum futures prices move independently in the long run by relying on the cointegration approach during 2002–2010. The author finds that the prices of the gold, palladium, platinum and silver futures contracts move independently, i.e. that there is no long-term relationship among them.

5.5.1.3 Gold and Crude Oil Prices

- Zhang and Wei (2010) analyze the cointegration between the crude oil and gold markets during 2000–2008. Indeed, the authors notice that the prices of these two commodities were not completely driven by demand and supply fundamentals but rather by the financial features of international commodity markets, and with a close interaction between them. They show that a significant cointegrating relationship can be identified between the crude oil and gold prices, i.e. that there exists a long-term equilibrium relationship which results from the fact that the two markets tend to be influenced by common factors (such as the US Dollar exchange rate, economic fundamentals, geopolitical events, etc.). Interestingly, Zhang and Wei (2010) also suggest that the surging crude oil price has driven up the gold price (but not vice versa), which implies that among commodity markets the role of crude oil outweighs that of gold.

These main results from academic research are conveniently summarized in Table 5.28.

Overall, we notice that meaningful equilibrium relationships can be detected in precious metals markets. Most studies agree on the fact that gold and silver on the one hand, and gold, palladium and platinum on the other hand are characterized by a common evolution in the long term (despite the occurrence of time periods during which the specific supply and demand fundamentals of each market may cause the price series to diverge). The cointegration relationship between gold and crude oil is also interesting from an economic viewpoint, since these two commodities can be valued for other uses than hedging or production alone. Indeed, they carry information on global economic fundamentals, and can be used as a vehicle for speculation (albeit this latter hypothesis constitutes a hotly debated topic in the academic literature).

Table 5.28   Precious metals: cointegrating relationships

Authors	Period	Cointegration Relationship	SS	SB
Gold and silver prices				
Wahab *et al.* (1994)	1982–1992	Gold ↔ Silver	No	No
Escribano and Granger (1998)	1971–1990	Gold ↔ Silver	Yes	Yes
Ciner (2001)	1992–1998	Gold Ø Silver	No	No
Lucey and Tully (2006)	1978–2002	Gold ↔ Silver	Yes	No
Gold, palladium and platinum prices				
Kearney and Lombra (2009)	1985–2006	Gold ↔ Platinum	Yes	No
Tsuchiya (2010)	2002–2010	Gold Ø Silver Ø Palladium Ø Platinum	No	No
Gold and crude oil prices				
Zhang and Wei (2010)	2000–2008	Gold ↔ Crude Oil	No	No

Note: ↔ indicates the presence of a cointegration relationship. Ø indicates the absence of a cointegration relationship. SS stands for 'Sub Sample' analysis in the paper considered. SB stands for 'Structural Break' analysis in the paper considered.

In what follows, we proceed with our own cointegration analysis between gold, silver, palladium and platinum.

5.5.2   Results of Granger Causality Tests for Precious Metals

Table 5.29 reports the results of pairwise Granger causality tests (with one lag) among precious metals. It is difficult to infer a causal relationship from this table, but it can be seen as a guide for the cointegration analysis. For instance, we note that gold and silver do not necessarily cause each other (at the 5% rejection rate), while the relationship between gold and platinum goes in both directions. Note that some additional tests have been conducted for gold, which will be re-used in the next chapter.

Table 5.29   Pairwise Granger causality tests for precious metals

From	To	p-value	F-statistic
Gold	Silver	0.3345	0.9314
Gold	Platinum	0.0216	5.2793
Gold	WTI	0.8239	0.0495
Gold	Brent	0.9831	0.0004
Gold	S&P 500 INDEX	0.6930	0.1559
Gold	US 10 Year	0.7880	0.0723
Gold	USD Trade Weighted	0.1621	1.9552
Gold	EUR-USD X-RATE	0.0028	8.9186
Silver	Gold	0.0725	3.2274
Silver	Platinum	0.0165	5.7555
Platinum	Gold	0.0098	6.6769
Platinum	Silver	0.7209	0.1276

Note: The p-value and the F-statistic of the pairwise Granger causality tests between X and Y are given with one lag. The null hypothesis is that X does not Granger cause Y.

Table 5.30 Cointegration analyses of precious metals: summary of the main results

Period	Cointegration Relationship	SB
1993–2011	Gold Ø Silver	No
1993–2000	Gold Ø Silver	No
2000–2011	Gold Ø Silver	No
1993–2011	Gold ↔ Silver	Yes
1993–2011	Gold Ø Platinum	No
1993–2000	Gold Ø Platinum	No
2000–2011	Gold ↔ Platinum	No
1993–2011	Gold ↔ Platinum	Yes
1993–2011	Gold Ø Silver Ø Platinum	No
1993–2000	Gold Ø Silver Ø Platinum	No
2000–2011	Gold ↔ Silver ↔ Platinum	No
1993–2011	Gold ↔ Silver↔ Platinum	Yes
1993–2011	Gold Ø Oil	No
1993–2000	Gold Ø Oil	No
2000–2011	Gold ↔ Oil	No
1993–2011	Gold ↔ Oil	Yes

Note: ↔ indicates the presence of a cointegration relationship. Ø indicates the absence of a cointegration relationship. SB stands for 'Structural Break' analysis.

5.5.3   Cointegration Analyses for Precious Metals

The results are summarized in Table 5.30.

5.5.3.1   *Gold and Silver*

Let us start with the most frequently studied pair of commodities in the category of precious metals, i.e. the relationship between gold and silver. Table 5.30 tells us that only one cointegrating relationship can be detected during the full period with the occurrence of a structural break.

In Table 5.31, we verify that the null hypothesis of no cointegration can be rejected at the 1% level in favor of the alternative hypothesis that there exists at least one cointegrating relationship between gold and silver during 1993–2011.

The estimation of the VECM, shown in Table 5.32, reveals that only the error-correction term for gold is negative (equal to -0.008) and statistically significant. Hence, we can infer that gold is the leader in the price discovery process among the two commodities. This result is not surprising given the common knowledge that gold constitutes the safest precious metal (in terms of returns on investment) in its category.

Table 5.31 Lütkepohl *et al.* (2004) cointegration test results with structural break for gold and silver

1993–2011	Max. Eigen.	10%	5%	1%
$r \leq 1$	9.23	5.42	6.79	10.04
$r = 0$	23.39	13.78	15.83	19.85

Table 5.32 VECM results with structural break (1993–2011) for gold and silver

Error-Correction Term		
Gold	1	
Silver	−0.508	

VECM	ΔGold	ΔSilver
ECT	−0.008	0.003
(*t*.stat)	(−2.06)	(0.61)
ΔGold(−1)	0.024	0.054
(*t*.stat)	(0.85)	(1.36)
ΔSilver(−1)	−0.027	−0.07
(*t*.stat)	(−1.35)	(−2.48)

Regarding the cointegration relationship, represented in Figure 5.14, it is readily observable that it is not stationary after the structural break on November 14, 1996. Indeed, past that date, the cointegrating relationship seems to diverge again from 2008 onwards, probably indicating the presence of more than one break. We cautiously conclude that there seems to be an unstable cointegrating relationship between gold and silver, which may be due to diverging market fundamentals between the two commodities – silver having more applications in industry than gold for instance, hence making the two time series periodically depart from each other. Our results are similar to Ciner (2001), but contradict the previous findings by Wahab *et al.* (1994), Escribano and Granger (1998) and Lucey and Tully (2006).

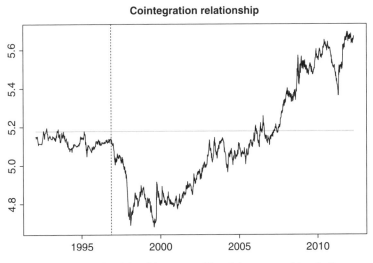

Figure 5.14 Cointegration relationship with structural break between gold and silver

Table 5.33   Cointegration test for the 2000–2011 sub-period, *without* structural break, between gold and platinum

2000–2011	Max. Eigen.	10%	5%	1%
$r \leq 1$	3.76	10.49	12.25	16.26
$r = 0$	21.57	16.85	18.96	23.65

5.5.3.2   Gold and Platinum

The second pair of precious metals considered here is composed of gold and platinum. For the first time in our cointegration analyses, we are able to detect a valid cointegrating relationship during a sub-period, namely 2000–2011.

Table 5.33 provides the results of the linear Johansen cointegration test during the recent period, i.e. 2000–2011. At the 5% level, we can assess that the rank of the cointegration r is at least equal to 1.

The estimation of the VECM in Table 5.34 provides only half of the expected results, since only the error-correction term for gold is negative and highly significant (at the 1% level). Similarly to the preceding case, gold can be seen as the leader in the price discovery process in that system as well. Any short-term departures from the long-run equilibrium will be corrected by the variations of the gold price to push back towards the fundamental value between these two precious metals.

The cointegration relationship displayed in Figure 5.15 appears extremely stable. Thus, we can undoubtedly conclude in favor of the presence of one cointegration relationship between gold and platinum. We therefore agree with the findings of Kearney and Lombra (2009).

As mentioned in Table 5.30, note that similar results could be achieved by modeling the cointegrating relationship with one structural break during 1993–2011. In that setting, we identified a break date on July 3, 2008. However, the VECM could not be validated, and

Table 5.34   VECM results for the 2000–2011 sub-period, *without* structural break, between gold and platinum

Error-Correction Term	
Gold	1
Platinum	−0.288
Trend	−0.001

VECM	ΔGold	ΔPlatinum
ECT	−0.027	0.001
(t.stat)	(−3.44)	(0.11)
Intercept	0.112	−0.004
(t.stat)	(3.47)	(−0.1)
ΔGold(−1)	0.032	0.032
(t.stat)	(0.91)	(0.75)
ΔPlatinum(−1)	−0.089	0.009
(t.stat)	(−3.02)	(0.25)

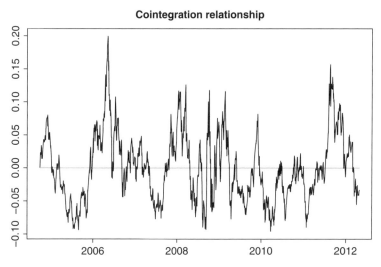

Figure 5.15 Cointegration relationship for the 2000–2011 sub-period, *without* structural break, between gold and platinum

gold and platinum seemed to obey different dynamics during 2008–2009 (with the possible spillover effects of the financial crisis). Hence, we do not reproduce these latter results.

5.5.3.3   Gold, Silver and Platinum

We now proceed with the most complete specification composed of gold, silver and platinum. In Table 5.30, we notice that the results are roughly similar to the case of gold and platinum with the possibility of detecting one cointegrating relationship either during the second sub-period (without structural break) or during the full period with the modeling of one break.

In Table 5.35, we can verify that the rank of the cointegration r is at least equal to 1 (at the 10% level).

The VECM results reproduced in Table 5.36 reveal that two error-correction terms are significantly negative for gold and silver. In addition, the magnitude of the coefficients estimated is higher than in the two preceding cases, indicating that there are stronger error-correction mechanisms at stake in this system composed of three precious metals. Most of the deviations from the long-run stationary equilibrium will be exclusively corrected by gold and/or silver in our setting.

Table 5.35   Cointegration test for the 2000–2011 sub-period, *without* structural break, between gold, silver and platinum

2000–2011	Max. Eigen.	10%	5%	1%
$r \leq 2$	3.65	10.49	12.25	16.26
$r \leq 1$	5.13	16.85	18.96	23.65
$r = 0$	23.91	23.11	25.54	30.34

Table 5.36   VECM results for the 2000–2011 sub-period, *without* structural break, between gold, silver and platinum

Error-Correction Term			
Gold	1		
Silver	−0.063		
Platinum	−0.239		
Trend	−0.001		

VECM	ΔGold	ΔSilver	ΔPlatinum
ECT	−0.031	−0.046	0.001
(*t*.stat)	(−3.6)	(−2.79)	(0.05)
Intercept	0.135	0.196	−0.002
(*t*.stat)	(3.63)	(2.81)	(−0.04)
ΔGold(−1)	0.059	0.08	0.052
(*t*.stat)	(1.27)	(0.91)	(0.92)
ΔSilver(−1)	−0.023	−0.094	−0.017
(*t*.stat)	(−0.94)	(−1.99)	(−0.55)
ΔPlatinum(−1)	−0.079	−0.033	0.015
(*t*.stat)	(−2.57)	(−0.56)	(0.41)

The graph of the cointegrating relationship, given in Figure 5.16, is stationary. Hence, we have been successful in specifying and estimating a cointegration relationship between gold, silver and platinum during 2000–2011. These three precious metals can be considered as having common fundamentals over the period, which trigger their adjustment towards their fundamental value. We disagree on this matter with Tsuchiya (2010), who was unable to identify a valid cointegration relationship between these commodities during 2002–2010 (besides palladium which is not included in our database).

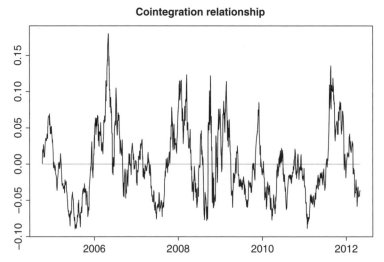

Figure 5.16   Cointegration relationship for the 2000–2011 sub-period, *without* structural break, between gold, silver and platinum

Table 5.37 Cointegration test for the 2000–2011
sub-period, *without* structural break, between gold and oil

2000–2011	Max. Eigen.	10%	5%	1%
$r \leq 1$	5.74	10.49	12.25	16.26
$r = 0$	16.88	16.85	18.96	23.65

Note also that Table 5.30 indicates the presence of another cointegration relationship during 1993–2011 with the occurrence of one structural break on July 15, 2008. In addition to the fact that the VECM could not be validated in that latter case, the cointegrating relationship did not appear stationary during the first regime (i.e. before the break date).

5.5.3.4 Gold and Oil

Next, we consider the case of cross-commodity linkages between two of the most liquid futures contracts contained in our database, i.e. gold and oil. Both assets can be considered by investment managers for inclusion in a diversified portfolio, gold being seen as a safe haven and oil for its interesting properties in terms of leverage. Therefore, it appears interesting to study the possibility that the two variables are moving together over time in a formal cointegration exercise. Conversely, the portfolio manager could be exposed to the risk of seeing the price of these two commodities embracing different paths through time.

Table 5.30 tells us that such a cointegration relationship could indeed be identified during the most recent sub-period (2000–2011), as well as during the full period with the detection of one structural break in the data.

In Table 5.37, the linear Johansen cointegration test confirms the presence of at least one cointegration relationship between gold and oil (at the 10% level).

Table 5.38 contains the VECM estimates, which feature the presence of two statistically significant error-correction terms. Surprisingly, only the ECT for gold is negative, at the highest

Table 5.38 VECM results for the 2000–2011 sub-period, *without*
structural break, between gold and oil

Error-Correction Term		
Gold	1	
WTI	−0.201	
Trend	−0.001	

VECM	ΔGold	ΔWTI
ECT	−0.019	0.019
(*t*.stat)	(−2.98)	(1.64)
Intercept	0.098	−0.097
(*t*.stat)	(3.01)	(−1.63)
ΔGold(−1)	−0.013	0.089
(*t*.stat)	(−0.46)	(1.71)
ΔWTI(−1)	−0.035	−0.063
(*t*.stat)	(−2.19)	(−2.2)

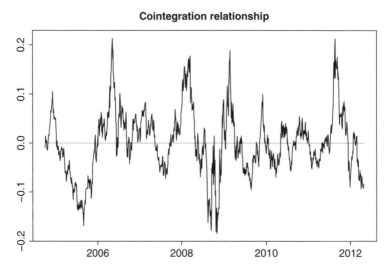

Figure 5.17   Cointegration relationship for the 2000–2011 sub-period, *without* structural break, between gold and oil

1% confidence level, which implies that gold is the driver in the price discovery process. This result is mostly unusual, since we could have expected the ECT for WTI to be negative as well (it is marginally significant at the 10% level). Overall, this cointegration exercise brings fruitful and new results regarding the behavior over time of two of the most actively traded commodities: gold and oil. To the best of our knowledge, these results highlight for the first time the possibility that gold pushes back the system toward the long-term equilibrium, and thereby compensates for short-term fluctuations in the oil price. This finding may be understood in the recent context of the 2008 oil price swing, which was affected strongly by that latter time series.

The cointegration relationship given in Figure 5.17 shows beyond any doubt that the cointegrating relationship is stationary over 2000–2011. Hence, we have successfully fine tuned our understanding of the relationship between gold and oil in our cointegration framework. These results are in line with the previous findings by Zhang and Wei (2010) and Natanelov *et al.* (2011) – except that these authors did not feature asymmetric ECT signs between gold and oil.

We do not further comment here on the cointegration results between gold and oil during 1993–2011 with one structural break detected on August 26, 2008. Indeed, the ECTs are not significantly negative in this setting, and the cointegration relationship does not appear to be stationary overtime.

5.5.3.5   Summary and Discussion on Cointegration Analyses for Precious Metals

The investigation of the cointegration relationships across precious metals (and the oil price) has proved to be most successful. Indeed, for each of the pair (or more) of commodities investigated, it has been possible to detect at least one cointegration relationship. Therefore, we could broadly conclude that there are more cross-commodity linkages than usually thought by market practitioners. Interestingly, most of the results hold during the recent 2000–2011 period, during which we have witnessed a commodity boom. Despite the worldwide growth in the demand for many commodities, it appears that some meaningful relationships still exist between precious metals, which share the characteristic of being safe havens in periods of economic turmoil. Overall, it cannot be challenged that common variations exist between the prices of precious metals, despite their growing inclusion in production processes for industry or jewellery. In troubled times, investors can then safely look for precious metals to store value, and their common behavior over the recent period allows us to validate this hypothesis.

Next, we will apply the cointegration tool to the case of energy prices.

5.6   COINTEGRATION IN ENERGY MARKETS

In this section, cointegration is used to analyze the long-term equilibrium relationships that may occur between energy markets. To illustrate the mechanisms at stake, consider the case where crude oil, unleaded gasoline and heating oil futures prices are cointegrated. This suggests that the crack spreads[12] will not deviate without bounds, and will revert to their 'normal' levels. On the other hand, if the futures prices of crude oil, unleaded gasoline and heating oil are not cointegrated, then the crack spreads can deviate without bounds, and using these spreads as a risk management tool or as a speculative vehicle will be questionable. Therefore, cointegration among these petroleum futures prices will make it possible to use statistical tools for determining extremes. The extremes in turn can then be used as a basis for trading strategies, and to explore risk arbitrage opportunities in crack spreads. Therefore, cointegration results will be used to identify relative mispricings that could be exploited.

As another illustrative example, we may refer to Gjolberg and Johnsen (1999), who argue that stable long-run equilibrium relationships may exist between crude and oil product prices. Despite physical limits as to the relative amounts of different products that can be distilled from a barrel of crude, refiners do have some flexibility in their product mix. This flexibility can be utilized when shifts in relative prices occur, and can be enhanced by stock adjustments. Consequently, while relative prices may fluctuate, they are likely to gravitate back towards some long-run equilibrium level. If such long-run equilibrium price relationships do, in fact, exist, they may represent valuable information for risk management in integrated oil companies, which both produce and refine crude oil.[13] Finally, if the price process can be described as an error-correction mechanism, this may be utilized for selective hedging, based on information about likely price movements back towards a long-term equilibrium price relationship. In their empirical application, Gjolberg and Johnsen (1999) find indeed that for all refined products (possibly excluding heavy fuel oil) prices are cointegrated with the crude price. Hence, the current product–crude margin deviations from a long-run equilibrium may contain significant

---

[12] Defined as the spread created by purchasing oil futures and offsetting the position by selling gasoline and heating oil futures. The name of this investment strategy is derived from the fact that cracking oil produces gasoline and heating oil. Therefore, oil refiners are able to generate residual income by entering into these transactions. During the summer of 2005, the effects of hurricanes in the Southeastern United States created large volatility in the crack spread.

[13] The net price risk for an integrated company will depend on the price variability of its portfolio of crude and refined products. Risk management should, therefore, take into account the covariance structure of all prices, and hedging should not be on a product-by-product basis. Furthermore, if product and crude prices are cointegrated, then the standard approach for establishing a risk-minimizing hedge may yield biased estimates.

information about the future changes in product prices and margins, which has implications in terms of product price forecasting and risk management.

Natural gas, coal and electricity prices are also characterized by equilibrium relationships in energy markets, especially from the perspective of power production. In the long run, Moutinho *et al.* (2011) underline that it is important to account for electricity generating technologies, given that fuels compete on a cost basis in electricity production. In addition, fuel substitution capabilities within the electricity sector, either at plant- or grid-level, should contribute to the cointegrating relationship between energy prices. Hence, substitutability between crude oil, coal and gas products in the industrial sector, through direct use and cogeneration of electricity, can also influence the commodity price relationship. In order to understand why coal, crude oil and gas prices sometimes diverge from their long-term equilibrium, it is also important to control for various short-term factors that establish trends in the prices of electricity and other commodities.

5.6.1 Literature Review

Cointegration among energy markets has been extensively documented in the academic literature. We present below the main results related to three groups: (i) petroleum products, (ii) oil, gas and coal prices and (iii) electricity and fuel prices.

5.6.1.1 Petroleum Products

- Chaudhuri (2001) tries to ascertain the role played by real oil prices in explaining the extremely volatile movements in real prices of primary commodities[14] by taking into account oil price shocks. The author shows that real commodity prices and real oil prices are cointegrated during 1973–1996, while the magnitude of oil price shocks could differ substantially among commodity markets. Additionally, the error-correction term stimulates the real commodity price adjustment (but not the real oil price adjustment).
- Asche *et al.* (2003) investigate the relationship between Brent crude oil and refined product prices during 1992–2000. They find empirical evidence of a long-run relationship between the prices of crude oil, gasoil, kerosene and naphtha. Evidence of a close relationship between the latter three refined products indicates that these markets are integrated. The crude oil price is found to be weakly exogenous, i.e. refined product prices are dependent on the crude oil price but not vice versa. No cointegration relationship can be found between crude and heavy fuel oil.
- Lanza *et al.* (2005) provide a comprehensive analysis of the price dynamics between 10 varieties of heavy crude oils[15] and product prices[16] in Europe and the USA during 1994–2002. They show that (i) product prices are statistically relevant in explaining short- and long-run adjustment in petroleum markets, and (ii) the long-run adjustment coefficients are sensitive to the gravity of the specific crude.[17]

---

[14] The commodities included in this analysis are: aluminum, bananas, beef, coal, cocoa beans, coffee, copper, cotton, groundnuts, hides, jute, lamb, lead, maize, manganese, nickel, plywood, potash, pulp, rice, rubber, silver, sugar, tea, tin, tobacco, wheat, wool and zinc.

[15] For example Brent, Urals, Iranian, Forcados, WTI, Maya, Boscan, Kern River, Thums.

[16] For example gasoline, gasoil, high sulfur fuel oil (HSFO) and low sulfur fuel oil (LSFO).

[17] Prices of crude oils whose physical characteristics are more similar to the marker are likely to converge more rapidly to the long-run equilibrium.

- Murat and Tokat (2009) analyze the crack spread[18] on the WTI crude oil by using weekly NYMEX futures during 2000–2008. They establish a causal impact of crack spread futures on crude oil markets both in the long and short run after 2003 (where they detected a structural break). Westgaard *et al.* (2011) also examine the spread between gasoil and Brent crude oil futures prices on ICE Futures – i.e. the crack spread – during 1994–2009. A cointegration relationship is found for the 1- and 2-month futures contracts during 1994–2009. However, no cointegration relationships can be found during 2002–2009. Hurricane Katrina, the economic boom and the following financial crises might explain these results. In such volatile periods the spread between gasoil and crude oil is likely to deviate, and it might take several years until it reverts to its equilibrium value. For energy traders and hedgers, the authors suggest that exposures to the crack spread should therefore be treated with great care in such market environments.

5.6.1.2   Oil, Gas and Coal Prices

- Serletis and Herbert (1999) identify shared trends among the US Henry Hub (HH) natural gas price and fuel oil prices during 1996–1997 (using daily data). Interestingly, they also feature feedback relationships, which presupposes the existence of effective arbitraging mechanisms across the two markets.
- Bachmeier and Griffin (2006) evaluate the degree of market integration both within and between crude oil, coal and natural gas markets during 1989–2004. They find that world crude oil prices[19] are cointegrated, but that the degree of market integration is much weaker for US coal prices.[20] Finally, they show that the crude oil, coal, and natural gas markets are only weakly integrated.
- Panagiotidis and Rutledge (2007) find a cointegrating relationship among UK gas prices and Brent oil prices during 1996–2003. Despite the highly liberalized nature of the UK gas market, they show that gas and oil prices were still moving together in the long run. This latter result is greatly debated in the literature. For instance, Villar and Joutz (2006) established earlier, based on a cointegration analysis, that the oil and natural gas prices may have appeared to decouple during 1989–2005. On the same topic, Brown and Yücel (2008) and Hartley *et al.* (2008) are able to identify a cointegration relationship between the WTI crude oil and HH natural gas prices during 1994–2007 and 1990–2006, respectively. While Brown and Yücel (2008) find that short-run deviations from the estimated long-run relationship could be explained by influences of weather, seasonality, natural gas storage and production in the Gulf of Mexico, Hartley *et al.* (2008) find that seasonal fluctuations and other factors such as weather shocks and changes in storage can have a significant influence on the short-run dynamic adjustment of prices.
- Moutinho *et al.* (2011) reveal that the prices of Zeebrugge gas, API coal, fuel oil and Brent crude oil are cointegrated in Spain during 2002–2005. In addition, the prices of Brent tend

---

[18] Recall that the crack spread is a term used in the oil industry and futures trading for the differential between the price of crude oil and petroleum products extracted from it – that is, the profit margin that an oil refinery can expect to make by cracking crude oil (i.e. breaking its long-chain hydrocarbons into useful shorter-chain petroleum products). In the futures markets, the crack spread is a specific spread trade involving simultaneously buying and selling contracts in crude oil and one or more derivative products, typically gasoline and heating oil. Oil refineries may trade a crack spread to hedge the price risk of their operations, while speculators attempt to profit from a change in the oil/gasoline price differential.

[19] For example, West Texas Intermediate (WTI) traded at Cushing, Oklahoma, Brent crude from the UK sector of the North Sea, Dubai crude from the Middle East, Arun crude from Indonesia and Alaskan North Slope (ANS) crude traded near Los Angeles.

[20] For example, Colorado, Utah and Wyoming in the West, Kentucky and Ohio in the East.

to move to re-establish the price equilibrium. The suggested economic mechanism is the following: if there is an increase in demand, and taking into account a fixed production capacity, fuel and the raw material from which it is made, crude oil, becomes scarcer, inherently making both commodities more expensive. Based on these characteristics, the authors predict that the tendency for crude oil and other fossil fuel prices (gas, coal and fuel oil) to move quickly and follow one another will strengthen, due to the substitutability of the four products in the heating and electricity markets.

5.6.1.3 Electricity and Fuel Prices

- Asche *et al.* (2006) find that natural gas, crude oil and electricity prices are cointegrated during 1995–1998 (i.e. after the deregulation of the UK gas market), with a leading role played by crude oil in the long-term relationship.
- Mjelde and Bessler (2009) find that the price series of natural gas, crude oil, coal and uranium are cointegrated with electricity prices from the US Pennsylvania–New Jersey–Maryland Interconnection (PJM) during 2001–2008. However, the authors are not able to detect one common trend, but that fuel prices tend to move electricity prices.
- In his cointegration analysis, Mohammadi (2009) challenges this result by showing that coal, natural gas and crude oil do not affect electricity prices significantly during 1960–2007. Significant long-run relationships are found only between electricity and coal prices.
- In a recent contribution, Bencivenga *et al.* (2011) analyze the relationships existing between crude oil, natural gas and electricity prices in the USA and Europe by using an error-correction model (ECM) framework during 2001–2010. Their results illustrate that a long-run equilibrium between the various pairs of energy commodities in Europe and the North American market exists.

In previous academic literature, the main findings of cointegration analyses that can be found across energy markets are summarized in Table 5.39.

Taken together, these studies provide overwhelming evidence in favor of a link between crude oil and other fuel prices in the long term. This result may be explained on solid economic grounds, given the indexation of many long-term energy futures contracts on the price of oil, and the determination of other energy prices based on various qualities of oil products as an input to production. However, the link between oil and gas may have disappeared in the recent period (as investigated by Bachmeier and Griffin (2006) and Brown and Yücel (2008)) due to industrial changes in the production of natural gas at the regional level (especially in the US with the development of shale gas). Note that our database does not include electricity prices. Hence, we are mostly interested in digging further into the cointegration relationships between the WTI and Brent crude oil, gasoil, natural gas and heating oil in the following empirical application.

5.6.2 Results of Granger Causality Tests for Energy Markets

Table 5.40 shows the estimation results of pairwise Granger causality tests (with one lag) for energy markets. We observe that the WTI price causes in the Granger sense (at the 5% level) aluminum, nickel, gasoil, corn, wheat and soybean. Hence, this energy time series exhibits linkages with many other commodities, be it metals or agricultural products, which will be further examined in the cointegration framework. Brent has a causal effect on gasoil. Natural

Table 5.39 Energy prices: cointegrating relationships

Authors	Period	Cointegration Relationship	SS	SB
Petroleum products				
Chaudhuri (2001)	1973–1996	Real Oil Prices ↔ Real Commodity Prices	No	No
Asche *et al.* (2003)	1992–2000	Crude Oil ↔ Gasoil, Kerosene, Naphtha	No	No
		Crude Oil Ø Heavy Fuel Oil		
Lanza *et al.* (2005)	1994–2002	Crude Oil ↔ Gasoline, Gasoil, HSFO, LSFO	No	No
Murat and Tokat (2009)	2000–2008	Crude Oil ↔ Gasoil (≈ Crack Spread)	Yes	Yes
Westgaard *et al.* (2011)	1994–2009	Brent Oil ↔ Gasoil (≈ Crack Spread)	Yes	No
Oil, gas and coal prices				
Serletis and Herbert (1999)	1996–1997	Fuel Oil ↔ Natural Gas	No	No
Bachmeier and Griffin (2006)	1989–2004	WTI ↔ Brent ↔ ANS ↔ Dubai ↔ Arun	No	No
		US Western Coal ↔ US Eastern Coal		
		WTI Ø Wyoming Coal Ø Natural Gas		
Villar and Joutz (2006)	1989–2005	WTI Oil ↔ Natural Gas	No	No
Panagiotidis and Rutledge (2007)	1996–2003	Brent Oil ↔ UK Natural Gas	No	No
Brown and Yücel (2008)	1994–2007	WTI Oil ↔ Natural Gas	No	No
Hartley *et al.* (2008)	1990–2006	WTI Oil ↔ Natural Gas	No	No
Moutinho *et al.* (2011)	2002–2005	Brent Oil ↔ Fuel Oil ↔ Gas ↔ Coal	No	No
Electricity and fuel prices				
Asche *et al.* (2006)	1995–1998	Crude Oil ↔ Natural Gas ↔ Electricity	No	No
Mjelde and Bessler (2009)	2001–2008	WTI ↔ Natural Gas ↔ Coal ↔ Uranium ↔ Elec	No	No
Mohammadi (2009)	1960–2007	Coal ↔ Electricity	No	No
		Crude Oil Ø Gas Ø Coal Ø Electricity		
Bencivenga *et al.* (2011)	2001–2010	Crude Oil ↔ Natural Gas ↔ Electricity	No	No

Note: ↔ indicates the presence of a cointegration relationship. Ø indicates the absence of a cointegration relationship. SS stands for 'Sub Sample' analysis in the paper considered. SB stands for 'Structural Break' analysis in the paper considered.

gas also displays causal links with heating oil and gasoil. Finally, heating oil causes gasoil in the Granger sense. Thus, these preliminary tests bring fruitful results, as they uncover deep inter-relationships among energy markets. Additional tests have also been performed for the WTI time series, which will be useful in the next chapters.

5.6.3 Cointegration Analyses for Energy Markets

In the context of energy markets, we are mainly interested in testing the hypothesis of cointegration in two categories: (i) petroleum products, and (ii) oil and gas prices. Note that the

Table 5.40   Pairwise Granger causality tests for energy markets

From	To	p-value	F-statistic
WTI	Gold	0.3664	0.8158
WTI	Silver	0.5900	0.2903
WTI	Platinum	0.2525	1.3100
WTI	Aluminum	0.0265	4.9239
WTI	Copper	0.0674	3.3474
WTI	Nickel	0.0052	7.7987
WTI	Zinc	0.3351	0.9294
WTI	Lead	0.9960	0.0000
WTI	Brent	0.9279	0.0082
WTI	Gasoil	0.0000	113.7337
WTI	Natural Gas	0.2111	1.5643
WTI	Heating Oil	0.6499	0.2061
WTI	Corn	0.0040	8.3071
WTI	Wheat	0.0049	7.9239
WTI	Coffee	0.9436	0.0050
WTI	Sugar	0.7846	0.0747
WTI	Cocoa	0.6804	0.1696
WTI	Cotton	0.3280	0.9570
WTI	Soybean	0.0004	12.5960
WTI	Rice	0.2191	1.5104
WTI	S&P 500 INDEX	0.3221	0.9805
WTI	US 10 Year	0.8592	0.0315
WTI	USD Trade Weighted	0.2929	1.1066
WTI	EUR-USD X-RATE	0.1894	1.7224
Brent	WTI	0.7646	0.0897
Brent	Gasoil	0.0000	120.9856
Brent	Natural Gas	0.0650	3.4059
Brent	Heating Oil	0.9599	0.0025
Gasoil	WTI	0.5255	0.4031
Gasoil	Brent	0.5769	0.3114
Gasoil	Natural Gas	0.7485	0.1028
Gasoil	Heating Oil	0.9036	0.0147
Natural Gas	WTI	0.1123	2.5220
Natural Gas	Brent	0.0412	4.1704
Natural Gas	Gasoil	0.0000	17.4077
Natural Gas	Heating Oil	0.0006	11.8816
Heating Oil	WTI	0.3376	0.9195
Heating Oil	Brent	0.9097	0.0129
Heating Oil	Gasoil	0.0000	169.8990
Heating Oil	Natural Gas	0.2998	1.0754

Note: The p-value and the F-statistic of the pairwise Granger causality tests between X and Y are given. The null hypothesis is that X does not Granger cause Y.

analysis cannot be performed on the entire spectrum of fuel prices, i.e. including coal. Indeed, coal futures contracts are mostly traded on a very long-term basis (i.e. several years ahead). Therefore, the availability of long time series is limited and not currently included in our Bloomberg database. Hence, we cannot fully replicate the results from previous literature dealing with coal data.

The third category from our literature review composed of electricity prices is not included in our current analysis for two main reasons. First, electricity prices are mostly studied by

Table 5.41   Cointegration analyses of energy prices: summary of the main results

Period	Cointegration Relationship	SB
Petroleum products		
1993–2011	WTI ↔ Gasoil	No
1993–2000	WTI ↔ Gasoil	No
2000–2011	WTI ↔ Gasoil	No
1993–2011	WTI ↔ Gasoil	Yes
1993–2011	Brent ↔ Gasoil	No
1993–2000	Brent ↔ Gasoil	No
2000–2011	Brent ↔ Gasoil	No
1993–2011	Brent ↔ Gasoil	Yes
1993–2011	WTI ↔ Heating Oil	No
1993–2000	WTI ↔ Heating Oil	No
2000–2011	WTI ↔ Heating Oil	No
1993–2011	WTI ↔ Heating Oil	Yes
1993–2011	Brent ↔ Heating Oil	No
1993–2000	Brent ↔ Heating Oil	No
2000–2011	Brent ↔ Heating Oil	No
1993–2011	Brent ↔ Heating Oil	Yes
Oil and gas prices		
1993–2011	Heating Oil Ø Natural Gas	No
1993–2000	Heating Oil ↔ Natural Gas	No
2000–2011	Heating Oil Ø Natural Gas	No
1993–2011	Heating Oil ↔ Natural Gas	Yes
1993–2011	WTI ↔ Natural Gas	No
1993–2000	WTI ↔ Natural Gas	No
2000–2011	WTI Ø Natural Gas	No
1993–2011	WTI ↔ Natural Gas	Yes

Note: ↔ indicates the presence of a cointegration relationship. Ø indicates the absence of a cointegration relationship. SB stands for 'Structural Break' analysis.

resorting to spreads, for instance documenting the cost to produce one MWh of electricity from a coal- vs. gas-fired power plant. This would lead us to many technicalities which are better dealt with in specialized books or articles. Second, the use of raw electricity prices is most often performed by using hourly data (24-hour) which is not compatible with the daily frequency of the data used in this chapter. Last but not least, the discussion about peak vs. base electricity prices complicates the treatment of the information in the rather simple framework of cointegration that we wish to develop here.

Our main results regarding energy prices are contained in Table 5.41. Let us start our investigation with the first category labeled as petroleum products.

5.6.4   Petroleum Products

5.6.4.1   *WTI and Gasoil*

Studying cointegration between the WTI crude oil futures price and gasoil consists, by definition, in testing the stationarity of the crack spread. In Table 5.41, we verify that this hypothesis

Table 5.42   Cointegration test for the 1993–2000 sub-period, *without* structural break, between WTI and gasoil

1993–2000	Max. Eigen.	10%	5%	1%
$r \leq 1$	5.76	10.49	12.25	16.26
$r = 0$	36.85	16.85	18.96	23.65

Table 5.43   VECM results for the 1993–2000 sub-period, *without* structural break, between WTI and gasoil

Error-Correction Term		
WTI	1	
Gasoil	−0.900	
Trend	−0.001	

VECM	ΔWTI	ΔGasoil
ECT	−0.028	0.038
(*t*.stat)	(−1.72)	(2.54)
Intercept	−0.046	0.064
(*t*.stat)	(−1.7)	(2.56)
ΔWTI(−1)	−0.034	0.294
(*t*.stat)	(−0.84)	(7.96)
ΔGasoil(−1)	−0.004	−0.238
(*t*.stat)	(−0.09)	(−6.02)

consistently holds during the full period (with or without break), as well as during the corresponding sub-periods.

In Table 5.42, we only reproduce the results obtained for the first sub-period. This sub-period was chosen among other possible results, since it provides us with the most satisfactory output concerning the estimation of the VECM. The remaining results can be obtained upon request to conserve space.[21] Table 5.42 clearly illustrates the fact that there exists a cointegration relationship between WTI and Gasoil during 1993–2000 (at the 1% level).

The corresponding VECM estimates can be found in Table 5.43. While both error-correction terms are statistically significant, only the sign for the WTI variable is negative. Hence, the stationarity of the crack spread is made possible through the feedback effects coming from the WTI crude oil futures price in this system.

As a final diagnostic check, we can observe in Figure 5.18 that the cointegrating relationship between WTI and gasoil is stable during 1993–2000. The same comments apply for the other graphs that could be produced out of this cointegration exercise between the two time series. Our results in this first category of petroleum products are in line with the findings by Murat and Tokat (2009), who analyzed previously the crack spread over the period 2000–2008. Note that we were able to identify one structural break in this relationship on January 4, 2011.

---

[21] This comment applies in the remainder of this chapter.

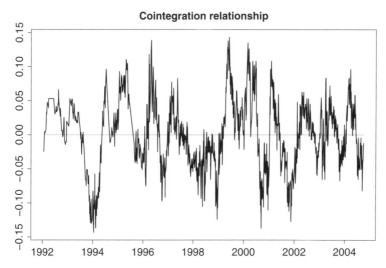

Figure 5.18   Cointegration relationship for the 1993–2000 sub-period, *without* structural break, between WTI and gasoil

5.6.4.2   *Brent and Gasoil*

Very similar results can be obtained when we perform the cointegration analysis between Brent and gasoil. Recall that Brent is mostly produced out of North European shores, while the WTI price is a world benchmark crude oil price delivered in Cushing, Oklahoma (USA). Apart from these geographical differences, the stationarity of the crack spread – defined as the difference between Brent and gasoil here – should still hold. Inspection of Table 5.41 indeed allows us to validate this statement, and we can only underline the remarkable stability of this relationship across all specifications designed to test for cointegration in this chapter.

In Table 5.44, we report again the results for the first sub-period (which bring the best fit to the data when looking at the VECM). The rank of the cointegration r is at least equal to 1 (at the 1% significance level).

In the VECM displayed in Table 5.45, only the error-correction term for gasoil is significant, but it is not positive. As concerns the ECT for Brent, we record as expected a negative sign, but it is not significant. Therefore, we cannot entirely validate this specification (despite the strong indication in favor of cointegration between Brent and gasoil) due to this lack of significance coming from the error-correction model. In that particular case, it is not guaranteed that the Brent price will be able to restore the long-term equilibrium should deviations occur from either of the two time series in the short term.

Table 5.44   Cointegration test for the 1993–2000 sub-period, *without* structural break, between Brent and gasoil

1993–2000	Max. Eigen.	10%	5%	1%
$r \leq 1$	5.82	10.49	12.25	16.26
$r = 0$	31.52	16.85	18.96	23.65

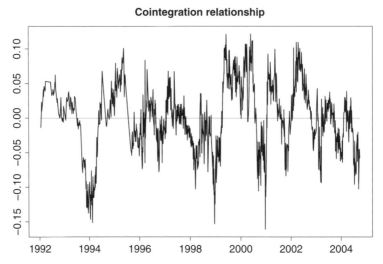

Figure 5.19 Cointegration relationship for the 1993–2000 sub-period, *without* structural break, between Brent and gasoil

Finally, we can investigate the stationarity of the crack spread as pictured in Figure 5.19. The relationship appears very stable around the mean. However, we discarded this model previously following the analysis of the VECM estimates. These results differ from the most recent analysis by Westgaard *et al.* (2011), who concluded in favor of the stationarity of the crack spread (defined as the difference between Brent and gasoil) during 1994–2009. Note that, in another specification, we have identified a structural break on September 24, 2003.

Table 5.45   VECM results for the 1993–2000 sub-period, *without* structural break, between Brent and gasoil

Error-Correction Term		
Brent	1	
Gasoil	−0.933	
Trend	−9.976	

VECM	ΔBrent	ΔGasoil
ECT	−0.015	0.044
(*t*.stat)	(−0.93)	(2.85)
Intercept	−0.028	0.084
(*t*.stat)	(−0.90)	(2.87)
ΔBrent(−1)	−0.045	0.332
(*t*.stat)	(−1.11)	(8.48)
ΔGasoil(−1)	0.009	−0.261
(*t*.stat)	(0.22)	(−6.51)

Table 5.46 Cointegration test for the 1993–2000 sub-period, *without* structural break, between WTI and heating oil

1993–2000	Max. Eigen.	10%	5%	1%
$r \leq 1$	6.14	10.49	12.25	16.26
$r = 0$	36.38	16.85	18.96	23.65

5.6.4.3 WTI and Heating Oil

The third specification tested in the context of petroleum products consists of the pair of commodities WTI and heating oil. According to Table 5.41, the same results apply here, as the validity of the cointegration model is accepted in all the cases considered.

In Table 5.46, we verify readily the presence of one cointegrating relationship between WTI and heating oil (at the 1% level).

However, in Table 5.47, the VECM model estimated is not entirely satisfactory. Indeed, we observe that the error-correction term for heating oil is significant but positive, while the ECT for WTI is negative but insignificant (i.e. it does not reach the 10% level). Therefore, we must reject the validity of the VECM model based on our observations.

In Figure 5.20, we could not detect any instability in the cointegration relationship displayed between WTI and heating oil. Thus, similarly to our previous case with Brent and gasoil, we must dismiss the validity of a cointegration relationship between WTI and heating purely based on the results from the VECM. We agree on this point with the conclusions by Asche *et al.* (2003), who rejected the cointegration between crude oil and heavy fuel oil (of which heating oil is one component) during the study period 1992–2000. Finally, note that a structural break could be detected here on January 4, 2011.

Table 5.47 VECM results for the 1993–2000 sub-period, *without* structural break, between WTI and heating oil

Error-Correction Term		
WTI	1	
Heating Oil	−0.928	
Trend	−8.161	

VECM	ΔWTI	ΔHeating Oil
ECT	−0.022	0.033
(*t*.stat)	(−1.40)	(2.06)
Intercept	−0.016	0.026
(*t*.stat)	(−1.34)	(2.11)
ΔWTI(−1)	−0.035	0.041
(*t*.stat)	(−0.72)	(0.82)
ΔHeating Oil(−1)	0.001	−0.075
(*t*.stat)	(−0.01)	(−1.52)

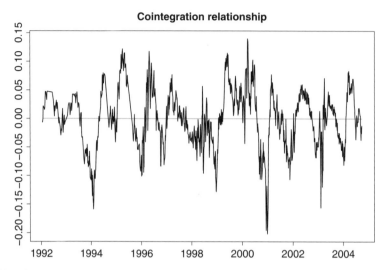

Figure 5.20   Cointegration relationship for the 1993–2000 sub-period, *without* structural break, between WTI and heating oil

5.6.4.4   Brent and Heating Oil

According to Table 5.41, similar conclusions can be reached when replacing WTI with Brent in the cointegration exercise. Indeed, the hypothesis of cointegration between Brent and heating oil can be accepted in all the specifications tested here.

Table 5.48 reflects the results obtained during the first sub-period, where the rank of the cointegration r is found to be equal to at least 1 (at the 1% level).

According to Table 5.49, we cannot accept any more the validity of the cointegration hypothesis by looking at the VECM estimates. Indeed, the error-correction term for heating oil is significant but positive. As concerns the Brent variable, the ECT is negative but not statistically significant. Hence, we cannot find evidence of any feedback mechanism to correct the deviations from the long-run equilibrium in this system.

Figure 5.21 tells us that the relationship is quite stable over time. But the cointegration hypothesis must still be rejected, given our comments at the stage of the VECM. Our results are the opposite of the recent findings by Moutinho *et al.* (2011), who concluded in favor of the cointegration hypothesis between Brent and fuel oil (among other fuels such as gas and coal). In another specification during the full period, note that we were able to isolate a structural break on July 15, 2008.

Table 5.48   Cointegration test for the 1993–2000 sub-period, *without* structural break, between Brent and heating oil

1993–2000	Max. Eigen.	10%	5%	1%
$r \leq 1$	5.98	10.49	12.25	16.26
$r = 0$	30.84	16.85	18.96	23.65

Table 5.49   VECM results for the 1993–2000 sub-period, *without* structural break, between Brent and heating oil

Error-Correction Term		
Brent	1	
Heating Oil	−0.964	
Trend	−6.963	

VECM	ΔBrent	ΔHeating Oil
ECT	−0.011	0.037
(*t*.stat)	(−0.79)	(2.42)
Intercept	−0.010	0.037
(*t*.stat)	(−0.74)	(2.46)
ΔBrent(−1)	−0.053	0.043
(*t*.stat)	(−1.10)	(0.85)
ΔHeating Oil(−1)	0.017	−0.076
(*t*.stat)	(0.37)	(−1.57)

5.6.5   Oil and Gas Prices

5.6.5.1   *Heating Oil and Natural Gas*

Moving to the next category of cointegration exercises dedicated to energy prices, we now focus our attention on the pair of commodities composed of heating oil and natural gas. Overall, the results contained in Table 5.41 are less satisfactory than for the previous category, since we are able to detect a cointegrating relationship in two of the four specifications tested only, i.e. during the first sub-period and during the full period with the modeling of one structural break.

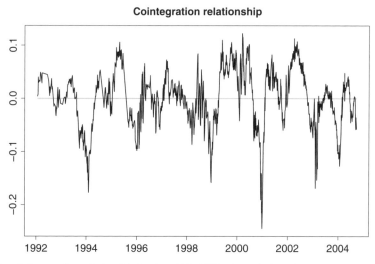

Figure 5.21   Cointegration relationship for the 1993–2000 sub-period, *without* structural break, between Brent and heating oil

Table 5.50   Cointegration test for the 1993–2011 full period, with structural break, between heating oil and natural gas

1993–2011	Max. Eigen.	10%	5%	1%
$r \leq 1$	13.21	5.42	6.79	10.04
$r = 0$	29.38	13.78	15.83	19.85

In Table 5.50, we have chosen to reproduce the results relative to the full period with one structural break. The null hypothesis of no cointegration ($r=0$) between heating oil and natural gas can be safely rejected at the 1% level.

As shown in Table 5.51, this specification is not valid, however, given that both error-correction terms are significant but positive.

In Figure 5.22, we notice indeed that the stability of the cointegration relationship cannot be granted as easily as in the former category. There remain some areas for instability in the cointegration relationship between heating oil and natural gas before and even after the structural break detected on July 7, 2008. Overall, our results contradict the previous findings by Serletis and Herbert (1999) who studied this relationship over the period 1996–1997.

5.6.5.2   WTI and Natural Gas

The next relationship under scrutiny consists of the pair of commodities WTI and natural gas, which is a central relation on energy markets. Indeed, the hypothesis that oil and natural gas could be cointegrated comes from the fact that both fuels can be seen as substitutes in the production of many intermediary consumption goods. Hence, when their prices diverge, market agents are able to arbitrate between both markets to adopt the cheapest energy source. But various idiosyncratic shocks can disrupt this relation, for instance the fact that gas markets are essentially more regional than the crude oil market. Another example lies in the fact that oil is storable while storing and transporting gas is more difficult (at least before the advent of shale gas, which is not discussed here). In Table 5.41, our results point to the fact that the

Table 5.51   VECM results for the 1993–2011 full period, with structural break, between heating oil and natural gas

Error-Correction Term		
Heating Oil	1	
Natural Gas	−4.066	

VECM	ΔHeating Oil	ΔNatural Gas
ECT	0.001	0.003
(*t*.stat)	(2.75)	(3.77)
ΔHeating Oil(−1)	−0.060	−0.020
(*t*.stat)	(−2.91)	(−0.57)
ΔNatural Gas(−1)	0.037	−0.028
(*t*.stat)	(3.06)	(−1.38)

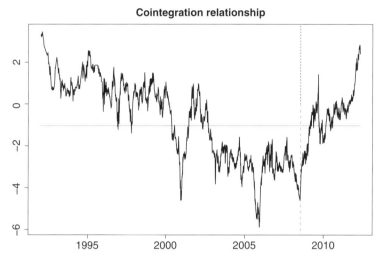

Figure 5.22   Cointegration relationship for the 1993–2011 full period, with structural break, between heating oil and natural gas

hypothesis of cointegration between oil and gas holds for most specifications, except during the second sub-period (2000–2011).

The results reproduced in Table 5.52 concern the 1993–2011 full period, without structural break. We infer from this table that the rank of the cointegration r between WTI and natural gas is equal to at least 1 (at the 10% level).

The VECM returns better results in Table 5.53 than previously for heating oil and natural gas. Indeed, both error-correction terms are significant. What is more, the sign of the ECT for WTI is negative, which allows us to validate the model. The main implication of this result is that if deviations occur between oil and gas, they will be corrected by the fluctuations of the WTI variable in order to ensure the stationarity of the system.

In Figure 5.23, the interested reader can detect some forms of non-stationarity at the beginning of the period (1993–1998), but the behavior of the cointegrating relationship is globally stable past that date. Based on this interpretation of the VECM, we confirm the validity of the cointegration hypothesis between WTI and natural gas, as identified previously by many authors (among others: Villar and Joutz (2006), Brown and Yücel (2008), Hartley *et al.* (2008)). In another specification, note that we have identified the presence of one structural break on July 7, 2008 (i.e. at the period of time corresponding to strong fluctuations in the WTI price series).

Table 5.52   Cointegration test for the 1993–2011 full period, *without* structural break, between WTI and natural gas

1993–2011	Max. Eigen.	10%	5%	1%
$r \leq 1$	5.26	10.49	12.25	16.26
$r = 0$	17.53	16.85	18.96	23.65

Table 5.53   VECM results for the 1993–2011 full period, *without* structural break, between WTI and natural gas

Error-Correction Term		
WTI	1	
Natural Gas	−0.454	
Trend	−0.001	

VECM	ΔWTI	ΔNatural Gas
ECT	−0.006	0.010
(t.stat)	(−2.45)	(2.61)
Intercept	0.013	−0.020
(t.stat)	(2.56)	(−2.57)
ΔWTI(−1)	−0.050	−0.033
(t.stat)	(−2.54)	(−1.08)
ΔNatural Gas(−1)	0.022	−0.030
(t.stat)	(1.74)	(−1.54)

Note that we will not further test the specifications by Bachmeier and Griffin (2006) who used several coal price series absent from our dataset, and who also focused on the issue of the Law of One Price between various qualities of crudes (which is deliberately left out of our research in the present chapter). Note also that, in the spirit of Panagiotidis and Rutledge (2007), the investigation of the cointegration relationship between Brent and natural gas cannot be performed in our setting. While these authors relied on the UK time series for natural gas (which makes sense to be compared with the European Brent time series), we have gathered in our dataset a US time series for natural gas (labeled Henry Hub).

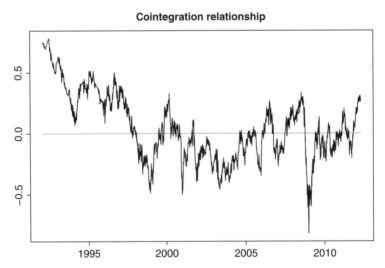

Figure 5.23   Cointegration relationship for the 1993–2011 full period, *without* structural break, between WTI and natural gas

5.6.5.3   *Summary and Discussion on Cointegration Analyses for Energy Prices*

Among the variety of cointegration analyses developed in this chapter, it is noteworthy to remark that energy markets seem strongly inter-related. Indeed, 21 of the 24 specifications tested confirmed the presence of cointegration either between petroleum products, or between oil and gas prices. The core of the results implies that energy markets share common trends over time, such as the worldwide demand for energy which has encountered an unprecedented growth over the last decades. Besides, energy sources offer the advantage of being substitutable technologically speaking, which allows producers and/or consumers to switch between their fuel inputs depending on the cheapest energy source. Our results globally point out the existence of shared trends among energy markets, despite the fact that idiosyncratic shocks (e.g. excess demand or supply, geopolitical events, etc.) can still affect one market in particular. Of all energy markets, the crude oil price (with the WTI as its benchmark) seems to be the leader in the price discovery process, since most of the time it triggers the adjustment towards the long-term stationary equilibrium between the variables in the cointegration system.

5.7   CONCLUDING REMARKS

We have attempted in Section 5.1.1 to provide a well-documented and exhaustive review of the literature on cross-commodity linkages based on the cointegration tool. This topic has been studied in the previous academic literature, but it appeared to lack a central and up-to-date body of knowledge to synthesize this information.

We have divided our database of commodities into four groups: (i) agricultural products, (ii) industrial metals, (iii) precious metals and (iv) energy prices. We have briefly summarized in the contents of the chapter the main insights obtained by replicating cointegration analysis for each group.

Compared to the systematic reproduction of the results from previous literature, the interest in resorting to the cointegration technique with the explicit modeling of one structural break has been clearly underlined, compared to linear cointegration tools or sub-period decomposition only. The main conclusion of our empirical work is therefore to indicate that there are more cross-commodity linkages at hand than is usually agreed upon among market practitioners. Even if the relationships at hand are not always stable, they do exist among the various groups of commodities investigated in our study.

Across our various econometric models, we have been able to identify sometimes (but not always) meaningful relationships between commodities. These pairs or groups of commodities seem to share common trends, which might explain why we observe the phenomenon of cointegration over specific periods (or sub-periods) of time. In terms of economic implications, when cointegration is detected, then the long-run stationary combination of the time series considered implies that idiosyncratic shocks will be corrected by feedback effects.

The forces at stake in the error-correction mechanisms can be related to substitutes and/or complementary relationships between pairs of groups of commodities. These characteristics are of primary importance for consumers and producers of the commodity, but also for investment managers and traders who would lose valuable information by ignoring them.

REFERENCES

Adrangi, B., Chatrath, A., Raffiee, K. 2003. Economic Activity, Inflation, and Hedging: The Case of Gold and Silver Investments. *Journal of Wealth Management* 6(2):60–77

Ai, C., Chatrath, A., Song, F. 2006. On the Comovement of Commodity Prices. *American Journal of Agricultural Economics* 88:574–588

Akram, QF. 2009. Commodity Prices, Interest Rates and the Dollar. *Energy Economics* 31:838–851

Ardeni, PG. 1989. Does the Law of One Price Really Hold for Commodity Prices? *American Journal of Agricultural Economics* 71(3):661–669

Aruga, K., Managi, S. 2011. Testing the International Linkage in the Platinum-group Metal Futures Markets. *Resources Policy* 36:339–345

Asche, F., Gjolberg, O., Völker, T. 2003. Price Relationships in the Petroleum Market: An Analysis of Crude Oil and Refined Product Prices. *Energy Economics* 25:289–301

Asche, F., Osmundsen, P., Sandsmark, M. 2006. The UK Market for Natural Gas, Oil and Electricity: Are the Prices Decoupled? *Energy Journal* 27(2):27–40

Aulton, AJ., Ennew, CT., Rayner, AJ. 1997. Efficiency Tests of Futures Markets for UK Agricultural Commodities. *Journal of Agricultural Economics* 48:408–424

Bachmeier, LJ., Griffin, JM. 2006. Testing for Market Integration: Crude Oil, Coal, and Natural Gas. *The Energy Journal* 27(2):55–71

Baffes, J. 1991. Some Further Evidence on the Law of One Price: The Law of One Price Still Holds. *American Journal of Agricultural Economics* 73(4):1264–1273

Baillie, RT., Myers, RJ. 1991. Bivariate GARCH Estimation of the Optimal Commodity Futures Hedge. *Journal of Applied Econometrics* 6:109–124

Beck, SE. 1994. Cointegration and Market Efficiency in Commodities Futures Markets. *Applied Economics* 26:249–257

Bencivenga, C., Sargenti, G., D'Ecclesia, R. 2011. Integration of Energy Commodity Markets in Europe and the USA. *Journal of Risk Management in Financial Institutions* 4(3):301–313

Bessler, DA., Covey, T. 1991. Cointegration: Some Results on U.S. Cattle Prices. *Journal of Futures Markets* 11(4):461–474

Bhar, R., Hamori, S. 2006. Linkages Among Agricultural Commodity Futures Prices: Some Further Evidence from Tokyo. *Applied Economics Letters* 13:535–539

Booth, GG., Brockman, P., Tse, Y. 1998. The Relationship Between US and Canadian Wheat Futures. *Applied Financial Economics* 8:73–80

Booth, GG., Ciner, C. 2001. Linkages Among Agricultural Commodity Futures Prices: Evidence from Tokyo. *Applied Economics Letters* 8:311–313

Brown, SPA., Yücel, MK. 2008. What Drives Natural Gas Prices? *Energy Journal* 29:45–60

Casassus, J., Liu, P., Tang, K. 2009. Commodity Prices in the Presence of Inter-commodity Equilibrium Relationships. *Working Paper SSRN* #1306022, Social Science Research Network, USA

Cerda, RA. 2007. Market Power and Primary Commodity Prices: The Case of Copper. *Applied Economics Letters* 14:775–778

Chaudhuri, K. 2001. Long-run Prices of Primary Commodities and Oil Prices. *Applied Economics* 33:531–538

Chavas, JP., Kim, K. 2005. Cointegration Relationships and Hedonic Pricing of Differentiated Commodities: An Application to Price Dynamics in the US Dairy Sector. *Applied Economics* 37:1813–1827

Chen, AS., Lin, JW. 2004. Cointegration and Detectable Linear and Nonlinear Causality: Analysis Using the London Metal Exchange Lead Contract. *Applied Economics* 36:1157–1167

Chng, MT. 2009. Economic Linkages Across Commodity Futures: Hedging and Trading Implications. *Journal of Banking and Finance* 33:958–970

Chong, J., Miffre, J. 2010. Conditional Correlation and Volatility in Commodity Futures and Traditional Asset Markets. *Journal of Alternative Investments* 12(3):61–75

Chowdhury, AR. 1991. Futures Market Efficiency; Evidence from Cointegration Tests. *Journal of Futures Markets* 11:577–589

Chunrong, A., Chatrath, A., Song, F. 2006. On the Comovement of Commodity Prices. *American Journal of Agricultural Economics* 88(3):574–588

Ciner, C. 2001. On the Longrun Relationship between Gold and Silver: A Note. *Global Finance Journal* 12:299–303

Cortazar, G., Milla, C., Severino, F. 2008. A Multicommodity Model Of Futures Prices: Using Futures Prices of One Commodity to Estimate the Stochastic Process of Another. *Journal of Futures Markets* 28:537–560

Crowder, WJ., Hamed, A. 1993. A Cointegration Test for Oil Futures Market Efficiency. *Journal of Futures Markets* 13(8):933–941

Dawson, PJ., White, B. 2002. Interdependencies Between Agricultural Commodity Futures Prices on the LIFFE. *Journal of Futures Markets* 22(3):269–280

Dickey, DA., Fuller, WA. 1979. Distribution of the Estimators for Autoregressive Time Series with a Unit Root. *Journal of the American Statistical Association* 74:427–431

Dickey, DA., Fuller, WA. 1981. Likelihood Ratio Statistics for Autoregressive Time Series with a Unit Root. *Econometrica* 49:1057–1072

Escribano, A., Granger, CWJ. 1998. Investigating the Relationship between Gold and Silver Prices. *Journal of Forecasting* 17(2):81–107

Fattouh, B. 2007. The Drivers of Oil Prices: The Usefulness and Limitations of Nonstructural Model, the Demand–Supply Framework and Informal Approaches. *Technical Report* #286084, Oxford Institute for Energy Studies, UK.

Fortenbery, TR., Zapata, HO. 1993. An Examination of Cointegration Between Futures and Local Grain Markets. *Journal of Futures Markets* 13:921–932

Fortenbery, TR., Zapata, HO. 1997. An Evaluation of Price Linkages Between Futures and Cash Markets for Cheddar Cheese. *Journal of Futures Markets* 17(3):279–301

Foster, KA. 1999. Cointegration and Settlement of Commodity Futures Contracts. *Macroeconomic Dynamics* 3:226–242

Franses, PH., Kofman, P. 1991. An Empirical Test for Parities between Metal Prices at the LME. *Journal of Futures Markets* 11(6):729–736

Garcia, P., Leuthold, RM. 2004. A Selected Review of Agricultural Commodity Futures and Options Markets. *European Review of Agricultural Economics* 31(3):235–272

Garner, CA. 1989. Commodity Prices: Policy Target or Information Variable? *Journal of Money, Credit, and Banking* 21(4):508–514

Girma, PB., Paulson, AS. 1999. Risk Arbitrage Opportunities in Petroleum Futures Spreads. *Journal of Futures Markets* 19:931–955

Gjolberg, O., Johnsen, T. 1999. Risk Management in the Oil Industry: Can Information on Long-run Equilibrium Prices be Utilized? *Energy Economics* 21:517–527

Goodwin, BK., Schroeder, TC. 1991. Cointegration Tests and Spatial Price Linkages in Regional Cattle Markets. *American Journal of Agricultural Economics* 73(2):452–464

Greene, WH. 2003. *Econometric Analysis.* Pearson Education, India

Hamilton, J. 1996. *Time Series Analysis, 2nd Edition*, Princeton, Princeton University Press, USA

Hartley, PR., Medlock III, KB., Rosthal, J. 2008. The Relationship Of Natural Gas to Oil Prices. *Energy Journal* 29(3):47–65

Johansen, S. 1988. Statistical Analysis of Cointegration Vectors. *Journal of Economic Dynamics and Control* 12:231–254

Johansen, S. 1991. Estimation and Hypothesis Testing of Cointegration Vectors in Gaussian Vector Autoregressive Models. *Econometrica* 59:1551–1580

Johansen, S., Juselius, K. 1990. Maximum Likelihood Estimation and The Demand for Money Inference on Cointegration with Application. *Oxford Bulletin of Economics and Statistics* 52:169–210

Kaldor, N. 1939. Speculation and Economic Stability. *Review of Economic Studies* 7:1–27

Karbuz, S., Jumah, A. 1995. Cointegration and Commodity Arbitrage. *Agribusiness* 11(3):235–243

Kearney, AA., Lombra, RE. 2009. Gold and Platinum: Toward Solving the Price Puzzle. *Quarterly Review of Economics and Finance* 49:884–892

Kellard, N., Newbold, P., Rayner, T., Ennew, C. 1999. The Relative Efficiency of Commodity Futures Markets. *Journal of Futures Markets* 19:413–432

Kilian, L. 2009. Not All Oil Price Shocks Are Alike: Disentangling Demand and Supply Shocks in the Crude Oil Market. *American Economic Review* 99(3):1053–1069

Kwiatkowski, DP., Phillips, PCB., Schmidt, P., Shin, Y. 1992. Testing the Null Hypothesis of Stationarity Against the Alternative of the Unit Root: How Sure are we that Economic Time Series are Non Stationary? *Journal of Econometrics* 54:159–178

Labson, BS., Crompton, PL. 1993. Common Trends in Economic Activity and Metals Demand: Cointegration and the Intensity of Use Debate. *Journal of Environmental Economics and Management* 25(2):147–161

Labys, WC., Lord, MJ. 1992. Inventory and Equilibrium Adjustments in International Commodity Markets: A Multi-cointegration Approach. *Applied Economics* 24:77–84

Lanza, A., Manera, M., Giovannini, M. 2005. Modeling and Forecasting Cointegrated Relationships Among Heavy Oil and Product Prices. *Energy Economics* 27:831–848

Lombardi, MJ., Osbat, C., Schnatz, B. 2011. Global Commodity Cycles and Linkages: A FAVAR Approach. *Empirical Economics* 36:546–555 DOI 10.1007/s00181-011-0494-8

Lord, MJ. 1991. Price Formation in Commodity Markets. *Journal of Applied Econometrics* 6(3):239–254

Lucey, BM., Tully, E. 2006. The Evolving Relationship between Gold and Silver 1978–2002: Evidence from a Dynamic Cointegration Analysis – a note. *Applied Financial Economics Letters* 2:47–53

Lütkepohl, H., Saikkonen, P., Trenkler, C. 2004. Testing for the cointegrating rank of a VAR with level shift an unknown time. *Econometrica* 72:647–662

MacDonald, R., Taylor, M. 1988. Metals Prices, Efficiency, and Cointegration: Some Evidence from the London Metal Exchange. *Bulletin of Economic Research* 40(3):235–240

Malliaris, AG., Urrutia, JL. 1996. Linkages between Agricultural Commodity Futures Contracts. *Journal of Futures Markets* 16:595–609

Marquis, MH., Cunningham, SR. 1990. Is There a Role for Commodity Prices in the Design of Monetary Policy? Some Empirical Evidence. *Southern Economic Journal* 57(2):394–412

McKenzie, AM., Holt, MT. 2002. Market Efficiency in Agricultural Futures Markets. *Applied Economics* 34:1519–1532

Mjelde, JW., Bessler, DA. 2009. Market Integration Among Electricity Markets and their Major Fuel Source Markets. *Energy Economics* 31(3):482–491

Mohammadi, H. 2009. Electricity Prices and Fuel Costs: Long-run Relations and Short-run Dynamics. *Energy Economics* 31(3):503–509

Moosa, IA., A-Loughani, INE. 1995. The Effectiveness of Arbitrage and Speculation in the Crude Oil Futures Market. *Journal of Futures Markets* 15:167–186

Moutinho, V., Vieira, J., Carrizo-Moreira, A. 2011. The Crucial Relationship Among Energy Commodity Prices: Evidence from the Spanish Electricity Market. *Energy Policy* 39:5898–5908

Murat, A., Tokat, E. 2009. Forecasting Oil Price Movements with Crack Spread Futures. *Energy Economics* 31:85–90

Nakajima, K., Ohashi, K. 2011. A Cointegrated Commodity Pricing Model. *Journal of Futures Markets* DOI: 10.1002/fut.20553

Natanelov V., Alam, MJ., McKenzie, AM., Van Huylenbroeck, G. 2011. Is there Co-movement of Agricultural Commodities Futures Prices and Crude Oil? *Energy Policy* 39:4971–4984

Nazlioglu, S. 2011. World Oil and Agricultural Commodity Prices: Evidence from Nonlinear Causality. *Energy Policy* 39:2935–2943

Ng, V., Pirrong, S. 1996. Price Dynamics in Refined Petroleum Spot and Futures Markets. *Journal of Empirical Finance* 2:359–388

Panagiotidis, T., Rutledge, E. 2007. Oil and Gas Markets in the UK: Evidence from a Cointegrating Approach. *Energy Economics* 29:329–347

Pfaff, B. 2008. *Analysis of Integrated and Cointegrated Time Series with R*. Springer, New York Dordrecht Heidelberg London, UK

Phillips, PCB., Peron, P. 1988. Testing for a unit root in time series regression. *Biometrika* 75:335–346

Pindyck, RS., Rotemberg, JJ. 1990. The Excess Co-Movement of Commodity Prices. *Economic Journal* 100:1173–1189

Pippenger, J., Phillips, L. 2008. Some pitfalls in testing the law of one price in commodity markets. *Journal of International Money and Finance* 27:915–925

Pynnonen, S., Vataja, J. 2002. Bootstrap testing for cointegration of international commodity prices. *Applied Economics* 34(5):637–647

Ramanujam, P., Vines, D. 1990. Commodity Prices, Financial Markets and World Income: A Structural Rational Expectations Model. *Applied Economics* 22:509–527

Reinhart, C., Wickham, P. 1994. Commodity prices: cyclical weakness or secular decline? *IMF Staff Papers* 41:175–213

Roll, R. 1984. Orange Juice and Weather. *American Economic Review* 74(5):861–880

Schroeder, TC., Goodwin, BK. 1991. Price Discovery and Cointegration for Live Hogs. *Journal of Futures Markets* 11:685–696

Schwarz, TV., Szakmary, AC. 1994. Price Discovery in Petroleum Markets: Arbitrage, Cointegration, and the Time Interval of Analysis. *Journal of Futures Markets* 14:147–167

Sephton, PS. 1991. Commodity Prices: Policy Target or Information Variable: A Comment. *Journal of Money, Credit, and Banking* 23:260–266

Serletis, A., Herbert, J. 1999. The Message in North American Energy Prices. *Energy Economics* 21(5):471–483

Stevens, SC. 1991. Evidence for a Weather Persistence Effect on the Corn, Wheat, and Soybean Growing Season Price Dynamics. *Journal of Futures Markets* 11:81–88

Trenkler, C. 2003. A New Set of Critical Values for Systems Cointegration Tests with a Prior Adjustment for Deterministic Terms. *Economics Bulletin* 3:1–9

Tsuchiya, Y. 2010. Linkages Among Precious Metals Commodity Futures Prices: Evidence from Tokyo. *Economics Bulletin* 30(3):1772–1777

Vataja, J. 2000. Should the Law of One Price be Pushed Away? Evidence from International Commodity Markets. *Open Economics Review* 11:399–415

Villar, JA., Joutz, FL. 2006. The Relationship Between Crude Oil and Natural Gas Prices. *Technical Report, Energy Information Administration*, Office of Oil and Natural Gas, Washington, DC, USA

von Hagen, J. 1989. Relative Commodity Prices and Cointegration. *Journal of Business and Economic Statistics* 7(4):497–503

Wahab, M., Cohn, R., Lashgari, M. 1994. The Gold–Silver Spread: Integration, Cointegration, Predictability, and Ex-ante Arbitrage. *Journal of Futures Markets* 14:709–756

Westgaard, S., Estenstad, M., Seim, M., Frydenberg, S. 2011. Co-integration of ICE Gas oil and Crude oil futures. *Energy Economics* 33:311–320

Working, H. 1949. The Theory of the Price of Storage. *American Economic Review* 39:1254–1262

Zapata, HO., Fortenbery, TR. 1996. Stochastic Interest Rates and Price Discovery in Selected Commodity Markets. *Review of Agricultural Economics* 18:634–654

Zhang, YJ., Wei, YM. 2010. The Crude Oil Market and the Gold Market: Evidence for Cointegration, Causality and Price Discovery. *Resources Policy* 35:168–177

6

Cointegration with Traditional Asset Markets

This chapter contains a cointegration analysis between representative indices of commodity markets (i.e. the GSCI indices) and traditional asset markets. More particularly, we are interested in determining the extent to which commodity markets may vary together with the time series of equities, bonds and exchange rates.

Following unit root test results, the cointegration analysis between commodities and asset markets unfolds as follows: we study first the influence of the S&P 500 and the US 10-year rate, and second the influence of exchange rates.

6.1 DATASET AND UNIT ROOT TEST RESULTS

Table 6.1 shows the descriptive statistics for the equities, bonds and exchange rate variables studied in Chapter 6, in conjunction with GSCI sub-indices (instead of individual commodity price series as in the previous chapter). In what follows, USD Trade Weighted is a trade-weighted index of the US Dollar, and EUR-USD X-RATE denotes the Euro–Dollar exchange rate. All the data comes from Bloomberg with a daily frequency.

The time series are shown in Figure 6.1 for the GSCI sub-indices, in Figure 6.2 for equities and bonds, and in Figure 6.3 for exchange rate variables. While we remark on the recent variability of the GSCI sub-indices (especially energy) following the summer of 2008, the other variables considered display an upward trend. Hence, this visual inspection validates the need for a cointegration exercise (except perhaps for the bond variable which has a distinct behavior from the other groups of variables).

Table 6.2 contains the unit root test results for the GSCI sub-indices, equities, bonds and exchange rates. We verify in this setting that all series are integrated of order 1 ($I(1)$), which validates the preliminary condition for cointegration.

6.2 COINTEGRATION BETWEEN THE GSCI SUB-INDICES, S&P 500 AND US 10-YEAR RATE

Let us now start our analysis with the linkages between commodities, bonds and equities. Indeed, commodities and equities are influenced by the variations in global demand, and more generally by the growth rate of industrial production. The same comment applies for the 10-year Treasury bill rate, and the link between commodity prices and expected inflation, which also impacts the 10-year rate. Hence, there is a strong economic rationale to find inter-relationships between these kinds of variables.

Table 6.1 Descriptive statistics for the GSCI sub-indices, equities, bonds and exchange rates

	Min	Max	Mean	Std. Dev.	Skew.	Kurt.	JB
GSCI Agri.	6.1641	7.3333	6.6218	0.2683	0.7131	2.0437	248.0559
GSCI Energy	5.5285	8.0179	6.7895	0.5704	−0.2476	2.8351	95.9719
GSCI Ind. Metals	5.9730	7.7908	6.8488	0.5467	0.2482	1.8157	299.9406
GSCI Prec. Metals	5.8233	7.8477	6.5609	0.5891	0.5601	4.9569	275.4209
S&P 500 INDEX	5.9989	7.3557	6.9459	0.3249	−1.3611	6.9170	982.9053
US 10 Year	0.5412	2.0807	1.4821	0.3124	−0.6260	5.3031	182.1007
USD Trade Weighted	4.2673	4.7876	4.4866	0.1234	0.5257	3.5913	151.2442
EUR–USD X-RATE	−0.1918	0.4694	0.2003	0.1438	−0.7134	3.7673	234.6386

Note: The number of observations is equal to 2,757. Std. Dev. stands for Standard Deviation, Kurt. for Kurtosis, Skew. for Skewness, and JB for the Jarque Bera test statistic.

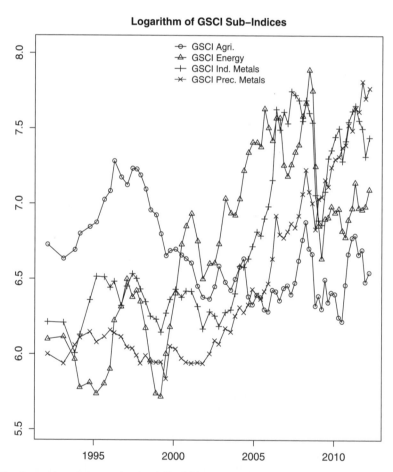

Figure 6.1 Logarithm of time series for daily GSCI sub-indices

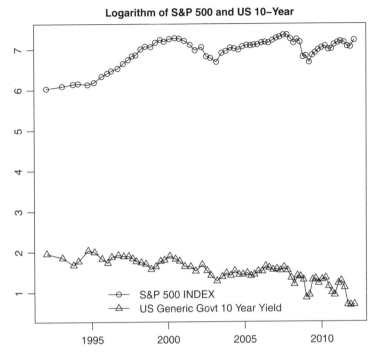

Figure 6.2 Logarithm of time series for equities and bonds

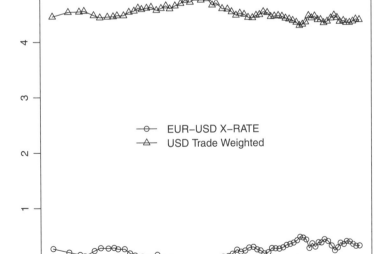

Figure 6.3 Logarithm of time series for exchange rate variables

Table 6.2   Unit root test results for the GSCI sub-indices, equities, bonds and exchange rates

	ADF None	ADF Drift	ADF Trend	PP Constant	PP Trend	KPSS
GSCI Agri.	−37.0906	−37.0848	−37.0782	−52.0888	−52.0795	0.0794
GSCI Energy	−37.1022	−37.1056	−37.1048	−53.7968	−53.7926	0.0767
GSCI Ind. Metals	−37.6441	−37.6694	−37.6628	−54.1199	−54.1105	0.1096
GSCI Prec. Metals	−37.6158	−37.7107	−37.7366	−53.2987	−53.3256	0.0385
S&P 500 INDEX	−39.7546	−39.8005	−39.8357	−57.3629	−57.4141	0.1175
US 10-Year	−38.6546	−38.6792	−38.6778	−55.6415	−55.6383	0.0283
USD Trade Weighted	−37.1928	−37.1877	−37.1886	−51.3511	−51.3483	0.0684
EUR–USD X-RATE	−36.9616	−36.9549	−36.9536	−52.7168	−52.7120	0.0826

Note: Test statistics are given. ADF stands for the Augmented Dickey–Fuller unit root test, PP for the Phillips–Perron unit root test, and KPSS for the Kwiatkowski–Phillips–Schmidt–Shin unit root test. Corresponding critical values (at 5% level) can be found in Greene (2003): −1.9409 for ADF None, −2.8623 for ADF Drift, −3.4114 for ADF Trend, −2.8623 for PP Constant, −3.4114 for PP Trend, and 0.4630 for KPSS.

6.2.1   Literature Review

We briefly recall below the findings from the two main studies dedicated to the linkages between asset markets and commodities.

- Zeng and Swanson (1998) investigate the cointegrating relationship between the S&P 500 index, treasury bonds, gold and crude oil during 1990–1995. Their results show that error-correction models provide a satisfactory fit to the data, compared to other models (random walks and VARs) for forecasting purposes.
- Büyükşahin *et al.* (2010) cannot find any cointegrating vector between the S&P 500 and GSCI sub-indices during 1991–2008 (although some unstable cointegration between the benchmark commodity and equity indices can be found during the sub-period 1997–1999 by using recursive estimates). They conclude that there is little evidence of a common long-term trend between investable commodity and equity indices, and no evidence of secular strengthening of any such trend. An implication is that passive investors are likely to achieve gains over the long run by diversifying portfolios across the two asset classes.

The information drawn from these studies is conveniently summarized in Table 6.3.

Hence, previous studies disagree concerning the existence of meaningful cointegration relationships between asset markets and commodities. Besides, we note that structural breaks have not been accounted for in these studies. That is why we proceed in the next section with our own empirical application to GSCI sub-indices, the S&P 500 and the US 10-year rate,

Table 6.3   Asset markets and commodity prices: cointegrating relationships

Authors	Period	Cointegration Relationship	SS	SB
Zeng and Swanson (1998)	1990–1995	Gold, Oil ↔ Treasury bonds, S&P 500	No	No
Büyükşahin *et al.* (2010)	1991–2008	GSCI sub-indices Ø S&P 500	Yes	No

Note: ↔ indicates the presence of a cointegration relationship. Ø indicates the absence of a cointegration relationship. SS stands for 'Sub Sample' analysis in the paper considered. SB stands for 'Structural Break' analysis in the paper considered.

based on sub-sample decomposition and the explicit modeling of structural changes in the cointegration framework.

6.2.2   Results of Granger Causality Tests Between the GSCI Sub-Indices, S&P 500 and US 10-Year Rate

Table 6.4 shows the Granger causality test results (computed with one lag) for the GSCI sub-indices, equities and exchange rates. We notice causal links in the Granger sense (at the 5% level) between the GSCI Agricultural sub-index and the GSCI Energy and Industrial Metals sub-indices. The reverse Granger causality is true between the GSCI Energy sub-index and the GSCI Agricultural and Industrial Metals sub-indices (at the 5 and 10% levels, respectively).

Table 6.4   Pairwise Granger causality tests for the GSCI sub-indices, equities and bonds

From	To	p-value	F-statistic
GSCI Agri.	GSCI Energy	0.0346	4.4656
GSCI Agri.	GSCI Ind. Metals	0.0046	8.0562
GSCI Agri.	GSCI Prec. Metals	0.1609	1.9660
GSCI Agri.	S&P 500 INDEX	0.5406	0.3745
GSCI Agri.	US 10 year	0.2221	1.4911
GSCI Energy	GSCI Agri.	0.0082	6.9955
GSCI Energy	GSCI Ind. Metals	0.0604	3.5265
GSCI Energy	GSCI Prec. Metals	0.6551	0.1995
GSCI Energy	S&P 500 INDEX	0.4536	0.5617
GSCI Energy	US 10 year	0.4456	0.5820
GSCI Ind. Metals	GSCI Agri.	0.0298	4.7242
GSCI Ind. Metals	GSCI Energy	0.8236	0.0497
GSCI Ind. Metals	GSCI Prec. Metals	0.4692	0.5240
GSCI Ind. Metals	S&P 500 INDEX	0.3097	1.0321
GSCI Ind. Metals	US 10 year	0.5526	0.3526
GSCI Prec. Metals	GSCI Agri.	0.0794	3.0788
GSCI Prec. Metals	GSCI Energy	0.2439	1.3585
GSCI Prec. Metals	GSCI Ind. Metals	0.2966	1.0897
GSCI Prec. Metals	S&P 500 INDEX	0.4871	0.4829
GSCI Prec. Metals	US 10 year	0.3766	0.7818
S&P 500 INDEX	Gold	0.0190	5.5073
S&P 500 INDEX	WTI	0.0269	4.8988
S&P 500 INDEX	GSCI Agri.	0.0422	4.1304
S&P 500 INDEX	GSCI Energy	0.0281	4.8239
S&P 500 INDEX	GSCI Ind. Metals	0.0000	23.2594
S&P 500 INDEX	GSCI Prec. Metals	0.0093	6.7683
S&P 500 INDEX	US 10 year	0.2852	1.1423
US 10 year	Gold	0.1861	1.7490
US 10 year	WTI	0.4390	0.5990
US 10 year	GSCI Agri.	0.8388	0.0414
US 10 year	GSCI Energy	0.5723	0.3189
US 10 year	GSCI Ind. Metals	0.0661	3.3775
US 10 year	GSCI Prec. Metals	0.1451	2.1239
US 10 year	S&P 500 INDEX	0.8755	0.0245

Note: The p-value and the F-statistic of the pairwise Granger causality tests between X and Y are given. The null hypothesis is that X does not Granger cause Y.

Table 6.5   Cointegration analyses of asset markets and commodity prices:
summary of the main results

Period	Cointegration Relationship	SB
1993–2011	Gold Ø Oil Ø S&P 500 Ø US10Y	No
1993–2000	Gold Ø Oil Ø S&P 500 Ø US10Y	No
2000–2011	Gold Ø Oil Ø S&P 500 Ø US10Y	No
1993–2011	Gold ↔ Oil ↔ S&P 500 ↔ US10Y	Yes
1993–2011	GSCI Agricultural Ø S&P 500	No
1993–2000	GSCI Agricultural Ø S&P 500	No
2000–2011	GSCI Agricultural Ø S&P 500	No
1993–2011	GSCI Agricultural ↔ S&P 500	Yes
1993–2011	GSCI Industrial Metals Ø S&P 500	No
1993–2000	GSCI Industrial Metals Ø S&P 500	No
2000–2011	GSCI Industrial Metals Ø S&P 500	No
1993–2011	GSCI Industrial Metals ↔ S&P 500	Yes
1993–2011	GSCI Precious Metals Ø S&P 500	No
1993–2000	GSCI Precious Metals Ø S&P 500	No
2000–2011	GSCI Precious Metals Ø S&P 500	No
1993–2011	GSCI Precious Metals ↔ S&P 500	Yes
1993–2011	GSCI Energy Ø S&P 500	No
1993–2000	GSCI Energy Ø S&P 500	No
2000–2011	GSCI Energy Ø S&P 500	No
1993–2011	GSCI Energy ↔ S&P 500	Yes

Note: ↔ indicates the presence of a cointegration relationship. Ø indicates the absence of a
cointegration relationship. SB stands for 'Structural Break' analysis.

Concerning the GSCI Industrial and Precious Metals sub-indices, we find Granger causalities
only with the GSCI Agricultural sub-index (at the 5 and 10% levels, respectively). Hence, we
are unable to show significant causal interactions between the various GSCI sub-indices and
the equities and bonds variables, at least in the framework of Granger causality testing. The
difference with the S&P 500 index is striking, since we uncover significant Granger causalities
for all the variables considered in Table 6.4, except the US 10-year rate. The bond variable is
only causing, in the Granger sense, the GSCI Industrial Metals sub-index (at the 10% level).
Overall, our results feature an asymmetry in the Granger causalities between the GSCI sub-
indices, the S&P 500 and the US 10-year rate: while GSCI sub-indices mainly affect each
other, the S&P 500 index is revealed as a driving force impacting nearly all other variables.
Hence, the effects coming from equity markets seem quite strong based on this preliminary
data analysis. We aim at confirming these results in the subsequent cointegration analysis.

6.2.3   Cointegration Analyses for the GSCI Sub-Indices, S&P 500 and US 10-Year Rate

The main results from our cointegration analyses dedicated to the linkages between commodities and asset markets are given in Table 6.18.

6.2.3.1   Gold, Oil, S&P 500 and US-10Y

We start by investigating the link between equities, bonds and the two key commodities of
interest: gold and oil. The former commodity is used by investors during flight-to-quality

Table 6.6 Lütkepohl *et al.* (2004) cointegration test results with structural break for gold, WTI, S&P 500 and US 10Y

1993–2011	Max. Eigen.	10%	5%	1%
$r \leq 3$	5.86	5.42	6.79	10.04
$r \leq 2$	13.58	13.78	15.83	19.85
$r \leq 1$	27.26	25.93	28.45	33.76
$r = 0$	58.50	42.08	45.2	51.6

episodes (i.e. during periods of recession and economic turmoil). The latter commodity has become increasingly traded over the last decade not for its physical content (i.e. the delivery of one barrel of oil), but for its characteristics in terms of portfolio diversification as a new financial asset. Hence, we may expect that this set of commodities will be connected to the traditional asset markets.

In Table 6.6, we remark that the rank of the cointegration r between the gold, WTI, S&P 500 and US 10-year variables is at least equal to 1 (at the 1% level) during the full period with the modeling of one structural break. Other specifications were not successful in Table 6.18.

The VECM estimates reproduced in Table 6.7 do not appear as satisfactory. Indeed, only the US 10-year variable records a negative (but not statistically significant) error-correction term. Therefore, we cannot validate the cointegration relationship between the variables under consideration here.

By looking at Figure 6.4, we notice that the cointegration relationship is not stable during the period 1993–2011, neither before nor after the structural break detected on July 15, 2008. As a conclusion on this first cointegration exercise, we cannot validate the findings by Zeng and Swanson (1998) concerning the existence of a robust cointegration relationship between

Table 6.7 VECM results with structural break (1993–2011) for gold, WTI, S&P 500 and US 10Y

Error-Correction Term				
Gold	1			
WTI	−2.812			
SP500	−1.268			
US 10Y	2.372			

VECM	ΔGold	ΔWTI	ΔSP500	ΔUS 10Y
ECT	0.001	0.006	0.002	−0.001
(*t*.stat)	(0.98)	(5.06)	(2.01)	(−0.88)
ΔGold(−1)	−0.001	0.016	−0.005	0.008
(*t*.stat)	(−0.03)	(0.43)	(−0.23)	(0.32)
ΔWTI(−1)	−0.006	−0.047	−0.014	−0.005
(*t*.stat)	(−0.53)	(−2.37)	(−1.11)	(−0.32)
ΔSP500(−1)	0.028	0.073	−0.062	−0.023
(*t*.stat)	(1.49)	(2.14)	(−2.85)	(−0.91)
ΔUS 10Y(−1)	−0.025	−0.002	−0.004	−0.049
(*t*.stat)	(−1.61)	(−0.07)	(−0.24)	(−2.42)

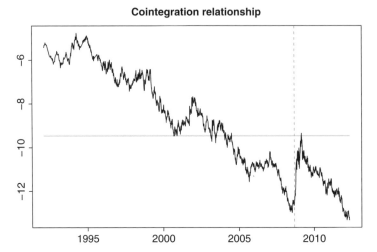

Figure 6.4   Cointegration relationship with structural break between gold, WTI, S&P 500 and US 10Y

two of the most actively traded commodities (e.g. gold and oil) and two variables relative to equity and bond markets.

6.2.3.2   GSCI Agricultural and S&P 500

Let us now focus more specifically on the interaction between equity markets – by taking the S&P 500 as a proxy – and the GSCI sub-indices for commodity markets. The first category studied here concerns agricultural markets. In Table 6.18, we observe that one cointegration relationship can be highlighted during the full period with the occurrence of a break.

Table 6.8 shows the presence of one cointegrating relationship between the GSCI Agricultural sub-index and the S&P 500 (at the 5% level).

In the VECM shown in Table 6.9, it is clear that both error-correction terms are statistically significant. However, only the ECT for the GSCI Agricultural sub-index is negative. This result is quite surprising, since it implies that deviations from the long-term equilibrium will be corrected by the agricultural commodity variable. As such, the results appear counter-intuitive with respect to the literature documenting that asset markets are leaders in the price formation process, since they reflect instantly the information available to all market participants.

When inspecting the cointegration relationship in Figure 6.5, we notice that it is quite stable after the structural break on October 28, 1997. Conversely, the cointegration relationship could

Table 6.8   Lütkepohl *et al.* (2004) cointegration test results with structural break for GSCI Agricultural and S&P 500

1993–2011	Max. Eigen.	10%	5%	1%
$r \leq 1$	5.44	5.42	6.79	10.04
$r = 0$	19.14	13.78	15.83	19.85

Table 6.9   VECM results with structural break (1993–2011) for GSCI Agricultural and S&P 500

Error-Correction Term		
GSCI Agri.	1	
S&P 500	−1.550	
VECM	ΔGSCI Agri.	ΔS&P 500
ECT	−0.003	0.004
(*t*.stat)	(−2.62)	(2.82)
ΔGSCI Agri.(−1)	0.004	−0.019
(*t*.stat)	(0.22)	(−0.85)
ΔS&P 500(−1)	0.005	−0.007
(*t*.stat)	(0.27)	(−0.39)

be judged as being non-stationary during the first regime. To sum up, we obtain puzzling results in this first specification, since agricultural commodities are found to be the main driving force pushing back its combination with the S&P 500 toward the long-term equilibrium. In a similar framework, Büyükşahin *et al.* (2010) failed to identify a cointegration relationship between the GSCI Agricultural sub-index and the S&P 500 during 1991–2008. We could agree with their findings given the relative instability detected in the cointegration relationship in our setting before the break date in 1997.

6.2.3.3   GSCI Industrial Metals and S&P 500

We continue our investigation of the linkages between equity and commodity markets by testing the cointegration between the S&P 500 and the GSCI sub-index for industrial metals.

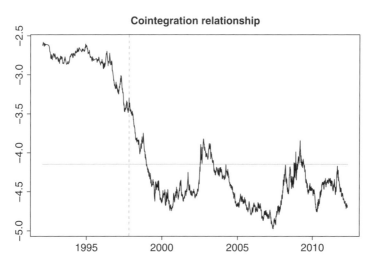

Figure 6.5   Cointegration relationship with structural break between GSCI Agricultural and S&P 500

Table 6.10 Lütkepohl *et al.* (2004) cointegration test results with structural break for GSCI Industrial Metals and S&P 500

1993–2011	Max. Eigen.	10%	5%	1%
$r \leq 1$	5.35	5.42	6.79	10.04
$r = 0$	15.83	13.78	15.83	19.85

In Table 6.18, we obtain similar results to the previous case, i.e. there is one cointegration relationship when selecting the specification during 1993–2011 and with one structural break.

Table 6.10 shows that the null of no cointegration between the two time series of interest can be safely rejected at the 5% level.

Table 6.11 contains interesting results, since it features two significantly negative error-correction terms. Since the coefficients obtained for the two variables are roughly equal (when rounding), we can interpret this table by stating that both variables correct equally the short-term deviations from the long-run equilibrium. Hence, we obtain a harmonious combination between the S&P 500 and the GSCI Industrial Metals sub-index, which means that the two variables are arguably strongly tied over time. The interpretation of this result unfolds as follows: periods of bullish equity markets could be regarded as reflecting surges in economic activity where industrial metals are globally needed to meet the needs of companies in terms of construction, equipment and provision of final goods.

In Figure 6.6, the cointegrating relationship is impacted by the occurrence of one structural break on June 3, 2008. It is also non-stationary during the first regime of our estimates, and more particularly during 1993–1998. To conclude, we have been able to identify one cointegration relationship between the S&P 500 and the basket of commodities relative to industrial metals. There are strong economic mechanisms at stake to relate these variables, such as the adjustment process to economic activity. However, the inspection of the graph of the cointegration relationship is not satisfactory during the full sample. Therefore, we might also agree with Büyükşahin *et al.* (2010), who denied the existence of such a cointegration relationship in their paper.

Table 6.11 VECM results with structural break (1993–2011) for GSCI Industrial Metals and S&P 500

Error-Correction Term		
GSCI Ind.Met.	1	
S&P 500	0.993	
VECM	ΔGSCI Ind.Met.	ΔS&P 500
ECT	−0.001	−0.001
(*t*.stat)	(−2.93)	(−2.22)
ΔGSCI Ind.Met.(−1)	−0.053	−0.005
(*t*.stat)	(−2.64)	(−0.22)
ΔS&P 500(−1)	0.083	−0.059
(*t*.stat)	(4.27)	(−2.96)

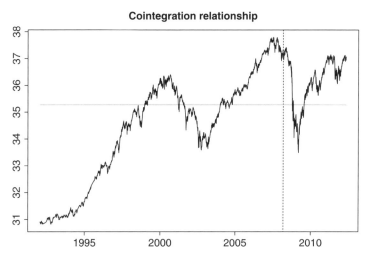

Figure 6.6 Cointegration relationship with structural break between GSCI Industrial Metals and S&P 500

Table 6.12 Lütkepohl *et al.* (2004) cointegration test results with structural break for GSCI Precious Metals and S&P 500

1993–2011	Max. Eigen.	10%	5%	1%
$r \leq 1$	7.51	5.42	6.79	10.04
$r = 0$	20.97	13.78	15.83	19.85

6.2.3.4 GSCI Precious Metals and S&P 500

Is the situation different when one looks at precious metals (instead of industrial metals)? Table 6.18 provides us with a first hint: there seems to be one cointegration relationship with asset markets during 1993–2011 and with the modeling of one structural break.

In Table 6.12, we are able to verify that the rank of the cointegration r between the GSCI Precious Metals sub-index and the S&P 500 is equal to at least 1 (at the 1% level).

The VECM results are less accurate than in the case of industrial metals. Indeed, in Table 6.13, we observe that both error-correction terms are significant. But only the coefficient for the GSCI Precious Metals sub-index is found to be negative. Similarly to the case of agricultural products, this finding would imply that the prices of precious metals are a driving force pushing back the two time series towards their equilibrium in the long run.[1] This result also appears counter-intuitive given the well-documented properties of asset markets to reflect efficiently the information available to all market participants, including the variations in the price of commodities.

The cointegration relationship pictured in Figure 6.7 is not stable during either of the two regimes separated by the structural break on September 6, 1996. Overall, our results can only

---

[1] It is also possible that the signs of the ECTs are symmetrically opposed in this setting so as to reflect flight-to-quality episodes, i.e. the price of gold rises during periods of declining equity markets and the converse.

Table 6.13   VECM results with structural break (1993–2011) for GSCI Precious Metals and S&P 500

Error-Correction Term		
GSCI Prec.Met.	1	
S&P 500	−0.574	
VECM	**ΔGSCI Prec.Met.**	**ΔS&P 500**
ECT	−0.006	0.006
(*t*.stat)	(−3.23)	(2.91)
ΔGSCI Prec.Met.(−1)	0.001	−0.009
(*t*.stat)	(−0.01)	(−0.38)
ΔS&P 500(−1)	0.022	−0.051
(*t*.stat)	(1.17)	(−2.47)

cautiously confirm the results by Büyükşahin *et al.* (2010), who rejected the hypothesis of cointegration between precious metals and equity markets.

6.2.3.5   GSCI Energy and S&P 500

In the last case, modeling the link between the GSCI Energy sub-index and the S&P 500, Table 6.18 indicates the presence of one cointegration relationship during the full period and with the occurrence of one break.

Table 6.14 allows us to verify that the rank of the cointegration *r* is at least equal to 1 (at the 1% level).

In Table 6.15, the estimation of the VECM appears extremely satisfactory. Indeed, we record two negative and statistically significant error-correction terms. By looking at the magnitude of the coefficients obtained, we may infer that the GSCI Energy sub-index slightly predominates the error-correction effects coming from the S&P 500. Compared to the previous categories of

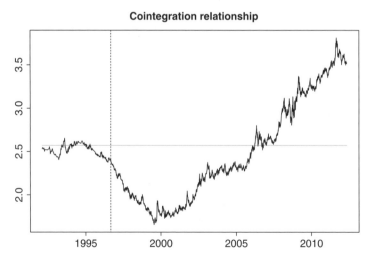

Figure 6.7   Cointegration relationship with structural break between GSCI Precious Metals and S&P 500

Table 6.14 Lütkepohl *et al.* (2004) cointegration test results with structural break for GSCI Energy and S&P 500

1993–2011	Max. Eigen.	10%	5%	1%
$r \leq 1$	5.92	5.42	6.79	10.04
$r = 0$	23.68	13.78	15.83	19.85

commodities, the results appear globally plausible in this setting, since we are able to isolate statistically significant adjustment processes coming from equity markets. Hence, we can judge favorably the existence of one cointegration relationship between energy commodities and asset markets. The interpretation could be viewed as quite similar to the case of industrial metals: energy can be seen as an input to production processes, whose needs are greater during periods of economic expansion (and asset prices can be viewed as an early warning signal of changes in the state of the economy).

The last test for our results consists in the examination of the behavior of the cointegration relationship during the period 1993–2011. In Figure 6.8, we uncover one structural break on September 3, 2008, which may be related to the period of intense market activity of the summer of 2008 and the oil price swing. While the combination between the two variables in the system is certainly stationary during the second regime (i.e. after the break), we cannot conclude in favor of the stationarity of the cointegrating relationship during 1993–2008. Therefore, we cannot ultimately consider that the cointegrating relationship between the GSCI Energy sub-index and the S&P 500 holds. Despite encouraging results at first sight, we must agree on this matter with the previous findings by Büyükşahin *et al.* (2010).

6.2.3.6 Summary and Discussion on Cointegration Analyses between Asset Markets and Commodity Prices

The relationship between various categories of commodities and asset markets appears quite elusive in our setting, given that the statistical tests that confirm the presence of cointegration are undermined either by the VECM estimates or by the non-stationarity of the long-term relationship. Therefore, the modeling of the linkages between commodities and asset markets

Table 6.15 VECM results with structural break (1993–2011) for GSCI Energy and S&P 500

Error-Correction Term		
GSCI Energy	1	
S&P 500	0.993	
VECM	ΔGSCI Energy	ΔS&P 500
ECT	−0.007	−0.005
(*t*.stat)	(−3.17)	(−3.89)
ΔGSCI Energy(−1)	−0.046	−0.007
(*t*.stat)	(−2.20)	(−0.60)
ΔS&P 500(−1)	0.092	−0.060
(*t*.stat)	(2.49)	(−2.85)

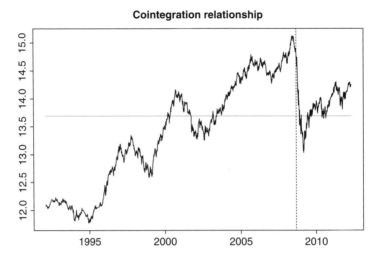

Figure 6.8   Cointegration relationship with structural break between GSCI Energy and S&P 500

should rely on another econometric framework based on multivariate GARCH volatilities, for instance (see Büyükşahin *et al.* (2010) for recent results on this topic).

Next, we extend our cointegration analysis to the links between commodities and exchange rates.

6.3   COINTEGRATION BETWEEN THE GSCI SUB-INDICES AND EXCHANGE RATES

Exchange rates have long been thought to have an important impact on the export and import of goods and services, and, thus, exchange rates are expected to influence the price of those products that are traded.

Real interest rates represent the opportunity costs of holding commodities either as one part of storage costs or as portfolio assets. If the interest rates become high, the costs of commodity storage are immediately more expensive. This leads the demand for primary commodities to fall until the net expected future gains of stocks is not inferior to zero according to the theory of storage (Working (1949), Brennan, (1958)), or to the marginal financial yield according to the portfolio adjustment theory of commodities (Heal and Barrow (1980), Deaton and Laroque (1992)).

High interest rates may also affect commodity prices either via the substitution effects of reducing investment (in the commodities sector as well as in the manufactured products sector) in favor of increasing saving, or via the rising of debt service obligations, or via the flight from capital of developing countries (Gilbert (1989)).

6.3.1   Literature Review

We present below the main findings from academic research on the link between exchange rates and commodity prices in a cointegration framework.

- Fraser *et al.* (1991) test the purchasing power parity (PPP) using disaggregated commodity data in the UK and the US during 1975–1980. While few markets (e.g. wood, lubricating oil) show evidence of cointegration, their results are unfavorable to the long-run proportionality of prices in a common currency. Hence, the hypothesis that the exchange rate and relative UK–US prices tend toward the PPP can be rejected.

- Sephton (1992) tests for cointegration between exchange rates and commodity prices of feed wheat, feed barley and canola traded on the Winnipeg Commodity Exchange during 1983–1988. In the long run, currency depreciation is shown to have no lasting impact on the rates of inflation in the three commodity prices.
- Dooley et al. (1995) test for the short and long-run influences of gold prices on exchange rates conditional on other monetary and real macroeconomic variables (e.g. M1, short-term interest rate, consumer prices and industrial production) during 1976–1990. Based on the concept of gold as an 'asset without a country' and the argument that changes in country preferences will be systematically reflected in the price of gold, the authors show that gold price movements have explanatory power with respect to exchange rate movements, over and above the effects of movements in monetary fundamentals and other variables.
- Hua (1998) tests by cointegration technique the hypothesis of a long-run quantifiable relationship between non-oil primary commodity prices and macroeconomic/monetary variables during 1970–1993. The author finds that fluctuations in industrial production and the effective exchange rate of the US Dollar appear to have significantly affected the real non-oil primary commodity prices in both long-run and short-run components, while the real interest rate has rather complex pricing dynamic effects.
- Cashin et al. (2004) examine whether the real exchange rates of commodity-exporting countries and the real prices of their commodity exports move together over time. By using data from the IMF on the world prices of 44 commodities during 1980–2002, they show evidence of a long-run relationship between national real exchange rates and real commodity prices for about one-third of the commodity-exporting countries investigated in their paper.
- Harri et al. (2009) examine the cointegration relationship between the primary agricultural commodities, exchange rates and oil prices during 2000–2008. The authors identify that commodity prices are linked to oil for corn, cotton and soybean, but not for wheat, and that exchange rates do play a role in the linkage of prices over time.
- He et al. (2010) investigate the cointegrating relationship between crude oil prices and global economic activity during 1988–2007. Indeed, it is well known that global economic activity is essential for modeling the demand side of the crude oil market and is, therefore, the key determinant of oil prices.[2] They find that real futures prices of crude oil are cointegrated with the Kilian economic index[3] and a trade-weighted US Dollar index.
- Sari et al. (2010) examine the cointegration among the four precious metals (e.g. gold, silver, platinum and palladium), the oil price and the US Dollar/Euro exchange rate during 1999–2007. The latter variable is expected to be the link that relates all these industrial commodities because they are priced in the US Dollar. The authors cannot identify a cointegration relationship among precious metals, oil prices and the exchange rate, implying that these variables are not collectively driving forces of each other in the long run (despite the strong correlations among precious metals in the short run). In addition, this result reflects the

---

[2] An increase (decrease) in demand for crude oil, caused by the global economic expansion (slump), shifts the demand curve to the right (left) in a price–quantity diagram, and consequently prices increase (decrease) since the supply curve is not completely elastic (Fattouh (2007)).

[3] Kilian (2009) uses a newly developed measure of global economic activity and proposes a structural decomposition of the real price of crude oil into three components: supply shocks, shocks to the global demand for all industrial commodities and demand shocks that are specific to the crude oil market.

Table 6.16   Exchange rates and commodity prices: cointegrating relationships

Authors	Period	Cointegration Relationship	SS	SB
Fraser *et al.* (1991)	1975–1980	UK/US Exchange Rate ↔ Wood, Lubricating Oil	No	No
Sephton (1992)	1983–1988	Exchange rates Ø Feed Wheat, Feed Barley, Canola	No	No
Dooley *et al.* (1995)	1976–1990	Exchange rates ↔ Gold	No	No
Hua (1998)	1970–1993	US Exchange Rate ↔ Non-Oil Primary Commodities	Yes	No
Cashin *et al.* (2004)	1980–2002	Real Exchange Rate ↔ Real Commodity Prices	No	Yes
Harri *et al.* (2009)	2000–2008	Oil ↔ Exchange Rates ↔ Corn, Cotton, Soybean	No	No
He *et al.* (2010)	1998–2007	Trade Weighted US Dollar Index ↔ Oil	No	No
Sari *et al.* (2010)	1999–2007	Gold Ø Silver Ø Platinum Ø Palladium Ø Oil Ø USD/EUR Ex. Rate	No	No

Note: ↔ indicates the presence of a cointegration relationship. Ø indicates the absence of a cointegration relationship. SS stands for 'Sub Sample' analysis in the paper considered. SB stands for 'Structural Break' analysis in the paper considered.

increasing disparity in economic, monetary and hedging uses between these commodities and exchange rates. Oil is controlled by OPEC and other oil-producing countries, and has its own seasonality, inventories and hedging strategies. Gold and silver have almost limited supplies, are considered safe haven assets and respond strongly to inflationary expectations. Since there is only rather weak evidence of a long-run relationship, Sari *et al.* (2010) conclude that investors may benefit from diversification into precious metals in the long run.

These findings are summarized in Table 6.16.

Overall, we notice that globally exchange rates indicate strong economic linkages between economic variables and commodity prices, more particularly through the prices of gold and oil (and, to a lesser extent, through a direct connection with agricultural prices). We develop in the next section our own empirical application on this issue.

6.3.2   Results of Granger Causality Tests Between the GSCI Sub-Indices and Exchange Rates

Table 6.17 summarizes the results of the pairwise Granger causality tests (with one lag) between the GSCI sub-indices and exchange rates. We observe that the GSCI Agricultural sub-index Granger causes the Euro–Dollar exchange rate (at the 5% level). Moreover, the USD trade-weighted index is found to Granger cause the GSCI Industrial and Precious Metals sub-indices as well as the Euro–Dollar exchange rate. Finally, the reverse Granger causality is true between the Euro–Dollar exchange rate and the USD trade-weighted index (at the 5% level). Thus, we uncover that the linkages between the GSCI sub-indices and exchange rates are rather weak pursuant to our Granger causality analysis. Next, we proceed with the formal cointegration tests.

Table 6.17   Pairwise Granger causality tests for the GSCI sub-indices and exchange rates

From	To	p-value	F-statistic
GSCI Agri.	USD Trade Weighted	0.1366	2.2166
GSCI Agri.	EUR–USD X-RATE	0.0254	5.0008
GSCI Energy	USD Trade Weighted	0.2452	1.3509
GSCI Energy	EUR–USD X-RATE	0.1096	2.5612
GSCI Ind. Metals	USD Trade Weighted	0.4887	0.4795
GSCI Ind. Metals	EUR–USD X-RATE	0.2650	1.2427
GSCI Prec. Metals	USD Trade Weighted	0.8308	0.0457
GSCI Prec. Metals	EUR–USD X-RATE	0.1339	2.2474
USD Trade Weighted	Gold	0.1278	2.3197
USD Trade Weighted	WTI	0.2107	1.5672
USD Trade Weighted	GSCI Agri.	0.6212	0.2443
USD Trade Weighted	GSCI Energy	0.2426	1.3658
USD Trade Weighted	GSCI Ind. Metals	0.0226	5.1991
USD Trade Weighted	GSCI Prec. Metals	0.0050	7.9039
USD Trade Weighted	EUR–USD X-RATE	0.0000	134.9402
EUR–USD X-RATE	Gold	0.6303	0.2317
EUR–USD X-RATE	WTI	0.2223	1.4899
EUR–USD X-RATE	GSCI Agri.	0.2558	1.2916
EUR–USD X-RATE	GSCI Energy	0.2524	1.3101
EUR–USD X-RATE	GSCI Ind. Metals	0.4240	0.6394
EUR–USD X-RATE	GSCI Prec. Metals	0.7803	0.0778
EUR–USD X-RATE	USD Trade Weighted	0.0462	3.9754

Note: The p-value and the F-statistic of the pairwise Granger causality tests between X and Y are given. The null hypothesis is that X does not Granger cause Y.

6.3.3   Cointegration Analyses for the GSCI Sub-Indices and Exchange Rates

Similarly to the previous chapter, we do not seek to replicate exhaustively the findings from previous literature, but rather the key findings common to previous studies which are accessible based on our dataset. The bulk of our cointegration analyses in this section is dedicated to the link between each category of the GSCI commodity index and the Euro–USD exchange rate. This latter exchange rate has been chosen as the main variable of interest in our setting. Additional attempts have been made with the USD trade-weighted index as another representative variable for exchange rates. They produced similar results, and are briefly mentioned in the text below. Besides, in Figure 6.3, we can observe that the EUR–USD FX and the USD trade-weighted variables exhibit a similar behavior during our study period. Hence, our choice of presenting most cointegration tests with the Euro–USD exchange rate is unlikely to affect qualitatively the nature of the results obtained in this section, which are summarized in Table 6.18.

6.3.3.1   GSCI Agricultural, Industrial Metals, Precious Metals and EUR–USD X-Rate

As shown in Table 6.18, we could not identify any cointegrating relationship between the Euro–USD exchange rate and the three following GSCI sub-indices: Agricultural products, Industrial and Precious Metals. When the USD trade-weighted index is used, the same comment applies for the GSCI Agricultural and Industrial Metals indices. The only cointegration relationship

Table 6.18 Cointegration analyses of exchange rates and commodity prices: summary of the main results

Period	Cointegration Relationship	SB
1993–2011	GSCI Agricultural Ø EUR–USD X-Rate	No
1993–2000	GSCI Agricultural Ø EUR–USD X-Rate	No
2000–2011	GSCI Agricultural Ø EUR–USD X-Rate	No
1993–2011	GSCI Agricultural Ø EUR–USD X-Rate	Yes
1993–2011	GSCI Industrial Metals Ø EUR–USD X-Rate	No
1993–2000	GSCI Industrial Metals Ø EUR–USD X-Rate	No
2000–2011	GSCI Industrial Metals Ø EUR–USD X-Rate	No
1993–2011	GSCI Industrial Metals Ø EUR–USD X-Rate	Yes
1993–2011	GSCI Precious Metals Ø EUR–USD X-Rate	No
1993–2000	GSCI Precious Metals Ø EUR–USD X-Rate	No
2000–2011	GSCI Precious Metals Ø EUR–USD X-Rate	No
1993–2011	GSCI Precious Metals Ø EUR–USD X-Rate	Yes
1993–2011	GSCI Energy Ø EUR–USD X-Rate	No
1993–2000	GSCI Energy Ø EUR–USD X-Rate	No
2000–2011	GSCI Energy Ø EUR–USD X-Rate	No
1993–2011	GSCI Energy ↔ EUR–USD X-Rate	Yes
1993–2011	Gold ↔ Silver ↔ Platinum ↔ WTI ↔ EUR–USD X-Rate	No
1993–2000	Gold ↔ Silver Ø Platinum Ø WTI Ø EUR–USD X-Rate	No
2000–2011	Gold ↔ Silver Ø Platinum Ø WTI Ø EUR–USD X-Rate	No
1993–2011	Gold ↔ Silver ↔ Platinum ↔ WTI ↔ EUR–USD X-Rate	Yes
1993–2011	Gold Ø EUR–USD X-Rate	No
1993–2000	Gold Ø EUR–USD X-Rate	No
2000–2011	Gold Ø EUR–USD X-Rate	No
1993–2011	Gold Ø EUR–USD X-Rate	Yes
1993–2011	WTI Ø EUR–USD X-Rate	No
1993–2000	WTI Ø EUR–USD X-Rate	No
2000–2011	WTI Ø EUR–USD X-Rate	No
1993–2011	WTI ↔ EUR–USD X-Rate	Yes
1993–2011	WTI Ø EUR–USD X-Rate Ø Corn Ø Cotton Ø Soybean	No
1993–2000	WTI Ø EUR–USD X-Rate Ø Corn Ø Cotton Ø Soybean	No
2000–2011	WTI Ø EUR–USD X-Rate Ø Corn Ø Cotton Ø Soybean	No
1993–2011	WTI ↔ EUR–USD X-Rate ↔ Corn ↔ Cotton ↔ Soybean	Yes

Note: ↔ indicates the presence of a cointegration relationship. Ø indicates the absence of a cointegration relationship. SB stands for 'Structural Break' analysis.

which could be found here is between the GSCI Precious Metals sub-index and the USD trade-weighted index, during the full period and when one allows for one structural break on April 16, 2002. In that specification, we obtain a significant (at the 1% level) and negative error-correction term from the USD trade-weighted variable. However, this relationship could not be considered stationary and these results are not reproduced here.[4] Hence, the main finding in that line of research is that it is difficult to relate any agricultural, precious or industrial metals commodity index with exchange rate variables.

---

[4] Available upon request.

Table 6.19 Lütkepohl *et al.* (2004) cointegration test results with structural break for GSCI Energy and EUR–USD X-rate

1993–2011	Max. Eigen.	10%	5%	1%
$r \leq 1$	5.76	5.42	6.79	10.04
$r = 0$	19.59	13.78	15.83	19.85

6.3.3.2   GSCI Energy and EUR–USD X-Rate

When turning to the GSCI Energy sub-index, we obtain a different picture. Indeed, Table 6.18 reveals the presence of one cointegration relationship with the Euro–USD exchange rate during 1993–2011 and with the occurrence of one structural break.

Table 6.19 allows us to verify this statement: the rank of the cointegration r between the GSCI Energy and the EUR–USD X-rate variables is equal to at least 1 (at the 5% confidence level).

In Table 6.20, we have been able to estimate successfully the VECM. Both error-correction terms are negative and significant, which indicates the presence of strong feedback effects coming from either the GSCI Energy sub-index or the Euro–USD exchange rate to correct short-term deviations. The economic insights explained at the beginning of Section 6.3 can therefore be verified statistically, at least in the case of energy commodities.

Figure 6.9 highlights the presence of one structural break on July 15, 2008. After that date, the cointegration relationship could be considered stationary. However, we detect significant instabilities prior to the break date. Indeed, the relationship is upward sloping during the first regime. Based on these comments, we shall reject cautiously the hypothesis stating the existence of cointegration between the GSCI Energy and the EUR–USD X-rate variables. Thus, after careful consideration, none of the commodity indices could be related convincingly to exchange rates.

Note that, when performing the same exercise between the GSCI Energy sub-index and the USD trade-weighted index, we could identify the presence of cointegration during the full period with one structural break on July 15, 2008. Despite the significant (at 1% level) and negative error-correction term coming from the GSCI Energy variable, the relationship could

Table 6.20 VECM results with structural break (1993–2011) for GSCI Energy and EUR–USD X-rate

Error-Correction Term		
GSCI Energy	1	
EUR–USD FX	−0.171	
VECM	ΔGSCI Energy	ΔEUR–USD FX
ECT	−0.007	−0.001
(*t*.stat)	(−3.08)	(−2.29)
ΔGSCI Energy(−1)	−0.034	0.005
(*t*.stat)	(−1.79)	(1.02)
ΔEUR–USD FX(−1)	0.121	−0.008
(*t*.stat)	(1.68)	(−0.43)

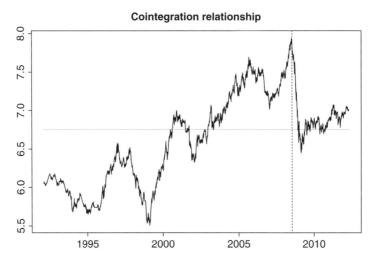

Figure 6.9 Cointegration relationship with structural break between GSCI Energy and EUR–USD X-rate

Table 6.21   Johansen cointegration test results for the 1993–2011 full period for gold, silver, platinum, WTI and EUR–USD FX

1993–2011	Max. Eigen.	10%	5%	1%
$r \leq 4$	4.38	10.49	12.25	16.26
$r \leq 3$	7.90	16.85	18.96	23.65
$r \leq 2$	9.33	23.11	25.54	30.34
$r \leq 1$	11.86	29.12	31.46	36.65
$r = 0$	37.52	34.75	37.52	42.36

not be considered stable over time. Hence, the conclusion reached in the previous paragraph still holds in that case.[5] These effects, to the best of our knowledge, are new and have not been tested explicitly in previous literature.

6.3.3.3   Gold, Silver, Platinum, WTI and EUR–USD X-Rate

Our next cointegration exercise is dedicated to the linkages between precious metals (i.e. gold, silver, platinum), the oil price and the Euro–USD exchange rate. The idea behind this combination of variables is to test whether exchange rates can be found as a buffer between various kinds of commodities. Indeed, most commodities are labeled in USD, while the remaining commodities are traded in other foreign currencies. In Table 6.18, we are able to identify two types of cointegration relationships: both occur during the full period, with and without the modeling of a structural break.

In Table 6.21, we reproduce the results relative to the full period *without* a structural break. It can be seen that the rank of the cointegration r for gold, silver, platinum, WTI and EUR–USD FX is equal to at least 1 (at the 5% level).

---

[5] These results are not shown to conserve space, and may be obtained upon request.

Table 6.22   VECM results for the 1993–2011 full period for gold, silver, platinum, WTI and EUR–USD FX

Error-Correction Term

Gold	1
Silver	0.069
Platinum	−14.160
WTI	10.869
EUR–USD FX	0.590
Trend	0.001

VECM	ΔGold	ΔSilver	ΔPlatinum	ΔWTI	ΔEUR–USD FX
ECT	0.001	0.001	0.001	−0.002	0.001
(*t*.stat)	(0.39)	(−0.55)	(0.28)	(−5.29)	(−2.53)
Intercept	0.003	−0.006	0.003	−0.075	−0.011
(*t*.stat)	(0.48)	(−0.49)	(0.33)	(−5.24)	(−2.54)
ΔGold(−1)	0.038	0.056	0.041	−0.015	0.028
(*t*.stat)	(1.33)	(1.04)	(1.02)	(−0.25)	(1.53)
ΔSilver(−1)	−0.018	−0.063	0.024	−0.021	0.014
(*t*.stat)	(−1.18)	(−2.21)	(1.13)	(−0.67)	(1.5)
ΔPlatinum(−1)	−0.037	−0.017	−0.047	0.039	−0.013
(*t*.stat)	(−2.22)	(−0.55)	(−2.06)	(1.11)	(−1.21)
ΔWTI(−1)	−0.003	−0.01	0.009	−0.052	0.002
(*t*.stat)	(−0.33)	(−0.57)	(0.71)	(−2.58)	(0.39)
ΔEUR–USD FX(−1)	0.023	0.013	−0.002	0.074	−0.027
(*t*.stat)	(0.72)	(0.22)	(−0.05)	(1.09)	(−1.35)

When investigating whether the exchange rates can act as a bridge between the prices of precious metal and oil commodities, we get the result in Table 6.22 that the error-correction term for EUR–USD FX is significant but positive. Hence, the main adjustment mechanism does not occur through the exchange rate variable. In fact, the other significant ECT belongs to the oil price variable, which records a negative sign. This specification therefore highlights that the modeling of exchange rates as a buffer between commodity prices is not necessary, since the price of oil is able to play that role. Short-term deviations will be corrected by the WTI price in this system.

The plot of the cointegrating relationship given in Figure 6.10 appears clearly stationary during 1993–2011. The same comment applies when visualizing the cointegration relationship with one structural break on July 15, 2008. Overall, the modeling of the cointegration link between gold, silver, platinum, WTI and EUR–USD FX can be considered valid with our dataset, with the oil price being identified as the driver in the price discovery process. These results contradict the recent findings by Sari *et al.* (2010) over the period 1999–2007.

Finally, note that when using the USD trade-weighted variable (instead of EUR–USD FX), the cointegrating relationship is also quite stable.

6.3.3.4   Gold and EUR–USD X-Rate

Let us now consider the interaction between the price of gold and the Euro–USD exchange rate. In Table 6.18, we cannot detect any cointegration between these two variables, neither during the full nor sub-periods. When replacing EUR–USD FX with the USD trade-weighted

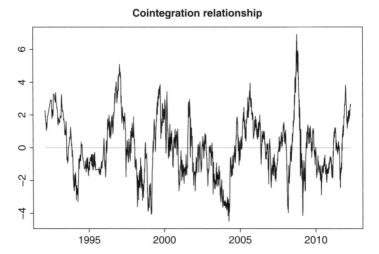

Figure 6.10   Cointegration relationship for the 1993–2011 full period for gold, silver, platinum, WTI and EUR–USD FX

Table 6.23   Lütkepohl *et al.* (2004) cointegration test results with structural break for WTI and EUR–USD X-Rate

1993–2011	Max. Eigen.	10%	5%	1%
$r \leq 1$	5.22	5.42	6.79	10.04
$r = 0$	24.91	13.78	15.83	19.85

index, one cointegrating relationship with a break on April 16, 2002 can be found (at the 5% level). While the exchange rate variable records a significantly negative error-correction term in that specification, the graph of the cointegrating relationship could not be considered stable.[6] Contrary to Dooley *et al.* (1995) during the period 1976–1990, we cannot assert that a valid cointegration relationship exists between gold and exchange rates with our dataset.

6.3.3.5   WTI and EUR–USD X-Rate

The next cointegration pair considered is composed of the price of oil and the Euro–USD exchange rate. As shown in Table 6.18, we can find one cointegrating relationship during 1993–2011 with the inclusion of a structural break.

Inspection of Table 6.23 reveals that the rank of the cointegration *r* for WTI and EUR–USD X-Rate is equal to at least 1 (at the 1% level).

The VECM has been successfully estimated: in Table 6.24, we uncover two negative and statistically significant error-correction terms. By looking at the magnitude of the coefficients and at the significance levels, we document the fact that WTI is the main driving force in the price discovery process. This result confirms our results in the case of gold, silver, platinum,

---

[6] These results are not displayed here to conserve space, and can be accessed upon request.

Table 6.24   VECM results with structural break (1993–2011) for WTI and
EUR–USD X-Rate

Error-Correction Term		
WTI	1	
EUR–USD FX	−1.034	
VECM	**ΔWTI**	**ΔEUR–USD FX**
ECT	−0.012	−0.001
(*t*.stat)	(−4.33)	(−1.62)
ΔWTI(−1)	−0.044	0.007
(*t*.stat)	(−2.30)	(1.18)
ΔEUR–USD FX(−1)	0.096	−0.001
(*t*.stat)	(1.46)	(−0.51)

WTI and EUR–USD FX: the oil price can be seen as an essential variable of adjustment in cointegrating processes linking various commodities together. These results do not undermine the likely role played by exchange rates, but they nonetheless indicate that oil has become a central commodity among the other categories studied here to trigger feedback mechanisms in the long run.

Figure 6.11 shows the presence of a structural break on July 15, 2008. Recall that the summer of 2008 and the subsequent price collapse can be seen as a key characteristic of oil price changes over the recent period. Before the break, we cannot consider that the cointegrating relationship is stationary.

Note that the same results were obtained with the USD trade-weighted index (instead of the EUR–USD FX). In that latter case, the WTI price is significantly negative (at the 1% level) in the VECM. However, the cointegrating relationship is not stable before the same break date. Consequently, we cannot validate the presence of one cointegrating relationship between oil

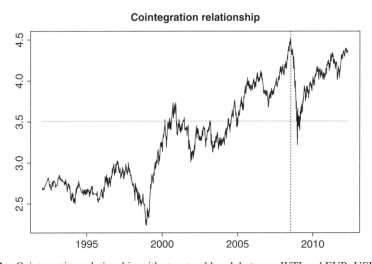

Cointegration relationship

Figure 6.11   Cointegration relationship with structural break between WTI and EUR–USD X-Rate

Table 6.25   Lütkepohl *et al.* (2004) cointegration test results with structural break for WTI, corn, cotton, soybean and EUR–USD FX

1993–2011	Max. Eigen.	10%	5%	1%
$r \leq 4$	5.04	5.42	6.79	10.04
$r \leq 3$	14.19	13.78	15.83	19.85
$r \leq 2$	29.57	25.93	28.45	33.76
$r \leq 1$	52.38	42.08	45.2	51.6
$r = 0$	78.10	61.92	65.66	73.12

and exchange rates with our dataset. This finding contradicts the previous study by He *et al.* (2010), which concerned the period going from 1998 to 2007.

6.3.3.6   WTI, EUR–USD X-Rate, Corn, Cotton, Soybean

The last combination studied in this section concerns the price of agricultural products (i.e. corn, cotton, soybean), the price of oil and the Euro–USD exchange rate. Similarly to the case with precious metals, this specification aims at testing whether the links between various commodities – which are labeled in different foreign currencies – may channel through the exchange rate variable. Table 6.18 tells us that such a cointegration relationship does indeed exist during the full period with one break.

Table 6.25 indicates that the null of no cointegration between WTI, corn, cotton, soybean and EUR–USD FX can be rejected at the 1% level.

As reproduced in Table 6.26, the VECM estimates are extremely satisfactory. It is remarkable to obtain five negative error-correction terms, which suggests that this specification has been

Table 6.26   VECM results with structural break (1993–2011) for WTI, corn, cotton, soybean and EUR–USD FX

Error-Correction Term					
WTI	1				
Corn	0.189				
Cotton	−0.591				
Soybean	0.406				
EUR–USD FX	−1.125				

VECM	ΔWTI	ΔCorn	ΔCotton	ΔSoybean	ΔEUR–USD FX
ECT	−0.009	−0.007	−0.001	−0.005	−0.001
(*t*.stat)	(−3.74)	(−3.63)	(−0.65)	(−2.87)	(−1.71)
ΔWTI(−1)	−0.051	−0.053	0.013	−0.053	0.005
(*t*.stat)	(−2.67)	(−3.28)	(0.79)	(−3.84)	(0.83)
ΔCorn(−1)	0.002	0.008	−0.015	0.001	0.006
(*t*.stat)	(0.08)	(0.34)	(−0.60)	(0.02)	(0.69)
ΔCotton(−1)	−0.026	−0.008	0.017	0.011	0.003
(*t*.stat)	(−1.09)	(−0.41)	(0.82)	(0.63)	(0.40)
ΔSoybean(−1)	0.078	0.018	0.014	0.025	0.015
(*t*.stat)	(2.22)	(0.61)	(0.46)	(1.00)	(1.44)
ΔEUR–USD FX(−1)	0.082	−0.038	−0.064	−0.015	− 0.018
(*t*.stat)	(1.23)	(−0.68)	(−1.12)	(−0.31)	(−0.93)

Cointegration relationship

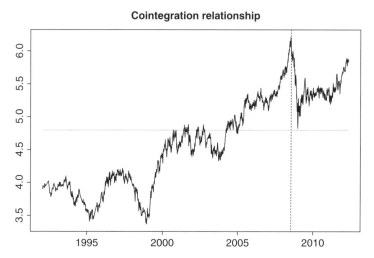

Figure 6.12 Cointegration relationship with structural break for WTI–corn–cotton–soybean–EUR–USD FX

carefully designed and contains meaningful indications as to the links between the selected variables. Nearly all ECTs are statistically significant (except cotton). Among the significantly negative ECTs, we may stress that oil and corn register the largest coefficients, indicating that the adjustment processes happen mainly through those two variables. Thanks to this specification containing oil and agricultural commodities, we add the knowledge that the price of corn can act as a significant feedback force to correct the deviations toward the long-term equilibrium in this system. The same cannot be said, however, for the exchange rate variable. Although its statistical impacts are unquestionable, it cannot be established as being the main variable facilitating the adjustment towards the stationary combination of variables in this setting.

Having these comments in mind, we need to comment on the cointegrating relationship displayed in Figure 6.12. We learn that a structural break occurred on July 15, 2008. Before the break date, the cointegration cannot be considered stationary (and is, on the contrary, upward sloping). Therefore, we failed to identify a correct cointegration relationship between the price of oil, agricultural products and the Euro–USD exchange rate.

Note that the same results hold with the USD trade-weighted index. In the latter case, the error-correction terms for the WTI, corn and soybean variables are significantly negative in the VECM. However, this relationship does not appear stable before the same break date. We must disagree on that matter with the previous findings by Harri *et al.* (2009), which covered the period 2000–2008.

6.3.3.7 *Some Concluding Remarks on Cointegration Analyses between Exchange Rates and Commodity Prices*

Overall, it appears difficult to identify a valid and stable cointegrating relationship between exchange rates and commodities, be it GSCI indices or individual price series. The hypothesis that the exchange rate can act as a buffer, or a connection, between the prices of various commodities – which are naturally traded in various currencies – does not hold in our cointe-gration framework. Apart from the effects of the GSCI Energy index, which can be found to be convincingly related to exchange rate variables, we can only underline in this chapter the central role played by the oil price (and to a lesser extent the corn price) to trigger adjustment mechanisms in cointegrated systems. The same cannot be said for gold. It therefore looks like the WTI crude oil futures could be used as the most representative commodity currency.

6.4 CONCLUDING REMARKS

In this chapter, we have attempted to deal with a difficult topic, i.e. to what extent are commodity and traditional asset markets related? Previous scholars could not conclude in favor of a clear link between equities, bonds and commodity markets. Based on our cointegration tool, during full and sub-periods as well as with structural break tests, we can only agree with these previous findings. Indeed, when a cointegration relationship is found between the S&P 500 and the GSCI sub-indices for agricultural products, industrial/precious metals or energy, the entire specification tests (e.g. negative and significant ECTs in conjunction with a stationary long-term relationship) cannot be verified. When introducing individual commodities such as oil, gold or corn, our main message is that the price of oil is able to trigger significant adjustment processes. From that perspective, it would appear more appropriate to look for linkages between commodity and traditional asset markets based on volatility models (e.g. univariate and multivariate GARCH). It appears that – in the long run – commodity markets on the one hand, and equities, bonds and exchange rates on the other hand cannot be established to be moving together. Again, this information could be useful for investors with a long-term view (such as pension funds).

REFERENCES

Brennan, MJ. 1958. The Supply of Storage. *American Economic Review* 49:50–72
Büyükşahin, B., Haigh, MS., Robe, MA. 2010. Commodities and Equities: Ever a 'Market of One'? *Journal of Alternative Investments* 12(3):76–95
Cashin, P., Cespedes, LF. Sahay, R. 2004. Commodity Currencies and the Real Exchange Rate. *Journal of Development Economics* 75:239–268
Chong, J., Miffre, J. 2010. Conditional Correlation and Volatility in Commodity Futures and Traditional Asset Markets. *Journal of Alternative Investments* 12(3):61–75
Deaton, A., Laroque, G. 1992. On the Behaviour of Commodity Prices. *Review of Economic Studies* 59:1–23
Dooley, MP., Isard, P., Taylor, MP. 1995. Exchange Rates, Country-specific Shocks, and Gold. *Applied Financial Economics* 5:121–129
Fattouh, B. 2007. *The Drivers of Oil Prices: The Usefulness and Limitations of Nonstructural Model, the Demand–Supply Framework and Informal Approaches*. Technical Report #286084, Oxford Institute for Energy Studies, UK
Fraser, P., Taylor, MP., Webster, A. 1991. An Empirical Examination of Long-run Purchasing Power Parity as Theory of International Commodity Arbitrage. *Applied Economics* 23:1749–1759
Gilbert, CG. 1989. The Impact of Exchange Rates and Developing Country Debt on Commodity Prices. *Economic Journal* 99:773–784
Greene, WH. 2003. *Econometric Analysis*. Pearson Education, India
Harri, A., Nalley, L., Hudson, D. 2009. The Relationship between Oil, Exchange Rates, and Commodity Prices. *Journal of Agricultural and Applied Economics* 41(2):501–510
He, Y., Wang, S., Lai, KK. 2010. Global Economic Activity and Crude Oil Prices: A Cointegration Analysis. *Energy Economics* 32:868–876

Heal, G., Barrow, M. 1980. The Relationship between Interest Rates and Metal Price Movements. *Review of Economic Studies* 47(1):161–181

Hua, P. 1998. On Primary Commodity Prices: The Impact of Macroeconomic/Monetary Shocks. *Journal of Policy Modeling* 20(6):767–790

Kilian, L. 2009. Not All Oil Price Shocks Are Alike: Disentangling Demand and Supply Shocks in the Crude Oil Market. *American Economic Review* 99(3):1053–1069

Lombardi, MJ., Osbat, C., Schnatz, B. 2011. Global Commodity Cycles and Linkages: A FAVAR Approach. *Empirical Economics* 36:546–555 DOI 10.1007/s00181-011-0494-8

Lütkepohl, H., Saikkonen, P., Trenkler, C. 2004. Testing for the cointegrating rank of a VAR with level shift an unknown time. *Econometrica* 72:647–662

Marquis, MH., Cunningham, SR. 1990. Is There a Role for Commodity Prices in the Design of Monetary Policy? Some Empirical Evidence. *Southern Economic Journal* 57(2):394–412

Sari, R., Hammoudeh, S., Soytas, U. 2010. Dynamics of Oil Price, Precious Metal Prices, and Exchange Rate. *Energy Economics* 32:351–362

Sephton, PS. 1991. Commodity Prices: Policy Target or Information Variable: A Comment. *Journal of Money, Credit, and Banking* 23:260–266

Sephton, PS. 1992. Modelling the Link between Commodity Prices and Exchange Rates: The Tale of Daily Data. *Canadian Journal of Economics* 25(1):156–171

Working, H. 1949. The Theory of Price of Storage. *American Economic Review* 39(6):1254–1262

Zeng, T., Swanson, NR. 1998. Predictive Evaluation of Econometric Forecasting Models in Commodity Futures Markets. *Studies in Nonlinear Dynamics and Econometrics* 2(4):159–177

7

Cointegration with Industrial Production and Inflation

This chapter deals with the inter-relationships between commodity markets and two major constituents of macroeconomic variables: (i) industrial production (as a proxy of economic activity) and (ii) inflation. These key indicators are being followed closely by analysts and market professionals, as detailed previously in Part II.

In what follows, we shall first explore the usual descriptive statistics and unit root tests of the dataset, and then develop two kinds of cointegration analyses between commodities on the one hand, and industrial production or inflation on the other hand. Then, we briefly conclude with the main results that have been achieved by following this standardized econometric procedure.

7.1 DATASET AND UNIT ROOT TEST RESULTS

Table 7.1 provides the descriptive statistics of the time series used in Chapter 7. To facilitate the exposition, we rely on the GSCI sub-indices to carry out our analysis, instead of the individual commodity price series. We use mainly industrial production and inflation indices from the USA, China (CH), Brazil (BR), Australia (AU), Canada (CA), the EU and Germany (GE). Other monetary aggregates include US M2 and the OECD inflation index. All the data used in this chapter comes from Bloomberg with monthly frequency (due to the availability of macroeconomic time series at monthly frequency at best).

The raw data can be seen in Figure 7.1 for the GSCI sub-indices, in Figures 7.2 and 7.3 for industrial production variables, and in Figures 7.4 and 7.5 for the inflation and monetary variables. We can remark that the evolution pattern is quite similar for all these time series, i.e. with an upward trend (except perhaps the GSCI energy sub-index which was characterized by a high degree of volatility during the summer of 2008). Besides, most industrial production variables record a decrease from the onset of the 2008 financial crisis and the recessionary period. Hence, the time series can be considered as good candidates to be regrouped in a cointegration analysis.

Unit root tests are presented in Table 7.2. This table allows us to verify that the time series are integrated of the same order ($I(1)$), as a pre-requisite for cointegration.

7.2 COINTEGRATION BETWEEN THE GSCI SUB-INDICES AND INDUSTRIAL PRODUCTION

When investigating the link between commodity markets and a central macroeconomic variable such as industrial production, several economic forces are of interest. First, in a context of sustained economic growth, the demand for commodity markets is strong. Hence, consumers'

Table 7.1   Descriptive statistics for the GSCI sub-indices, industrial production, monetary and inflation variables

	Min	Max	Mean	Std. Dev.	Skew.	Kurt.	JB
GSCI Agri.	6.1964	7.2869	6.6240	0.2862	0.8215	0.6213	3.3815
GSCI Energy	5.5698	7.9818	6.8226	0.5273	−0.1528	0.9402	11.7205
GSCI Ind. Metals	6.1480	7.7478	6.7902	0.5358	0.5176	3.2463	94.8298
GSCI Prec. Metals	5.8347	7.7111	6.4565	0.5347	0.7049	1.6517	23.4517
US M2	8.2031	9.1342	8.6779	0.2744	−0.1232	4.8955	235.7902
OECD Index Inflation	4.4296	4.7238	4.5749	0.0860	0.0737	4.2170	162.6011
Industrial Production US	4.2816	4.6126	4.4968	0.0736	−0.8004	7.2675	510.8818
Inflation US	5.0415	5.4184	5.2307	0.1131	0.0154	11.5886	1150.9830
Industrial Production CH	6.1620	8.0959	7.0780	0.5845	0.1568	4.2581	150.3156
Inflation CH	4.4027	4.7198	4.5178	0.0825	0.8425	1.5263	25.3705
Industrial Production BR	4.4403	4.8752	4.6579	0.1311	0.1944	10.8290	1039.6271
Inflation BR	7.1396	8.1092	7.6474	0.2938	−0.1238	7.1327	513.4509
Industrial Production AU	4.3412	4.6220	4.4925	0.0813	−0.1928	6.2129	343.1431
Inflation AU	4.7749	5.1835	4.9562	0.1280	0.0832	16.5446	2491.5800
Industrial Production CA	4.5726	4.7562	4.6432	0.0449	0.6319	14.7366	1902.8239
Inflation CA	4.4773	4.7925	4.6311	0.0933	−0.0575	0.7023	6.6728
Industrial Production EU	4.4116	4.7113	4.5651	0.0721	−0.1375	2.4034	77.0835
Inflation EU	4.4269	4.7283	4.5709	0.0902	0.0771	2.0633	35.8680
Industrial Production GE	4.3981	4.7493	4.5654	0.0943	0.2663	2.8235	85.0722
Inflation GE	4.4762	4.7131	4.5840	0.0699	0.2159	0.3982	7.2013

Note: The number of observations is equal to 187. Std. Dev. stands for Standard Deviation, Kurt. for Kurtosis, Skew. for Skewness, and JB for the Jarque Bera test statistic.

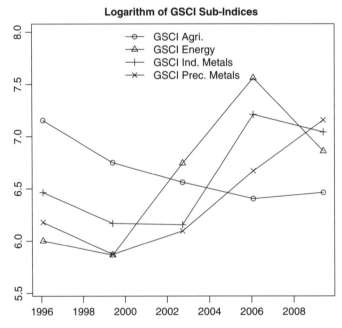

Figure 7.1   Logarithm of time series for GSCI monthly sub-indices

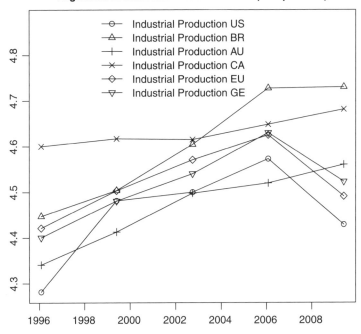

Figure 7.2   Logarithm of industrial production variables (except China)

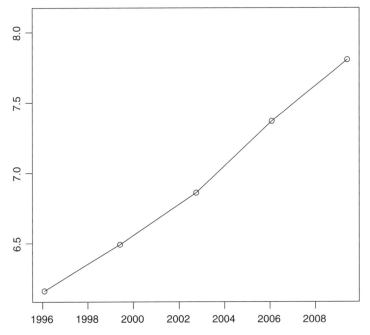

Figure 7.3   Logarithm of time series for industrial production variables: China

Logarithm of Inflation and Monetary Indices (except US M2 and Inflation Brazil)

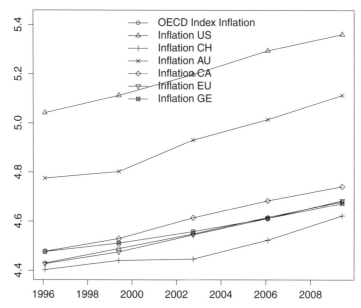

Figure 7.4   Logarithm of time series for inflation and monetary variables (except US M2 and Inflation Brazil)

Logarithm of Inflation and Monetary Indices: US M2 and Inflation BR

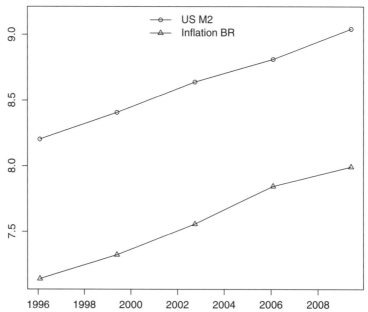

Figure 7.5   Inflation and monetary variables: US M2 and Inflation Brazil

Table 7.2 Unit root test results for the GSCI sub-indices, industrial production, monetary and inflation variables

	ADF None	ADF Drift	ADF Trend	PP Constant	PP Trend	KPSS
GSCI Agri.	−8.5965	−8.6006	−8.6885	−13.1401	−13.1983	0.0308
GSCI Energy	−8.7648	−8.7632	−8.7578	−11.3029	−11.2997	0.0473
GSCI Ind. Metals	−7.4832	−7.5426	−7.5796	−11.0095	−11.0279	0.0757
GSCI Prec. Metals	−10.4528	−11.0234	−11.8022	−15.7345	−16.7938	0.0407
US M2	−2.8570	−6.8931	−6.8518	−10.3996	−10.3736	0.0661
OECD Index Inflation	−6.7599	−8.7509	−8.7336	−7.5931	−7.5706	0.0264
Industrial Production US	−5.8379	−6.0067	−6.2046	−11.0378	−11.3245	0.1112
Inflation US	−6.6637	−9.2071	−9.1812	−8.4595	−8.4342	0.0427
Industrial Production CH	−4.4308	−10.1549	−10.3068	−13.6028	−13.7126	0.1076
Inflation CH	−5.9677	−6.7962	−7.2895	−10.5848	−10.9085	0.1353
Industrial Production BR	−9.4054	−9.5636	−9.5373	−12.9916	−12.9550	0.0233
Inflation BR	−3.3869	−5.9940	−6.0345	−6.3833	−6.4019	0.1278
Industrial Production AU	−9.6923	−10.1436	−10.1178	−14.0240	−14.0226	0.0236
Inflation AU	−9.5159	−14.3953	−14.7282	−17.1996	−17.4439	0.1026
Industrial Production CA	−8.5891	−8.6350	−8.6271	−10.9285	−10.9168	0.0255
Inflation CA	−7.0432	−8.6870	−8.6654	−11.2812	−11.2494	0.0304
Industrial Production EU	−6.8494	−6.9180	−6.9579	−13.1694	−13.1965	0.0538
Inflation EU	−7.8080	−10.2733	−10.2645	−12.0554	−12.0308	0.0495
Industrial Production GE	−8.4634	−8.6225	−8.5971	−14.0966	−14.0637	0.0552
Inflation GE	−8.5411	−10.6193	−10.6968	−18.9745	−19.1241	0.0350

Note: Test statistics are given. ADF stands for the Augmented Dickey–Fuller unit root test, PP for the Phillips–Perron unit root test and KPSS for the Kwiatkowski–Phillips–Schmidt–Shin unit root test. Corresponding critical values (at 5% level) can be found in Greene (2003): −1.9409 for ADF None, −2.8623 for ADF Drift, −3.4114 for ADF Trend, −2.8623 for PP Constant, −3.4114 for PP Trend and 0.4630 for KPSS.

demand triggers extra production effort from companies, which resort to various commodities as an input to their production.[1]

Conversely, in a context of decreasing economic activity, some segments of the economy will be characterized by declining demand, and thus the associated demand in terms of commodities will be lower. We can thus expect cyclical movements in commodity prices, if they are synchronized with economic activity. Obviously, we can also detect counter-cyclical effects. For instance, when industrial production decreases, the price of gold increases as a refuge for value.

With respect to other theories on macroeconomic effects, we can also evoke the hypothesis whereby high commodity prices dampen increases in industrial production, because the prices of goods increase relative to consumers' income. Low commodity prices can also lower costs of production and stimulate the demand for goods, as well as industrial production.

Having these economic mechanisms in mind, we aim at developing cointegration analyses between industrial production in various countries and a broad set of commodity prices. If the evolutions are similar in the long term, then we may think of meaningful economic forces linking these variables over time. Let us start our study of this topic with a brief review of previous academic literature on this subject.

---

[1] Assuming the income elasticity of commodity demand to be near 1.

7.2.1 Literature Review

- Cody and Mills (1991) evaluate the macroeconomic interactions between industrial production in the US and the Commodity Research Bureau (CRB) basket of commodities by using monthly data over the period 1959–1987. To do so, the authors test for cointegration between the two series, and cannot reject the null hypothesis of no cointegration. In a subsequent VAR analysis, while commodity prices do not respond to changes in the macroeconomic variable of interest here, they are significant in explaining the future path of industrial production. Overall, the authors conclude that commodity prices are an early indicator of the current state of the economy.

- Labys and Maizels (1993) resort to Granger causality tests to analyze the commodity price fluctuations and macroeconomic adjustments in developed countries (France, Germany, Italy, Japan, UK, USA) during 1953–1987. They use various IMF commodity indices and the industrial production index to carry out their econometric work. The main results suggest a causality in the direction of commodity prices to industrial production (except for France).

- Labys *et al.* (1999) aim at determining the impact of macroeconomic influences on LME metal price fluctuations during 1971–1995 by using factor models. Their study comprises five industrial metals: aluminum, copper, lead, tin and zinc. Industrial activity was found to influence metal prices most strongly for France, Italy, Japan and the OECD. Hence, the direct influence of industrial production on metal price cycles has been paramount during this time period.

- Hua (1998) establishes the cointegration between commodity prices and economic activity in 22 developed countries during 1970–1993. The results are supportive of the hypothesis that the non-oil primary commodity prices are cointegrated with macroeconomic variables, and that long-run relationships exist between them. The author is also able to confirm the existence of an equilibrium adjustment in commodity prices to macroeconomic shocks through a feedback mechanism. The strong significance of the error correction coefficients supports the view that non-oil primary commodity prices in particular vary together with the fluctuations in economic activity. The results are more complex to interpret for agricultural commodities.

- Awokuse and Yang (2003) report Granger causality test results between IMF commodity indices and US industrial production during 1975–2001. They find unambiguously that commodity prices may provide signals about the future direction of the economy, including inflation and other macroeconomic activities such as industrial production.

- Cunado and de Gracia (2003) examine the oil price–macroeconomy relationship by means of estimating the impact of oil price changes on industrial production indices for 15 European countries during the period 1960–1999. The authors cannot identify a cointegrating long-run relationship between oil prices and economic activity, which suggests that the impact of oil shocks on this variable is limited to the short run. In addition, they do not find evidence of a long-run relationship between these two variables even when allowing for a structural break.[2]

- Bloch *et al.* (2006a; 2006b) examine the linkages between all commodities (exclusive of fuels) as reported in the World Bank's Development Indicators and industrial production data from the OECD countries covering the 102-year period from 1900 to 2001. Their regression results feature that a reduction in the rate of economic growth can lead to reducing the rate

---

[2] In order to capture the oil market collapse which occurred in 1985.

of increase in commodity prices. Hence, according to the authors, there is a weak linkage between world economic growth and the rate of change of commodity prices over the past century.

- Bloch *et al.* (2006a; 2006b) use IMF commodity indices and industrial production indices to show that world commodity prices move pro-cyclically with world industrial production. Their study validates the link between the use of commodities such as raw materials and increases in industrial production in the case of Australia and Canada during 1960–2001.

- Pieroni and Ricciarelli (2005) utilize 1955–2000 US copper data to investigate the properties of a vector error-correction model extended to macroeconomic variables such as industrial production.[3] It can be shown that price adjustments depend on the short-run dynamic component of the model, whereas the long-run dynamic is statistically rejected. Hence, there is no cointegration between copper and industrial production during this time period.

- Ai *et al.* (2006) examine the interactions between five agricultural commodity prices (wheat, barley, corn, oats, soybean) and US industrial production during 1957–2002. They fail to identify significant cointegration relationships between macro indicators such as industrial production and agricultural commodity prices in this setting.

- Cheung and Morin (2007) evaluate the cointegration between the Bank of Canada Commodity Price Index and industrial production in the OECD during 1980–2006, with the possible occurrence of structural breaks. While the authors cannot detect statistically the presence of cointegration, they highlight the role played by emerging Asia's industrial activity in driving the price of oil and industrial metals in particular.[4]

- Hamori (2007) provides Granger causality tests between the Bank of Japan Commodity Price Index and industrial production in Japan during 1990–2005. The author finds no causal relationships between the Bank of Japan commodity index and the industrial production index, even when considering a structural break in February 1999.

- Bhar and Hamori (2008) analyze whether commodity prices (Commodity Research Bureau indicator) have causal relationships with industrial production, and vice versa by using monthly US data during 1957–2005. Based on Granger causality tests, the authors validate the hypothesis that commodity price indices provide information on future changes in production.

These results are usefully summarized in Table 7.3. Despite the existence of a strong economic theory background to link commodity prices with industrial production, we observe overall that the conclusions of these various empirical studies seem to vary depending on the commodity, the country and the period considered. We attempt to replicate the best available evidence to date, i.e. the most successful cointegration relationships identified in previous academic literature, in our own empirical application.

Let us start classically with Granger causality tests.

7.2.2   Results of Granger Causality Tests Between the GSCI Sub-Indices and Industrial Production

Pairwise Granger causality tests (with one lag) for the GSCI and industrial production variables are given in Tables 7.4 to 7.6. The main results may be summarized as follows. Concerning the

---

[3] When analyzing US copper consumption, the authors identify two important industrial demands: (i) refined copper is largely used in wire rod mills, while brass mills prefer using copper scraps, and (ii) wire rod mills and brass mills are both used for the production of cathodes.

[4] As manufacturing activity has been increasingly outsourced for production in that region since 1997.

Table 7.3   Industrial production and commodity prices: cointegrating relationships

Authors	Period	Cointegration Relationship	SS	SB
Cody and Mills (1991)	1959–1987	US Ind. Prod. Ø CRB	No	No
Labys and Maizels (1993)	1953–1987	IMF Commodity Indices ↔ Ind. Prod. (OECD)	No	No
Labys et al. (1999)	1971–1995	Aluminum, Copper, Lead, Tin, Zinc ↔ Ind. Prod. (OECD)	No	No
Hua (1998)	1970–1993	IMF Commodity Indices ↔ Ind. Prod. (OECD)	No	No
Awokuse and Yang (2003)	1975–2001	IMF Commodity Indices ↔ Ind. Prod. (US)	No	No
Cunado and de Gracia (2003)	1960–1999	Oil Ø Ind. Prod. (Europe)	No	Yes
Bloch et al. (2006a; 2006b)	1900–2001	WB Commodity Prices Ø Ind. Prod. (OECD)	No	No
Bloch et al. (2006a; 2006b)	1960–2001	IMF Commodity Indices ↔ Ind. Prod. (AU, CA)	No	No
Pieroni and Ricciarelli (2005)	1955–2000	Copper Ø Ind. Prod. (US)	No	No
Ai et al. (2006)	1957–2002	Wheat, Barley, Corn, Oats, Soybean Ø Ind. Prod. (US)	No	No
Cheung and Morin (2007)	1980–2006	BoC Commodity Price Index Ø Ind. Prod. (OECD)	Yes	Yes
Hamori (2007)	1990–2005	BoJ Commodity Price Index Ø Ind. Prod. (JA)	Yes	No
Bhar and Hamori (2008)	1957–2005	CRB ↔ Ind. Prod. (US)	No	No

Note: ↔ indicates the presence of a cointegration relationship. Ø indicates the absence of a cointegration relationship. SS stands for 'Sub Sample' analysis in the paper considered. SB stands for 'Structural Break' analysis in the paper considered. Ind. Prod. is for Industrial Production. AU stands for Australia, CA for Canada, BoC for Bank of Canada, JA for Japan, BoJ for Bank of Japan, WB for World Bank.

GSCI sub-indices (Table 7.4), we can notice that the GSCI Agricultural sub-index has many Granger causalities with the industrial production variables in China, Brazil, Canada and the EU (at the 5% level). The same can be said for the GSCI Energy sub-index in all countries (at the 10% level). In the case of industrial metals, the industrial production variables which reveal Granger causalities can be found in all countries except Australia and Canada. Finally, precious metals appear to cause, in the Granger sense, only the US and Chinese industrial production variables (at the 5% level). Overall, we highlight significant interactions between the GSCI sub-indices and the selected industrial production proxies, which may bring fruitful results during our cointegration analysis.

Interestingly, concerning the industrial production variables (Tables 7.5 and 7.6), the reverse Granger causalities seem to hold as well. In the case of the US Industrial Production index, we uncover, for instance, a clear effect on the four GSCI sub-indices (at the 5% level). In China, industrial production seems to Granger cause the GSCI Energy and Industrial Metals sub-indices, thereby illustrating the link between sustained consumption of raw materials and economic growth. However, we are unable to find significant Granger causalities from the industrial production indices in the other countries. We do not comment here on the interactions between industrial production variables themselves, but they are readily available to the reader in these tables.

7.2.3   Cointegration Analyses for Industrial Production and Commodity Prices

To study the relationship between industrial production and commodity prices in the cointegration framework, we have attempted to reproduce most of the results from previous literature based on our updated dataset.

By following the methodology outlined in Chapter 5, we consider systematically cointegration with sub-samples and with structural breaks.

Table 7.4 Pairwise Granger causality tests for the GSCI sub-indices and industrial production variables (1/3)

From	To	p-value	F-statistic
GSCI Agri.	GSCI Energy	0.3791	0.3791
GSCI Agri.	GSCI Ind. Metals	0.5260	0.5260
GSCI Agri.	GSCI Prec. Metals	0.1426	0.1426
GSCI Agri.	Industrial Production US	0.9718	0.9718
GSCI Agri.	Industrial Production CH	0.0067	0.0067
GSCI Agri.	Industrial Production BR	0.0033	0.0033
GSCI Agri.	Industrial Production AU	0.2178	0.2178
GSCI Agri.	Industrial Production CA	0.0804	0.0804
GSCI Agri.	Industrial Production EU	0.0419	0.0419
GSCI Agri.	Industrial Production GE	0.2917	0.2917
GSCI Energy	GSCI Agri.	0.7361	0.7361
GSCI Energy	GSCI Ind. Metals	0.2698	0.2698
GSCI Energy	GSCI Prec. Metals	0.6795	0.6795
GSCI Energy	Industrial Production US	0.0279	0.0279
GSCI Energy	Industrial Production CH	0.0551	0.0551
GSCI Energy	Industrial Production BR	0.0001	0.0001
GSCI Energy	Industrial Production AU	0.0758	0.0758
GSCI Energy	Industrial Production CA	0.0062	0.0062
GSCI Energy	Industrial Production EU	0.0015	0.0015
GSCI Energy	Industrial Production GE	0.0014	0.0014
GSCI Ind. Metals	GSCI Agri.	0.4684	0.4684
GSCI Ind. Metals	GSCI Energy	0.0900	0.0900
GSCI Ind. Metals	GSCI Prec. Metals	0.8518	0.8518
GSCI Ind. Metals	Industrial Production US	0.0091	0.0091
GSCI Ind. Metals	Industrial Production CH	0.0002	0.0002
GSCI Ind. Metals	Industrial Production BR	0.0006	0.0006
GSCI Ind. Metals	Industrial Production AU	0.2300	0.2300
GSCI Ind. Metals	Industrial Production CA	0.1036	0.1036
GSCI Ind. Metals	Industrial Production EU	0.0000	0.0000
GSCI Ind. Metals	Industrial Production GE	0.0000	0.0000
GSCI Prec. Metals	GSCI Agri.	0.2556	0.2556
GSCI Prec. Metals	GSCI Energy	0.2675	0.2675
GSCI Prec. Metals	GSCI Ind. Metals	0.7136	0.7136
GSCI Prec. Metals	Industrial Production US	0.0276	0.0276
GSCI Prec. Metals	Industrial Production CH	0.0031	0.0031
GSCI Prec. Metals	Industrial Production BR	0.1767	0.1767
GSCI Prec. Metals	Industrial Production AU	0.6363	0.6363
GSCI Prec. Metals	Industrial Production CA	0.5210	0.5210
GSCI Prec. Metals	Industrial Production EU	0.1771	0.1771
GSCI Prec. Metals	Industrial Production GE	0.2510	0.2510

Note: The p-value and the F-statistic of the pairwise Granger causality tests between X and Y are given. The null hypothesis is that X does not Granger cause Y. US stands for USA, CH for China, BR for Brazil, AU for Australia, CA for Canada, EU for European Union and GE for Germany.

Table 7.5 Pairwise Granger causality tests for the GSCI sub-indices and industrial production variables (2/3)

From	To	p-value	F-statistic
Industrial Production US	GSCI Agri.	0.0087	0.0087
Industrial Production US	GSCI Energy	0.0004	0.0004
Industrial Production US	GSCI Ind. Metals	0.0168	0.0168
Industrial Production US	GSCI Prec. Metals	0.0238	0.0238
Industrial Production US	Industrial Production CH	0.2685	0.2685
Industrial Production US	Industrial Production BR	0.3901	0.3901
Industrial Production US	Industrial Production AU	0.1320	0.1320
Industrial Production US	Industrial Production CA	0.8438	0.8438
Industrial Production US	Industrial Production EU	0.0000	0.0000
Industrial Production US	Industrial Production GE	0.0008	0.0008
Industrial Production CH	GSCI Agri.	0.1538	0.1538
Industrial Production CH	GSCI Energy	0.0286	0.0286
Industrial Production CH	GSCI Ind. Metals	0.0034	0.0034
Industrial Production CH	GSCI Prec. Metals	0.3711	0.3711
Industrial Production CH	Industrial Production US	0.1591	0.1591
Industrial Production CH	Industrial Production BR	0.0254	0.0254
Industrial Production CH	Industrial Production AU	0.7295	0.7295
Industrial Production CH	Industrial Production CA	0.0202	0.0202
Industrial Production CH	Industrial Production EU	0.1976	0.1976
Industrial Production CH	Industrial Production GE	0.9757	0.9757
Industrial Production BR	GSCI Agri.	0.7931	0.7931
Industrial Production BR	GSCI Energy	0.3151	0.3151
Industrial Production BR	GSCI Ind. Metals	0.3772	0.3772
Industrial Production BR	GSCI Prec. Metals	0.2167	0.2167
Industrial Production BR	Industrial Production US	0.0032	0.0032
Industrial Production BR	Industrial Production CH	0.0567	0.0567
Industrial Production BR	Industrial Production AU	0.9412	0.9412
Industrial Production BR	Industrial Production CA	0.6435	0.6435
Industrial Production BR	Industrial Production EU	0.0002	0.0002
Industrial Production BR	Industrial Production GE	0.0000	0.0000
Industrial Production AU	GSCI Agri.	0.8603	0.8603
Industrial Production AU	GSCI Energy	0.9800	0.9800
Industrial Production AU	GSCI Ind. Metals	0.4409	0.4409
Industrial Production AU	GSCI Prec. Metals	0.2151	0.2151
Industrial Production AU	Industrial Production US	0.2528	0.2528
Industrial Production AU	Industrial Production CH	0.4796	0.4796
Industrial Production AU	Industrial Production BR	0.2237	0.2237
Industrial Production AU	Industrial Production CA	0.9728	0.9728
Industrial Production AU	Industrial Production EU	0.0128	0.0128
Industrial Production AU	Industrial Production GE	0.0073	0.0073

Note: The p-value and the F-statistic of the pairwise Granger causality tests between X and Y are given. The null hypothesis is that X does not Granger cause Y. US stands for USA, CH for China, BR for Brazil, AU for Australia, CA for Canada, EU for European Union and GE for Germany.

Table 7.6   Pairwise Granger causality tests for the GSCI sub-indices and industrial production variables (3/3)

From	To	p-value	F-statistic
Industrial Production CA	GSCI Agri.	0.2819	0.2819
Industrial Production CA	GSCI Energy	0.3920	0.3920
Industrial Production CA	GSCI Ind. Metals	0.2820	0.2820
Industrial Production CA	GSCI Prec. Metals	0.8775	0.8775
Industrial Production CA	Industrial Production US	0.7092	0.7092
Industrial Production CA	Industrial Production CH	0.6315	0.6315
Industrial Production CA	Industrial Production BR	0.1560	0.1560
Industrial Production CA	Industrial Production AU	0.1772	0.1772
Industrial Production CA	Industrial Production EU	0.0941	0.0941
Industrial Production CA	Industrial Production GE	0.0667	0.0667
Industrial Production EU	GSCI Agri.	0.5845	0.5845
Industrial Production EU	GSCI Energy	0.2005	0.2005
Industrial Production EU	GSCI Ind. Metals	0.7135	0.7135
Industrial Production EU	GSCI Prec. Metals	0.2673	0.2673
Industrial Production EU	Industrial Production US	0.0000	0.0000
Industrial Production EU	Industrial Production CH	0.2563	0.2563
Industrial Production EU	Industrial Production BR	0.4298	0.4298
Industrial Production EU	Industrial Production AU	0.0851	0.0851
Industrial Production EU	Industrial Production CA	0.3794	0.3794
Industrial Production EU	Industrial Production GE	0.0060	0.0060
Industrial Production GE	GSCI Agri.	0.2499	0.2499
Industrial Production GE	GSCI Energy	0.6030	0.6030
Industrial Production GE	GSCI Ind. Metals	0.5240	0.5240
Industrial Production GE	GSCI Prec. Metals	0.2996	0.2996
Industrial Production GE	Industrial Production US	0.0139	0.0139
Industrial Production GE	Industrial Production CH	0.4698	0.4698
Industrial Production GE	Industrial Production BR	0.6221	0.6221
Industrial Production GE	Industrial Production AU	0.1041	0.1041
Industrial Production GE	Industrial Production CA	0.9184	0.9184
Industrial Production GE	Industrial Production EU	0.3349	0.3349

Note: The p-value and the F-statistic of the pairwise Granger causality tests between X and Y are given. The null hypothesis is that X does not Granger cause Y. US stands for USA, CH for China, BR for Brazil, AU for Australia, CA for Canada, EU for European Union and GE for Germany.

The main findings are summarized in Table 7.7.

7.2.3.1   GSCI Sub-Indices and Industrial Production in the US

Let us start by looking at the relationship between GSCI sub-indices (Agricultural Products, Industrial Metals, Precious Metals, Energy Markets) and the US Industrial Production index. The US economy could be considered in this setting as a proxy for world GDP (or economic activity) growth. Table 7.7 tells us that one cointegration relationship exists during the first sub-period (1993–2000), as well as during the full period 1993–2011 with the occurrence of one structural break.

To conserve space, we reproduce in what follows the results of the best model only, i.e. the econometric model which is the most satisfactory statistically speaking.[5]

---

[5] Additional results can be obtained upon request.

Table 7.7   Cointegration analyses of industrial production and commodity prices: summary of the main results

Period	Cointegration Relationship	SB
1993–2011	GSCI Sub-Indices Ø Industrial Production US	No
1993–2000	GSCI Sub-Indices ↔ Industrial Production US	No
2000–2011	GSCI Sub-Indices Ø Industrial Production US	No
1993–2011	GSCI Sub-Indices ↔ Industrial Production US	Yes
1993–2011	GSCI Sub-Indices Ø Industrial Production CH	No
1993–2000	GSCI Sub-Indices Ø Industrial Production CH	No
2000–2011	GSCI Sub-Indices Ø Industrial Production CH	No
1993–2011	GSCI Sub-Indices ↔ Industrial Production CH	Yes
1993–2011	GSCI Sub-Indices ↔ Industrial Production BR	No
1993–2000	GSCI Sub-Indices Ø Industrial Production BR	No
2000–2011	GSCI Sub-Indices Ø Industrial Production BR	No
1993–2011	GSCI Sub-Indices ↔ Industrial Production BR	Yes
1993–2011	GSCI Sub-Indices Ø Industrial Production AU	No
1993–2000	GSCI Sub-Indices Ø Industrial Production AU	No
2000–2011	GSCI Sub-Indices Ø Industrial Production AU	No
1993–2011	GSCI Sub-Indices ↔ Industrial Production AU	Yes
1993–2011	GSCI Sub-Indices ↔ Industrial Production CA	No
1993–2000	GSCI Sub-Indices Ø Industrial Production CA	No
2000–2011	GSCI Sub-Indices ↔ Industrial Production CA	No
1993–2011	GSCI Sub-Indices ↔ Industrial Production CA	Yes
1993–2011	GSCI Sub-Indices Ø Industrial Production EU	No
1993–2000	GSCI Sub-Indices Ø Industrial Production EU	No
2000–2011	GSCI Sub-Indices Ø Industrial Production EU	No
1993–2011	GSCI Sub-Indices ↔ Industrial Production EU	Yes
1993–2011	GSCI Sub-Indices Ø Industrial Production GE	No
1993–2000	GSCI Sub-Indices Ø Industrial Production GE	No
2000–2011	GSCI Sub-Indices Ø Industrial Production GE	No
1993–2011	GSCI Sub-Indices ↔ Industrial Production GE	Yes
1993–2011	Aluminum ↔ Copper ↔ Lead ↔ Zinc ↔ Industrial Production US	No
1993–2000	Aluminum Ø Copper Ø Lead Ø Zinc Ø Industrial Production US	No
2000–2011	Aluminum ↔ Copper ↔ Lead ↔ Zinc ↔ Industrial Production US	No
1993–2011	Aluminum ↔ Copper ↔ Lead ↔ Zinc ↔ Industrial Production US	Yes
1993–2011	Copper ↔ Industrial Production US	No
1993–2000	Copper ↔ Industrial Production US	No
2000–2011	Copper ↔ Industrial Production US	No
1993–2011	Copper ↔ Industrial Production US	Yes
1993–2011	Wheat ↔ Corn ↔ Soybean ↔ Industrial Production US	No
1993–2000	Wheat ↔ Corn ↔ Soybean ↔ Industrial Production US	No
2000–2011	Wheat Ø Corn Ø Soybean Ø Industrial Production US	No
1993–2011	Wheat ↔ Corn ↔ Soybean ↔ Industrial Production US	Yes
1993–2011	Oil Ø Industrial Production EU	No
1993–2000	Oil Ø Industrial Production EU	No
2000–2011	Oil Ø Industrial Production EU	No
1993–2011	Oil ↔ Industrial Production EU	Yes

Note: ↔ indicates the presence of a cointegration relationship. Ø indicates the absence of a cointegration relationship. SB stands for 'Structural Break' analysis. US stands for USA, CH for China, BR for Brazil, AU for Australia, CA for Canada, EU for European Union and GE for Germany.

Table 7.8 Lütkepohl *et al.* (2004) cointegration test results with structural break for GSCI sub-indices and industrial production US

1993–2011	Max. Eigen.	10%	5%	1%
$r \leq 4$	1.62	5.42	6.79	10.04
$r \leq 3$	7.96	13.78	15.83	19.85
$r \leq 2$	18.40	25.93	28.45	33.76
$r \leq 1$	42.37	42.08	45.2	51.6
$r = 0$	72.10	61.92	65.66	73.12

In our current setting, the best results were obtained with the full sample estimates in the presence of one structural break. Hence, we shall comment on these results below.

First, we verify in Table 7.8 that at least one cointegration relationship exists between the GSCI sub-indices and the US Industrial Production index, i.e. the rank of the cointegration r is at least equal to 1 (at the 5% level).

Second, we obtain the VECM estimates as reproduced in Table 7.9. They show, by and large, that the VECM has been correctly specified, since three error-correction terms are negative (GSCI Agri., GSCI Energy, Prod. Ind. US). However, only the ECT for the US Industrial Production index is statistically significant (at the 1% level), which implies that the deviations from the long-term equilibrium are solely corrected by the macroeconomic variable in this system. This result means that variations in the industrial production index in the US are able to correct for the short-term deviations in the various commodity markets, provided that a long-term and meaningful relationship between these variables indeed exists.

Table 7.9 VECM results with structural break (1993–2011) for GSCI sub-indices and industrial production US

Error-Correction Term					
GSCI Agri.	1				
GSCI Ind. Met.	−0.642				
GSCI Prec. Met.	−1.008				
GSCI Energy	0.178				
Prod. Ind. US	−0.323				

VECM	ΔGSCI Agri.	ΔGSCI Ind. Met.	ΔPrec. Met.	ΔGSCI Energy	ΔProd. Ind. US
ECT	−0.045	0.079	0.100	−0.043	−0.015
(*t*.stat)	(−1.29)	(1.68)	(3.30)	(−0.85)	(−4.18)
ΔGSCI Agri.(−1)	0.065	0.116	0.142	0.058	−0.014
(*t*.stat)	(0.75)	(0.99)	(1.86)	(0.46)	(−1.60)
ΔGSCI Ind. Met.(−1)	−0.048	0.043	0.006	0.211	0.001
(*t*.stat)	(−0.66)	(0.43)	(0.09)	(1.98)	(0.02)
ΔGSCI Prec. Met.(−1)	0.142	0.053	−0.056	−0.134	0.003
(*t*.stat)	(1.36)	(0.38)	(−0.62)	(−0.88)	(0.29)
ΔGSCI Energy(−1)	−0.087	−0.016	−0.066	0.124	0.015
(*t*.stat)	(−1.76)	(−0.23)	(−1.53)	(1.71)	(2.95)
ΔProd. Ind. US(−1)	1.529	2.513	1.934	2.337	0.189
(*t*.stat)	(2.11)	(2.58)	(3.06)	(2.22)	(2.60)

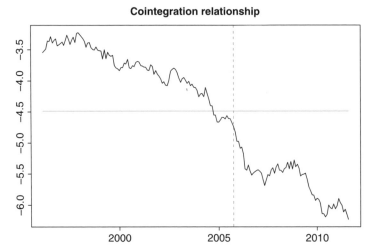

Figure 7.6 Cointegration relationship with structural break for GSCI sub-indices and industrial production US

Third, we examine the validity of the cointegration relation in Figure 7.6. This graph clearly shows that the relationship is not stationary over the 1993–2011 full period. On the contrary, it is downward sloping with the presence of one structural break on September 30, 2005. Therefore, we cannot consider that the cointegration exercise between the GSCI sub-indices and the US Industrial Production index has been successful from an econometric viewpoint. Indeed, some key characteristics of cointegration are missing, such as the presence of several negative and significant ECTs, as well as the stationarity of the long-term relationship observed.

With respect to previous literature on this subject, we agree with the early findings by Cody and Mills (1991) pointing out the absence of a cointegration relationship between the US Industrial index and commodity indices during 1959–1987. However, our results contradict the findings by Awokuse and Yang (2003) – who used IMF indices instead of GSCI indices – during 1975–2001, and those of Bhar and Hamori (2008) – who used CRB indices – during 1957–2005. We believe that the systematic inclusion of sub-periods and structural breaks enriches the results in this literature. Besides, we use an updated database compared to these latter authors to account for the effect of the 2008 financial crisis in the adjustment mechanism under consideration.

7.2.3.2   GSCI Sub-Indices and Industrial Production in China

Next, we consider the relationship between the GSCI sub-indices and the Chinese industrial production index. This region is of particular interest, since China has recorded the world's fastest growing GDP rate over the last two decades. Hence, it attracts much of the demand in terms of raw materials and primary commodities for production and construction. We learn from Table 7.7 that only one cointegration relationship could be detected during the full period with the modeling of one structural break.

Table 7.10 confirms this view, i.e. the rank of the cointegration r is equal to at least 1 (at the 5% confidence level).

Table 7.10   Lütkepohl *et al.* (2004) cointegration test results with structural break for GSCI sub-indices and industrial production CH

1993–2011	Max. Eigen.	10%	5%	1%
$r \leq 4$	4.68	5.42	6.79	10.04
$r \leq 3$	12.58	13.78	15.83	19.85
$r \leq 2$	24.19	25.93	28.45	33.76
$r \leq 1$	39.90	42.08	45.2	51.6
$r = 0$	67.47	61.92	65.66	73.12

In Table 7.11, the VECM estimates provide very interesting results. Indeed, four (out of five) error-correction terms are negative. Two of them are highly significant (at the 1% level) for GSCI Agricultural Products and GSCI Industrial Metals. One of them is barely significant (at the 10% level). However, in this practical example, the ECT for the Chinese industrial production index is negative but not significant. We could infer that the economic logic whereby higher demand from the industry translates into higher consumption of raw materials does not hold in the context of China. On the contrary, the variation of the commodity sub-indices in agricultural and industrial metals markets (and to a lesser extent in energy markets) is found to correct the deviations from the long-term equilibrium in this system of equations. Therefore, this result is both original and surprising, since we could have intuitively expected opposite effects.

When examining the cointegration relationship in Figure 7.7, we notice that it is stationary before and after the structural break detected on September 30, 2008. This break could be characteristic of the commodity price boom and bust during the summer of 2008. Consequently,

Table 7.11   VECM results with structural break (1993–2011) for GSCI sub-indices and industrial production CH

Error-Correction Term					
GSCI Agri.	1				
GSCI Ind. Met.	0.470				
GSCI Prec. Met.	−2.154				
GSCI Energy	0.189				
Prod. Ind. CH	1.280				

VECM	ΔGSCI Agri.	ΔGSCI Ind. Met.	ΔPrec. Met.	ΔGSCI Energy	ΔProd. Ind. CH
ECT	−0.076	−0.081	0.059	−0.087	−0.004
(*t*.stat)	(−2.51)	(−2.94)	(2.25)	(−1.54)	(−0.97)
ΔGSCI Agri.(−1)	−0.018	0.073	0.076	0.227	0.013
(*t*.stat)	(−0.23)	(1.00)	(1.10)	(1.53)	(1.10)
ΔGSCI Ind. Met.(−1)	−0.007	0.057	−0.073	0.051	0.025
(*t*.stat)	(−0.09)	(0.74)	(−1.00)	(0.32)	(2.01)
ΔGSCI Prec. Met.(−1)	0.137	0.027	0.108	−0.360	0.036
(*t*.stat)	(1.35)	(0.30)	(1.24)	(−1.93)	(2.41)
ΔGSCI Energy(−1)	−0.057	−0.056	−0.059	−0.058	0.001
(*t*.stat)	(−1.33)	(−1.44)	(−1.60)	(−0.73)	(0.20)
ΔProd. Ind. CH(−1)	0.737	1.533	0.891	1.768	−0.051
(*t*.stat)	(1.47)	(3.39)	(2.07)	(1.91)	(−0.69)

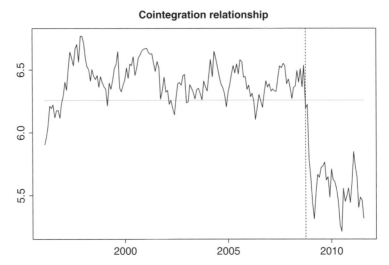

Figure 7.7 Cointegration relationship with structural break for GSCI sub-indices and industrial production CH

we conclude our analysis of the relationship between the GSCI sub-indices and the Chinese industrial production index by uncovering new (original) but also puzzling results. On the one hand, we have been able to estimate satisfactorily a VECM between these variables. On the other hand, the results contradict the macroeconomy–commodity markets view, whereby changes in industrial production induce a higher demand, and thus higher consumption of commodities. Why agricultural and industrial metals prices are able to act as a feedback mechanism when faced with deviations from the long-term equilibrium in this system needs to be investigated with further research on this topic.

To the best of our knowledge, most of the results (as well as subsequent results on OECD countries) are new with respect to the econometric methodology used and the sample data contained in this study.

7.2.3.3   GSCI Sub-Indices and Industrial Production in Brazil

Brazil constitutes another area of potential strong economic growth, in terms of associated commodity demand as well. We examine here the link between the various GSCI sub-indices and the Brazilian industrial production index. In Table 7.7, we detect two cointegration relationships during the full period with and without a structural break. We reproduce below the results obtained during 1993–2011 with a break.

In Table 7.12, we verify that the null hypothesis of no cointegration between the variables of interest can be safely rejected (at the 1% level).

Table 7.13 contains the VECM estimates. Again, we obtain mostly satisfactory results, since four error-correction terms (out of five) record a negative sign. Among them, the ECTs for the GSCI Industrial Metals and the Brazilian industrial production index are statistically significant at the 1% level. Unlike in the Chinese case, we highlight here that a clear mechanism exists linking the variation of commodity prices and economic activity in the long term. The feedback mechanism governing the adjustment of short-term deviations from the long-term equilibrium

Table 7.12   Lütkepohl *et al.* (2004) cointegration test results with structural break for GSCI sub-indices and industrial production BR

1993–2011	Max. Eigen.	10%	5%	1%
$r \leq 4$	6.48	5.42	6.79	10.04
$r \leq 3$	14.73	13.78	15.83	19.85
$r \leq 2$	27.64	25.93	28.45	33.76
$r \leq 1$	52.10	42.08	45.2	51.6
$r = 0$	85.65	61.92	65.66	73.12

is driven in this setting by the demand for industrial metals and the level of industrial production. These results correspond to the following intuitive reasoning: in a context of high demand for goods, industrial production capacities are tense, and hence the demand for raw materials is high (and vice versa). If some categories of commodity markets do not fit temporarily in this price profile, then the long-term relationship between the macroeconomic and commodity variables will be restored by the variation of the industrial production index and the variation of industrial metals prices. By looking at the magnitude of the coefficients for the ECTs, we could even state that the feedback mechanism coming from industrial metals (-0.043) is slightly stronger than that coming from the industrial production index (-0.020).

The last step to confirm the validity of this model is to examine the cointegration relationship, which is pictured in Figure 7.8. Despite the occurrence of one structural break on September 30, 2008 (which could also be due to the episode of strong price adjustment of all commodities to the economic context of financial crisis), we clearly observe visually that the relationship is stable and stationary in each of the two regimes highlighted by the structural break test. Hence,

Table 7.13   VECM results with structural break (1993–2011) for GSCI sub-indices and industrial production BR

Error-Correction Term					
GSCI Agri.	1				
GSCI Ind. Met.	0.133				
GSCI Prec. Met.	-2.815				
GSCI Energy	-0.349				
Prod. Ind. BR	11.854				

VECM	ΔGSCI Agri.	ΔGSCI Ind. Met.	ΔPrec. Met.	ΔGSCI Energy	ΔProd. Ind. BR
ECT	-0.014	-0.043	0.011	-0.010	-0.020
(*t*.stat)	(-1.07)	(-3.68)	(1.01)	(-0.43)	(-5.23)
ΔGSCI Agri.(-1)	-0.017	0.096	0.104	0.248	0.055
(*t*.stat)	(-0.21)	(1.31)	(1.49)	(1.65)	(2.28)
ΔGSCI Ind. Met.(-1)	-0.003	0.007	-0.061	0.072	0.014
(*t*.stat)	(-0.03)	(0.09)	(-0.78)	(0.43)	(0.53)
ΔGSCI Prec. Met.(-1)	0.230	0.110	0.090	-0.212	-0.036
(*t*.stat)	(2.30)	(1.24)	(1.06)	(-1.16)	(-1.24)
ΔGSCI Energy(-1)	-0.072	-0.078	-0.054	-0.079	0.027
(*t*.stat)	(-1.63)	(-1.96)	(-1.44)	(-0.98)	(2.08)
ΔProd. Ind. BR(-1)	0.116	0.474	-0.095	0.101	0.058
(*t*.stat)	(0.45)	(2.07)	(-0.44)	(0.21)	(0.78)

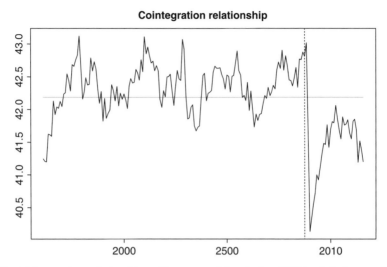

Figure 7.8 Cointegration relationship with structural break for GSCI sub-indices and industrial production BR

we can confirm that the VECM is valid concerning the relationship between the GSCI sub-indices and the Brazilian industrial production index. This cointegration exercise has brought us a wealth of insights, since we have been able to validate empirically the macroeconomy–commodity markets link in Brazil.

7.2.3.4   GSCI Sub-Indices and Industrial Production in Australia

Moving to the adjustment between industrial production in Australia and the GSCI sub-indices, we obtain from Table 7.7 that a cointegration relationship could only be detected during the 1993–2011 full period with the modeling of a structural break.

Table 7.14 reveals that the rank of the cointegration r between these variables is at least equal to 1 (i.e. $r = 1$) at the 1% level.

The VECM reproduced in Table 7.15 provides fruitful results. Indeed, four error-correction terms (except for precious metals) are negative. GSCI Industrial Metals stand out as the most significant variable (at the 1% level), followed by the GSCI Agricultural Products and the Australian industrial production index (at the 5% level). The GSCI Energy Prices are close to the 10% significance level. The economic logic developed in the case of Brazil seems to

Table 7.14   Lütkepohl *et al.* (2004) cointegration test results with structural break for GSCI sub-indices and industrial production AU

1993–2011	Max. Eigen.	10%	5%	1%
$r \leq 4$	5.20	5.42	6.79	10.04
$r \leq 3$	14.30	13.78	15.83	19.85
$r \leq 2$	27.81	25.93	28.45	33.76
$r \leq 1$	49.08	42.08	45.2	51.6
$r = 0$	82.66	61.92	65.66	73.12

Table 7.15 VECM results with structural break (1993–2011) for GSCI sub-indices and industrial production AU

Error-Correction Term					
GSCI Agri.	1				
GSCI Ind. Met.	0.646				
GSCI Prec. Met.	−1.745				
GSCI Energy	0.162				
Prod. Ind. AU	8.625				

VECM	ΔGSCI Agri.	ΔGSCI Ind. Met.	ΔPrec. Met.	ΔGSCI Energy	ΔProd. Ind. AU
ECT	−0.052	−0.123	0.004	−0.067	−0.006
(*t*.stat)	(−2.05)	(−5.65)	(0.20)	(−1.45)	(−2.07)
ΔGSCI Agri.(−1)	0.005	0.013	0.095	0.266	0.017
(*t*.stat)	(0.06)	(1.85)	(1.35)	(1.77)	(1.70)
ΔGSCI Ind. Met.(−1)	−0.026	−0.016	−0.076	0.032	−0.001
(*t*.stat)	(−0.30)	(−0.21)	(−0.98)	(0.20)	(−0.11)
ΔGSCI Prec. Met.(−1)	0.194	0.020	0.066	−0.286	−0.024
(*t*.stat)	(1.93)	(0.23)	(0.77)	(−1.55)	(−2.01)
ΔGSCI Energy(−1)	−0.059	−0.037	−0.052	−0.057	0.007
(*t*.stat)	(−1.33)	(−0.98)	(−1.37)	(−0.70)	(1.28)
ΔProd. Ind. AU(−1)	0.369	−0.121	−0.633	−0.366	−0.018
(*t*.stat)	(0.59)	(−0.22)	(−1.17)	(−0.32)	(−0.24)

apply in the case of Australia as well. In a context of high economic growth (and associated tensions on industrial production capacities), the demand for commodities is inherently higher which triggers price adjustments, especially in the agricultural and industrial metals sectors. The magnitude of the ECTs is the strongest for industrial metals (−0.123), which implies that the feedback mechanism occurs especially through this channel. However, we verify as well that changes in macroeconomic conditions (i.e. industrial production) in Australia are able to produce adjustment mechanisms in the long term. Also, we may suggest another interpretation: Australia has become one of the main exporters of industrial metals over the period in question. Therefore, when the worldwide demand for industrial metals falls, the Australian economy may be adversely impacted.

This hypothesis of a macroeconomic link in Australia with commodity markets is further validated by the stationarity of the cointegration relationship, which is visible in Figure 7.9. Indeed, it appears stable during each of the two regimes separated by the structural break date on September 30, 2008. Hence, we can make a strong case for linkages between macroeconomic variables and commodity markets (in various segments such as agricultural products, industrial metals and perhaps even energy markets) in the Australian region.

Our results conform to the previous findings by Bloch *et al.* (2006a; 2006b), who found evidence in favor of a cointegration relationship between IMF commodity indices and industrial production in Australia during 1960–2001.

7.2.3.5 *GSCI Sub-Indices and Industrial Production in Canada*

In the case of the Canadian economy, we uncover in Table 7.7 the existence of cointegration relationships between its industrial production index and the GSCI sub-indices in all

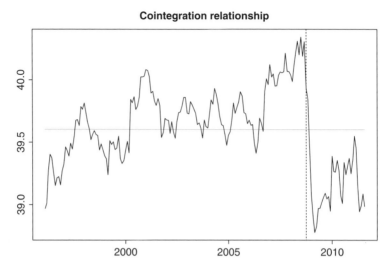

Figure 7.9 Cointegration relationship with structural break for GSCI sub-indices and industrial production AU

specifications (except the first 1993–2000 sub-period). In what follows, we choose to reproduce the results relative to the 1993–2011 full period with one break.

Table 7.16 states that there exists at least one cointegration relationship between the GSCI sub-indices and the Canadian industrial production index (at the 1% level).

The VECM estimates shown in Table 7.17 are extremely satisfactory. In this specification, all error-correction terms are negative. Three of them are statistically significant: the Canadian industrial production index and the GSCI Agricultural Products sub-index (at the 1% level), as well as the GSCI Industrial Metals sub-index (at the 5% level). By examining the magnitude of the ECTs, we can establish in this setting that agricultural products produce the strongest feedback mechanism (−0.051). It is therefore very interesting to confirm for a fourth world region that the link between the macroeconomy and the commodity markets holds. In light of the Canadian economy, it can indeed be said that the Industrial Production index, Agricultural Products and Industrial Metals prices will correct any deviations from the long-term equilibrium in this system. Thus, the existence of a meaningful economic mechanism can be inferred from this cointegration exercise: in the long run, the variation in industrial production is able to trigger price adjustment in commodity prices (as an input to production). The size of the

Table 7.16 Lütkepohl *et al.* (2004) cointegration test results with structural break for GSCI sub-indices and industrial production CA

1993–2011	Max. Eigen.	10%	5%	1%
$r \leq 4$	5.54	5.42	6.79	10.04
$r \leq 3$	12.89	13.78	15.83	19.85
$r \leq 2$	31.09	25.93	28.45	33.76
$r \leq 1$	57.88	42.08	45.2	51.6
$r = 0$	88.94	61.92	65.66	73.12

Table 7.17 VECM results with structural break (1993–2011) for GSCI sub-indices and industrial production CA

Error-Correction Term					
GSCI Agri.	1				
GSCI Ind. Met.	−0.267				
GSCI Prec. Met.	−2.043				
GSCI Energy	0.661				
Prod. Ind. CA	14.129				

VECM	ΔGSCI Agri.	ΔGSCI Ind. Met.	ΔPrec. Met.	ΔGSCI Energy	ΔProd. Ind. CA
ECT	−0.051	−0.030	−0.013	−0.016	−0.008
(*t*.stat)	(−4.23)	(−2.59)	(−1.25)	(−0.68)	(−4.37)
ΔGSCI Agri.(−1)	−0.065	0.049	0.089	0.215	0.009
(*t*.stat)	(−0.82)	(0.65)	(1.26)	(1.43)	(0.75)
ΔGSCI Ind. Met.(−1)	−0.050	0.043	−0.103	0.057	−0.005
(*t*.stat)	(−0.59)	(0.54)	(−1.36)	(0.35)	(−0.38)
ΔGSCI Prec. Met.(−1)	0.170	0.126	0.049	−0.224	−0.012
(*t*.stat)	(1.81)	(1.41)	(0.58)	(−1.25)	(−0.83)
ΔGSCI Energy(−1)	−0.040	−0.060	−0.047	−0.075	0.019
(*t*.stat)	(−0.95)	(−1.50)	(−1.25)	(−0.92)	(3.05)
ΔProd. Ind. CA(−1)	−0.157	0.957	0.277	1.388	0.211
(*t*.stat)	(−0.34)	(2.18)	(0.67)	(1.58)	(3.07)

Canadian economy in terms of production of agricultural products and its role in the industrial metals industry also allows us to establish a reverse relationship.

In Figure 7.10, we can observe the occurrence of the structural break on September 30, 2008. Before and after that date, the two regimes can be considered broadly stationary. The stability of the cointegration relationship is not as neat in this graph as it was in the case of the

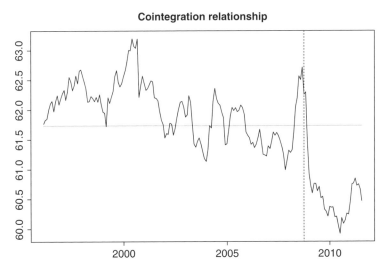

Figure 7.10 Cointegration relationship with structural break for GSCI sub-indices and industrial production CA

Table 7.18 Lütkepohl *et al.* (2004) cointegration test results with structural break for GSCI sub-indices and industrial production EU

1993–2011	Max. Eigen.	10%	5%	1%
$r \leq 4$	6.96	5.42	6.79	10.04
$r \leq 3$	16.39	13.78	15.83	19.85
$r \leq 2$	29.69	25.93	28.45	33.76
$r \leq 1$	54.40	42.08	45.2	51.6
$r = 0$	84.52	61.92	65.66	73.12

Chinese, Brazilian and Australian economies. Nevertheless, it could be considered broadly stationary. Consequently, we can validate the results highlighted in this section.

Note also that, similarly to the previous case for Australia, our results confirm the previous findings by Bloch *et al.* (2006a; 2006b), who found evidence in favor of a cointegration relationship between IMF commodity indices and industrial production in Canada during 1960–2001.

7.2.3.6   GSCI Sub-Indices and Industrial Production in the EU

We now turn to the study of the relationship between industrial production in the EU and commodity markets. According to Table 7.7, only one cointegration relationship could be found during the 1993–2011 full period and with the modeling of one break.

From Table 7.18, we get the insight that the rank of the cointegration matrix r is indeed at least equal to 1 (at the 1% level).

Table 7.19 contains the VECM estimates, which are also quite satisfactory. We record

Table 7.19 VECM results with structural break (1993–2011) for GSCI sub-indices and industrial production EU

Error-Correction Term					
GSCI Agri.	1				
GSCI Ind. Met.	0.684				
GSCI Prec. Met.	−2.219				
GSCI Energy	0.364				
Prod. Ind. EU	4.186				

VECM	ΔGSCI Agri.	ΔGSCI Ind. Met.	ΔPrec. Met.	ΔGSCI Energy	ΔProd. Ind. EU
ECT	−0.034	−0.079	0.030	−0.100	−0.008
(*t*.stat)	(−1.73)	(−4.63)	(1.78)	(−2.82)	(−1.77)
ΔGSCI Agri.(−1)	−0.027	0.060	0.078	0.212	0.019
(*t*.stat)	(−0.33)	(0.85)	(1.13)	(1.44)	(0.94)
ΔGSCI Ind. Met.(−1)	0.003	0.062	−0.018	0.049	0.038
(*t*.stat)	(0.03)	(0.78)	(−0.24)	(0.30)	(1.72)
ΔGSCI Prec. Met.(−1)	0.184	−0.001	0.045	−0.416	−0.052
(*t*.stat)	(1.79)	(−0.01)	(0.51)	(−2.25)	(−2.08)
ΔGSCI Energy(−1)	−0.045	0.001	−0.016	0.013	0.008
(*t*.stat)	(−0.92)	(0.01)	(−0.39)	(0.15)	(0.67)
ΔProd. Ind. EU(−1)	−0.217	−0.722	−0.846	−0.877	−0.160
(*t*.stat)	(−0.55)	(−2.09)	(−2.52)	(−1.23)	(−1.66)

Cointegration relationship

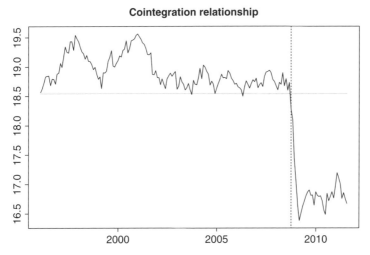

Figure 7.11 Cointegration relationship with structural break for GSCI sub-indices and industrial production EU

four negative error-correction terms (except for precious metals). The GSCI Industrial Metals record an ECT equal to −0.079 significant at the 1% level, followed by the GSCI Energy Markets equal to −0.100 significant at the 5% level. Both the error-correction terms of the GSCI Agricultural Products (−0.034) and the EU industrial production (−0.008) are significant at the 10% level. Hence, we find results similar to previous regions where the macroeconomy–commodity markets link has been established previously, with the exception that the magnitude of the ECT is the strongest in this setting for energy markets. Therefore, it could be said that all commodity markets (except precious metals) play a role here in correcting the errors towards the long-term fundamental value between these time series, in addition to the role played by the macroeconomic variable (that is, the industrial production index).

Examination of Figure 7.11 allows us to conclude that the cointegration relationship identified between the GSCI sub-indices and the European industrial production index is valid. Indeed, the graph appears roughly stationary before and after the structural break date on September 30, 2008. This stands in sharp contrast with the results obtained for the USA, where the results could not be validated at this stage. Significant differences seem to exist in the linkages between economic activity and commodity markets between both sides of the Atlantic.

7.2.3.7   GSCI Sub-Indices and Industrial Production in Germany

With respect to Germany, which constitutes the economic stronghold of the EU in terms of growth, our specifications in Table 7.7 reveal that only one cointegration relationship is valid during the full period and with the occurrence of one structural break.

Table 7.20 is able to confirm this statement: we can detect at least one cointegration relationship between the GSCI sub-indices and the German industrial production index (at the 1% level).

We record four negative error-correction terms (except precious metals) in the VECM, as shown in Table 7.21. By order of significance, we can state that the GSCI Industrial

Table 7.20   Lütkepohl *et al.* (2004) cointegration test results with structural break for GSCI sub-indices and industrial production GE

1993–2011	Max. Eigen.	10%	5%	1%
$r \leq 4$	7.20	5.42	6.79	10.04
$r \leq 3$	16.88	13.78	15.83	19.85
$r \leq 2$	29.57	25.93	28.45	33.76
$r \leq 1$	51.62	42.08	45.2	51.6
$r = 0$	82.10	61.92	65.66	73.12

Metals (1% level) precede the GSCI Energy and the EU industrial production index (5% level), followed by the GSCI Agricultural Products (10% level). Similarly to the EU case, the strongest ECT is registered for GSCI Energy. As a matter of fact, deviations from the long-run equilibrium relationship between these variables will be primarily corrected by the energy variable, followed by industrial metals, agricultural products and the German industrial production index.

According to Figure 7.12, this overall cointegration exercise is valid, since we can see that the cointegration relationship is stationary in each of the two regimes delimited by the structural break date on September 30, 2008. Therefore, we obtain very successful results in the EU and German cases (as a proxy of the EU 27 economic region), where we document that the macroeconomy–commodity markets link is active.

Having dealt with the link between industrial production and commodity markets in various geographical regions, we now turn to another kind of cointegration exercise. In what follows, we will aim at replicating precise case studies taken from previous literature.

Table 7.21   VECM results with structural break (1993–2011) for GSCI sub-indices and industrial production GE

Error-Correction Term					
GSCI Agri.	1				
GSCI Ind. Met.	0.609				
GSCI Prec. Met.	−2.593				
GSCI Energy	0.427				
Prod. Ind. GE	4.618				

VECM	ΔGSCI Agri.	ΔGSCI Ind. Met.	ΔPrec. Met.	ΔGSCI Energy	ΔProd. Ind. GE
ECT	−0.028	−0.070	0.024	−0.089	−0.010
(*t*.stat)	(−1.69)	(−4.73)	(1.70)	(−2.92)	(−2.26)
ΔGSCI Agri.(−1)	−0.022	0.081	0.104	0.239	0.006
(*t*.stat)	(−0.28)	(1.14)	(1.53)	(1.64)	(0.30)
ΔGSCI Ind. Met.(−1)	0.004	0.024	−0.025	−0.015	0.048
(*t*.stat)	(0.04)	(0.30)	(−0.32)	(0.09)	(1.99)
ΔGSCI Prec. Met.(−1)	0.175	0.036	0.059	−0.340	−0.037
(*t*.stat)	(1.74)	(0.41)	(0.70)	(−1.87)	(−1.37)
ΔGSCI Energy(−1)	−0.037	−0.026	−0.027	−0.041	0.009
(*t*.stat)	(−0.79)	(−0.63)	(−0.69)	(−0.48)	(0.71)
ΔProd. Ind. GE(−1)	−0.434	−0.342	−0.736	0.034	−0.094
(*t*.stat)	(−1.39)	(−1.24)	(−2.78)	(0.06)	(−1.13)

Cointegration relationship

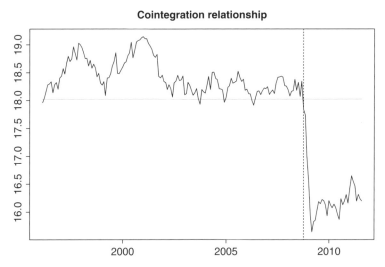

Figure 7.12 Cointegration relationship with structural break for GSCI sub-indices and industrial production GE

7.2.3.8 *Aluminum, Copper, Lead, Zinc and Industrial Production US*

The first topic deals with the link between some industrial metals (aluminum, copper, lead, zinc) and industrial production in the US, in light of the previous work by Labys *et al.* (1999). As summarized in Table 7.7, we could detect cointegration relationships in every specification except for the 1993–2000 first sub-period. We choose to reproduce the results of the 1993–2011 full period with one break.

Table 7.22 indicates that the rank of the cointegration *r* between aluminum, copper, lead, zinc and the US Industrial Production index is at least equal to 1 (at the 1% level).

The results from the estimation of the VECM, as shown in Table 7.23, are not entirely satisfactory. While three error-correction terms are negative, only the US Industrial Production index is strongly significant (at the 1% level), while aluminum could not be considered as significant at the minimum 10% level. If deviations occur from the long-run equilibrium, variations in industrial production would act here as a feedback mechanism. Therefore, we could find a weak rationale for the existence of an econometric link between these industrial metals price changes and the evolution of the macroeconomic variable.

Table 7.22 Lütkepohl *et al.* (2004) cointegration test results with structural break for aluminum, copper, lead, zinc and industrial production US

1993–2011	Max. Eigen.	10%	5%	1%
$r \leq 4$	8.98	5.42	6.79	10.04
$r \leq 3$	20.25	13.78	15.83	19.85
$r \leq 2$	41.78	25.93	28.45	33.76
$r \leq 1$	72.31	42.08	45.2	51.6
$r = 0$	115.86	61.92	65.66	73.12

Table 7.23   VECM results with structural break (1993–2011) for aluminum, copper, lead, zinc and industrial production US

	Error-Correction Term				
Aluminum	1				
Copper	2.225				
Lead	−0.945				
Zinc	3.594				
Prod. Ind. US	9.035				

VECM	ΔAluminum	ΔCopper	ΔLead	ΔZinc	ΔProd. Ind. US
ECT	−0.012	−0.010	0.021	0.010	−0.008
(*t*.stat)	(−1.50)	(−0.71)	(1.34)	(0.73)	(−6.95)
ΔAluminum(−1)	0.094	0.279	0.347	0.233	0.009
(*t*.stat)	(0.86)	(1.52)	(1.63)	(1.27)	(0.61)
ΔCopper(−1)	0.112	0.160	−0.048	0.065	0.027
(*t*.stat)	(1.37)	(1.16)	(−0.30)	(0.47)	(2.33)
ΔLead(−1)	0.060	0.123	0.223	0.115	−0.013
(*t*.stat)	(1.06)	(1.30)	(2.02)	(1.20)	(−1.70)
ΔZinc(−1)	−0.144	−0.357	−0.229	−0.200	−0.021
(*t*.stat)	(−1.79)	(−2.63)	(−1.46)	(−1.48)	(−1.87)
ΔProd. Ind. US(−1)	0.688	1.283	1.352	1.965	0.011
(*t*.stat)	(1.25)	(1.39)	(1.26)	(2.11)	(0.14)

However, this statement does not pass the investigation of the cointegration relationship, which cannot be considered stationary in Figure 7.13. Despite the occurrence of one structural break on June 30, 2006, there are still large variations visible before and after that date which impact the stability of the system as a whole. As a consequence, we cannot validate the cointegration relationship between aluminum, copper, lead, zinc and the US Industrial Production index within our econometric framework and given our updated dataset.

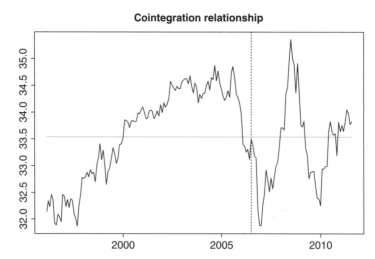

Figure 7.13   Cointegration relationship with structural break for aluminum, copper, lead, zinc and industrial production US

Table 7.24   Lütkepohl *et al.* (2004) cointegration test results with structural break for copper and industrial production US

1993–2011	Max. Eigen.	10%	5%	1%
$r \leq 1$	4.77	5.42	6.79	10.04
$r = 0$	13.78	13.78	15.83	19.85

We disagree on that point with the findings by Labys *et al.* (1999) during 1971–1995 (although they used a proxy of industrial production for the OECD, which is not easily reproducible in our setting).

7.2.3.9   *Copper and Industrial Production US*

Next, we consider a more restricted case, with the adjustment between the price of copper and the US Industrial Production index, building on the previous work by Pieroni and Ricciarelli (2005). In Table 7.7, we establish that a remarkable stability of the cointegration relationship seems to exist across all the periods and econometric specifications considered. We focus here on the results for the full period with the occurrence of one structural break.

Table 7.24 documents the fact that the rank of the cointegration r between copper and the US industrial index is at least equal to 1 (exactly at the 10% level).

Table 7.25 shows that the VECM could be considered valid, since we obtain at least one negative and statistically significant error-correction term for the price of copper. Although difficult to grasp, it seems that the copper price acts as the feedback mechanism in this cointegration exercise.

However, the validity of this latter result is undermined by the non-stationarity of the cointegration relationship pictured in Figure 7.14. The structural break date was identified as July 31, 2009.

This set of results corroborates the previous findings by Pieroni and Ricciarelli (2005) during 1955–2000. We cannot conclude that changes in macroeconomic conditions in the US are linked over time with the evolution of the price of copper (as an industrial metal which is heavily used in construction).

Table 7.25   VECM results with structural break (1993–2011) for copper and industrial production US

Error-Correction Term		
Copper	1	
Prod. Ind. US	−6.997	
VECM	ΔCopper	ΔProd. Ind. US
ECT	−0.024	0.004
(*t*.stat)	(−2.11)	(2.27)
ΔCopper(-1)	0.207	0.015
(*t*.stat)	(2.94)	(1.48)
ΔProd. Ind. US(-1)	1.247	0.124
(*t*.stat)	(2.56)	(1.72)

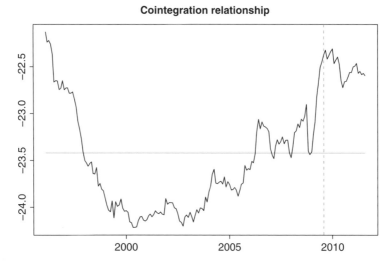

Figure 7.14 Cointegration relationship with structural break between copper and industrial production US

7.2.3.10   Wheat, Corn, Soybean and Industrial Production US

Next, we focus on a subset of agricultural commodities (wheat, corn, soybean) and their relation to the US industrial production, as studied previously by Ai *et al.* (2006). Our investigation of this issue reveals in Table 7.7 that a cointegration relationship can be established in all of our specifications, except for the 2000–2011 second sub-period. We comment upon the full period results with one break.

Table 7.26 allows us to conclude that there exists at least one cointegration relationship between wheat, corn, soybean and US industrial production (at the 5% level).

As concerns the VECM estimates, we learn from Table 7.27 that there is only one negative error-correction term (for the US industrial production) but it is not statistically significant. Therefore, we cannot explore further the issue of cointegration between these individual time series of agricultural commodities and the US macroeconomic variable.

Note that this comment holds irrespective of the apparent stationarity of the cointegration relationship in Figure 7.15, before and after the structural break on July 31, 2009. Indeed, it is a mandatory condition for cointegration that we record at least one statistically significant and negative ECT which should trigger the adjustment mechanisms over time.

On this topic, we are able to confirm the results by Ai *et al.* (2006), concerning the period 1957–2002.

Table 7.26 Johansen cointegration test results for the 1993–2011 full period for wheat, corn, soybean and industrial production US

1993–2011	Max. Eigen.	10%	5%	1%
$r \leq 3$	9.05	10.49	12.25	16.26
$r \leq 2$	11.54	16.85	18.96	23.65
$r \leq 1$	14.88	23.11	25.54	30.34
$r = 0$	33.95	29.12	31.46	36.65

Table 7.27 VECM results for the 1993–2011 full period for wheat, corn, soybean and industrial production US

Error-Correction Term				
Wheat	1			
Corn	−0.543			
Soybean	−0.567			
Prod. Ind. US	−0.434			
Trend	0.001			

VECM	ΔWheat	ΔCorn	ΔSoybean	ΔProd. Ind. US
ECT	0.075	0.239	0.205	−0.004
(*t*.stat)	(1.42)	(4.99)	(4.60)	(−0.95)
Intercept	0.202	0.647	0.557	−0.010
(*t*.stat)	(1.42)	(4.99)	(4.61)	(−0.87)
ΔWheat(−1)	−0.036	0.045	0.039	−0.008
(*t*.stat)	(−0.39)	(0.53)	(0.50)	(−1.10)
ΔCorn(−1)	−0.123	−0.043	0.078	0.004
(*t*.stat)	(−1.13)	(−0.43)	(0.84)	(0.43)
ΔSoybean(−1)	0.037	−0.115	−0.157	0.005
(*t*.stat)	(0.33)	(−1.14)	(−1.67)	(0.53)
ΔProd. Ind. US(−1)	1.569	2.493	1.504	0.254
(*t*.stat)	(1.76)	(3.07)	(1.99)	(3.54)

7.2.3.11   Oil and Industrial Production EU

As our last case study, we consider the adjustment between the oil price and the EU industrial production index, as studied initially by Cunado and de Gracia (2003). Table 7.7 reveals that a cointegration relationship could be identified only during the full period with the modeling of a break.

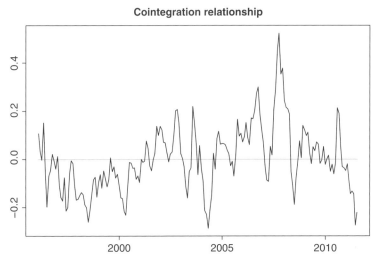

Figure 7.15 Cointegration relationship for the 1993–2011 full period for wheat, corn, soybean and industrial production US

Table 7.28   Lütkepohl *et al.* (2004) cointegration test results with structural break for oil and industrial production EU

1993–2011	Max. Eigen.	10%	5%	1%
$r \leq 1$	6.50	5.42	6.79	10.04
$r = 0$	16.17	13.78	15.83	19.85

Table 7.28 verifies that the rank of the cointegration r between the two variables of interest is at least equal to 1 (at the 5% level).

As for the VECM estimated in Table 7.29, we record one negative and statistically significant (at the 1% level) error-correction term for oil. Thus, it would seem that – concerning such a contentious issue in academic papers – deviations from the long-run relationship are restored by means of oil price changes. Furthermore, we cannot establish that changes in European industrial production act as a feedback mechanism in this setting.

These comments are discarded by the non-stationarity of the cointegration relationship between oil and EU industrial production, as observed in Figure 7.16. Indeed, the cointegration relationship can be seen as upward sloping here. Besides, we detect the presence of one structural break on July 31, 2009, i.e. during a recovery period from the financial crisis.

Our results are broadly in line with the previous findings by Cunado and de Gracia (2003), who also resorted to structural break techniques to further strengthen their results.

7.2.3.12   Some Concluding Remarks on Cointegration Analyses Between Industrial Production and Commodity Prices

With respect to the adjustment between industrial production (as a proxy of economic activity) and commodity markets, we have considered various cointegration exercises depending on the geographic zone and the sectors covered by commodities: agricultural products, industrial and precious metals, energy markets. The main results feature a satisfactory long-term relationship between industrial production and various segments of commodity markets. Most of the time, precious metals are unable to trigger this adjustment, whereas industrial metals and

Table 7.29   VECM results with structural break (1993–2011) for oil and industrial production EU

Error-Correction Term		
Oil	1	
Prod. Ind. EU	−1.505	

VECM	ΔOil	ΔProd. Ind. EU
ECT	−0.087	0.001
(*t*.stat)	(−3.12)	(0.32)
ΔOil(−1)	0.115	0.011
(*t*.stat)	(1.57)	(1.30)
ΔProd. Ind. EU(−1)	0.945	0.114
(*t*.stat)	(1.53)	(1.55)

Cointegration relationship

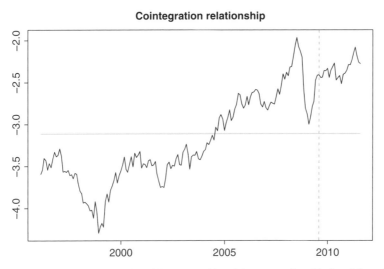

Figure 7.16   Cointegration relationship with structural break between oil and industrial production EU

agricultural products play a prime role. In terms of geographic coverage, we could verify that the adjustment of macroeconomic conditions to (and from) commodity markets is especially valid in China, Brazil, Australia, Canada, the EU and Germany – but not in the US. In China and in some other regions, we also find that commodity markets act as the central feedback mechanisms, which implies that they will be leader in the recovery towards the long-run state should any short-term deviations occur. Overall, we can certainly verify that changes in macroeconomic conditions induce higher demand for construction, production and therefore higher demand for raw materials and commodities as an input. But we have also documented firmly that the cross-market linkages are especially strong when developing that kind of cointegration exercise.

Compared to previous academic literature, we can consider the similarities between our results and various studies which included industrial production in the OECD. Indeed, our results for the economic regions aforementioned broadly confirm the findings by Labys and Maizels (1993) and Hua (1998) – who used IMF commodity indices instead of GSCI indices – during 1953–1987 and 1970–1993, respectively. We are therefore successful in updating their results on this matter, which were favorable to the existence of a cointegration relationship between commodity markets and industrial production. Note, however, that we disagree with Bloch *et al.* (2006a; 2006b), who could not find evidence of such a phenomenon during 1900–2001. Perhaps the difference between these latter authors and the present study comes from their choice of World Bank Indicators of Commodity Markets, or the period under consideration.

When looking at the adjustment between a subset of industrial metals and US industrial production, the cointegration relationship could not be firmly established (contrary to Labys *et al.* (1999)). Even with a dataset restricted to copper, the relationship with the macroeconomic variable could not be documented (in line with Pieroni and Ricciarelli (2005)). Therefore, it seems that the feedback mechanisms that we are looking for between commodities and the macroeconomy are only valid for baskets of commodities (as represented by the GSCI sub-indices), while a credible body of evidence in favor of that hypothesis is lacking for individual commodity price series. The same kind of conclusion holds for agricultural prices, or for the adjustment between EU industrial production and the oil price. Our results are globally in line with previous literature on this topic. The originality of the present work lies in the systematic inclusion of sub-periods and structural breaks, as well as in the use of an updated dataset compared to most of the previous studies. Finally, note that we have not further considered cointegration exercises with the gold price, since it seemed that there were few (or no) feedback mechanisms at stake in that category of commodities when using the GSCI sub-index for precious metals (which nearly all lacked conclusive evidence of acting as effective error-correction effects).

7.3 COINTEGRATION BETWEEN THE GSCI SUB-INDICES, INFLATION AND MONETARY INDICES

In this section, we wish to address the following research question: why is it so important to examine the nature of the relationship between *inflation* and *commodity prices*?

As Kyrtsou and Labys (2006) put it, commodity price increases can lead to periods of inflation, the latter reflected in changes in the producer and consumer price indexes. For manufacturers and processors, higher commodity prices lead to lower corporate profits, higher unemployment and result in less consumer spending. Because a rise in inflation will lower profits for many producers, they will have to reduce the work force, thus creating unemployment. This rise in unemployment will reduce disposable income, reduce commodity demand and thus cause a surplus if there is not a reduction in commodity production. The combination of lower wages, higher unemployment and an increased CPI will increase the recessionary cycle: decreased commodity demand in addition to overall demand, a fall in GDP, further decline in disposable income, increased decline in elastic goods demand, inventory surplus, increased exports coupled with decreased imports, worsened trade imbalance, etc.

Moosa (1998) recalls two main reasons why commodity prices may also be seen as a leading indicator of inflation. First, higher commodity prices imply higher costs of production which feed through (with a time lag) into prices. Second, commodity prices are more flexible than the prices of consumer goods and services because they are largely determined in flexible auction markets that respond quickly to demand. A rise in aggregate demand will be reflected in commodity prices first, then on consumer prices because the former react faster to news about future inflation whereas the latter are rather sticky.

Hence, there seem to exist strong inter-relationships between inflation and commodity prices, which we aim at exploring in a cointegration analysis.

7.3.1 Literature Review

Let us discuss below the main findings from previous academic literature on this topic.

- Garner (1989) investigates the cointegrating relationship between the Commodity Research Bureau (CRB) index of spot commodity prices, the *Journal of Commerce* (JOC) index, the Producer Price index for crude materials (PPICM), the gold price and the Consumer Price index (CPI) during 1980–1988. The empirical results consistently support the view that commodity prices (either gold or the CRB) and consumer prices are not cointegrated. However, the tests cannot reject the null hypothesis that the PPI for crude materials and the CPI are not cointegrated.

- Furlong and Ingenito (1996) examine the empirical relationship between changes in the CRB index for Raw Materials and the CPI during 1955–1995. Their results indicate that the empirical link between commodity prices and inflation has changed dramatically over time. Whereas commodity prices were relatively strong and statistically robust leading indicators of overall inflation during the 1970s and early 1980s, their influence as stand-alone indicators of inflation has diminished since the early 1980s. When considered in conjunction with other likely indicators of inflation (i.e. trade-weighted exchange value of the US Dollar, Federal funds, oil), non-oil commodity prices have had a somewhat more statistically robust relationship with inflation in the mid-1990s.

- Madhavi and Zhou (1997) find some evidence of cointegration between commodity prices (gold, industrial materials),[6] the nominal 3-month T-Bill rate, real GDP, and the CPI during 1958–1994. They recall that the use of gold or commodity prices as a guide for the direction of monetary policy relies upon the argument that these prices are determined in flexible markets with forward-looking expectations. Therefore, they can quickly incorporate events and news which might affect the expected inflation rate. Prices of goods and services included in the CPI basket, on the other hand, generally adjust more slowly as sellers gradually react to changing market conditions.

- Moosa (1998) tests the presence of cointegration between metals, raw materials, food prices (taken from the IMF *International Financial Statistics* database) and the OECD CPI during 1972–1993. The Johansen cointegration tests fail to reject the null hypothesis of zero cointegrating vectors. Although the author cannot show evidence for a long-run relationship between commodity prices and consumer prices, the study documents strong evidence for a short-run dynamic relationship in which causality runs from the former to the latter.

- Worthington and Pahlavani (2007) test for the presence of a stable long-run relationship between the price of gold and the US inflation rate during 1945–2006. Their results provide abundant evidence of a stable long-run relationship between the price of gold and inflation in both the post-war and post-1970s period, by accounting explicitly for structural changes in the US gold market and US inflationary regimes in 1972–1973 and 1978–1979. Since the long-run price of gold and inflation move together, the authors conclude that investment in gold can indeed serve as an inflationary hedge.

- Belke *et al.* (2010) examine the interactions between money (M2 to M4), the CPI and commodity prices (CRB and CRB Raw Industrials indices) during 1970–2008. By using a cointegrated VAR model, they document both long-run and short-run relationships among these variables, while the adjustment processes are mainly driven by global liquidity (i.e. monetary aggregates).

- Browne and Cronin (2010) study the long-run and dynamic relationships between commodity prices (CRB, CRB Raw Industrials and Conference Board's Sensitive Materials index (SENSI) indices), Consumer Prices Index (CPI) and money (M2) during 1959–2008. Based on a cointegrated VAR model for the USA and Canada, they are able to identify equilibrium relationships between money, commodity prices and consumer prices, with both commodity and consumer prices proportional to the money supply in the long run.

A summary of these findings can be found in Table 7.30.

---

[6] The study uses the *Journal of Commerce* index of industrial materials prices, which is composed of cotton, polyester, burlap, print cloth, steel scrap, zinc, copper scrap, aluminum, tin, hides, rubber, tallow, plywood, red oak, benzene and crude petroleum.

Table 7.30   Monetary variables and commodity prices: cointegrating relationships

Authors	Period	Cointegration Relationship	SS	SB
Garner (1989)	1980–1988	Producer Price Index for Crude Materials ↔ CPI Gold, CRB ∅ CPI	No	No
Furlong and Ingenito (1996)	1955–1995	CRB Raw Materials ↔ CPI	Yes	No
Madhavi and Zhou (1997)	1958–1994	Gold, Industrial Metals ↔ T-Bill, GDP, CPI	No	No
Moosa (1998)	1972–1993	IMF metals, raw materials, food prices ∅ OECD CPI	No	No
Worthington and Pahlavani (2007)	1945–2006	Gold ↔ US Inflation Rate	Yes	Yes
Belke et al. (2010)	1970–2008	CRB, CRB Raw Industrials ↔ M2–M4, CPI	No	No
Browne and Cronin (2010)	1959–2008	CRB, CRB Raw Industrials, SENSI ↔ M2, CPI	No	No

Note: ↔ indicates the presence of a cointegration relationship. ∅ indicates the absence of a cointegration relationship. SS stands for 'Sub Sample' analysis in the paper considered. SB stands for 'Structural Break' analysis in the paper considered.

Therefore, previous cointegration studies seem to agree that there is a strong connection, both in the short and long run, between indicators of inflation and commodity prices. This literature also highlights the presence of instability of this relationship depending on the period considered, and eventually the inclusion of structural breaks (as in Worthington and Pahlavani (2007)). In what follows, we aim at updating these results with a more recent dataset and the systematic modeling of structural changes.

7.3.2   Results of Granger Causality Tests Between the GSCI Sub-Indices, Inflation and Monetary Indices

The results of pairwise Granger causality tests (with one lag) between the GSCI sub-indices, inflation and monetary indices can be found in Tables 7.31 to 7.33. Broadly speaking, the following comments arise. The GSCI Agricultural sub-index causes, in the Granger sense, the OECD index inflation and the US and Chinese inflation indices (at the 5% level). The GSCI Energy sub-index exhibits Granger causalities with nearly all inflation and monetary indices (at the 10% level), except Inflation Brazil. The same comment applies for the GSCI Industrial Metals sub-index. Precious metals display significant Granger causalities with the OECD index inflation, and the inflation indices in the USA, China, the EU and Germany. Taken together, the results of the Granger causality tests for the GSCI sub-indices contain useful information on their potential impact on the inflation and monetary indices, which will be under scrutiny in the cointegration framework.

Concerning the monetary variables, we note that the US M2 aggregate and the OECD index inflation cause, in the Granger sense, the GSCI Industrial and Precious Metals, respectively. The US inflation index also records a significant Granger causality with precious metals. In the case of China, only the effect with energy is significant (at the 10% level). For the other economies, we remark especially that Inflation Brazil and Inflation Canada respectively cause, in the Granger sense, the GSCI Energy and Precious Metals sub-indices, whereas no Granger causality link occurs with the other indices. Hence, inspection of Tables 7.31 to 7.33 informs us that the inter-relationships between commodity markets and monetary/inflation variables is not as straightforward as indicated by the theory and previous empirical studies.

Table 7.31   Pairwise Granger causality tests for GSCI sub-indices, monetary and inflation variables (1/3)

From	To	p-value	F-statistic
GSCI Agri.	US M2	0.6399	0.2193
GSCI Agri.	OECD Index Inflation	0.0001	15.6509
GSCI Agri.	Inflation US	0.0000	19.5225
GSCI Agri.	Inflation CH	0.0374	4.3626
GSCI Agri.	Inflation BR	0.9767	0.0009
GSCI Agri.	Inflation AU	0.2828	1.1572
GSCI Agri.	Inflation CA	0.3178	1.0008
GSCI Agri.	Inflation EU	0.2894	1.1258
GSCI Agri.	Inflation GE	0.2093	1.5815
GSCI Energy	US M2	0.0632	3.4714
GSCI Energy	OECD Index Inflation	0.0000	82.4075
GSCI Energy	Inflation US	0.0000	119.7487
GSCI Energy	Inflation CH	0.0119	6.3948
GSCI Energy	Inflation BR	0.4191	0.6543
GSCI Energy	Inflation AU	0.0769	3.1469
GSCI Energy	Inflation CA	0.0062	7.5917
GSCI Energy	Inflation EU	0.0000	20.7597
GSCI Energy	Inflation GE	0.0000	18.3643
GSCI Ind. Metals	US M2	0.0056	7.7567
GSCI Ind. Metals	OECD Index Inflation	0.0002	14.2344
GSCI Ind. Metals	Inflation US	0.0003	13.2355
GSCI Ind. Metals	Inflation CH	0.0020	9.6590
GSCI Ind. Metals	Inflation BR	0.8082	0.0590
GSCI Ind. Metals	Inflation AU	0.8755	0.0246
GSCI Ind. Metals	Inflation CA	0.0537	3.7455
GSCI Ind. Metals	Inflation EU	0.0058	7.7130
GSCI Ind. Metals	Inflation GE	0.0028	9.0814
GSCI Prec. Metals	US M2	0.3347	0.9330
GSCI Prec. Metals	OECD Index Inflation	0.0188	5.5705
GSCI Prec. Metals	Inflation US	0.0019	9.7546
GSCI Prec. Metals	Inflation CH	0.0345	4.5034
GSCI Prec. Metals	Inflation BR	0.2018	1.6354
GSCI Prec. Metals	Inflation AU	0.8872	0.0202
GSCI Prec. Metals	Inflation CA	0.7852	0.0744
GSCI Prec. Metals	Inflation EU	0.0125	6.3027
GSCI Prec. Metals	Inflation GE	0.0175	5.6980
US M2	GSCI Agri.	0.1189	2.4437
US M2	GSCI Energy	0.1500	2.0807
US M2	GSCI Ind. Metals	0.0019	9.7837
US M2	GSCI Prec. Metals	0.2008	1.6426
US M2	OECD Index Inflation	0.8099	0.0580
US M2	Inflation US	0.3446	0.8956
US M2	Inflation CH	0.1566	2.0149
US M2	Inflation BR	0.3135	1.0188
US M2	Inflation AU	0.3629	0.8299
US M2	Inflation CA	0.6674	0.1850
US M2	Inflation EU	0.3545	0.8596
US M2	Inflation GE	0.1711	1.8806

Note: The p-value and the F-statistic of the pairwise Granger causality tests between X and Y are given. The null hypothesis is that X does not Granger cause Y.

Table 7.32 Pairwise Granger causality tests for GSCI sub-indices, monetary and inflation variables (2/3)

From	To	p-value	F-statistic
OECD Index Inflation	GSCI Agri.	0.1035	2.6646
OECD Index Inflation	GSCI Energy	0.7472	0.1041
OECD Index Inflation	GSCI Ind. Metals	0.8559	0.0330
OECD Index Inflation	GSCI Prec. Metals	0.0078	7.1485
OECD Index Inflation	US M2	0.0009	11.1782
OECD Index Inflation	Inflation US	0.3668	0.8165
OECD Index Inflation	Inflation CH	0.1504	2.0769
OECD Index Inflation	Inflation BR	0.7107	0.1378
OECD Index Inflation	Inflation AU	0.0301	4.7415
OECD Index Inflation	Inflation CA	0.0006	11.9488
OECD Index Inflation	Inflation EU	0.0000	18.5513
OECD Index Inflation	Inflation GE	0.3027	1.0651
Inflation US	GSCI Agri.	0.1848	1.7654
Inflation US	GSCI Energy	0.8002	0.0641
Inflation US	GSCI Ind. Metals	0.7263	0.1227
Inflation US	GSCI Prec. Metals	0.0050	7.9860
Inflation US	US M2	0.0003	13.4910
Inflation US	OECD Index Inflation	0.6570	0.1975
Inflation US	Inflation CH	0.2761	1.1898
Inflation US	Inflation BR	0.1111	2.5513
Inflation US	Inflation AU	0.1158	2.4845
Inflation US	Inflation CA	0.2408	1.3804
Inflation US	Inflation EU	0.0471	3.9685
Inflation US	Inflation GE	0.0388	4.3011
Inflation CH	GSCI Agri.	0.4245	0.6393
Inflation CH	GSCI Energy	0.0610	3.5308
Inflation CH	GSCI Ind. Metals	0.6624	0.1910
Inflation CH	GSCI Prec. Metals	0.7545	0.0979
Inflation CH	US M2	0.1319	2.2800
Inflation CH	OECD Index Inflation	0.0604	3.5476
Inflation CH	Inflation US	0.0627	3.4850
Inflation CH	Inflation BR	0.6267	0.2370
Inflation CH	Inflation AU	0.0838	3.0052
Inflation CH	Inflation CA	0.2051	1.6117
Inflation CH	Inflation EU	0.1134	2.5187
Inflation CH	Inflation GE	0.0036	8.5749
Inflation BR	GSCI Agri.	0.6960	0.1530
Inflation BR	GSCI Energy	0.0318	4.6477
Inflation BR	GSCI Ind. Metals	0.5847	0.2992
Inflation BR	GSCI Prec. Metals	0.4210	0.6491
Inflation BR	US M2	0.6978	0.1510
Inflation BR	OECD Index Inflation	0.2614	1.2653
Inflation BR	Inflation US	0.6961	0.1528
Inflation BR	Inflation CH	0.7993	0.0647
Inflation BR	Inflation AU	0.2954	1.0982
Inflation BR	Inflation CA	0.4943	0.4680
Inflation BR	Inflation EU	0.0653	3.4168
Inflation BR	Inflation GE	0.0275	4.9014

Note: The p-value and the F-statistic of the pairwise Granger causality tests between X and Y are given. The null hypothesis is that X does not Granger cause Y.

Table 7.33 Pairwise Granger causality tests for GSCI sub-indices, monetary and inflation
variables (3/3)

From	To	p-value	F-statistic
Inflation AU	GSCI Agri.	0.7055	0.1430
Inflation AU	GSCI Energy	0.2871	1.1367
Inflation AU	GSCI Ind. Metals	0.8805	0.0226
Inflation AU	GSCI Prec. Metals	0.4363	0.6072
Inflation AU	US M2	0.5133	0.4282
Inflation AU	OECD Index Inflation	0.0513	3.8236
Inflation AU	Inflation US	0.2060	1.6048
Inflation AU	Inflation CH	0.6479	0.2090
Inflation AU	Inflation BR	0.0079	7.1444
Inflation AU	Inflation CA	0.3088	1.0387
Inflation AU	Inflation EU	0.0040	8.3797
Inflation AU	Inflation GE	0.5316	0.3921
Inflation CA	GSCI Agri.	0.0505	3.8512
Inflation CA	GSCI Energy	0.3901	0.7403
Inflation CA	GSCI Ind. Metals	0.6507	0.2054
Inflation CA	GSCI Prec. Metals	0.0037	8.5167
Inflation CA	US M2	0.0746	3.1964
Inflation CA	OECD Index Inflation	0.0147	6.0129
Inflation CA	Inflation US	0.0779	3.1263
Inflation CA	Inflation CH	0.7124	0.1361
Inflation CA	Inflation BR	0.3738	0.7930
Inflation CA	Inflation AU	0.0277	4.8842
Inflation CA	Inflation EU	0.0000	29.3275
Inflation CA	Inflation GE	0.0008	11.3284
Inflation EU	GSCI Agri.	0.7553	0.0973
Inflation EU	GSCI Energy	0.7244	0.1245
Inflation EU	GSCI Ind. Metals	0.8416	0.0400
Inflation EU	GSCI Prec. Metals	0.3810	0.7694
Inflation EU	US M2	0.1409	2.1777
Inflation EU	OECD Index Inflation	0.5568	0.3459
Inflation EU	Inflation US	0.9201	0.0101
Inflation EU	Inflation CH	0.4807	0.4983
Inflation EU	Inflation BR	0.1750	1.8471
Inflation EU	Inflation AU	0.0266	4.9560
Inflation EU	Inflation CA	0.0822	3.0372
Inflation EU	Inflation GE	0.6002	0.2751
Inflation GE	GSCI Agri.	0.6467	0.2104
Inflation GE	GSCI Energy	0.5317	0.3919
Inflation GE	GSCI Ind. Metals	0.7702	0.0854
Inflation GE	GSCI Prec. Metals	0.2139	1.5500
Inflation GE	US M2	0.1210	2.4158
Inflation GE	OECD Index Inflation	0.0761	3.1645
Inflation GE	Inflation US	0.1454	2.1288
Inflation GE	Inflation CH	0.6179	0.2492
Inflation GE	Inflation BR	0.5478	0.3619
Inflation GE	Inflation AU	0.4221	0.6459
Inflation GE	Inflation CA	0.0655	3.4121
Inflation GE	Inflation EU	0.0001	15.6772

Note: The p-value and the F-statistic of the pairwise Granger causality tests between X and Y are given. The null
hypothesis is that X does not Granger cause Y.

7.3.3   Cointegration Analyses for Commodities, Inflation and Monetary Indices

In what follows, we proceed with our own cointegration analysis of the relationship that may exist between commodities, inflation and monetary indices. Similarly to Chapters 5 and 6, we consider systematically sub-periods in our econometric tests, as well as the explicit modeling of structural breaks. We attempt to reproduce the main results that could be gathered from previous academic literature and provide new evidence on this topic based on our updated dataset. Table 7.34 contains a summary of our main results.

Table 7.34   Cointegration analyses of inflation, monetary indices and commodity prices: summary of the main results

Period	Cointegration Relationship	SB
1993–2011	GSCI Agricultural Ø US M2 Ø Inflation US	No
1993–2000	GSCI Agricultural Ø US M2 Ø Inflation US	No
2000–2011	GSCI Agricultural Ø US M2 Ø Inflation US	No
1993–2011	GSCI Agricultural ↔ US M2 ↔ Inflation US	Yes
1993–2011	GSCI Prec. Met. ↔ GSCI Ind. Met. ↔ M2 ↔ Inflation US	No
1993–2000	GSCI Prec. Met. Ø GSCI Ind. Met. Ø US M2 Ø Inflation US	No
2000–2011	GSCI Prec. Met. Ø GSCI Ind. Met. Ø US M2 Ø Inflation US	No
1993–2011	GSCI Prec. Met. ↔ GSCI Ind. Met. ↔ US M2 ↔ Inflation US	Yes
1993–2011	GSCI Energy Ø US M2 Ø Inflation US	No
1993–2000	GSCI Energy Ø US M2 Ø Inflation US	No
2000–2011	GSCI Energy Ø US M2 Ø Inflation US	No
1993–2011	GSCI Energy ↔ US M2 ↔ Inflation US	Yes
1993–2011	GSCI Agricultural ↔ Inflation EU	No
1993–2000	GSCI Agricultural Ø Inflation EU	No
2000–2011	GSCI Agricultural ↔ Inflation EU	No
1993–2011	GSCI Agricultural ↔ Inflation EU	Yes
1993–2011	GSCI Prec. Met. Ø GSCI Ind. Met. Ø Inflation EU	No
1993–2000	GSCI Prec. Met. Ø GSCI Ind. Met. Ø Inflation EU	No
2000–2011	GSCI Prec. Met. Ø GSCI Ind. Met. Ø Inflation EU	No
1993–2011	GSCI Prec. Met. ↔ GSCI Ind. Met. ↔ Inflation EU	Yes
1993–2011	GSCI Energy Ø Inflation EU	No
1993–2000	GSCI Energy Ø Inflation EU	No
2000–2011	GSCI Energy Ø Inflation EU	No
1993–2011	GSCI Energy ↔ Inflation EU	Yes
1993–2011	Gold ↔ Inflation US	No
1993–2000	Gold Ø Inflation US	No
2000–2011	Gold Ø Inflation US	No
1993–2011	Gold ↔ Inflation US	Yes
1993–2011	WTI Ø Inflation US	No
1993–2000	WTI Ø Inflation US	No
2000–2011	WTI Ø Inflation US	No
1993–2011	WTI ↔ Inflation US	Yes
1993–2011	Gold ↔ GSCI Ind. Met. ↔ US10Y ↔ Ind. Prod. US ↔ Inflation US	No
1993–2000	Gold ↔ GSCI Ind. Met. ↔ US10Y ↔ Ind. Prod. US ↔ Inflation US	No
2000–2011	Gold ↔ GSCI Ind. Met. ↔ US10Y ↔ Ind. Prod. US ↔ Inflation US	No
1993–2011	Gold ↔ GSCI Ind. Met. ↔ US10Y ↔ Ind. Prod. US ↔ Inflation US	Yes

Note: ↔ indicates the presence of a cointegration relationship. Ø indicates the absence of a cointegration relationship. SB stands for 'Structural Break' analysis. GSCI Prec. Met. stands for GSCI Precious Metals, GSCI Ind. Met. for GSCI Industrial Metals, and Ind. Prod. for Industrial Production.

Table 7.35 Lütkepohl *et al.* (2004) cointegration test results with structural break for GSCI Agricultural, US M2 and Inflation US

1993–2011	Max. Eigen.	10%	5%	1%
$r \leq 2$	6.62	5.42	6.79	10.04
$r \leq 1$	15.80	13.78	15.83	19.85
$r = 0$	36.60	25.93	28.45	33.76

7.3.3.1 GSCI Agricultural, US M2 and Inflation US

In our first specification, we wish to examine jointly the evolution over time of the GSCI Agricultural sub-index, the US M2 and CPI. Table 7.34 tells us that one cointegrating relationship could be detected during 1993–2011 with a structural break.

Indeed, we observe in Table 7.35 that there exists at least one cointegrating relationship between these three variables (at the 1% level).

Moving to the estimation of the VECM, we notice in Table 7.36 that only the US M2 variable records a negative error-correction term. But it is barely significant (at the 10% level). Therefore, we cannot conclude that we have highlighted a significant adjustment mechanism over the long run between agricultural markets on the one hand, and the US CPI and M2 on the other hand.

This statement is further confirmed by Figure 7.17, where the cointegration relationship is downward sloping. Hence, it is non-stationary, which would otherwise have been required to validate the VECM model. In addition, the slope of the cointegration relationship is slightly impacted by the structural break occurring on August 29, 2008.

7.3.3.2 GSCI Precious and Industrial Metals, US M2 and Inflation US

Second, we move to the relationship that could potentially exist between metals prices (industrial metals and precious metals) on the one hand, and US inflation and monetary variables

Table 7.36 VECM results with structural break (1993–2011) for GSCI Agricultural, US M2 and Inflation US

Error-Correction Term			
GSCI Agri.	1		
US M2	−2.176		
Inflation US	−46.771		

VECM	ΔGSCI Agri.	ΔUS M2	ΔInflation US
ECT	0.022	−0.001	0.002
(*t*.stat)	(1.91)	(−1.56)	(4.09)
ΔGSCI Agri.(−1)	0.020	−0.004	0.008
(*t*.stat)	(0.26)	(−0.80)	(2.22)
ΔUS M2(−1)	−3.001	0.240	0.001
(*t*.stat)	(−2.44)	(3.22)	(0.02)
ΔInflation US(−1)	−3.925	−0.204	0.439
(*t*.stat)	(−2.86)	(−2.45)	(7.02)

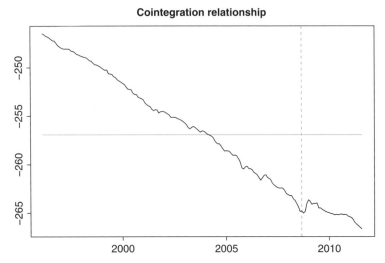

Figure 7.17   Cointegration relationship with structural break between GSCI Agricultural, US M2 and Inflation US

(M2, CPI) on the other hand. Table 7.34 indicates that a cointegration relationship could be identified during the full period, either with or without a structural break. The best results were obtained for the model with a break, hence only those results are reproduced below.[7]

Table 7.37 underlines that the rank of the cointegration r between metals prices, inflation and monetary variables in the US is equal to at least 1 (at the 1% level).

When examining the VECM results in Table 7.38, it appears that the GSCI Precious Metals sub-index and the US CPI register a negative sign. Among them, only the US CPI is statistically significant (at the 1% level). Hence, short-term deviations from the long-term equilibrium between metals prices, inflation and monetary variables will be corrected by the US CPI in this system. It seems as if inflation is the central variable through which all the interactions between markets occur.

This interesting result, however, cannot be entirely validated by looking at Figure 7.18. The cointegrating relationship is downward sloping again (similar to the case of agricultural markets). It may be slightly more stationary following the break, but this fact is not enough to validate the cointegration exercise in this setting.

Table 7.37   Lütkepohl *et al.* (2004) cointegration test results with structural break for GSCI Precious Metals, GCSI Industrial Metals, US M2 and Inflation US

1993–2011	Max. Eigen.	10%	5%	1%
$r \leq 3$	4.86	5.42	6.79	10.04
$r \leq 2$	15.77	13.78	15.83	19.85
$r \leq 1$	36.54	25.93	28.45	33.76
$r = 0$	70.52	42.08	45.2	51.6

---

[7] Other results can be obtained upon request.

Table 7.38 VECM results with structural break (1993–2011) for GCSI Precious Metals, GCSI Industrial Metals, US M2 and Inflation US

Error-Correction Term				
GSCI Prec. Metals	1			
GSCI Ind. Metals	−3.559			
US M2	−34.187			
Inflation US	75.242			

VECM	ΔGSCI Prec Met	ΔGSCI Ind Met	ΔM2	ΔUS CPI
ECT	−0.012	−0.012	0.002	−0.001
(*t*.stat)	(−1.46)	(−1.28)	(4.64)	(−3.43)
ΔGSCI Prec Met(−1)	−0.127	−0.023	−0.001	0.004
(*t*.stat)	(−1.69)	(−0.28)	(−0.25)	(0.95)
ΔGSCI Ind Met(−1)	−0.008	0.151	0	0.007
(*t*.stat)	(−0.11)	(1.77)	(−0.02)	(1.92)
ΔM2(−1)	−1.323	−2.954	0.142	0.044
(*t*.stat)	(−1.22)	(−2.49)	(2.04)	(0.82)
ΔUS CPI(−1)	−3.118	0.901	−0.35	0.4
(*t*.stat)	(−2.31)	(0.61)	(−4.04)	(5.9)

7.3.3.3 GSCI Energy, US M2 and Inflation US

Third, we extend this specification to the case of energy markets. According to Table 7.34, one cointegrating relationship can be found between the GSCI Energy sub-index, US M2 and CPI during the 1993–2011 period with the occurrence of a structural break.

As shown in Table 7.39, the rank of the cointegration r is equal to at least 1 (at the 10% level) between these three variables.

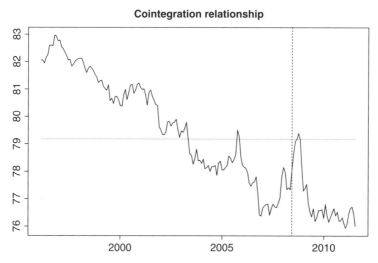

Figure 7.18 Cointegration relationship with structural break between GSCI Precious Metals, GCSI Industrial Metals, US M2 and Inflation US

Table 7.39   Lütkepohl *et al.* (2004) cointegration test results with structural break for GSCI Energy, US M2 and Inflation US

1993–2011	Max. Eigen.	10%	5%	1%
$r \leq 2$	6.23	5.42	6.79	10.04
$r \leq 1$	14.64	13.78	15.83	19.85
$r = 0$	27.30	25.93	28.45	33.76

The estimation of the VECM returns the results presented in Table 7.40. US M2 appears to be the central variable of interest here, since its error-correction term is significantly negative. Therefore, it could be said that the US monetary variable triggers feedback mechanisms toward the long-run equilibrium between energy markets and inflation, should this relationship be judged stable.

As displayed in Figure 7.19, the preceding statement cannot be verified. For the third time in a row, we obtain a downward-sloping cointegration relationship, which is mildly impacted by the structural break on October 31, 2008.

Thus, we cannot verify empirically that there exists any cointegrating relationship between the GSCI sub-indices, the US monetary and inflation variables. Our results contradict previous findings in this literature, namely those of Belke *et al.* (2010) and Browne and Cronin (2010) who studied this adjustment during 1970–2008 and 1959–2008, respectively, based on CRB indices – instead of GSCI indices. It should be noted that none of these previous studies included sub-periods or structural breaks in their cointegration framework. To a lesser extent, we also disagree with Furlong and Ingenito (1996), who found evidence of cointegration between CRB raw materials and the US CPI during 1955–1985.

7.3.3.4   GSCI Agricultural and Inflation EU

Let us now replicate this analysis with respect to the EU inflation variable. Concerning the interactions with agricultural markets, Table 7.34 reveals that cointegration relationships could be identified in each specification, except during the 1993–2000 first sub-period. We reproduce

Table 7.40   VECM results with structural break (1993–2011) for GSCI Energy, US M2 and Inflation US

Error-Correction Term			
GSCI Energy	1		
US M2	−4.147		
Inflation US	−86.033		

VECM	ΔGSCI Energy	ΔUS M2	ΔInflation US
ECT	0.008	−0.001	0.001
(*t*.stat)	(0.68)	(−2.39)	(2.32)
ΔGSCI Energy(−1)	−0.003	−0.004	0.006
(*t*.stat)	(−0.04)	(−1.23)	(2.79)
ΔUS M2(−1)	−2.062	0.202	−0.165
(*t*.stat)	(−1.08)	(2.78)	(−3.22)
ΔInflation US(−1)	−1.673	−0.355	0.135
(*t*.stat)	(−0.62)	(−3.44)	(1.85)

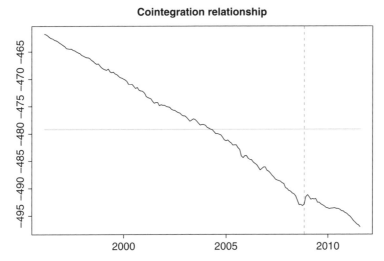

Figure 7.19 Cointegration relationship with structural break between GSCI Energy, US M2 and Inflation US

below only the results for the full period with one break, which yields the most satisfactory econometric results.

Table 7.41 highlights that there exists at least one cointegrating relationship (at the 1% level) between the GSCI Agricultural sub-index and EU Inflation.

From Table 7.42, we get the insight that the VECM has been correctly estimated, since the GSCI Agricultural variable records a negative and statistically significant (at the 10% level) error-correction term.

Nevertheless, Figure 7.20 plots a downward-sloping (i.e. non-stationary) cointegrating relationship with a break on July 30, 2010. Similar to the US case (where we included in addition the M2 component), we cannot validate econometrically speaking the cointegration exercise between agricultural commodities and inflation.

7.3.3.5 GSCI Precious and Industrial Metals and Inflation EU

Moving to the specification with metals prices, Table 7.34 shows that one cointegration relationship is present during the 1993–2011 full period with the modeling of one structural break.

Table 7.43 points out that the rank of the cointegration r between the GSCI Industrial and Precious Metals sub-indices on the one hand, and EU inflation on the other hand, is at least equal to 1 (at the 1% level).

Table 7.41 Lütkepohl *et al.* (2004) cointegration test results with structural break for GSCI Agricultural and Inflation EU

1993–2011	Max. Eigen.	10%	5%	1%
$r \leq 1$	4.77	5.42	6.79	10.04
$r = 0$	26.84	13.78	15.83	19.85

Table 7.42   VECM results with structural break (1993–2011) for GSCI Agricultural and Inflation EU

Error-Correction Term		
GSCI Agri.	1	
Inflation EU	−29.995	

VECM	ΔGSCI Agri.	ΔInflation EU
ECT	−0.049	0.006
(*t*.stat)	(−1.82)	(4.74)
ΔGSCI Agri.(−1)	0.023	−0.001
(*t*.stat)	(0.31)	(−0.16)
ΔInflation EU(−1)	−0.649	0.177
(*t*.stat)	(−0.42)	(2.44)

Cointegration relationship

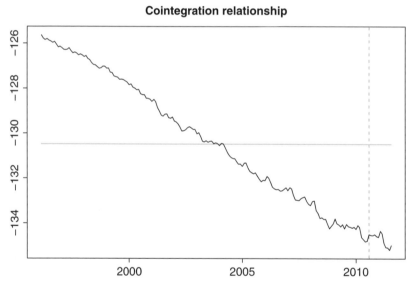

Figure 7.20 Cointegration relationship with structural break between GSCI Agricultural and Inflation EU

Table 7.43   Lütkepohl *et al.* (2004) cointegration test results with structural break for GSCI Precious and Industrial Metals and Inflation EU

1993–2011	Max. Eigen.	10%	5%	1%
$r \leq 2$	3.69	5.42	6.79	10.04
$r \leq 1$	16.67	13.78	15.83	19.85
$r = 0$	47.95	25.93	28.45	33.76

Table 7.44   VECM results with structural break (1993–2011) for GSCI Precious and Industrial Metals and Inflation EU

	Error-Correction Term		
GSCI Prec. Met.	1		
GSCI Ind. Met.	−0.353		
Inflation EU	−16.652		

VECM	ΔGSCI Prec. Met.	ΔGSCI Ind. Met.	ΔInflation EU
ECT	−0.013	0.184	0.009
(*t*.stat)	(−0.32)	(4.32)	(4.20)
ΔGSCI Prec. Met.(−1)	0.149	0.087	−0.001
(*t*.stat)	(1.78)	(1.00)	(−0.15)
ΔGSCI Ind. Met.(−1)	−0.094	−0.001	0.005
(*t*.stat)	(−1.34)	(−0.01)	(1.30)
ΔInflation EU(−1)	−0.973	−0.380	0.118
(*t*.stat)	(−0.74)	(−0.28)	(1.66)

Table 7.44 informs us of the quality of the adjustment mechanism between these variables. It can be seen that only the sign of the error-correction term for the GSCI Precious Metals is negative. However, it is not statistically significant, which leads us inevitably to discard this VECM.

A look at Figure 7.21 confirms our analysis: the cointegrating relationship is not stationary during the period (with a break on September 30, 2008). In the case of metals prices, we therefore reach the same conclusion as for agricultural prices.

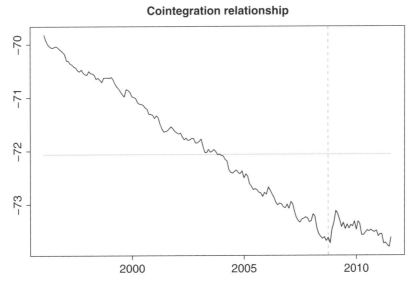

Figure 7.21   Cointegration relationship with structural break between GSCI Precious and Industrial Metals and Inflation EU

Table 7.45   Lütkepohl *et al.* (2004) cointegration test results with structural break for GSCI Energy and Inflation EU

1993–2011	Max. Eigen.	10%	5%	1%
$r \leq 1$	9.93	5.42	6.79	10.04
$r = 0$	24.57	13.78	15.83	19.85

7.3.3.6   GSCI Energy and Inflation EU

In the third and last specification, we now examine the link between the GSCI Energy sub-index and EU inflation. According to Table 7.34, there exists one cointegration relationship during the full period with the modeling of one break.

Table 7.45 highlights that the rank of the cointegration r between these two variables is at least equal to 1 (at the 1% level).

In the VECM, we note in Table 7.46 that the error-correction term for the energy variable is negative and significant (at the 1% level). Hence, any deviations from the long-term equilibrium between energy markets and inflation in the EU will be corrected by the former variable in this system. This result highlights the significant interactions that could channel between the increase in energy prices and the overall level of inflation in the EU economy.

Figure 7.22 plots the cointegration relationship, with the occurrence of a structural break on July 31, 2008. This graph cannot be judged as being stationary. As a consequence, we must dismiss this cointegration model as well, despite the promising results that arose from the VECM estimates.

To conclude on this topic, we cannot show empirically that a significant adjustment mechanism exists between each sub-category of GSCI indices (agricultural products, metals prices and energy prices) and the level of inflation in the EU. At least, it cannot be shown that such a link exists in the long run.

Compared to previous work, we agree with the findings by Moosa (1998) who reached a similar conclusion (in the wider context of the OECD) by using IMF indices instead of GSCI indices.

Table 7.46   VECM results with structural break (1993–2011) for GSCI Energy and Inflation EU

Error-Correction Term		
GSCI Energy	1	
Inflation EU	−38.796	

VECM	ΔGSCI Energy	ΔInflation EU
ECT	−0.074	0.002
(*t*.stat)	(−2.39)	(2.85)
ΔGSCI Energy(−1)	0.161	0.005
(*t*.stat)	(2.15)	(2.55)
ΔInflation EU(−1)	1.048	0.103
(*t*.stat)	(0.38)	(1.40)

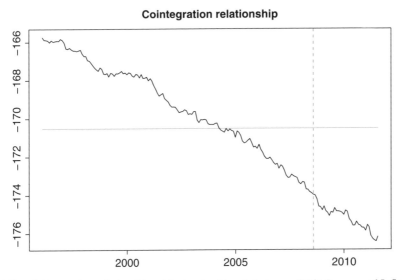

Figure 7.22 Cointegration relationship with structural break between GSCI Energy and Inflation EU

Having dealt with the linkages between inflation, monetary variables and indices of commodity markets in the US and the EU, we now investigate some case studies which have originated in previous literature.

7.3.3.7 Gold and Inflation US

First, the link between gold and the US CPI appears of paramount importance. In Table 7.34, we show that a cointegrating relationship could be detected during the 1993–2011 full period, either with or without the modeling of a break. In what follows, we choose to reproduce the results based on the inclusion of a structural break in the econometric modeling.

In Table 7.47, it is clear that the rank of the cointegration r between gold and Inflation US is at least equal to 1 (at the 1% level).

In Table 7.48, the quality of the adjustment in the VECM does not appear satisfactory. Indeed, no error-correction term records a negative sign.

This econometric model is further undermined by the non-stationarity of the cointegration relationship, given in Figure 7.23 (with a break on October 31, 2008).

Therefore, our results clearly reject the possibility of cointegration between the price of gold and the US Inflation Index, based on our updated dataset. As such, we are able to confirm

Table 7.47 Lütkepohl *et al.* (2004) cointegration test results with structural break for gold and Inflation US

1993–2011	Max. Eigen.	10%	5%	1%
$r \leq 1$	7.59	5.42	6.79	10.04
$r = 0$	21.41	13.78	15.83	19.85

Table 7.48   VECM results with structural break (1993–2011) for gold and Inflation US

	Error-Correction Term	
Gold	1	
Inflation US	−42.853	
VECM	**ΔGold**	**ΔInflation US**
ECT	0.033	0.002
(*t*.stat)	(2.17)	(3.04)
ΔGold(−1)	−0.220	0.019
(*t*.stat)	(2.83)	(6.27)
ΔInflation US(−1)	−2.000	0.261
(*t*.stat)	(−1.27)	(4.16)

the previous findings by Garner (1989), who also denied the existence of such a relationship during 1980–1988. But we disagree with Worthington and Pahlavani (2007), who studied this adjustment during 1945–2006.

7.3.3.8   WTI and Inflation US

Another important cointegration pair concerns the price of oil – one of the most traded commodity futures worldwide – and the US CPI. In Table 7.34, we identify one cointegration relationship during the full period with one break.

Table 7.49 establishes that at least one cointegration relationship exists between the two variables (at the 1% level).

In Table 7.50, we remark that the quality of the adjustment mechanism is not satisfactory. Indeed, no ECT records a negative sign in the VECM.

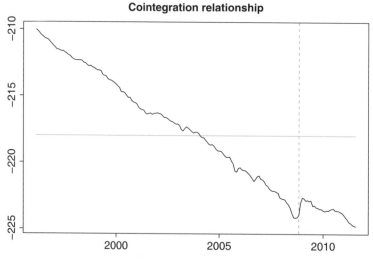

Figure 7.23   Cointegration relationship with structural break between gold and Inflation US

Table 7.49 Lütkepohl *et al.* (2004) cointegration test results with structural break for oil and Inflation US

1993–2011	Max. Eigen.	10%	5%	1%
$r \leq 1$	10.87	5.42	6.79	10.04
$r = 0$	26.70	13.78	15.83	19.85

Table 7.50 VECM results with structural break (1993–2011) for oil and Inflation US

Error-Correction Term		
WTI	1	
Inflation US	−23.398	
VECM	ΔWTI	ΔInflation US
ECT	0.022	0.005
(*t*.stat)	(0.56)	(4.19)
ΔWTI(−1)	0.021	0.011
(*t*.stat)	(0.26)	(4.66)
ΔInflation US(−1)	−3.402	0.058
(*t*.stat)	(−1.47)	(0.90)

Besides the identification of a structural break on October 31, 2008, in Figure 7.24 we fail to highlight a stationary cointegration relationship.

Similarly to the case between gold and Inflation US, it cannot be concluded empirically that there exists a link over the long run between the price of oil (i.e. the WTI price series in our setting) and the US CPI. This result implies that changes in oil prices cannot be related to changes in the level of inflation for the US economy from a long-term perspective.

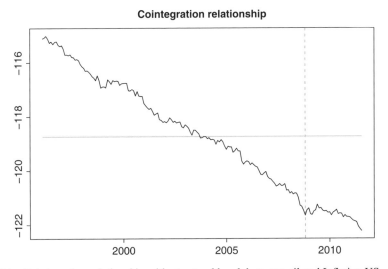

Cointegration relationship

Figure 7.24 Cointegration relationship with structural break between oil and Inflation US

Table 7.51   Johansen cointegration test results for the 1993–2011 full period for gold, GSCI Industrial Metals, US 10-year, industrial production US and Inflation US

1993–2011	Max. Eigen.	10%	5%	1%
$r \leq 4$	8.02	10.49	12.25	16.26
$r \leq 3$	11.69	16.85	18.96	23.65
$r \leq 2$	22.75	23.11	25.54	30.34
$r \leq 1$	36.34	29.12	31.46	36.65
$r = 0$	83.74	34.75	37.52	42.36

7.3.3.9   Gold, GSCI Industrial Metals, US 10-Year, Industrial Production US and Inflation US

The last case study that we choose to include in this section is dedicated to cross-market linkages. Indeed, we wish to examine the relationship between commodities, bonds, industrial production and inflation in the US. The existence of such a relationship was first hypothesized by Madhavi and Zhou (1997). The rationale behind this hypothesis is that the link between commodity markets and inflation could channel through other variables which have been highlighted in our previous experiments, such as the state of the macroeconomic environment. Table 7.34 reveals that this adjustment works in all of our specifications (sub-periods included). Among these remarkable results, we detail the case of the full period *without* break which gave us the best econometric results.

In Table 7.51, we establish that at least one cointegrating relationship exists (at the 1% level) between the price of gold,[8] the price of industrial metals (as captured by the respective GSCI sub-index), the US 10-year rate, the US Industrial Production index, and the US CPI.

Next, we move to the most interesting part of the empirical work with the interpretation of the VECM results. In Table 7.52, we record four negative error-correction terms for the GSCI Industrial Metals, the US 10-year, the US Industrial Production index, and US inflation. By looking at the magnitude of the coefficients, the ECT for the US 10-year (equal to −0.052) appears the most important variable in this system, followed by the US Industrial Production index (ECT equal to −0.010) and US inflation (ECT equal to −0.002). For the three variables, the order of significance is the 1% level. The ECT for the GSCI Industrial Metals sub-index is not statistically significant. Thus, we find, surprisingly, that the bond market can act as a transmission mechanism across commodities and other variables of the economy (such as inflation). Bonds are naturally supplemented by the influence of the industrial production index, which can be seen as a proxy of economic activity.[9] Besides, we are finally able to find a direct link between inflation and commodities in the long run thanks to this specification. Therefore, the long-term equilibrium between the five variables contained in this system will be restored by the feedback mechanisms triggered by bonds, industrial production and inflation.

The cointegration relationship appears reasonably stationary in Figure 7.25. In the specification with break, we could narrow down the period where the graph peaks as being August 29, 2008 (i.e. a period of strong price adjustment in all commodity markets following a commodity boom in the previous years).

---

[8] Note that the price of gold has been preferred in this specification to the GSCI sub-index for precious metals in order to reproduce the results by Madhavi and Zhou (1997).

[9] When the economy is in a boom, the associated demand for commodities is expected to rise as well as an input to production activities.

Table 7.52   VECM results for the 1993–2011 full period for gold, GSCI Industrial Metals, US 10-year, industrial production US and Inflation US

Error-Correction Term					
Gold	1				
GSCI Ind.Met.	−1.803				
US 10Y	0.330				
Ind.Prod. US	3.007				
Inflation US	42.287				
Trend	−0.080				

VECM	ΔGold	ΔGSCI Ind.Met	ΔUS 10Y	ΔInd.Prod. US	ΔInflation US
ECT	0.018	−0.002	−0.052	−0.010	−0.002
(*t*.stat)	(−1.84)	(−0.17)	(−3.50)	(−7.24)	(−3.69)
Intercept	−4.049	0.495	11.603	2.181	0.474
(*t*.stat)	(−1.84)	(0.17)	(3.50)	(7.24)	(3.70)
ΔGold(−1)	−0.029	0.080	−0.050	0.011	0.010
(*t*.stat)	(−0.36)	(0.74)	(−0.42)	(0.97)	(2.12)
ΔGSCI Ind.Met.(−1)	−0.025	0.175	0.206	0.012	0.010
(*t*.stat)	(−0.42)	(2.14)	(2.25)	(1.46)	(2.77)
ΔUS 10Y(−1)	0.052	0.001	−0.058	0.008	0.001
(*t*.stat)	(1.00)	(0.02)	(−0.74)	(1.10)	(0.01)
ΔInd.Prod. US(−1)	1.565	1.474	3.438	−0.033	−0.042
(*t*.stat)	(2.89)	(2.02)	(−4.22)	(−0.45)	(−1.34)
ΔInflation US(−1)	−3.185	0.279	1.645	0.068	0.285
(*t*.stat)	(−2.70)	(0.18)	(0.93)	(0.42)	(4.15)

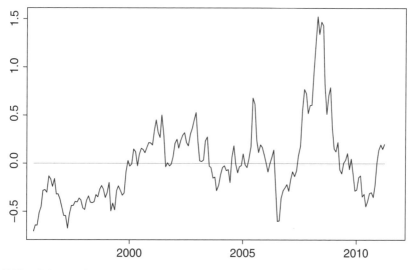

Figure 7.25   Cointegration relationship for the 1993–2011 full period for gold, GSCI Industrial Metals, US 10-year, industrial production US and Inflation US

This case study with many cross-market linkages has provided fruitful results. Indeed, it is possible to show empirically that precious metals (with gold), industrial metals and inflation are finally related directly in the VECM, and indirectly with the influences of the bond market and the industrial production index. We must note as well the remarkable stability of these results across all our specifications (within sub-periods and with break), and the overall stationarity of the cointegration relationship. Compared to our previous case studies, it seems that the relationship between inflation and commodity markets cannot be shown to exist in standard cases (i.e. by considering pairs of variables), but can in an extended framework where significant cross-market interactions seem to occur. Our results therefore confirm the previous work by Madhavi and Zhou (1997) over the period 1958–1994.

7.3.3.10   Some Concluding Remarks on Cointegration Analyses Between Inflation, Monetary Indices and Commodity Prices

Concerning the link between commodity markets on the one hand, and inflation and monetary variables on the other hand, we could not reach any definite conclusion on the existence of a meaningful adjustment mechanism between these variables in the long term. Our investigation of the GSCI sub-indices, including agricultural products, metals prices and energy markets, points toward a downward-sloping (hence not stationary) cointegration relationship in nearly all cases. This comment applies in the case of the US as well as in the EU economy. In the former region, our results contradict previous findings by Furlong and Ingenito (1996), Belke *et al.* (2010) and Browne and Cronin (2010). In the latter region, our results fall in line with the previous analysis by Moosa (1998).

Concerning the link between inflation and specific commodities, such as gold and oil, we could not identify empirically strong linkages. These results conform to Garner (1989), but contradict Worthington and Pahlavani (2007). Finally, it appears that the interactions between commodity markets and inflation should be studied in a broader framework. Indeed, we have successfully reproduced the specification by Madhavi and Zhou (1997), whereby precious and industrial metals could be related directly to inflation in a VECM, in conjunction with the influences of the US bond and industrial production indices. Therefore, the link between inflation and commodity markets does not appear as clear cut as in standard textbooks, and must be examined by tailoring specific cases involving various commodities, markets and periods of time.

7.4   CONCLUDING REMARKS

In this chapter, we have been investigating the cross-market linkages between commodities on the one hand, and macroeconomic and monetary variables on the other hand. While our cointegration analyses were quite successful in identifying linkages between various commodity markets and industrial production indices, the results are more difficult to interpret when entering monetary and inflation variables in our cointegrated systems.

First, it appears immediately that in a context of high demand for production goods, the demand for commodities is high, and that a cointegration link should exist. This linkage differs obviously from commodity to commodity, and depending on the geographical region, as shown by our analysis.

Second, the idea of linking commodities to inflation or monetary variables stems from rising price trends that may be transmitted to or come from the sphere of commodity markets. Our results show instead that such a link is rather indirect, with other variables such as bonds or industrial production playing a role in channeling these effects.

Overall, we have enriched our standing of the inter-relationships not only within the class of commodities, but with other categories of variables within the global economy. These effects are especially interesting to highlight in the wider context of the 2008–2009 financial crisis, where commodities seemed to adjust quite well to the changes in the macroeconomic conditions.

REFERENCES

Ai, C., Chatrath, A., Song, F. 2006. On the Comovement of Commodity Prices. *American Journal of Agricultural Economics* 88(3):574–588

Awokuse, TO., Yang, J. 2003. The Informational Role of Commodity Prices in Formulating Monetary Policy: A Reexamination. *Economics Letters* 79:219–224

Belke, A., Bordon, IG., Hendricks, TW. 2010. Global Liquidity and Commodity Prices – A Cointegrated VAR Approach for OECD Countries. *Applied Financial Economics* 20:227–242

Bhar, R., Hamori, S. 2008. Information Content of Commodity Futures Prices for Monetary Policy. *Economic Modelling* 25:274–283

Bloch, H., Dockery, AM., Sapsford, D. 2006a. Commodity Prices, Wages, and U.S. Inflation in the Twentieth Century. *Journal of Post Keynesian Economics* 26(3):523–545

Bloch, H., Dockery, AM., Sapsford, D. 2006b. Commodity Prices and the Dynamics of Inflation in Commodity-Exporting Nations: Evidence from Australia and Canada. *Economic Record* 82:S97–S109

Browne, F., Cronin, D. 2010. Commodity Prices, Money and Inflation. *Journal of Economics and Business* 62:331–345

Cheung, C., Morin, S. 2007. The Impact of Emerging Asia on Commodity Prices. *Bank of Canada, Working Paper* #2007-55, Canada

Cody, BJ., Mills, LO. 1991. The Role of Commodity Prices in Formulating Monetary Policy. *Review of Economics and Statistics* 73(2):358–365

Cunado, J., de Gracia, FP., 2003. Do Oil Price Shocks Matter? Evidence for Some European Countries. *Energy Economics* 25:137–154

Furlong, F., Ingenito, R. 1996. Commodity Prices and Inflation. *FRBSF Economic Review* 2:27–47

Garner, CA. 1989. Commodity Prices: Policy Target or Information Variable? *Journal of Money, Credit, and Banking* 21(4):508–514

Greene, WH. 2003. *Econometric Analysis.* Pearson Education, India

Hamori, S. 2007. The Information Role of Commodity Prices in Formulating Monetary Policy: Some Evidence from Japan. *Economics Bulletin* 5(13):1–7

Hua, P. 1998. On Primary Commodity Prices: The Impact of Macroeconomic/Monetary Shocks. *Journal of Policy Modeling* 20(6):767–790

Kyrtsou, C., Labys, WC. 2006. Evidence for Chaotic Dependence Between US Inflation and Commodity Prices. *Journal of Macroeconomics* 28:256–266

Labys, WC., Maizels, A. 1993. Commodity Price Fluctuations and Macro-economic Adjustments in the Developed Countries. *Journal of Policy Modeling* 15(3):335–352

Labys, WC., Achouch, A., Terraza, M. 1999. Metal Prices and the Business Cycle. *Resources Policy* 25:229–238

Lütkepohl, H., Saikkonen, P., Trenkler, C. 2004. Testing for the cointegrating rank of a VAR with level shift an unknown time. *Econometrica* 72:647–662

Madhavi, S., Zhou, S. 1997. Gold and Commodity Prices as Leading Indicators of Inflation: Tests of Long-Run Relationship and Predictive Performance. *Journal of Economics and Business* 49:475–489

Marquis, MH., Cunningham, SR. 1990. Is There a Role for Commodity Prices in the Design of Monetary Policy? Some Empirical Evidence. *Southern Economic Journal* 57(2):394–412

Moosa, IA. 1998. Are Commodity Prices a Leading Indicator of Inflation? *Journal of Policy Modeling* 20(2):201–212

Pieroni, L., Ricciarelli, M. 2005. Testing Rational Expectations in Primary Commodity Markets. *Applied Economics* 37:1705–1718

Worthington, AC., Pahlavani, M. 2007. Gold Investment as an Inflationary Hedge: Cointegration Evidence with Allowance for Endogenous Structural Breaks. *Applied Financial Economics Letters* 3: 259–262

Ziramba, E. 2009. Disaggregate Energy Consumption and Industrial Production in South Africa. *Energy Policy* 37:2214–2220

Index

Note: Italic page numbers refer to figures and tables. The letter *n* after a page number indicates a note.